THE BATTLE OF LINCOLN PLACE

AN EPIC FIGHT BY TENANTS TO SAVE THEIR HOMES

DENNIS HATHAWAY

The Battle of Lincoln Place
An Epic Fight by Tenants to Save Their Homes

ISBNs:
978-1-7324762-3-3 (paperback)
978-1-7324762-2-6 (hardcover)
978-1-7324762-4-0 (eBook)

CRANIA

PRESS

Published by Crania Press
Venice, California
www.crania.com.

To the memory of Carol Beck,
Lincoln Place activist and free spirit.

ACKNOWLEDGMENTS

I could not have written this book without the generous help and support of many people. Sheila Bernard, Jan Book, Ingrid Mueller, and Laura Burns provided invaluable memories of their time as Lincoln Place tenants, along with notes, documents, transcripts, and recordings that helped recreate the long tenant struggle against the corporate landlords who wanted to get rid of them. Tenants Barbara Eisenberg and Sara Sakuma shared their memories of dramatic moments in that struggle and helped me flesh out those scenes. I'm deeply grateful to them.

I owe a debt of gratitude to others who didn't live at Lincoln Place, but played important parts in its story. Amanda Seward's memories and insights were a crucial help in sorting out the complicated elements of the fight for historic recognition of Lincoln Place and its architect. Karen Brodkin's audio and video recordings, made with the help of Mary Hardy, were critical when it came to describing meetings, demonstrations, and other tenant activities. Other community members involved in facets of the Lincoln Place story who provided important memories and insights were David and Sandy Moring, Anne Murphy, David Ewing, Suzanne Thompson, Jataun Valentine, and Ken Medlock. And I want to thank Bill Megalos, Lydia Ponce, Margaret Molloy, Hans Adamson, and Jim Smith for technical help and photographs that were key to visualizing important events.

I want to give a special thanks to Marcia Scully, Elena Popp, and John Murdock, the attorneys who represented the tenants at different phases of their struggle. The book would not be complete without their generosity in talking to me and freely sharing facts and insights. Also to Gail Sansbury, an early supporter of the tenant struggle who generously shared her master's thesis on the history of Lincoln Place.

Finally, I want to thank my wife, Laura Silagi, who was not only involved in the tenant movement, but whose support and critical eye were crucial to me in undertaking this project. Without her steadfast love and belief in my efforts, it would not have been possible.

CONTENTS

1

LOCKED OUT

ON A COOL DECEMBER morning in 2005, Laura Burns was sitting at the dining table in her Venice, California, apartment drinking coffee when she glanced out the window and saw a line of black-and-white patrol cars pulling up in front of the building. With a distinct sense of unease, she got up and stood at the window and watched a dozen deputies get out of the cars and gather on the sidewalk. She called to her husband, Bernard Perroud, who was in their bedroom getting dressed.

"Come look," she said. "They're here," She knew that he would understand what she was talking about. *They're here.* She turned away from the window, started up her computer, and typed this message into an email to a friend who lived in another building in the garden apartment complex, then picked up the phone and started dialing numbers and delivering the same message to whomever answered.

But it wasn't long before she heard a thud of feet and muffled voices on the landing outside the apartment, and after a moment that seemed like an eternity, a sharp staccato of raps on the door followed by a loud, authoritarian voice.

"Sheriff's department, we're here for eviction! Open the door!" Before Burns could hang up the phone, there was another series of heavy raps that chilled her like some horror-film contrivance. The voice echoed through the apartment. "Occupants of apartment two, come to the door!"

Burns, a freelance film editor who had lived in the 795-unit complex for nine years, opened the door to see the uniformed sheriff's deputies along with a man she recognized as one of the property's maintenance workers. Two of the deputies were standing off to either side of the door as if to block any attempt at escape, while a third was filming the scene with a camcorder. One of the deputies asked Burns and Perroud if there was anyone else in their apartment, then told them to stay where they were while another looked into the rooms and even the closets to confirm that they had told them the truth. The first deputy then told Burns and Perroud that they had five minutes to leave the apartment. If they wanted to take anything with them, they should get it right now.

Fifteen years later, some details have faded in Burns's memory. What she was wearing. Whether she had eaten breakfast. What she had planned to do that day. How many people she had called. But her emotions at that moment are deeply etched into her psyche.

"I felt like a criminal," she says, the southern lilt in her voice a remnant of her Texas childhood. "I felt like we were pieces of garbage being thrown out with the trash."

Not knowing where she and Perroud would be staying the next few days, she decided to use their five minutes to gather some items of underwear. Even if they had to live on the street, she wouldn't be forced to wear dirty underthings. The five minutes went by like seconds, and once they were out of the apartment, the maintenance man set about changing the lock on the door and then screwing the windows shut. Perroud was visibly angry—they weren't being evicted because they were behind on their rent or had hosted too many loud parties or had dealt drugs from their apartment. They hadn't violated any provisions in their rental agreement. In almost anyone's eyes, they had been model tenants, and now they no longer had a place to call home.

They're here. On the far side of the leafy, expansive complex called Lincoln Place, Sara Sakuma was at her computer checking messages when the email from Burns popped up. She didn't know how long it would take the deputies to reach her apartment, so she hurriedly packed a suitcase with items of clothing and other essentials she would need for the next few days. At that moment, her mind was busy with the question of where she would go, who would take her in, and she didn't have time to reflect upon the lamentable echoes of her family history, the day sixty-five years before when her parents, her grandparents, and a great-grandmother were all forced to pack the belongings they could carry and climb onto trucks to be transported to an internment camp. To leave the places they had long called home without knowing if they would ever come back.

Sakuma managed to fill the suitcase and a couple of boxes before she heard noises on the landing and then the sharp rap of knuckles on the door.

"They weren't nasty or anything, just really businesslike," she says. "But I was in a state of shock. I had lived there twelve years, I had paid my rent and not caused any trouble, and I was being told I had five minutes to get out."

Burns and Perroud, an Italian-born Frenchman and sculptor who had been working on an environmental installation in the Mojave Desert, walked down Elkgrove Avenue, the main street that curved through the center of the thirty-eight-acre complex. It seemed that patrol cars were everywhere, and helicopters noisily thrashed the air overhead. Other people were outside, gathered in clusters on the sidewalks, often next to suitcases and boxes of belongings. There were single people, couples, families with children. One woman hadn't had time to dress and was still in her bathrobe. Another was trying to find someone to let her back into her apartment because she had forgotten her insulin. A woman hadn't been able to find her cat before the lock was changed on her apartment, and she was afraid the pet was still inside. A mother with a young daughter was distraught because she feared that she might have to return to her abusive husband. A man who had moved to Lincoln Place from the inner city after his brother-in-law was killed in a gang shooting was afraid he would have to move back to that neighborhood. Some people were crying. Others were angry, cursing the landlord, the sheriff's deputies, the city, anyone or anything seen as part of a conspiracy to throw them out of their homes.

In all, sixty-five adults and twenty-one children were forced from their apartments that December day, less than three weeks before Christmas. The term of art for such a proceeding is *lockout*, and the Lincoln Place evictions represented the largest single-day lockout in Los Angeles history. By the time the deputies who had gone methodically from building to building got back into their cars and drove away a scant three hours after they arrived, only eighty-one units were still occupied. Many of the two-story, midcentury modern-style buildings were entirely vacant. Seven of the original fifty-two buildings had previously been demolished; others had been gutted and sat as windowless hulks in weedy patches enclosed by chain-link fencing. In the common areas where children once played, where tenants had gotten together for cookouts and birthday celebrations, the once-lush grass was brown and brittle. Almost all the remaining tenants were elderly or suffered disabilities. Some of them joined the locked-out tenants gathered outside, to sympathize, to wonder when their turns would come to see the black-and-white patrol cars and hear the banging on their apartment doors. The question in everybody's minds: What will come next?

Later that day, Burns and Perroud walked to a Pizza Hut on Lincoln Boulevard, the neighborhood's major commercial street, and bought two personal pizzas. They found a pair of lawn chairs, sat outside the carport behind their building, and ate the pizzas as they stared at the windows of their apartment, officially vacant now but still holding pieces of their furniture, books, clothing, dishes, artworks. Pieces of their lives. They would be allowed into the apartment to retrieve those possessions, but only after making an appointment with the Lincoln Place management for a two-hour slot of time. They had already arranged to stay the night with a tenant who hadn't been locked out, but once they got access to the apartment, they would load up their Volvo station wagon with whatever they could carry and then make the long, two-day drive to Austin, Texas, where Burns grew up and where they would stay for the time being with two of her brothers who still lived in their childhood home.

A small woman with an animated manner, Burns responds to her own question. "Did we think we'd be back? We hoped so. Because we loved everything about the place. It was hard to think about living anywhere else." Speaking rapidly, her voice rising, she adds, "We knew this was wrong, and I knew that for every wrong there's a legal remedy. But right then I didn't know if there would be anything to come back to."

After the maintenance man changed the lock on her apartment door, Sakuma put her suitcase and boxes in her car and then found a telephone to call an ex-boyfriend who lived a few blocks away. He agreed to let her spend the night. Like Burns and Perroud and the others, she would have to call or visit the management office and make an appointment to get her belongings. In this respect, she was better off than her parents and grandparents who had been strawberry farmers on Bainbridge Island in Washington and had lost their homes and property and everything they couldn't carry when the trucks arrived to take them to the ferry and then to a train on a trip that ended at the Manzanar internment camp in California's Owens Valley. Still, she didn't know where she would go after leaving the ex-boyfriend's apartment; she didn't know if she would be able to find a decent place that she could afford on her income as a graphic artist; she didn't know if she would ever live in a place where she felt as much at home as she had at Lincoln Place. Like Burns, she knew that she wanted to come back, to walk beneath the large Brazilian pepper trees that shaded the curving sidewalks, to see the plots of flowers that people had tended outside their buildings, to hear children playing on the parklike lawns. But this was, at best, an uncertain dream. "Even if we could go back," she says, "I wondered what we would be going back to, what was going to be there."

Others locked out of their apartments felt varying degrees of fear about the future. The woman with the abusive husband was forced to get a motel room for herself and her daughter, while others camped out with friends or family members. One man spent the night in his car, while another went to a homeless shelter. In fact, the Venice community had—and still has—the largest homeless population in Los Angeles outside downtown's Skid Row, and evicted tenants wouldn't need to go far to see a man or woman sleeping on the sidewalk and imagine that kind of miserable existence for themselves. Evicted not because they had fallen behind on their rent or broken rules but because the corporate owners of the property simply wanted them out. Had been trying to get them out by one means or another for as long as some of them could remember.

The reason why was plain enough, although knowing the reason did nothing to assuage the fear and anger. Since Lincoln Place first advertised one- and two-bedroom apartments for rent in the fall of 1950, the property had increased more than tenfold in value, but because of its appeal both to families with children and seniors living on fixed incomes, and because

Venice is part of Los Angeles and subject to the city's rent control law, people were inclined to stay put once they had moved in. And because that rent control law applied only to multifamily properties built before 1979, the rents charged at older apartment complexes like Lincoln Place gradually fell farther and farther behind the rents landlords were able to charge at newly developed projects. Lincoln Place was owned by the family of one of the original builders for thirty-seven years, but in 1986, it was sold to a pair of Northern California real estate developers, and winds of change began to blow through the gnarled, densely leafed pepper trees. And tenants began to suspect that this change was going to affect their lives in ways that nobody could predict.

At the time of the sale, there were nearly two thousand occupants, including a woman born when her parents lived there and several who had rented their apartments when the complex first opened its doors. The 1970s and '80s had seen a rapid increase in Los Angeles property values, along with the inevitable real estate speculation, and Venice, with shabby, raffish neighborhoods and gang activity despite its proximity to the Pacific Ocean and origins as a middle-class beach resort, had become a hotbed of gentrification. Apartment complexes like Lincoln Place would have no problem attracting new tenants even at significantly higher rents, and it soon became obvious that the new owners wanted to do just that. Their only obstacle was the current tenants, and the laws that protected them from being arbitrarily kicked out of their homes.

When Sheila Bernard rented a two-bedroom apartment in Lincoln Place in the summer of 1988, she had no inkling of the brewing storm that would upend the lives of almost every occupant in the coming years. The single mother of three was an adult education teacher in the Los Angeles public school system, but in her twenties she had managed a warehouse food cooperative, where she had developed a keen interest in that model not only for food distribution but for other sectors of the economy.

"You can have political democracy," she says in the earnest, mildly urgent tone of the teacher working to get her point across to pupils. "But if you don't have economic democracy, the political democracy is always fragile." She moved to Lincoln Place after breaking up with her live-in boyfriend, and a major attraction was a reawakening of her earlier passion for cooperative ventures. "When I saw it," she says, "It hit me right away that these folks would be the kind of people willing to be part of a cooperative. It would give people a stake, a sense of ownership of things around them."

She soon learned that the $800 a month she was paying for her apartment was at least double the rent charged many long-term tenants, and that the new owners of the property had given some of them notices that they would have to leave. She also learned that concerned tenants had formed a group called the Lincoln Place Tenants Association, or LPTA, as everyone called it, and her interest in social and political movements led her to quickly join and begin attending meetings to discuss possible actions tenants might take to resist the landlord's efforts to get rid of them. When the group's president decided to step down, she volunteered to take on the position even though she was working full-time and caring for three minor children.

Bernard was still head of the LPTA on that December day in 2005 when the sheriff's deputies arrived with their lockout orders, but because her then-adult daughter had developed a disability, her household was one of those spared eviction, although that reprieve was scheduled to end in just a few months. She also knew that throwing up her hands and moving elsewhere wasn't an option.

"I had committed to this fight, and even if they threw me out on the street I wasn't going to give up."

A tenant who wasn't home when sheriff's deputies rapped on her apartment door was Jan Book, who was recently divorced when she moved into the complex in 1984. A certified public accountant with a law degree, Book moved into her future husband's condominium in nearby Marina Del Rey five years later, but she kept the Lincoln Place apartment, as a studio and place to display the artwork she created in her spare time. She wasn't an active LPTA member then, but a neighbor, Ingrid Mueller, kept her up to date on the doings of the group and the landlord's effort to get rid of long-term tenants so that rents could be raised. Mueller was among those who escaped immediate eviction because she had just turned sixty-two and was classified as a senior. Literally born in a bunker during the Allied bombing of Germany in World War II, Mueller had emigrated to the United

States as a young woman, eventually ended up in Southern California, and moved into Lincoln Place after her two daughters grew up and left the nest. When she saw the deputies fanning out through the complex, she called Book, who dropped what she was doing and drove through the morning rush hour traffic to see what was going on firsthand and give whatever aid and comfort she could to those locked out of their apartments.

Mueller and Book, along with Burns, Bernard, and a fifth woman named Amanda Seward, an entertainment lawyer who lived with her husband in a tract of historically designated houses a mile away, would play critical roles in what some observers had come to see as a lost cause, a David-and-Goliath battle that would end, not as the biblical tale ended, but in a victory of the powerful over the weak. The fight had already been carried to city hall, to the state capital, to the courts. Many tenants had helped in various ways, the support of politicians and advocacy groups had been enlisted, newspaper articles had been written, and films produced, but to some of the people out on the sidewalks with their possessions, it seemed that nothing could stop the juggernaut of presumptive progress, and they just had to get on with their lives elsewhere. As the sheriff's cars pulled away, it looked like a quixotic fight, not only nullifying the evictions so people could come back to their homes, but keeping those homes from literally disappearing, being wiped off the face of the earth.

2

THE BEAN FIELD

FOUR YEARS BEFORE THE first ads for Lincoln Place apartments appeared in local newspapers, a Federal Housing Administration official named Wilson Wyatt declared during a visit to Los Angeles that the city had "the biggest housing problem in the country."[1] That problem, shared by other major cities like New York, Philadelphia, and Chicago, was an acute shortage of housing for the millions of GIs coming home from the battlefields and other venues of World War II. It was especially severe in Southern California, where a concentration of aircraft factories and defense-related businesses was shifting to civilian production. Workers were needed both for expanded assembly lines and to replace women who had worked in the factories during the war but were laid off when the labor pool began to fill with returning GIs.

An article in the August 26, 1946, issue of *Newsweek* quoted a disgruntled young Los Angeles veteran who had lived the past six months with his wife and two young daughters in a dilapidated car. "I've damn well had enough of it," he told the writer as he waited in a veterans' housing office to find out if any apartments or houses had become available.[2] Other GIs and their families camped out with friends and relatives, or lived in basements, garages, and makeshift shelters. Estimates of the number of veterans in the city without homes to call their own ranged as high as forty thousand, and the need to address this appalling fact on a nationwide basis was the subject of a statement issued three months later by President Harry S. Truman. A mixture of high-minded sentiment and specific policy proposals, the three-page statement emphasized the need to greatly expand the construction of rental housing. And not just housing for the well-to-do, but housing that returning veterans and their families could easily afford.

"We, as a Nation, owe the veterans an opportunity to have homes," Truman's statement concluded. "We will see that they get them."[3]

Today, more than seventy years later, Los Angeles again faces a housing crisis—thousands of homeless men and women sleeping on sidewalks or in tents and other temporary shelters, many thousands more living in motels or illegally converted garages, crowded into substandard apartments and houses, or paying rent that swallows up half or more of their incomes. Promises by politicians to rectify this situation are often met with justifiable cynicism, but Truman's declaration was followed by action, most notably the adoption of policies to stimulate the construction of multifamily housing projects. One of those projects was Lincoln Place, which broke ground in 1949 on the site of a lima bean field just over a mile from the Pacific Ocean. At the time, it was the largest apartment complex under construction in California financed with a federally guaranteed loan.

That site, on the east side of Lincoln Boulevard, which is also the route of iconic Highway 1, had almost nothing in common with the community that lay to the west. Bordered by the city of Santa Monica on the north and a seasonal waterway called Ballona Creek on the south, the area west of Lincoln Boulevard was developed just after the turn of the twentieth century as a resort called Venice of America and later known as Venice Beach or simply Venice. The brainchild of a tobacco magnate turned developer named Abbot Kinney, Venice of America had an amusement pier, Italian-style colonnaded buildings, a miniature railway, and an extensive system of canals complete with gondoliers. But the canals tended to stagnate and silt up, and when financial problems led to Venice's annexation by Los Angeles in 1925, all but a handful were filled and turned into streets.

The 1920s also saw the discovery of oil in the tidelands upon which Venice of America had risen, and by the mid-1930s, more than a hundred wells were pumping away on stretches of the beach as well as inland, some right in the backyards of houses. Venice even had its own ghetto, a half-mile square area called Oakwood that had been set aside for African Americans who worked in the construction of Kinney's extravaganza and served the needs of pleasure-seeking white people who could afford to make the trip by train from the city's more populated neighborhoods near downtown and points beyond. At that time, it was the only neighborhood where Black people were able to live.

At the end of World War II, there was only scattered development east of Lincoln Boulevard, almost all of it consisting of single-family houses amid the bean fields that thrived in what was once an expansive wetlands frequented only by the native Tongva people. But on higher ground immediately to the north of Venice was the city of Santa Monica, the home of Douglas Aircraft and its factories that turned out military aircraft during the war and then geared up for a burgeoning civilian market when hostilities were finally over. And just three miles away, rising from the marshes south of Ballona Creek, were the buildings of Hughes Aircraft, where parts and systems for military planes were produced, and where the infamous "Spruce Goose" transport plane was built and embarked upon its first and only flight. After the war, Hughes turned to the development of guided missiles and related systems and, by the late 1940s, had become the largest employer in the area. Los Angeles Airport, later to be known as Los Angeles International Airport, or LAX, opened in 1947 just a few miles farther south, while in the nearby community of Hawthorne, the Northrop Corporation was building upon its success developing World War II fighter planes to become a major player in the postwar aerospace industry. These companies and supporting businesses needed skilled workers and offered decent pay, and former GIs, many with wives and children, looked for housing they could afford in Venice and other communities in the Santa Monica bay area. They were the population that Lincoln Place was designed to serve.

The dire housing shortage in Los Angeles and elsewhere had been in the making since the onset of the 1930s Depression, which severely inhibited new housing construction as well as the repair and renovation of existing houses and apartment buildings. In 1933, it was estimated that as many as half the nation's home mortgages were in default, and banks were understandably loath to make new home loans. Despite opposition from some politicians who declared that the federal government had no business intervening in the private housing market, the Roosevelt administration proposed and Congress passed the National Housing Act of 1934, which established the Federal Housing Administration and the Federal Savings and Loan Insurance Corporation.[4] The FHA would insure mortgage loans as well as establish standards for housing construction and finance, while the FSLIC would guarantee deposits in savings and loan institutions, many of which had failed in the Depression's early years and wiped out their depositors' savings.

This landmark legislation didn't magically cure the crisis, but it did significantly reduce the number of mortgage defaults and helped restore people's faith that their money would be safe in their local savings and loan, drawing interest instead of sitting idle and losing value to inflation. Housing construction slowly picked up, but after the bombing of Pearl Harbor and United States' entry into the war, the government restricted the use of steel, lumber, and other materials. Activity was then concentrated on military-related facilities, including housing for military personnel and war workers, rather than new single-family houses and apartment buildings. But once the war ended, the Truman administration prodded Congress to adopt measures to stimulate new housing construction. The FHA had originally guaranteed mortgages only for single-family houses, but an amendment to the National Housing Act called Section 608 extended those guarantees to apartment complexes, and after the war, the section was liberalized by allowing developers to get government-backed mortgages for up to ninety percent of a project's cost. It also lengthened the maturity period for the loans, reduced working capital requirements, and streamlined the loan approval process.

In March 1948, a Los Angeles company called Union Housing Plan, Inc. applied for FHA mortgage insurance on a $5,167,700 loan to build a 795-unit garden apartment complex in Venice. Two of the company's principals were brothers Ray and R. Reese Myers, who had made names for themselves building, among other things, movie sound stages, and gas stations. Joining them in the venture was a real estate developer named Samuel Bialac, a Polish immigrant and former advertising man, and his son Jerry, who had recently been mustered out of the air force. Bialac had acquired the undeveloped site in 1945, but it wasn't until Section 608 was liberalized that he set about arranging financing and organizing the myriad details involved in designing and constructing such a project.

Years later, Jerry Bialac told an interviewer that "it was our intention to build the finest and largest FHA-insured project in the country." He said that he and his father toured other garden-style apartment complexes in Southern California in a quest to identify the architect they believed had done the best job of design within the guidelines for such projects, which called for airy, spacious units along with amenities like common spaces and greenery while remaining affordable to working people and families. According to Bialac, the name that quickly rose to the top of the list was Ralph Vaughn. "He had not only the best footprints but had an incredible flair for design and ability to deliver affordable housing that looked like luxury housing. We were a perfect fit."[5]

Before the Bialacs sought out Vaughn and offered him the job of designing Lincoln Place, they were unaware of the fact that he was a rarity in the city's architectural circles, an African American in an overwhelmingly white profession. The son of an architect and public school teacher, Vaughn got his degree in architecture from the University of Illinois in 1932 and worked as an architectural draftsman in Washington, DC, before going to work for Hilyard Robinson, an African American architect and Howard University lecturer who designed the historic Langston Terrace Dwellings, the first publicly funded housing project in the nation's capital. Vaughn also taught at Howard, and it was there that he met architect Paul Williams, a guest lecturer at the university and a member of Robinson's design team. Williams, who had grown up in Los Angeles, was the most prominent African American architect in that city, and after completion of Langston Terrace he offered Vaughn a job in his Los Angeles office. There the younger man worked on the design of several notable projects, including the MCA headquarters building and the Saks Fifth Avenue department store in Beverly Hills. Williams had developed the reputation of "architect to the stars," and in the course of his four years with Williams, Vaughn also worked on the design of residences for celebrities like Bert Lahr, Tyrone Power, and Bill "Bojangles" Robinson.

The construction slump at the onset of World War II meant a severe drop in architectural commissions, and Williams could no longer afford to keep Vaughn on his staff, although by all accounts the two worked well together and admired each other's talents. Fortunately, Vaughn's work with Williams meant that he had gotten to know people in the movie industry, and was able to use those connections to find work at MGM as a set designer. There he worked with Cedric Gibbons, who had won Academy Awards for art direction and set design, and a cinematic influence can be seen in Vaughn's later architectural designs. When the war ended and the construction business began to stir, he left MGM to start an independent design practice even though he wasn't licensed as an architect by the state of California. This posed a problem for the builders of Lincoln Place because FHA-insured projects required the official involvement of a licensed architect, but the issue was settled when Vaughn teamed up with another architect he had met when both worked at MGM. That man, Heth Wharton, was not only licensed but had worked for Myron Hunt, one of Southern California's most noted architects, before striking out on his own and gaining a degree of fame designing houses in the 1920s and '30s for prominent Los Angeles residents. They called their firm Wharton & Vaughn Associates.

At first glance, it was unlikely partnership. Wharton, who was fifteen years older than Vaughn, had been born into a prominent Virginia family that counted well-to-do plantation owners and slaveholders in its ancestry. His grandfather, Gabriel Wharton, and great-uncle, Henry Heth, were both generals in the Confederate army during the Civil War, and his grandmother was a Radford, the family after which the city in southwest Virginia is named. But Heth Wharton, who spent two years at Harvard University's School of Architecture, was known to hold liberal views on such subjects as politics and race, and had no misgivings about working with a Black architect, although some members of the public weren't as enlightened—Jerry Bialac told the interviewer that he and his father actually received death threats because of their employment of Vaughn during the Lincoln Place construction.[6]

Vaughn's design was strongly influenced by the Bauhaus style, which originated in Germany at the end of World War I, and had its roots in the modernist movement of the late nineteenth century. This style calls for the integration of form and function and shuns architectural ornamentation in favor of clean, simple lines. Its emphasis on building design as an artistic venture appealed to Vaughn, who considered himself a creative artist and not just a glorified draftsman. Another major influence on Vaughn's design was the garden city movement, which first arose in England at the turn of the twentieth century and quickly spread to other countries, including the United States. In its original conception, a garden city would be built outside large urban areas beset by such ills as poverty, overcrowding, crime, and pollution. A garden city would be a self-contained city surrounded by green-belts, with plentiful open space, parkland, and communal areas. It would be a healthy place for families and children, unlike the dirty, gray urban cores of London, New York, and many other major metropolitan centers.

Vaughn and the Bialacs were clearly sympathetic to the goals of the garden city movement, many of which were expressed in FHA guidelines for projects built under the Section 608 program. Elements like housing blocks with units facing inner courtyards, the separation of car and pedestrian traffic, amenities for families with children, and ample green space were conspicuous features of Lincoln Place. The FHA guidelines also encouraged modernist design principles like the aforementioned lack of ornamentation, the straightforward geometric shapes, and the liberal use of glass. The fifty-two buildings of the Lincoln Place complex, which varied in size, exterior detail, and orientation on the site, were distinctive examples of those principles in practice.

The guidelines called for rents in section 608 projects to be affordable to working families, and for rental complexes to be located near services and amenities like shopping districts, parks, and schools. By the time the Lincoln Place developers broke ground in 1949, plans were underway for a thirteen-acre public park with a baseball field and playground adjacent to one corner of the complex, and beyond it a new elementary school within easy walking distance. A nine-acre strip of land between the Lincoln Place site and Lincoln Boulevard had been set aside for a shopping center with a Market Basket supermarket and Thrifty drugstore that would serve the needs of tenants and others in the community. In keeping with the idealized view of family in those postwar years, the male head of household would go off to work each day at Douglas Aircraft or one of the other aerospace plants, the wife and mother would shop at the supermarket and drugstore, the children would walk to the school, and on weekends, the entire family would go to the park or have a cookout or picnic in the courtyard area outside their apartment building. If this picture wasn't perfectly consistent with reality, it had a strong appeal to many looking for a place to rent that they could genuinely call their homes and not just temporary places to hang their hats.

By the time the design work was finished and the FHA had given its stamp of approval to the plans, the Myers brothers had sold their interest in the project to a contractor and real estate developer named Philip Yousem. Both Samuel Bialac and Yousem had grown up in Omaha, Nebraska, where Yousem had worked in a family plumbing and heating business before migrating to southern California. Yousem's son-in-law, Earl Schafer, who also grew up in Omaha and moved to Los Angeles after getting out of the army, became a member of the development team. The actual construction work proceeded quickly. Two model units were fully furnished and made available for inspection by prospective tenants, and just thirty months after Union Housing Plan applied for FHA mortgage insurance, the first group of units was ready for occupancy.[7] By March 1951, all 795 units were ready for tenants, and in July of that year, the complex was fully occupied.

A color brochure distributed by the developers aimed to entice tenants with the myriad details that made Lincoln Place a desirable place to live. Features that would later become common in apartment construction but at the time were relative rarities in all but upper-class housing were breakfast nooks with tables, window cornices with built-in drapery rods, TV and telephone outlets, tiled kitchens and bathrooms, oak floors, and garbage disposers. Many of the units had patios and balconies, and outside each building was a laundry room with automatic washers and dryers. There were both single-car garages and open carports with built-in storage cabinets, all set apart from the buildings so that car and pedestrian traffic wouldn't mix. One page of the brochure was a simplified map showing Lincoln Place's proximity to Douglas and Hughes Aircraft as well as the MGM studios in nearby Culver City and Twentieth Century Fox studios in West Los Angeles. Interestingly, the Pacific Ocean just over a mile to the west wasn't touted as an attraction—among many salient features listed in the brochure was the fact that Lincoln Place was *away* from the salt-air atmosphere of the beach.

With fifty-two buildings set on thirty-eight acres, there was ample open space with lawns, shrubbery, and more than three hundred trees. The two-story buildings varied in size, shape, number of units, and perhaps most significantly, in their orientation. Those on Elkgrove Avenue, the central street, followed the curve of that thoroughfare, while others were set at angles to each other instead of perfectly geometric rows. The buildings all had low, hipped roofs with broad eaves, which gave an impression of flatness but were easier to maintain than the truly flat roofs popular in modernist design. Rather than being regularly spaced, the double-hung wood windows were placed together in groups of three in the living rooms and two in the bedrooms, which afforded greater light and a feeling of spaciousness. Simple decorative elements of wood and glass were placed above the building entrances, and wood siding was installed below balconies and between living room windows on the first and second floors to break up the monotony of long stucco walls.

A 1951 ad in the *Los Angeles Times* listed one-bedroom apartments for $63.50 a month, and two bedrooms for $73.50, including garages. The ad touted the apartments as ideal for school-age children, with drawings of grinning youngsters with book bags hurrying off to school. Lincoln Place, the ad copy declared, was close to elementary, middle, and high schools, as well as a junior college in Santa Monica and UCLA in the community of Westwood just seven miles away. The median household income in Los Angeles was then just under $5,000 a year, meaning that a family would be spending about seventeen percent of its income to rent a two-bedroom apartment, a far cry from today, when the median household income is $68,000 a year but the average two-bedroom apartment rents for $2,700, or almost half that household's income.[8]

This rosy picture of happy families living in pleasant surroundings without straining their budgets had some darker undertones, however. Section 608 of the Housing Act had worked as intended by fueling a postwar boom in rental-housing construction, with 465,000 units built nationwide before the program expired in 1950, but a congressional investigation later revealed that builders had reaped millions in illicit profits by getting FHA-insured mortgages in excess of project costs and then pocketing the difference.[9] Which meant that tenants in those projects were paying higher rents to cover those inflated costs. One of the witnesses called to testify before a Senate committee was Philip Yousem, who admitted that the loan for Lincoln Place exceeded the actual costs of land and construction by $142,000. Although that would be more than $1.5 million in today's dollars, it was relatively small change compared to amounts pocketed by some builders, who inflated items like land costs and design fees by three and four times what they would actually pay.[10]

An even darker element of Lincoln Place history concerns the subject of race and housing discrimination. Jataun Valentine, a longtime community activist who was born and still lives in the nearby Oakwood neighborhood, says that some people in that once predominately African American neighborhood called Lincoln Place "the white projects." After graduating from high school in 1955, Valentine heard there were vacant apartments in the complex, but when she inquired at the rental office, she was told that nothing was available. Her older sister had the same experience. "She saw ads for apartments for rent there, but when she asked, they told her there weren't any. We were sure they just didn't want to rent to African Americans."

Given that Lincoln Place was designed by an African American architect, this presents a definite irony, although it's unknown whether Vaughn ever discussed with the Bialacs and Yousem the question of who would be allowed to live in the complex. Although he apparently wasn't as outspoken on racial issues as some of his contemporaries, Vaughn was friends with some prominent figures who were. A 1948 photograph shows him and his wife at a table in a Los Angeles nightclub with Leon Washington, the founding publisher of the *Los Angeles Sentinel*, the city's preeminent Black newspaper and a vocal advocate for civil rights. Also at the table is Washington's cousin, Loren Miller, an attorney who specialized in housing discrimination cases and was chief counsel in a case that led to a landmark 1948 US Supreme Court ruling that a state's legal powers couldn't be used to enforce the restrictive racial covenants that were common in Los Angeles and other cities.[11]

Sixteen years after that photograph was taken, and nine years after Jataun Valentine was told that no apartments were available, the local chapter of the Congress of Racial Equality (CORE) organized pickets at the Lincoln Place rental office to protest alleged discrimination. According to a March 3, 1964, article in the *Los Angeles Times*, four of the picketers—two men and two women—were arrested and charged with trespassing after blocking the office doorway and being bodily carried from the premises by the police. Meanwhile, according to the article, other CORE picketers paraded on nearby sidewalks and passed out leaflets accusing management of refusing to rent to Black people. A month later, an article in the newspaper quoted J. L. Yousem, identified as the Lincoln Place manager, saying that a settlement of the issue had been reached with CORE. This presumably meant that the complex would rent to African Americans, although the manager—Philip Yousem's nephew—said that both sides had agreed not to disclose the terms without the other's consent. The trespassing charges against the four picketers were dropped.[12]

Samuel Bialac and his son Jerry had sold their interest in Lincoln Place to Philip Yousem shortly after the complex opened its doors. Yousem died in 1963, but Lincoln Place remained in the family, with his daughter and son-in-law managing its operations. Rents remained affordable to working people and families, and tenant turnover and vacancy rates were low. All the land around Lincoln Place had been subdivided, and by the end of the 1960s, houses and a smattering of small apartment buildings had risen on virtually every lot. Because of the Cold War and space race with Russia, as well as the war in Vietnam, the large aerospace firms and military suppliers in the area were hiring skilled workers and operating at a brisk clip, but the advent of the 1970s saw the beginning of changes not only in that picture but also in the fortunes of people looking for houses to buy and apartments to rent.

Inflation ratcheted up in the early years of the decade, contributing to a rapid rise in real estate values that put single-family houses out of reach for many would-be homeowners and fueled a boom in both construction of new condominiums and conversions of existing apartments to for-sale units. That phenomenon touched Lincoln Place in 1972, when the Yousem family made a deal to sell the complex to a company that intended to convert all 795 units to condominiums. The conversion required public hearings and city approval, and housing experts told a Los Angeles City Council committee that a two-bedroom apartment then renting for an average of $112 a month would require a monthly payment of at least $175 as a condominium, in addition to a sizable down payment. Many current tenants were elderly and lived on fixed incomes, and they wouldn't be able to afford to buy one of the units, even if they wanted to. When the matter moved to the full city council a group of some thirty tenants, mostly senior citizens, came to protest this threat to the place they had long called home. And they soon got a reprieve when the company balked at the fees the city intended to charge, and the sale fell through.[13]

It was the first time Lincoln Place tenants had acted together to oppose something their landlord wanted, but no formal organization arose and for the next fourteen years under Yousem family ownership things were quiet and tenant fears of being pushed out of their homes gradually faded. Then the property was put up for sale again in 1986, and that date marked the beginning of changes that would affect the lives of every tenant and unfold in ways that nobody could predict.

3

A PLACE TO MAKE A HOME

As renters, we may feel we have no right to make demands of landlords and government officials. After all, we don't own, we only rent. But renting a home is not like renting a car. We are entitled to stability and security, the same as owners are. After all, we are paying the mortgages on these buildings, and contributing enormously to the wealth of the owners. It is ethically ridiculous for an owner to increase his wealth at our expense, and then threaten the stability of our community in order to become even wealthier.

—LPTA flyer

ON MAY 30, 1986, every tenant of Lincoln Place received a one-page notice informing them that the property had been sold to a real estate investment firm called Lincoln Place Investors. The notice was signed by James C. Coxeter, identified as the managing general partner of the firm. Along with some information regarding the addressing of rent checks, the notice said, "No immediate changes are anticipated in the operation of Lincoln Place Apartments." Coxeter was, in fact, a general partner in TransAction Financial Corp., an Oakland, California-based real estate investment firm that had been developing commercial property in Berkeley and other northern California locales. TransAction CEO Robert Bisno and Coxeter had formed Lincoln Place Investors to buy Lincoln Place Apartments, which represented the pair's first foray into real estate development in Southern California. Had people known anything about TransAction's activities, they might have felt some skepticism about the statement in the tenants' notice regarding changes, but nobody did, and therefore had little reason not to take it at face value.

Most people living at Lincoln Place when the notice appeared in their mail have long since moved away or are deceased. The few whose tenancies date back that far say that nothing seemed to change in the following months, with management clearly trying to create goodwill by sending out breezily cheerful newsletters and organizing a tenant get-together with free food, games for kids, and a raffle. But rumors soon began to circulate about newly vacated units being rented for as much as twice the rent paid by long-term tenants. That was worrisome, particularly to the elderly on fixed incomes and others for whom paying rent and putting food on the table was an ongoing struggle. Some also noticed that the newest tenants appeared to be younger and more affluent than those who had lent the complex a working-class and family atmosphere ever since it opened its doors. But turnover was low, and residents knew they were protected by the Rent Stabilization Ordinance Los Angeles had adopted eight years earlier to control rent increases, so few felt seriously threatened.

The change came without warning. On July 17, 1987, ten Lincoln Place tenants found the following notice under their doors.

TO: _____and to all others in possession of Unit Number _____, located at

_____

Venice, California, 90291.

PLEASE TAKE NOTICE that the rental agreement under which you occupy the above described premises is hereby terminated effective thirty (30) days after the date of service upon you of this notice and requires you to quit and vacate the premises at the expiration of the said thirty (30) day period.

This notice is given you under the provisions of Section 1946 of the California Civil Code which requires no specific reason. Additional grounds for this notice, if required under local ordinance, are as follows:

<u>We seek possession under Section 151.09 (9) of the Rent Stabilization Ordinance wherein we will be performing major rehabilitation on your unit in excess of $10,000.</u>

News of the eviction notices spread quickly through the complex. Because the tenants who got them were paying substantially less than those who had recently moved in, it was widely assumed that the owners wanted to evict them in order to rent their apartments at higher rates. But how could they legally do this? Before passage of the RSO, as the city's rent control ordinance was commonly called, the landlord could have simply given those tenants a thirty-day notice to leave, but the RSO not only had frozen rents and restricted future increases, but also had done away with no-fault evictions. Under the new ordinance, tenants in rent-controlled properties could only be evicted for cause, which ranged from the obvious—failure to pay rent, violation of a rental agreement, use of an apartment for illegal purposes—to the more obscure, like a landlord's plans to move a family member or resident manager into the unit. But what about the ordinance section cited in the underlined part of the eviction notice? What was "major rehabilitation"? What was the significance of $10,000? Few tenants at Lincoln Place or other renters in the city had heard of that section of the RSO, although they would soon be learning about it in great detail, and it would become a topic of intense conversation not only among apartment dwellers but city officials, politicians, landlords, and activists in the fields of housing and tenants' rights.

To fully understand the drama that unfolded after the eviction notices went out, it is necessary to look at the social and economic forces that led the Los Angeles City Council to enact rent controls in the first place. The 1970s inflation and attendant rise in real estate values had been good for speculators and others in the realty business, but bad for homeowners who wanted to stay put, particularly the elderly and people living on fixed incomes who saw their properties reassessed and their taxes shoot upward. These homeowners were the poster children in the successful campaign in 1978 to pass Proposition 13, a statewide initiative that capped property taxes at one percent of the assessed value of single-family homes, apartment

23

buildings, and commercial properties. Apartment-house owners got behind the initiative in a major way, blaming rent increases on high property tax bills and implying and sometimes even promising that rents would be rolled back if the measure passed.

Predictably, this only happened in a few isolated cases, and as property values continued their upward climb, many apartment dwellers actually saw their monthly rent bills increase. Movements for rent control had already been gathering steam in some urban areas, and in August 1978, three months after passage of Proposition 13 and the windfall it provided for apartment-house owners, the Los Angeles City Council approved a six-month moratorium that forced a rollback of recently imposed rent hikes and prohibited new increases at most multifamily residential properties. The ensuing months saw the drafting of the RSO that limited rent increases to a certain percentage, depending upon when a landlord had last raised the rent on a particular unit. To nobody's surprise, this triggered an onslaught of lobbying by landlord groups and real estate interests, who predicted dire consequences if it became law. Apartment-house owners, many of the mom-and-pop variety, would be forced out of business. Those who stayed in the business wouldn't be able to afford needed maintenance, and their properties would fall into disrepair. No developer with any sense would build new multifamily housing, notwithstanding the fact that the proposed ordinance would only affect properties constructed before October 1978, the moratorium's inception date. On the other side of the contentious debate were advocates for tenants forced to pay more and more of their incomes for rent, who had to move to smaller, shabbier apartments in less desirable areas of the city, or who faced the appalling prospect of joining a growing population of people with nowhere to live but the city streets.

On March 15, 1979, the ordinance came to the city council floor for a final vote. In the chamber packed with lobbyists and landlord groups as well as tenants and their advocates, the measure squeaked by with eight votes, the bare majority of the fifteen-member body. Tenants and their supporters celebrated while landlords vowed to work for repeal, although in truth, the latter had won major concessions prior to passage, and the measure fell significantly short of the mark tenant advocates first aimed for. The most glaring, perhaps, was that it would only be in effect for one year unless renewed by the city council. This meant that unhappy landlords and real estate lobbyists would be working city hall offices in an effort to convince council members that rent control was ill-advised and harmful to the city, while tenant advocates would hardly be able to take a breath before getting back into the fray.

Another fractious dispute arose over the issue of what would happen when a tenant vacated an apartment voluntarily or was evicted for good cause. Tenant advocates argued that rents shouldn't be affected by a change of occupants, while landlords wanted to be able to charge new renters whatever the market would bear. The city council settled the dispute in favor of landlords by allowing what was called "vacancy decontrol," but stipulated that the newly rented units would again be subject to the RSO limits on annual rent increases, which would be set by a rent control board and ostensibly linked to the rate of inflation. Supporters of this compromise tried to dampen fears that landlords would simply evict their current tenants and re-rent the apartments at higher rates. After all, a landlord would no longer be able to hand a tenant a notice to move but would have to cite a specific, legally defined cause. Unsurprisingly, this failed to mollify many tenant advocates, who argued that renters would be forced to stay in their apartments even if they needed more room, or a shorter commute, or suffered under a landlord from hell, since many wouldn't be able to find anything they could afford at market rates. They also argued that unscrupulous landlords would always be able to find loopholes or other creative means to get rid of low-paying renters despite the RSO restrictions designed to protect them.

That fear proved to be prophetic. On Sept. 17, 1979, less than six months after the city council approved the RSO, the *Los Angeles Times* published an article titled "Flaws in Rent Law Not Lost on Landlords." The article quoted the unnamed owner of an apartment building about the ease with which rents could be raised by taking advantage of an RSO provision allowing a landlord to evict a tenant in order to move a family member into the unit.

"You have relatives, don't you?" the landlord said. "You just notify the rent control people downtown that you want your tenants out so your relatives can move in. There won't be any argument. You let your relatives stay for a few months and move out voluntarily. Then you can raise the rent as high as you want."

Another avenue to getting higher-paying tenants was a section of the RSO allowing rents to be raised to recover the costs of capital improvements. An anonymous real estate broker handling the sale of a building near downtown told the *Times* reporter how easy it would be to take advantage of this pass-through-costs provision.

"This building is in good shape but you can doll it up some more and pass on the costs," he said.

"That will get some of the tenants out, because they won't want to pay higher rent. When they move out, you can raise the rent to whatever level you want."

But the RSO provision that came to threaten the largest number of renters, including those at Lincoln Place, was the one that allowed landlords to evict tenants in order to do rehabilitation work on their units. A Hollywood apartment owner was quoted in the *Times* article as saying that this work didn't have to be extensive or costly, just the kind that couldn't be done while an apartment was occupied. At that time, work on a unit had to cost at least $5,000 to qualify as major rehabilitation, but the owner quoted in the article said he was able to evict his tenants and raise the rents by "putting a little tile around the kitchen sinks and bathrooms and putting in new linoleum floors. It's no problem."

The fears—or hopes—that rent control would be a transient phenomenon were laid to rest when the RSO was renewed each of the two years following its passage, and then made permanent in 1982. By that time, a number of tenants throughout the city had complained about landlords abusing what had come to be known as the "major rehab" provision, and to close or at least narrow what many viewed as a major loophole, the city council raised the threshold cost of repairs to $10,000 and required landlords to file a notice with the city's housing department before proceeding with the work. But despite these changes, the pace of major rehab evictions actually picked up, and in 1985, landlords filed the required notices for a total of 416 units in 140 buildings.[14] In February 1986, the city council responded to this growing onslaught of evictions by amending the RSO to require landlords to pay "relocation assistance" in the amount of $1,000 for regular tenants and $2,500 for those sixty-two and older, handicapped, or living with dependent children. Still, tenant advocates believed the major rehab provision gave landlords a powerful motive to evict people by doing work on their apartments regardless of whether it was needed. And most alarming to tenant groups and people involved in social justice movements was the fact that the main targets appeared to be the elderly and people with low incomes, the very population the RSO had been designed to protect.

There was speculation that the new owners of Lincoln Place intended from the very beginning to use this loophole to evict long-term tenants, despite James Coxeter's statement about no immediate changes.[15] But the ten eviction notices were a definite harbinger of serious change, because two weeks later the *Los Angeles Times* published an article that quoted Barbara Zeidman, the city's rent control coordinator, saying that her office had been notified by Lincoln Place owners that a total of two hundred evictions were planned.[16] The subject of that article was a public meeting called by city Councilwoman Ruth Galanter in response to complaints from Lincoln Place residents, who were taking the first nascent steps in what would become an organized resistance to the evictions and the owners' future plans for the complex.

The councilwoman, who lived in Venice just a few blocks from Lincoln Place, would be deeply drawn into that conflict, but at the time of the public meeting, she was a political neophyte who had only a month earlier taken her seat on the city council. In what was widely regarded as a major upset, she had defeated five-term Councilwoman Pat Russell, who was painted by Galanter supporters as being too cozy with real estate developers and other powerful business interests in the racially and economically diverse district that encompassed the majority white communities of Venice, Mar Vista, and Westchester as well as the majority-Black Crenshaw district. In a dramatic incident just weeks before the election, an intruder broke into Galanter's home and stabbed her multiple times, and at the city council swearing-in ceremony on July 2, she was still confined to a wheelchair. With her record of activism in the environmental movement and calls for protecting affordable housing, she had gotten strong support from historically liberal Venice, and

Lincoln Place tenants had reason to see her as an ally in their eviction battle and breathe a sigh of relief at her recovery from the attack.

The public meeting on July 29 was held at the Westchester Municipal Center, one of the satellite offices in each of the city council's fifteen districts. According to the *Times* account, the place was crowded with angry Lincoln Place residents, including most of the ten who had gotten eviction notices two weeks earlier. One of them, Maria Johnson, was quoted as saying, "I just can't believe they can get away with this," and another, Francisco Romo, who lived at Lincoln Place with his wife and children, said, "Thirty days is not enough time to find a new place, especially if you have kids." A third, Marcia Misuis, said she had retained a lawyer and would refuse to vacate her apartment at the end of the thirty-day period. Also at the meeting, according to the article, were US Senator Alan Cranston, Representative Mel Levine, and former antiwar figure and then State Assemblyman Tom Hayden, who had become an issue in the recent city council campaign because of his friendship with Galanter, a fact some of her opponent's supporters had used to paint her as dangerously radical.

Because there was no organized tenants' association at Lincoln Place when the eviction notices went out, the owners may have expected little more than some grumbling from the people directly affected. But that was a miscalculation. For one thing, tenants in other parts of the city had been subjected to these major rehab evictions, and city Councilman Joel Wachs, a primary sponsor of the RSO, had submitted a motion calling for an emergency moratorium on all evictions of that type. Wachs, who represented a San Fernando Valley district with a significant proportion of renters, referred in his motion to "an increasing trend to remove the current low-income and elderly tenants in an effort to appeal to the young urban professionals, who can pay significantly higher rents. This has caused a great deal of hardship on low-income and senior tenants, causing them to be evicted from their homes of many years. The search for a new apartment in many cases can double or triple their current rent." Furthermore, Venice had long been a haven for political activism, and when news of the Lincoln Place eviction notices spread through the community, there were people ready to take up arms against what they regarded as a serious injustice.

Such movements seldom survive without strong leadership, however, and Lincoln Place residents were fortunate to find within their own ranks a person who bore the scars of social and political battles going back more than half a century. Her name was Ethel Shapiro-Bertolini, a seventy-seven-year-old whose family fled Jewish persecution in Ukraine when she was a child and settled in Chicago, where she became active in the union movement while still a teenager, taking part in demonstrations and writing articles for a union newspaper. Throughout the thirties and forties, she worked in labor organizing and in efforts to advance civil liberties and other causes seen by some as communist-inspired, which brought the unwelcome attention of the federal government in the McCarthy era of the early 1950s. By then she was living in Los Angeles, and in 1956, federal agents arrested her under the McCarran-Walter Act of 1952, which restricted immigration and broadened the reasons noncitizens could be deported, including, as alleged in her case, membership in the Communist Party. A long legal fight against the deportation followed, during which time she worked as a secretary and wrote and published novels set in the Great Depression and the McCarthy era, and a collection of correspondence she had conducted with prison inmates. Finally, after nearly thirty years of appeals, the deportation order was dismissed, and in 1985, she stood with other immigrants at the federal courthouse in downtown Los Angeles and took the oath to become an American citizen.[17]

Shapiro-Bertolini died in 1998, but those who knew her during her Lincoln Place years remember a woman who was small in stature but large in personality, with a fiery, outspoken temperament. She and her husband, Angelo Bertolini, a character actor who had appeared in such films as *Lady in White*, moved to Lincoln Place in 1974, and she soon became an active member of the Venice Town Council, a citizen's group set up by Pat Russell to give input on real estate development and other community issues. The eviction of longtime tenants who would have trouble finding new places they could afford obviously struck a nerve with someone who had spent her life fighting the perceived injustices of social, racial, and economic inequality. Employing skills from her union organizing days, she went knocking on her neighbors' doors, telling them about the evictions and inviting them to a meeting at her apartment to talk about a plan for resistance.

One of those neighbors, a twenty-nine-year-old woman named Lisa Weilmann, helped produce a one-page flyer titled "Statement of Lincoln Place Neighbors" and she and other volunteers distributed it throughout the complex prior to the July 29 public meeting called by Galanter. The flyer noted the sale of the property, the raising of rents for new tenants, and the eviction notices under the major-rehabilitation section of the RSO. It stated, "We, the Lincoln Place Neighbors, feel that these 'rehabilitations' are simply a ploy to decontrol the units. The apartments have always been very well maintained, and the new owners have not been 'rehabilitating' apartments vacated under normal turnover." It noted that some of the families facing eviction had lived at Lincoln Place for more than fifteen years, and concluded with, "We intend to take political action, as well as legal action."

A second flyer, titled "Strength in Numbers, Tenants Unite," quickly appeared. Addressed to "Lincoln Place Neighbors" and distributed to all the units in the complex, the flyer again noted the ten eviction notices and said, "It appears that these evictions are intended to enable the Lincoln Place Apartments investors to double or triple the rents and increase their cash flow and profits by destroying moderate-income opportunities." It included the names and phone numbers of key city council members and state and congressional representatives, and ended by urging people to call the offices of those persons and register their concerns. Yet another flyer notified tenants that on August 4 the city council would vote on the Wachs motion for an emergency moratorium on major rehab evictions, and it urged people to attend the meeting if possible.

The call for people to get themselves to city hall for the meeting was a big success. According to an *L.A. Times* account, some seventy-five Lincoln Place tenants were in the council chamber the day of the meeting.[18] One of them, Nick Zonen, told council members that Lincoln Place units were in good condition and didn't need rehabbing. "The so-called improvements are a sham, an insidious ruse to increase rents," he said. Another tenant who addressed the council was Marcia Misius, who had vowed at the July 29 public meeting to fight her eviction with the help of an attorney. She told council members that she had lived at Lincoln Place for thirteen years and was paying $300 a month in rent, but had been informed by management that if she wanted to return after the rehab work on her unit was finished the rent would be $875. A third tenant, eighty-eight-year-old Sol Weingast, told the council that he lived on a $444 a month Social Security check and paid $390 in rent. He hadn't gotten an eviction notice, but assumed that he would be getting one in the near future. "Where would I go but on the streets of Los Angeles?" he said.

On the other side the debate, a spokesman for the Los Angeles Housing Council, a coalition of major property owners, told the council that the moratorium on evictions "is a moratorium on rehabilitation." He warned that raising the financial threshold might encourage owners to simply demolish old buildings rather than fixing them up, which would lead to a decrease in badly needed housing.

Many people believed the council was under the influence of real estate and development interests, but it may have been swayed by the sight of so many tenants at one of its often sparsely attended meetings, because the moratorium was approved by a 13–0 vote. The action meant an immediate reprieve for tenants facing eviction at Lincoln Place and other apartment complexes in the city, but almost everyone expected a vigorous, if not acrimonious, debate on any permanent changes to the major rehab provision and other sections of the RSO. In addition to raising the $10,000 threshold, some tenant advocates wanted to allow evictions only for work required by the city's building code, such as repairs or improvements to the electrical and plumbing systems. Others wanted to try to remove the major rehab provision entirely, while still others saw the upcoming debate as an opportunity to try to get rid of vacancy decontrol. But powerful interests were lined up on the other side; real estate developers, apartment-house owners, and others who might see an opportunity to persuade the council to repeal rent control altogether after eight years of what they believed to have been an ill-advised and failed experiment.

In the meantime, Shapiro-Bertolini, along with Weilmann and several other members of an ad hoc steering committee, decided to reorganize Lincoln Place Neighbors as the Lincoln Place Tenants Association, or LPTA. In a bulletin distributed on August 10, 1987, this change was announced, along with a basic membership fee of fifteen dollars per adult or twenty-five per family. Also announced was a general tenant meeting to be held on August 13 at the city-owned Penmar Park recreation center, which was just a short walk from most of the Lincoln Place apartments.

Several dozen tenants turned out for the meeting in the center's multipurpose room, a large, blandly institutional space used for a variety of community activities. The evening meeting was chaired by Weilmann, who went over the proposed structure of the LPTA, with a fifteen-member steering committee as well as other committees to handle such matters as publicity, legal affairs, political action, and anything else deemed to be relevant. And perhaps most importantly, each of the fifty-two buildings in the complex would have an appointed captain whose job would be to pass out flyers and other materials, answer questions, and generally act as liaison between the steering committee and tenants.

A month after the Penmar Park meeting, the city council voted to increase the required relocation payments to $2,000 and $5,000, respectively. But action on the major rehab provision and other parts of the RSO had to await recommendations from the city's Rent Adjustment Commission. That body met on a Thursday afternoon at the city housing department offices in a turn-of-the-century office building downtown that, in a twist some might find ironic, has since been converted to apartments that are listed for rent between $1,600 and $3,500 a month. The seven commissioners appointed by Mayor Tom Bradley heard from tenant activists and landlord representatives before recommending a change in the $10,000 threshold for major rehabilitation. The total amount would remain the same, but in the future ninety percent would have to be for code-required repairs. This came to be known as the 90/10 provision, and commissioners clearly believed that it addressed complaints that landlords were evicting tenants to do purely cosmetic work on their units. As for vacancy decontrol, the commissioners listened to arguments for and against it, but decided to keep hands off this holy grail of landlords and *bête noire* of tenant activists.

The next stop in the tenants' quest to stop what they believed were grossly unfair evictions was the city council's government operations committee, which would take up the 90/10 proposal as well as other possible changes in the RSO. How it would fare in the three-member committee became a topic of vigorous discussion. Chairman Michael Woo, the first Asian-American elected to the city council, was a liberal Democrat, and his district, which encompassed Hollywood and the communities of Silverlake and Highland Park, had a large percentage of renters. A second member, Gloria Molina, was the first Latina elected to the council and represented a heavily Latino district east of downtown, which also had a significant percentage of renters. The third member, Joan Flores, was a pro-business Republican who had expressed negative views in the past about rent control, although neither she nor Woo and Molina were council members in 1979 when the RSO was adopted.

The committee was scheduled to meet at city hall on February 3, 1988. On January 30, the LPTA put out a notice calling for tenants to do everything in their power to attend. The meeting would begin at 8:30 a.m., and a pair of buses chartered to take people downtown would be ready for boarding at seven in the large cul-de-sac in the center of the Lincoln Place called Elkgrove Circle. "This is the time we need everyone to be there," the notice said. "This is a very important hearing!"

Because a large number of people were expected, the committee met in the city hall's council chamber rather than in one of the smaller rooms where committee meetings were typically held. Many consider the thirty-two-story building in downtown's civic center one of the city's finest art deco landmarks, but when people entered the main rotunda for the first time, they might have imagined themselves in a Byzantine church, with marble columns, soaring arches, and highly decorated mosaic floor, wall, and ceiling panels. That design was carried into the council chamber just off the south side of the rotunda, with marble columns marching along both sides of the high-ceilinged space from the entry doors in the back to the semicircle of council members' desks. Public seating consisted of two rows of polished pew-like benches on either side of a central aisle that led to a podium with microphone where speakers could address the council or whatever body was meeting in the chamber.

Woo, a trim thirty-eight-year-old whose round, dark-framed glasses lent him a professorial look, was considered a potential tenant ally, but activists worried about Flores, because of her past views on rent control and representation of a district with a majority of homeowners. And while

Molina's district contained a good proportion of renters, it also suffered from substandard housing, and she had spoken of the need for the city to provide incentives for landlords to rehabilitate their properties. Taking away the major rehab provision of the RSO could be a problem for her.

More than a hundred Lincoln Place tenants heeded the call and boarded the buses for the forty-five-minute trip on the I-10 freeway to downtown and city hall. When the meeting got underway, some members of the LPTA spoke of their fears of being evicted and having to desperately search for new places to live that they could afford. Other speakers demanded that the major rehab provision either be eliminated, or rewritten to raise the $10,000 threshold and require that work on a unit be done to comply with orders by the city's building, health, and fire departments, or to repair damage resulting from fire, earthquake, or other natural disaster.

The committee discussed the issue without taking a formal vote. Two weeks later, at another meeting packed with tenants, activists, and real estate lobbyists, it recommended adoption of the 90/10 provision but kept hands off the contentious subject of vacancy decontrol. Woo had seemed open to the idea of completely eliminating the major rehab provision, but Molina expressed concern about the effect on owners of buildings with units that genuinely needed repairs. Among members of the full council, Ruth Galanter appeared most strongly in favor of jettisoning the provision, but when the committee's report landed on council members' desks, there wasn't a clear majority in favor of that or any other specific position. As a result, the council did what detractors often called "kicking the can down the road" and voted to extend the soon-expiring moratorium and send the matter back to the committee for further analysis and discussion.

Despite the delay, the LPTA felt confident that positive changes were on the horizon. An April 1988 newsletter declared, "WE ARE COMING INTO THE HOME STRETCH! The moratorium on major-rehabilitation evictions has once again been extended for sixty days. Our work is paying off!" But tenant activists at Lincoln Place and elsewhere knew how much clout landlords and other real estate interests wielded at city hall and they weren't about to let down their guard while lobbyists buttonholed city council members to argue against more stringent rent control measures.

That spring and summer the government operations committee met but failed to reach consensus on the major rehab provision. This was where matters stood when Sheila Bernard rented a two-bedroom apartment at Lincoln Place in August of 1988. She was born in Los Angeles, but her accountant father and homemaker mother were always looking for a better house in a better neighborhood, and every few years, she and her three brothers found themselves facing the prospect of having to make friends in a new community and new school. "I was never in one place long enough to really feel that it was home," she says. "And when I had kids of my own, I really wanted that for them. When I saw Lincoln Place, I thought that maybe I had found it. A place to genuinely call home."

That was twenty years after she graduated from high school in Anaheim, the Orange County city most widely known as the home of Disneyland, and enrolled in the freshman class at UCLA. Her parents were politically and socially liberal, and dinner table conversations often touched on such subjects as politics and civil rights. She developed a strong interest in social movements that fought inequality and promoted democratic principles, but in her first two years at UCLA, she "kept her head down," as she puts it, and concentrated on her studies rather than get involved in the Vietnam War protests and other social and political stirrings common on college campuses in the late 1960s. At UCLA she also met her future husband, whose views about alternative ways of living helped kindle the fervent interest in cooperative ideals that would take so much of her time and energy after she got to Lincoln Place.

After graduating in 1971 with a degree in public service, she married and moved to the San Fernando Valley, where she gave birth to a daughter, Nerisha, and two years later, a son, Aryeh. She and her husband became involved in the organic farming and food movement, and she helped establish the warehouse cooperative to distribute organic food to retail outlets and managed the operation for the next seven years. But when she and her husband separated in 1980, she decided to change course and applied for a teaching job with the Los Angeles Unified School District. After a stint teaching seventh grade math, she moved to the district's continuing education program, where she taught subjects like math and English to adults whose education had been interrupted for various reasons, including incarceration and the need to work to support a family. Teachers in the program were commonly moved from school to school, depending upon need, and the next few years she lived in different parts of the city. A short-lived relationship resulted in the birth of her youngest son, Avi, and she often felt a kind of longing to give him the permanence she had never felt as a child, moving so often from place to place. In 1987 she met a man who lived in Venice, and made yet another move with her children to live with him and his two children in the seaside community that she knew little about. That relationship, however, didn't last, and in the summer of 1988, she found herself looking for a place where she could settle down and try again to make something resembling a permanent home for herself and her children.

Ads for Lincoln Place Apartments were then appearing in the *Los Angeles Times* classifieds, but she didn't see them. Instead, she was driving around one day looking for rental signs and found herself on the east side of Lincoln Blvd, where the shopping center with its supermarket, drugstore, and home improvement store mostly hid Lincoln Place buildings from the view of motorists on the busy thoroughfare. When she got a closer look, it was a kind of love at first sight.

"I knew that was the place," she says. "We could make a home there. And it could be a cooperative, too. That's what came to my mind."

She found the rental office, where the resident manager told her that a two-bedroom apartment would shortly be available. The rent was $800 a month, which she could manage on her teacher's salary, although making ends meet with three children was always a challenge and had taught her to be frugal. Her daughter, Nerisha, was then twelve years old, and Aryeh and Avi were ten and four, respectively. The building was part of an irregular arrangement of seven attached structures in the southwest part of the complex, with an entrance to the building's four units from a courtyard set back from the street. Like all units in the complex, the ground-floor apartment had oak floors, built-in bookcases, and liberal amounts of ceramic tile in the kitchen and single bathroom. It wasn't particularly large, but it was light and airy, with the living room windows looking out onto the courtyard with its leafy Brazilian pepper tree.

"I took one look and said I'd take it," Bernard recalls. Her daughter got one bedroom, and her sons the other, and she bought some four-by-fours and plywood and built a sleeping loft for herself in the living room. Her mother had taught her to sew, and she had made some pieces of clothing for herself and the children with a sewing machine that she installed on a table beneath the loft, a place where she would also stow the bicycle that she came to use as a means of daily transportation. As a woman with a sociable personality, she quickly began to get to know her neighbors, a diverse group from all walks of life. One woman was a retired farm worker in her sixties who had labored in the fields since she was sixteen years old. There was a restaurant worker who had grown up in Mexico, and a couple who were both artists. There was a fellow public school teacher. She describes them as positive and friendly, although all was not idyllic—some young people were dealing drugs from the apartment across the hall, but they were eventually rousted by the police and evicted.

When Bernard moved into Lincoln Place, she had no inkling of the drama that had unfolded almost exactly a year earlier after the first ten residents got eviction notices. She had never heard of the LPTA. But one day a flyer from the tenants' group appeared under her door, a notice of an LPTA meeting that weekend at the Penmar Park recreation center. The topic of discussion would be evictions.

Evictions? The property manager hadn't said anything about people being evicted. In her brief contacts with her new neighbors, the subject hadn't been mentioned. What could it mean? She decided that she had to find out.

"I walked into the Penmar room on the day of the meeting," she says, "And what I saw was a sea of white hair. I also found out that my rent of $800 a month was twice what most of those seniors were paying, and that it was those seniors who were being threatened with eviction."

Many of them, she learned, had worked during World War II at the nearby Douglas Aircraft plant, and some had lived at Lincoln Place since it had first opened its doors. It struck her as very wrong that these people could be thrown out of their homes just so the landlord could charge higher rents. She didn't know anything about the subjects discussed at the meeting, like major rehabilitation and changes to the rent stabilization ordinance.

But when she left the room that day, she knew that in some way she was going to get involved. The fact that people had organized and were fighting back against what they viewed as an injustice heartened her and confirmed her sense that Lincoln Place was the right setting for her dream of a society organized around the principle of mutual benefit and cooperative ownership. But she knew that she had much more to learn about the issues involved, more meetings to attend, before she could begin to advance her vision. Thus, a long and ultimately harrowing education began.

4

WHERE WILL I GO?

We hope that 1989 will be the year when those of us who rent our homes will find some justice and security.

—LPTA Bulletin

SHORTLY AFTER TEN O'CLOCK on the morning of October 4, 1989, Los Angeles City Council President John Ferraro took his seat on the dais above the arc of council members' desks and gaveled the regular Wednesday meeting to order. On the agenda that morning were permanent changes to the Rent Stabilization Ordinance, and the chamber was packed with tenants, housing advocates, landlords, and real estate lobbyists. Council members who looked out over this crowd could hardly miss seeing all the gray and white heads, along with a profusion of yellow tags that read *Close The Loopholes.* They could also see the smaller number of landlords and their supporters congregated on one side of the chamber, which presented council members with the political dilemma at the heart of rent control—a vote against tighter regulations could put those senior citizens at risk of eviction, while a vote to make the law more stringent could jeopardize support from powerful real estate interests that poured millions into city election campaigns.

For Lincoln Place tenants who arrived at city hall that morning in buses chartered by the LPTA, the two years since the city council adopted the first in a series of moratoriums on major rehab evictions felt like an eternity. They had answered calls to show up at meetings of the rent adjustment commission, the council's government operations committee, and the council itself, which more than once had treated the issue of rent control and evictions like a hot potato and tossed it back to the committee for further study. They had written letters, made phone calls, and waited with varying degrees of patience through the 1989 city election campaign, a period when action on controversial issues tends to be put on hold until council races are decided. But now the last of the moratoriums was about to expire, and everyone expected a vote on the rent control changes that tenants hoped would protect them from being rudely thrown out of their homes.

Tenant advocates had pressed for elimination of the major rehab provision and strict limits on the capital improvement costs that landlords could pass on to tenants. Almost all those advocates wanted to get rid of vacancy decontrol. But landlords vociferously opposed these changes. They were especially passionate about vacancy decontrol, which was the one thing, they argued, that gave them hope of a reasonable return on their investments.

Adding fuel to this volatile debate were media reports of a growing affordable-housing crisis in the city. One oft-repeated news story told of an elementary schoolteacher who sold flowers at night in upscale restaurants in order to make ends meet. Other stories documented cases of large families forced to crowd into small apartments or illegally converted garages. And there were the indignities and outright horrors faced by those forced to live in makeshift shelters on city streets. In November 1988, the *Los Angeles Times* had published a three-part series titled "Through the Roof: L.A.'s Crisis in Rental Housing" that found, among other things, that some 150,000 families in the city paid more than a third of their income for rent, and that a significant percentage of those paid more than half, a group dominated, unsurprisingly, by Latinos and African Americans. It was no surprise, either, that tenant advocates pointed to these facts as demonstrating the need for stronger rent control, while landlords contended that rent control was actually the culprit because it gave owners an incentive to convert their properties to condominiums or simply demolish them and put up new buildings with units that could be rented at market rates.

Michael Woo, chairman of the government operations committee, had initially supported elimination of the major rehab provision, but he couldn't muster enough support and the committee ended up recommending the 90/10 provision. Additionally, landlords evicting tenants for major rehabilitation would have to keep the units vacant for a minimum of forty-five days, and could re-rent only seventy-five percent of them at market rates, with the remainder kept affordable to lower-income tenants. And finally, evicted tenants would have a first right of refusal if they wanted to come back to their apartments when work was finished. The vexatious issue of vacancy decontrol wasn't on the agenda at all, having been relegated by the committee to the wilderness of future study and discussion.

Ferraro, who would become the longest serving council member in the city's history, had been an All-American football player at the University of Southern California, and at six-five and well over two hundred pounds, he cut an imposing figure in city hall. He ran council meetings with a firm hand, but was also known for his impartiality and frequent display of dry wit. The RSO changes were item nine on the agenda, but those who had piled into buses at Lincoln Place and driven from other areas of the city were hopeful that the council would take the item out of order and not force the large number of tenant supporters to sit through mostly routine matters that had nothing to do with them. Before that could happen, though, Ferraro announced that police chief Daryl Gates was present and would give council members details of a dramatic drug bust just six days earlier in the San Fernando Valley that had resulted in the seizure of twenty tons of cocaine.[19]

Gates took nearly an hour talking about the bust and answering council members' questions. The long-serving chief had already aroused criticism, especially in minority communities, for his aggressive approach to law enforcement, including the use of military tactics and equipment, and he would resign under pressure less than three years later amid the storm that raged in the wake of the infamous Rodney King beating. But at the October 4 meeting, Gates and some of the council members fulminated about the state of the US-Mexican border, even calling for then-President Ronald Reagan to send troops to help staunch the flow of cocaine and other drugs into the United States. The police chief called the porous condition of the border "a national disgrace," a portent, perhaps, of a view that would gain high visibility with the election almost exactly twenty years later of Donald Trump.

Some Lincoln Place tenants and others waiting to hear debate on the RSO changes were fuming when Ferraro finally called item number one on the agenda. Councilman Zev Yaroslavsky, who represented a west-side district with affluent communities like Westwood and Bel Air but was considered a rent control supporter, moved to take item nine out of order, and asked people in the audience who had come to speak and listen to the debate on the RSO changes to stand up. Councilwoman Gloria Molina observed that people were also waiting for agenda item one, and called it "ridiculous" to choose based on the numbers of people in the audience. Councilman Nate Holden also argued for taking items in order, but the council voted 11–2 for Yaroslavsky's motion, and debate on the issues that had caused so much grief and consternation to Lincoln Place tenants and others in the city finally got underway.

Barbara Zeidman, the city's Rent Stabilization director, outlined the changes proposed by Woo's committee. Ferraro then opened the floor to public comment, with pro and con sides each allotted ten minutes. The first speaker was Larry Gross, executive director of the Coalition for Economic Survival, the city's major renters' advocacy group, who contended that the 90/10 provision would be ineffective due to the large number of things that technically required permits; for example, installing a garbage disposer or a dishwasher. He called for raising the major rehab threshold to $15,000 and said that keeping twenty-five percent of rehabbed units at affordable rents was "too little, too late."

"You are about to take an important step in closing rent control loopholes that result in a loss of affordable housing," he told the council. "Why take half a step when you can take a full step?"

But a dire scenario was painted by speakers who opposed changes to the rent control law. Taking away incentives for landlords to maintain their properties would just lead to less badly needed affordable housing. Buildings would be boarded up, or torn down, turning large swaths of the city into slums. The very concept of rent control came under attack—the law mainly benefited drug dealers who would turn entire buildings into crack houses; rent control was something befitting Russia, not the United States of America.

While council members didn't appear to share these apocalyptic views, several were concerned about keeping incentives for landlords to maintain their properties. One of those was Molina, who spoke of the need to maintain a "delicate balance" between protecting tenants and encouraging the rehabilitation of deteriorated buildings. Along with Woo and Flores, she had visited Lincoln Place earlier in the year for a firsthand look at the epicenter of the eviction controversy, and she told her fellow council members that it was obvious the owner wasn't trying to kick out tenants in order to make badly need repairs, but to "gentrify" the apartments. Nevertheless, she opposed Ruth Galanter's call to raise the major rehab cost threshold to $15,000, arguing that it would be too high for many landlords in her predominately working class, Latino district. Councilman Richard Alatorre, who represented an adjacent and also heavily Latino district, concurred with Molina, predicting that adoption of a $15,000 threshold could mean the loss of badly needed housing in his area.

In the end, with strong expressions of support from Woo, Yaroslavsky, and a plea from Councilman Joel Wachs, who said, "If we're going to err, I want to err on the side of the tenants, I'll tell you that," the council voted to approve the 90/10 provision. While this would allow Lincoln Place tenants and others to breathe a little easier, nobody in the audience applauded when Ferraro announced the result. Cosmetic changes of the kind made to Lincoln Place units would no longer be a legal justification for evictions, but the lure of increased rents and profits would remain a powerful incentive to get rid of tenants paying less than the going rates. It's doubtful that any tenant in the council chamber that day believed that it was the last time he or she would be asked to climb onto buses and make the trip downtown to city hall.

Two months before that council meeting, Sheila Bernard had been elected president of the LPTA. The first president, Lisa Weilmann, stepped down earlier in the year, and a man served briefly in the position before buying a house with his wife and moving away. "It kind of fell to me by default," Bernard says. "Nobody else really wanted it." Since attending her first LPTA meeting in the fall of 1988, she had been getting more deeply involved in the group's affairs, but had been cautious about airing her vision of tenants owning the complex. By the end of 1989, though, with the RSO changes and stronger tenant protections in place, she felt the time had come to try to rally the LPTA in support of a plan to buy the property. Given the fact that the owner, TransAction Companies Ltd., had failed to realize the goal of increasing revenues by evicting low-paying tenants, she was optimistic that the company's principals, James Coxeter and Robert Bisno, would be willing to listen to a serious offer.

TransAction had taken over day-to-day management of the complex from an outside management company in the summer of 1989. The change was announced in the monthly newsletter put out by management, now called *Lincoln Place News* instead of the former *Lincoln Place Times* and sporting a much more professional appearance in terms of layout and graphics. The issue announcing the management change included a message to residents from Coxeter, who wrote, "We hope to enter a new era of tenant-manager relations. We believe that some regrettable mistakes were made in the past due to miscommunication. Our hope is to start fresh with open communication right from the beginning."

Many took this to mean that Coxeter and Bisno recognized that the attempted evictions had been a public relations disaster, and were trying to put a kinder, gentler face on management, although few were ready to believe that the place would now be run in the benign way it had during the thirty-seven years of ownership by one of the original builders and his heirs. For readers of the newsletter, a clue could be found in a reference to the complex's "downhill slide" and the need to address such things as deteriorated plumbing and electrical systems. The question this raised wasn't whether the owners had plans for the complex, but just what those plans were and how they would ultimately affect residents' lives.

In fact, many tenants believed that the "downhill slide" could be laid directly at the feet of TransAction. In June 1989, a tenant wrote to the LPTA to complain about peeling paint, poorly tended landscaping, and the dirty condition of common areas like laundry rooms. Other long-term tenants recalled that the previous owners had kept the property in immaculate condition, and decried what they saw as deliberate neglect. Many noticed that the security guards who had roved the property for a number of years had disappeared along with the change in ownership. Was TransAction cutting back on maintenance and security just to save money, or was this part of a larger plan being developed in lieu of the thwarted evictions?

The answer began to emerge with the advent of the new year. Tenants responding to knocks on their doors were greeted by a woman from a firm called Sweeney and Associates, who said she was conducting a "Community Profile Survey." The tenants were asked to fill out a two-page form with detailed questions about age, marital status, occupation, names and ages of children, and disabilities, among other things. The survey ended by asking the tenants to describe their feelings and impressions about living at Lincoln Place.

Some objected to the questions as intrusive, and others wondered who had authorized the survey and how the results would be used. But those who questioned the survey taker were able to glean some ominous though not particularly surprising information, which was that the gathering of data on tenants was part of the prelude to a plan for redeveloping the property.

At first, it was unclear what form this redevelopment might take. But as the news made its way through the tenant grapevine, people began calling Ruth Galanter's office and questioning employees in the Lincoln Place management office. While those employees would only confirm that redevelopment was being considered, an aide to Galanter told a tenant that TransAction had shared a rough outline of its plan with the councilwoman. According to the aide, the redevelopment would likely involve the demolition of most of the buildings and construction of new condominiums. Before any work could begin, of course, the plan would have to go through environmental review and public hearings, a process the company estimated would take about three years.

These facts convinced Bernard that the time had come for a major push to build support for cooperative ownership. She had already broached the subject with the ten-member LPTA steering committee, and while most favored the idea in concept they were skeptical that a tenants' group with no experience in buying and operating such a large complex could succeed. "It was scary," she says. "Where would we get the money? And if we somehow got the money, how would we manage the property? They liked the idea, but I think in the beginning they just thought it was a crazy dream." Bernard, who seldom raises her voice but projects a quiet intensity, worked hard to overcome that initial skepticism. During the fight against major rehab evictions, the LPTA had become a member of Housing L.A., a coalition of tenant associations and community organizations working to preserve and create affordable housing in the city, and two steering committee members had been delegated to attend the group's meetings. Bernard knew that a UCLA urban planning professor named Allan Heskin was active in Housing L.A. and actually lived in a cooperatively owned housing development near downtown L.A. called the Route 2 Project. "Ask him what he thinks," she told the steering committee members, Frieda Marlin and Harriet Wood. "Ask him if he thinks we could buy Lincoln Place."

Heskin, who had extensive experience with tenant movements and was about to publish a book on the Route 2 Project, told Marlin and Wood that, yes, tenants could buy Lincoln Place.[20] It wouldn't be easy, and they would need the help of professionals, but it was certainly possible. When the women brought this message back to the steering committee, the opposition to Bernard's pie-in-the-sky fantasy melted away. She assured everyone that a professional management company would be hired for day-to-day operations. Money would be raised not only to purchase the complex but also to make needed repairs. Other than the fact that tenants would no longer have to fear eviction or large rent increases, their daily lives at Lincoln Place would be largely unchanged.

Bernard convinced her colleagues that it was worth meeting with Coxeter to find out if TransAction might be amenable to a sale. On May 17, 1990, she and three steering committee members met with the owner in a ground-floor apartment that had been converted by the landlord into a public meeting room. According to a brief description of the meeting in the June issue of the LPTA newsletter, Coxeter told the three tenants that the property was always for sale "at the right price." He said he was open to further dialogue and would consider a request for details about Lincoln Place's income and expenses, something that would be needed in order to put together a realistic purchase offer.

That newsletter opened with an article titled "Why Are We Discussing Cooperative Ownership?" Written by Bernard, it presented tenant options for the future, beginning with being left alone—living, that is, without the threat of eviction or any demolition and redevelopment. Other options included being paid to relocate, being allowed to return to new units at current rents, and cooperatively owning the complex. The LPTA steering committee, the article said, overwhelmingly preferred the first option, but since that was apparently unrealistic, the next best would be tenant ownership of the entire property. A second article, titled "Why Cooperative Ownership of Lincoln Place Makes Sense," posed some questions and answers, including a rebuttal to Coxeter's frequently repeated claim that the buildings were in poor condition. "It is true," Bernard wrote, "that our buildings may need work at some point, and eventually will need to be rebuilt. But for the foreseeable future, they are very comfortable, and do not need to be demolished, thrown into a landfill, replaced with newer, taller, denser and more expensive buildings." That message concluded with, "We want to stay here, strengthen our social bonds, sink roots, plant trees, and live in a stable community." Finally, the newsletter announced a general meeting on the evening of June 21 at the Penmar Park recreation center where experts on the subject of tenant ownership would answer residents' questions.

More than a hundred tenants showed up for this meeting, along with aides to Councilwoman Galanter and State Senator David Roberti, whose district encompassed Venice. Speakers included a private housing consultant and a professor in the UCLA Graduate School of Architecture and Urban Planning. In summarizing the meeting, the July issue of the LPTA newsletter said, "The message of the speakers came through loud and clear: a tenant buyout at Lincoln Place is possible and similar events have occurred in Los Angeles and throughout the country." Encouraged by this positive response, the LPTA steering committee voted to initiate a search for a professional consultant to perform a feasibility study and handle the financial and legal aspects of what most understood would be a formidable challenge, even if TransAction was willing to sell at a reasonable price.

While the LPTA was taking these nascent steps toward Bernard's dream, James Coxeter began inviting small groups of tenants to meetings for the stated purpose of gathering feedback about the future of the complex. One attendee was Ingrid Mueller, who moved to Lincoln Place in October 1988 and became an active LPTA member after Bernard assumed the presidency. An energetic woman with liberal political views, Mueller volunteered to help with meetings and communications, including design and paste-up work on a longer, more polished newsletter. She recalls meeting with Coxeter and a handful of other tenants at a Marie Callender's restaurant in Marina Del Rey, the upscale apartment and condominium community just south of Venice.

Coxeter was "very congenial," Mueller says, buying coffee and donuts for everyone and projecting a genuine desire to hear what the tenants thought about Lincoln Place. But Mueller, whose father had died when she was a sixteen-year-old in Germany and who navigated different parts of the world on her own before coming to the United States, wasn't taken in. "What he really wanted was for us to support his project," she says. "He had us all sign in, and we found out later that our signatures were used to show that tenants really favored the new development when most of us were totally against it." She left that meeting, she says, with a strengthened feeling that tenants should get behind Bernard's plan to turn Lincoln Place into some kind of cooperative. "I thought it was great," she says. "We wouldn't always be under some awful landlord's thumb. We could do community gardens, lots of good things."

Another tenant who failed to be swayed by Coxeter's blandishments was Jan Book, who attended a meeting with the landlord and other residents on August 22, 1990. By that time, specific details of the proposed redevelopment had emerged. Lincoln Place as it had stood for forty years would cease to exist. In place of the fifty-two buildings in their parklike setting, TransAction proposed to build 655 for-sale townhouses and 205 rental units in a gated complex with a pool and the other amenities people looking to buy or rent in a gentrifying area of the city would expect. The construction would be done in phases over ten years, with existing units not re-rented when they became vacant but used to temporarily house tenants whose buildings were scheduled to be demolished. In that way, according to Coxeter, nobody would have to be evicted.

Book, who had gone to law school for four years at night while working full-time as an accountant, was not persuaded. The next day she wrote Coxeter a three-page letter detailing her objections to the redevelopment plan, focusing on the fact that the plan would result in a severe reduction in the existing number of 795 rental units. "You were very clever," she wrote, "To steer away from the fact that within ten years, there will be 595 fewer rental units available in Venice."

Coxeter had promoted the redevelopment, in large part, as a solution not only to maintenance issues but to parking problems and crime, but Book contended in her letter that parking issues were caused by tenants using their garages and carports for storage, and that crime could be addressed by having continuous patrols through the complex. She wrote, "I have a great affection for LPA [Lincoln Place Apartments]. I love the 50s look of the buildings. I love the neighborhood feeling here. I cannot afford a house, but at LPA, I feel like I live in a house with a lawn and good neighbors." She concluded by asking, "In ten years, where will I and my young neighbors live?"

Another tenant reacted to the proposed redevelopment in a letter to the LPTA signed only as "Concerned Resident." He or she wrote, "I like living here just the way it is, aside from the deplorable maintenance neglect as perpetrated by the present management. These apartments have a certain open, low-key sturdy ambiance that will surely be destroyed if they are surgically altered with underground parking, additional high-density buildings, etc. Why should a group of greedy, insensitive investors have the right to displace and alter the lives of so many people?"

Undeterred by the swelling chorus of opposition, Coxeter and TransAction continued the sales pitch for the redevelopment plan. In November 1990, Coxeter sent Book, Bernard and other tenants who had attended the so-called planning meetings a letter thanking them for their participation and announcing that Sweeney and Associates would be conducting another survey focused on the future of Lincoln Place. Enclosed with the letter was a brochure with the heading "Lincoln Place: helping shape the future." Below this piece of marketing jargon was a photo of Coxeter in rolled-up sleeves talking to a pair of tenants outside one of the buildings, an image obviously intended to convey the message that TransAction was seriously listening to tenant concerns. But inside the brochure, under the heading, "A possible solution: 'rethinking' Lincoln Place," there was a clear statement of the company's intentions, which had little to do with gathering tenant feedback and everything to do with pushing forward a plan that would mean the end of the vision that unfolded after Samuel Bialac bought the thirty-eight acres of vacant land at the end of World War II.

"After devoting the past year to 'hands-on' management of the apartments," the brochure said, "as well as studying the results of January's Community Profile Survey and examining maintenance records, crime statistics, and vacancy trends—Mr. Coxeter concluded that even extensive rehabilitation of the existing apartments could not bring the current plumbing and electrical systems in line with current demands or answer parking, circulation, safety and security concerns." In obvious anticipation of a major question, another heading read, "But Where Will I go?" The answer was notably vague. "For many Lincoln Place residents, especially seniors," the brochure declared, "their apartments are their permanent home. With this fact foremost in mind, Jim Coxeter and the TransAction team crafted a redevelopment concept designed to address resident concerns about meeting their housing needs. Taking advantage of the turnover rate at Lincoln Place, while implementing an eight to ten-year multiphased development, the entire site could be gradually redeveloped. In Jim Coxeter's words, 'the idea is to preserve the community, not destroy it.'"

This struck Book, Bernard, and others as highly disingenuous. The plan put forward by TransAction would absolutely destroy the Lincoln Place community in a physical sense, and despite promises that elderly and low-income tenants would have a home in the new development, it would drive out others who couldn't afford to buy the new condominiums or rent the new apartments and thus destroy the community of neighbors who had gotten to know each other, who cared about each other, who considered Lincoln Place their home and not just a stop on the way to another destination.

Not every resident of Lincoln Place opposed TransAction's plans, though. Despite a dearth of details, including the prices to be charged for the townhouses and the rents for the apartments, there were those who welcomed the idea that they might be able to live in a brand-new condominium or apartment. While well built, the existing apartments were forty years old and lacked the modern touches in new buildings like air conditioning, sliding glass doors, and built-in appliances. Regardless of the causes, parking was a problem. And crime was on the upswing, creating fear not only at Lincoln Place but also throughout Venice.

As the new year approached, holiday cheer in many Lincoln Place apartments was muted by uncertainty about the future. Even if elderly tenants were allowed to stay at affordable rents, what of the rigors, both physical and psychological, of moving to a new place? How would those with physical disabilities manage? What would happen to all those bonds of friendship that had developed over the years? There was uncertainly, and there was fear and anger over what many regarded as a product of wealthy investors' greed. But there was also a spark of optimism that Bernard and some other tenant leaders were trying to kindle into a full-fledged fire, the possibility that tenant ownership could not only save their homes but usher a new and exciting chapter into their lives.

5

LET'S OWN IT

AT THE BEGINNING OF 1991, which would prove for unrelated reasons to be one of the most consequential in Los Angeles history, the LPTA faced two formidable tasks. One was to come up with a tenant-purchase offer that TransAction couldn't refuse; the other was to stop the company's redevelopment plan before bulldozers rumbled onto the property and started knocking down buildings. Sheila Bernard and the LPTA leadership knew they had two years—three at the most—to save their homes and begin to create a Lincoln Place that would be a haven for its residents and serve as a statement that renters didn't have to be treated as second-class citizens.

Bernard and the steering committee members who met with James Coxeter the year before had come away with the sense that he would listen to a serious offer even though TransAction had no active plans to sell. According to public records, the company paid $28.7 million for the property in 1986, an amount some local realtors considered a bargain. But four years later, the country's eight-year economic expansion screeched to a halt, along with the upward spiral in real estate prices and the inevitable speculation that had helped fuel rent increases and the conversion of apartments to condominiums. Now, with an economic recession that was especially acute in urban areas of California, the redevelopment of Lincoln Place might not look quite so lucrative.

The LPTA's search for a consultant to conduct a feasibility analysis, identify funding sources, and handle negotiations with the owner led to the Agora Group, a northern California firm that specialized in low-income housing projects, including those organized as tenant cooperatives. In February of 1991, the LPTA signed a contract with the firm, which had its offices in Oakland, also the home city of TransAction. The contract obligated the LPTA to pay a hundred dollars per consultant hour plus travel expenses. While modest compared to fees charged by many consulting firms working in the private sector, it was a daunting commitment for an organization that depended upon contributions from tenants who were mostly seniors living on fixed incomes and people who worked at jobs that paid little more than enough to cover the rent and put food on the table.

In March, the Agora Group's principals, Edward Kirshner and Jennifer Bigelow, met with James Coxeter for the first time. Joining them for the meeting at Lincoln Place were Bernard and two members of the LPTA steering committee. Bernard recalls that Coxeter listened politely to the tenant proposal but wasn't forthcoming on the question of what TransAction would consider a reasonable offer for the property. His attitude was unchanged from their initial meeting, when he told committee members, in Bernard's words, that "everything's for sale at the right price." He also raised questions about the ability of tenants to manage such a large apartment complex, which struck Bernard and others as odd, since that would be the tenants' problem, not his. And finally, Coxeter told the gathering that TransAction was fully committed to its redevelopment plan and expected to start the process of getting needed city approvals in just a few months.

Bernard and the others left the meeting feeling a degree of frustration, but also determined to push forward. There was money to raise, not only to pay the consultants but for ongoing expenses like putting out newsletters and chartering buses to take people to meetings at city hall. The purchase plan would only work if a large majority of tenants embraced it, and an organized effort would have to be made to explain its benefits to everyone, not just those who came to LPTA meetings. City Councilwoman Ruth Galanter's endorsement of the plan could be critical too, which meant that the LPTA was well-advised to reach out and build support among her constituents in the Venice community, especially in the single-family neighborhoods surrounding Lincoln Place. In other words, the LPTA would need to take a page from Coxeter's and TransAction's book and conduct a vigorous marketing campaign to win over tenants, politicians, and community members.

To that end, Bernard hit upon the catchphrase "Let's Own It," which took its place at the top of the monthly LPTA newsletters and came to serve as a rallying cry for supporters of a tenant purchase. To reach a significant number of Spanish-speaking tenants, a volunteer was found to translate the newsletters and bulletins into that language. Each week, a "Talking Newsletter" was produced and recorded as a three-minute telephone message that people could hear by dialing a toll-free number. The steering committee brainstormed ideas for tenant outreach and fundraising—yard sales, holiday parties, raffles, silent auctions. The LPTA incorporated as a 501(c)(3) nonprofit organization and even followed TransAction's lead by joining the Venice Chamber of Commerce, an action Bernard hoped would help build support in the business community, particularly with the small business owners along nearby Lincoln Boulevard whose shops were patronized by many Lincoln Place tenants.

The vision of "Let's Own It" went beyond simply exchanging greedy corporate ownership for the benevolence of a structure that would protect tenants from eviction and exorbitant rent increases. Under the heading, "PICTURE THIS," an LPTA newsletter painted the following scene: "You go out your front door on a balmy summer evening and stroll a block or two to another unit just like yours. Inside is a cozy little restaurant, filled with your neighbors, some known to you and others new. On the menu are light snacks and beverages, and on the agenda are live music and a poetry reading. On the walls and on shelves are pottery and other fine art by your neighbors, who are displaying their work either for fun or for sale. On other nights at the Lincoln Place Pub, there are birthday and anniversary parties, speakers, videos, slide shows, discussions, pot luck dinners, meetings, game nights, and anything else tenants wish to schedule. Let's dare to dream and create! Let's Own it!" Those who called the talking newsletter heard similar appeals. "The good stuff we envision includes tall trees at full height and additional trees bearing everything from avocados to apricots." Another asked the listener to picture a large meeting room for residents. "Inside the community room is a dining area and a kitchen equipped with commercial appliances for preparing large community meals. Do we want it? We can get it! Stay informed. Let's own it!"

Were these just the starry musings of a hopeless romantic? Some may have believed that Bernard's head was indeed in the clouds, but her vision of Lincoln Place as a community where people knew and cared about their neighbors was consistent with principles of the garden city movement, which emphasized communal ownership and affordability. While TransAction's plan proposed some affordable rental units, the dominant element of the new Lincoln Place would be townhouses priced at the upper end of the area market, likely between three and four hundred thousand dollars. Even if the many seniors living at Lincoln Place were allowed to move into new apartments at their old rents, they wouldn't be around that long, and then what? Coxeter had told some tenants that the rental units would remain permanently affordable, but these apartments would be clustered in one corner of the property rather than scattered throughout the complex, which would create what Bernard and others regarded as a kind of low-income ghetto. That plan was completely antithetical to the principles that had guided Ralph Vaughn and his team in their design of Lincoln Place.

The seniors and other long-term tenants regarded Lincoln Place as home in the largest sense of that word, a place where they could live without fear of being uprooted, where they could plant flowers in the beds alongside their buildings, where they could take a lawn chair outside and sit beneath a pepper tree and chat with their neighbors, where they could be comfortable in the sense of that word as derived from the Latin root *confortare,* which means "to strengthen and console." Those tenants didn't have the most up-to-date appliances and latest stereo systems and fanciest chairs and sofas and the other consumer items marketers deemed essential to a "comfortable" lifestyle, but their homes gave them comfort by providing a sense of permanence and community. The Lincoln Place that glittered in the pages of TransAction's brochure promised the features seen in the pages of architectural magazines, but all of the landlord's renderings and descriptions did nothing to give anything resembling comfort to tenants staring into the uncertain future.

At that time, cooperatively owned housing projects were—and still are—relatively rare in Los Angeles. After all, the city grew from a sleepy hamlet in the early part of the nineteenth century to the urban behemoth it is today on the backs of successive real estate booms fueled by the promise that people could own their own homes on discrete plots of land. They wouldn't have to live cheek by jowl with others in the apartment buildings and row houses that distinguished eastern cities like Boston and New York. There would be apartment buildings in Los Angeles, of course, but they would be for families too poor to buy a single-family house, or for persons who, for various reasons, didn't want to put down permanent roots.

By the time TransAction bought Lincoln Place, however, the city was no longer dominated by single-family houses, and more than half the population lived in multifamily complexes of rental units or condominiums. Almost all of these, like Lincoln Place, were privately owned and operated, although a growing awareness of the problems of poverty and substandard housing in the 1960s had spurred the passage of government programs that provided money for affordable-housing cooperatives. In the latter part of that decade and into the 1970s, a half-dozen of these were developed in Los Angeles, all much smaller than Lincoln Place. But with the 1980 election of Ronald Reagan, with his tax-cutting, small-government philosophy, this financial support all but dried up. It wasn't until the election of George H. W. Bush in 1988 and his appointment of Jack Kemp as secretary of Housing and Urban Development that the picture brightened for those who believed in the principle of apartment dwellers owning and managing their own properties.

Kemp, a former professional football star and self-described "bleeding heart conservative," embraced such conservative orthodoxy as supply-side economics, but not the Reagan administration's hands-off approach to the social and economic problems that plagued the inner cities. The urban poor, Kemp believed, were caught in a cycle of dependency, but that cycle could be broken by giving them a genuine sense of ownership and responsibility for their own lives. To that end, he pushed the idea of tenants in public housing owning their own apartments. While that model wouldn't apply to a privately owned complex like Lincoln Place, Sheila Bernard believed that the secretary's rhetoric could have a positive effect on the LPTA's efforts. "The concept of cooperative housing and tenant ownership was being talked about on the federal level," she says. "And that was a good thing. If HUD could help public housing tenants own their units, it could show people what was possible, how low-income people could benefit. And programs could be expanded for people in private complexes, not just public housing."

One of the first steps the LPTA took to move "Let's Own It" forward was to form the nonprofit Lincoln Place Housing Corporation, the entity that would own the property. Under the structure proposed by the Agora Group, tenants wouldn't own their units as in a classic cooperative housing project, but would continue to pay rent. However, they would be given lifetime tenancy and rents would be strictly limited to comply with the city's Rent Stabilization Ordinance and HUD's affordability guidelines. Through a tenant-elected board of directors, all residents would have a voice in the decisions and actions that affected their homes and their lives, everything from rent increases to maintenance work to pet ownership policies.

Another necessary step before lining up financing and making a purchase offer was answering the question: Who lives at Lincoln Place? Statistics regarding such things as age, income level, and family size would likely be required by potential funding sources. Furthermore, Bernard and other LPTA leaders were skeptical of James Coxeter's claim that normal turnover—people leaving for reasons like wanting more space, moving for a job or buying a house—meant that over the ten-year construction period everyone who wanted to stay at Lincoln Place would be able to do so. Bernard even doubted that the proposed new rental units would accommodate all the seniors, single-parent families, and tenants with disabilities, let alone others who had no desire to move. But data was needed to prove it.

Some tenants were highly suspicious of surveys, believing with a degree of justification that the surveys conducted by Sweeney & Associates had been used to further TransAction's redevelopment plans. To assuage those fears, tenants were allowed to answer the LPTA questions anonymously, on forms they could fill out and return in sealed, unmarked envelopes. With the help of two student interns from UCLA's Graduate School of Architecture and Urban Planning, responses were collected from 488 Lincoln Place households, a number deemed sufficient for extrapolation to the resident population as a whole. By the end of July, a demographic picture of Lincoln Place had emerged.[21]

One of the most striking features of this picture was that almost twenty-seven percent of approximately fifteen hundred residents were over sixty-five. Another was that the median income of Lincoln Place households was only sixty percent of the median for all of Los Angeles County. In addition, thirty-four percent of those households had incomes classified by HUD guidelines as very low, meaning fifty percent or less than the area median income. Another twenty-four percent had incomes classified as low, or eighty percent or less than the median. In short, this meant that Lincoln Place residents were notably older and poorer than people in the rest of Venice and communities on the west side of Los Angeles. For Bernard and other LPTA members, it also showed that Lincoln Place was an important source of affordable housing, and should be preserved as such, not redeveloped into a complex affordable primarily to the so-called yuppies who were steadily becoming a more visible part of Venice's population.

The LPTA survey wasn't limited to the gathering of factual data, but asked tenants to state a preference among three alternatives: TransAction's redevelopment plan, tenant ownership of the property, or no change at all. Seventy-one percent of the respondents favored tenant ownership; only three percent supported the plan to tear everything down and build new apartments and condominiums.

While the results were heartening, the LPTA leadership was aware that some tenants were reluctant to express these sentiments publicly, fearing— with or without justification—that the landlord might retaliate by evicting them. Active LPTA members like Ingrid Mueller had no such qualms. She had come up with the graphic design and the bright yellow color for news-letters and bulletins, and she arranged for the printing of "Let's Own It" and "Preserve Lincoln Place" signs that people could put in their windows. "You could walk around and see all these signs in other people's windows," she says. "It was great to know that it wasn't just a few of us." Mueller was angry that the management hadn't said anything about the redevelopment plan when she moved in, although it was likely on the drawing boards. "I wouldn't have rented here," she says. "Not if I knew they were just planning to tear this wonderful place down."

But Bernard, Mueller, and other active LPTA members knew that tenant support alone wouldn't be enough to stop the redevelopment and make "Let's Own It" a success. They needed to be sure that Ruth Galanter was on their side. For one thing, federal housing programs were administered by the city, and the city council could have a voice in the use of funds that might be available to help the tenants buy the complex. For another, the city council operated, as a rule, on the unstated principle that when a council member supported or opposed a project in his or her own district, the other members would follow suit. This rule wasn't without exceptions, but both TransAction and the LPTA understood that getting Galanter's support was critical to their efforts.

This calculation was complicated by the fact Galanter was running for reelection, and there was more than the token opposition often faced by incumbents. While her 1987 campaign hammered at her opponent's alleged coziness with developers, the tables in the 1991 campaign were turned, and the half-dozen candidates running for the seat made the same accusation against her. In Venice, the most politically active part of the district, the subject of real estate development dominated the campaign. Community activists and others decried large projects that would bring added traffic, parking problems, and the gentrification seen as destructive of the economic and ethnic diversity that made the community so much more appealing than more homogeneous areas of the city. Galanter's strongest opponents tapped into this sentiment, and while she went into the campaign as the favorite, nobody was ready to declare her the winner before the ballots were cast.

The councilwoman fell short of the fifty percent needed to win outright in the April primary and faced a runoff in June. In the two-month general election campaign, though, the idea that she was a tool of development forces didn't gain serious traction and she won a second term by a comfortable margin. At that point, Sheila Bernard had seen and spoken briefly to her at public meetings, but had never had a private meeting to talk about Lincoln Place. "I didn't know how to talk to politicians," she says. "I guess I was intimidated by the idea." The political system was a foreign country, but she knew that she would have to get to know its customs if she wanted the city help push "Let's Own It" from the realm of catchy slogan to reality.

She hoped that a purchase offer could be presented to Coxeter before the end of the year. A nonprofit foundation called Liberty Hill had given the group a $5,000 grant to help pay the Agora Group, and the consultants were working to determine the size of a mortgage that could be supported by current rental income. The LPTA was told that an attorney's services would be needed at some point to work out legal details, which was yet another daunting prospect, given the group's limited resources. Fortunately, Bernard had learned of a public interest law firm called Public Counsel, established by the Los Angeles County Bar Association to provide free legal services to disadvantaged families, immigrants, and nonprofit institutions working to address poverty and civil rights issues. The firm had connections with large law firms that, as a matter of policy, took certain cases on a pro bono basis, and agreed to contact these and explain the LPTA's activities and its need for legal representation.

As the summer of 1991 wore on, tenants reading TransAction's *Lincoln Place News* still saw the monthly feature titled "From Jim Coxeter's Desk," but the face of TransAction most often seen on the property was that of Jim Merlino, a TransAction vice president. Tenants who met the boyish-looking thirty-one-year-old often remarked on his friendliness, and while the sincerity of this manner wasn't questioned, his presence was considered by Bernard and other active LPTA members to be part of TransAction's campaign to win the hearts and minds of tenants and Lincoln Place neighbors. If such a nice young man promised that the redevelopment would improve the lives of all the tenants and be a great boon to the neighborhood, then who were they to disagree?

TransAction sponsored several tenant events that the LPTA also regarded as part of the company's marketing campaign. There was a bus trip in August to the J. Paul Getty Museum in Malibu, and an "End of Summer Picnic" in September on Lincoln Place lawns. The latter featured catered food, live music by a local Russian folk group, and unsurprisingly, a display of plans and architectural renderings of the new Lincoln Place that would rise from the ashes of the relic that so many tenants wanted—inexplicably, in some people's view—to buy. Another measure TransAction took that would curry favor with almost all tenants was the hiring of a private security service to patrol the property. Among the redevelopment's selling points were the security fences and gates that would keep would-be thieves and vandals from freely wandering the property and stepping inside any building without constraint. Some of the more conspiracy-minded believed that TransAction actually viewed a high degree of concern about crime as an aid in building support for the redevelopment. Otherwise, why had the company dismissed the old security guards when it bought the property five years earlier?

On August 8, 1991, TransAction took the first steps toward getting city permission for its plans. This was the preparation of an environmental impact report, or EIR, that would study the impacts on traffic, noise, air pollution, energy use, aesthetics, and housing, among others. Required by the California Environmental Quality Act—commonly called CEQA (See'kwa)—an EIR for a large project like the Lincoln Place redevelopment could run to hundreds of pages and take more than a year to complete. Once the city certified the EIR, the project would move to the public hearing phase. The road to approval would begin with a hearing before a city planning department official, whose decision would be final unless appealed to the city planning commission. Depending upon that decision, either the LPTA or TransAction was virtually certain to file such an appeal, which meant at least one public hearing before the five appointed members of the commission. That was unlikely to be the end of the road, however, because the commission's action could in turn be appealed to the city council, going first to the council's planning and land-use management committee and finally, to the full fifteen-member body. For a project the size of the Lincoln Place redevelopment, all this meant multiple public hearings, an arduous prospect for the LPTA, which would need to repeatedly mobilize tenants and others to make telephone calls, write letters, and get themselves to city hall. But it also meant multiple opportunities to make the case for opposing the redevelopment and preserving Lincoln Place as a haven for the working families and elderly tenants who considered it their permanent home.

The LPTA steering committee knew it couldn't sit on its hands while waiting for the Agora Group to complete its feasibility study and put the finishing touches on a purchase offer. Flyers bearing the LPTA name and logo were posted on tenants' doors and laundry-room bulletin boards. "Dear Neighbor," the message in bold type on bright yellow paper began. "Where are you going to live after 1993? Like most of us you probably won't be able to live here at Lincoln Place if the owner gets his plans approved by the tenants, L.A. City Council, the L.A. City Planning Commission, etc. That's right—in as little as 24 months you could be looking for a new place to live, and good luck in today's inflated market. In fact, start looking around the neighborhoods now. See if you can find something close by with which to replace your present home." After asking for support of the LPTA's efforts to buy the property, the message concluded with, "Together we can preserve affordable housing in Venice, and fend off the agony of forced relocation."

Shortly before this flyer appeared, TransAction had sent all tenants an invitation to attend a "planning forum" for the expressed purpose of gathering feedback on the redevelopment. At that point, the company's plan was essentially a more detailed version of the one James Coxeter had presented to small groups a year earlier. All existing buildings with their 795 apartments would be demolished. Built in their place would be 850 brand-new units—654 townhouses for sale at market rates, fifty-two "affordable" townhouses, and 144 apartments set aside for current tenants at the rents they were now paying.

Bernard and other LPTA members didn't believe that these "planning forums" were anything more than public relations exercises designed to get tenants to support the redevelopment. After all, the company had already begun the process of getting city approval, and the overall scope of the project wasn't up for discussion, if it ever had been. Those who attended the earlier forums had only been asked to weigh in on such matters as window treatments and styles of carpeting. Anyone who came to complain about the propriety of tearing down a perfectly functional complex and disrupting the lives of so many people was wasting their breath. The meetings were for those excited about the prospect of living in a new, modern apartment, or even buying one of the townhouses and realizing lifelong dreams of owning their own homes.

According to Coxeter, elderly tenants would have first priority for the new apartments, while those with disabilities and single parents living with minor children would be given second and third priority, respectively. Any remaining units would be offered to tenants who didn't fall into these categories. Rents would remain affordable to people with low incomes even when the apartments changed hands. As for the "affordable" townhouses, Coxeter said he expected them to sell somewhere between $120,000 and $150,000, figures that raised skepticism since they were less than half the going market rate at the time.

The most glaring smudge on this rosy picture was pointed out by tenant Jan Book in her letter to Coxeter the previous fall—the landlord's plan would destroy 795 rental units while building only 144 new ones. "Where are you going to live after 1993?" the LPTA had asked, although that date for the start of construction was widely considered unrealistic, given the time required to prepare the EIR and shepherd the project through what was almost sure to be multiple public hearings. Still, the fact remained that machines could arrive and start knocking down buildings within a few years, and people now living in those buildings might not have any choice but to move out of Lincoln Place.

Coxeter had repeatedly tried to allay these concerns by stressing TransAction's plan to phase the construction over ten years. Due to the normal turnover of around 150 apartments each year, newly vacated units would be set aside as temporary housing for tenants whose buildings were scheduled for demolition. Once the new apartments were ready for occupancy, those tenants would be moved in. Over the course of the ten years, many tenants would voluntarily move—because of work, needing more space, buying a home, and so forth. There would be no need to evict anyone, least of all the elderly and others who had been subjected, in the landlord's apparent view, to LPTA fearmongering.

Bernard believed that these calculations were based on faulty assumptions. But even if had been correct, the plan to move people around the property while it was a major construction zone struck her as notably insensitive and even callous. "There were people in their eighties and even nineties," she says. "They had been living at Lincoln Place for as long as twenty or thirty years. They just wanted to be left alone to live out their lives in peace and quiet and here was the landlord telling them they would have to pack up everything and move to another unit, then do it all over again when their new apartment was ready."

By then, news that the Lincoln Place owners planned to demolish the existing complex and build new condominiums had spread beyond the surrounding neighborhoods to other parts of Venice, where fears of gentrification often clashed with the visions of those who welcomed development that would make the community more affluent and, as a consequence, raise everyone's property values. People in other parts of Los Angeles became aware of the proposed redevelopment and the LPTA's effort to buy the property when an article on the subject appeared in the September 15 issue of the *Los Angeles Times*.[22] The article noted that, between 1980 and 1990, the median rent in Venice had risen from $286 to $762 a month, and quoted an organizer for the Coalition for Economic Survival on the threat TransAction's redevelopment plan posed to the community. "Venice is the most diverse beach community around," he said. "If we keep losing low-income housing like Lincoln Place it will become another Newport Beach." While the specter of Venice turning into the Orange County city known for its wealthy, yacht-owning residents may have been hyperbole, the fact that the recession had officially ended in the spring of 1991 meant renewed incentives for apartment-house owners to find ways to raise rents, convert to condominiums, or, as in TransAction's case, completely redevelop their properties.

While the LPTA and TransAction continued to engage in a duel to win tenants to their respective sides, the Agora Group moved forward with a purchase proposal. One point of contention that needed to be resolved was Coxeter's claim that the buildings were in such poor condition that they weren't worth saving.[23] If the tenants bought the complex, they would have to spend untold millions on rehabilitation work. The LPTA disputed this, saying that a person only needed to take a walk around to see that the buildings weren't run-down. Peeling paint and cracked stucco—due, in many tenants' views to landlord neglect—were primarily cosmetic. As for the plumbing and electrical problems cited by Coxeter, most LPTA members said these systems were working fine in their apartments. To resolve the question, the LPTA arranged for rehabilitation specialists from the city's housing department to inspect the grounds and a selected number of units occupied by LPTA members. These inspections failed to support Coxeter's dire view of the property's condition, finding that the buildings needed painting but were structurally sound, and that the units themselves were in good condition, with only minor issues needing to be addressed, such as the lack of GFI outlets, leaking faucets, and plaster cracks.

In mid-January of 1992, the formal purchase offer was finally ready to be presented to Coxeter. Sheila Bernard and LPTA steering committee members had been apprised of most of the details, but it was still exciting to see the actual numbers in writing and imagine the landlord reviewing them and deciding that it was to his benefit to sell. The nonprofit Lincoln Place Housing Corporation would pay TransAction $47.7 million in cash, meaning that five years after buying the property, the company would walk away with a $19 million profit. The tenant corporation would need to raise another $6 million for rehabilitation, landscaping, and other site improvements, plus expenses associated with the sale. FHA-insured mortgage revenue bonds would provide approximately $50 million, while another $7 million would come from various government housing programs.

Coxeter was asked to respond to the offer by the end of February, so now it was a matter of waiting for news. But Bernard was sure that the seed planted in her mind when she first saw Lincoln Place in the summer of 1988 was ready to bear fruit. "I was definitely excited," she says. "I was sure we were off and running and were going to succeed." Other tenants infected by her contagious optimism were excited as well, although there were still many details to be taken care of before they could call themselves owners of their own homes. Those involved in the battle to stop the major rehab evictions could remember the 1989 city council meeting and the sense of euphoria that arose with the vote to tighten up the regulations. That feeling of being safe had only lasted a few months before news surfaced about the redevelopment plan, and until the landlord turned over the keys, so to speak, nobody was quite ready to say that a new day had dawned.

6

NOTICE TO QUIT

"Landlord" is a clear word. It reminds us of medieval lords of the manor, who allowed peasants to farm the land in return for large taxes which kept the lords rich and the peasants poor.

Today, landlords are advised by public relations firms to refer to themselves using nice, softer words like "owner" or "president of the corporation." They are advised to refer to tenants as "residents."

When they hold meetings to tell you they want to demolish your apartment, they are advised to call them "community planning forums."

When they intend to dump tons of useful housing into a landfill for their personal enrichment, they are advised to donate some money to a local program to educate children about the environment, so it will look like they are socially responsible.

They put up big signs that say, "Protected by Westec," when in reality Westec does nothing but drive through, even on New Year's Eve while arsonists are starting fires in the carports.

Jim Coxeter and TransAction are landlord. We are tenants. They hold meetings not to ask us, but to tell us what they want to do. They want to destroy our housing. In so doing, they will damage our physical and social environment, and they do not care. They are motivated by the desire for enormous personal profit.

Tenants are motivated by the desire for stable lives and rent we can afford. We can have these things at Lincoln Place only when we gain control of our own housing.

—LPTA Newsletter "What Is a Landlord?"

ON FEBRUARY 6, 1992, the lead article in the *Los Angeles Times* Metro section concerned the beginning of jury selection in the trial of four white police officers accused of the violent beating of Rodney King, the Black motorist who became a household name when a bystander's videotape of the beating was repeatedly aired on local and national media. Farther along, in that issue's Westside section, was a single column item under the heading "Panel to Air Tenants' Offer." The panel referred to was the Venice Community Planning Advisory Committee, or CPAC, a group of fifteen Venice residents appointed by Councilwoman Ruth Galanter to hold public meetings for input on development and planning issues. It had no official power, but Sheila Bernard and the LPTA steering committee regarded it as an important venue for explaining the purchase offer and, hopefully, broadening support beyond Lincoln Place itself.

On a warm, humid evening that held a portent of rain, some seventy persons packed the community room of the Westchester Municipal Center. Many were Lincoln Place residents wearing "Let's Own It" tags; others were from the Penmar neighborhood adjacent to the apartment complex. In a paisley dress and her hair cut short with bangs, Bernard stood by easels with charts and photographs and laid out the basics of the plan, stressing the fact that the LPTA wasn't trying to create a public housing project. The purchase would be financed almost entirely by private sources. A professional management company would be hired for day-to-day operations, and tenants would be carefully screened, just as they were now. The financing package included money for improvements like painting and landscaping. The major difference was that units would remain permanently affordable to seniors, working families, and others who couldn't afford rents that could take half or more of their incomes. Since the LPTA survey had shown that this group moved far less often than more affluent tenants, the new Lincoln Place would actually create a stable environment that everyone could agree would be an asset to the community.

Or so Bernard thought. But when she wrapped up her presentation, audience members were allowed to ask questions and comment, and members of a homeowners' group called the Penmar Neighborhood Association expressed skepticism about the ability of tenants to operate such a large complex. Some appeared openly hostile to the idea, airing the fear that the place would turn into a slum and drag down everyone's property values. In contrast, the TransAction plan promised benefits for everyone; getting rid of aging structures with little architectural merit and building handsome townhouses that would be a point of pride in the community.

"It was the first time we'd seen public opposition to the buyout," Bernard says, although she wasn't surprised by the undertone of classism, the attitude that renters were second-rate citizens and less desirable than those who could afford to own their homes. "We knew we had work to do to educate people. Some were beyond reach, I knew. But we had to get a bunch of them to see that destroying affordable housing and driving people out of their homes was not to the community's benefit. We had to go out into the neighborhood and convince them that Lincoln Place should be saved, and that our buyout plan was the best way to do it."

The meeting was covered by the *Argonaut*, a weekly newspaper that reported on doings in Venice and surrounding communities. The article that appeared a week later quoted a tenant named Jennifer Reif, who, according to the reporter's account, was in tears as she spoke. "I've lived at Lincoln Place for twelve years, and if they tear it down, I'll be evicted with no place to go. I love my home. I'm attached to it. I don't have much money, but I want it to look beautiful."

That kind of appeal—protecting the vulnerable from being pushed out of the community—was at the heart of the LPTA's quest to win the support of Lincoln Place neighbors. But how well it would resonate with a population of homeowners was an open question. A week after its report on the CPAC meeting, the *Argonaut* published a letter from Judith Pressman, who lived just north of Lincoln Place and was cochair of the Penmar Neighborhood Association. After complaining that her group wasn't represented on the CPAC, she wrote, "What many of the homeowners are fearful of is living extremely close to an aging, unimproved forty acres of nonprofit-run housing. Eventually, good tenants will not want to live at Lincoln Place and bad tenants will replace them—people with antisocial outlooks who don't care at all about the property. When this happens, property values decline, and the city loses part of its tax base as owners move out."

Intended or not, this apocalyptic view of undesirables invading the neighborhood and driving out the good people had unfortunate echoes of the 1950s and 1960s in Los Angeles, when the phenomenon of "white flight" saw homeowners fleeing en masse to the suburbs because of fear that African Americans moving into their neighborhoods would drag down property values. Bernard could have attacked the attitude expressed in the *Argonaut* letter as implicitly racist, but she chose instead to emphasize the positive aspects of "Let's Own It." At every opportunity, she pointed to the Agora Group's feasibility study, which showed that even with rents below-market rates, the tenant corporation would bring in enough revenue for needed maintenance and improvements. Nobody would be thrown out so that the landlord could raise the rent, but serious rules violations—repeatedly holding loud parties, for example, or using an apartment for drug sales—could definitely lead to eviction. A professional security detail would patrol the property. TransAction, a private for-profit company, had neglected needed maintenance and failed to provide effective security for a number of years. The corporation run by and for the tenants could and would do better.

Councilwoman Ruth Galanter was on record in support of the concept of tenant ownership, but there was a fear that she might waver or fail to use her position to publicly promote the plan and help persuade Coxeter to sell.[24] In a letter to Jennifer Reif, the tenant who spoke so emotionally at the CPAC meeting, Galanter allayed those fears to a degree by writing that she had recently met with the Agora Group and "found their presentation very encouraging."[25] The letter was in response to one Reif had written to the councilwoman urging her to oppose TransAction's redevelopment plan and support both the tenant-purchase plan and a citywide moratorium on the demolition of affordable housing. "I oppose the redevelopment of Lincoln Place," Galanter wrote, "and I doubt that I can say it any more clearly than that." But she went on to write, "If my statements of support for your position were all it took to stop a property owner from exercising his or her property rights, you'd be home free right now. But unfortunately, there's a lot more to it than that." She praised the LPTA purchase proposal but added that "the laws and constitutional property rights are not on our side. We can delay the process and we can make a lot of noise, but ultimately we have to either buy the property or allow the owner to do what the law allows." As for a moratorium, she was in favor of adopting one, but questioned whether a majority of the city council would vote for such a dramatic measure.

That letter was dated April 21, the same day that James Coxeter was guest speaker at a luncheon meeting of the Venice Chamber of Commerce. His appearance was announced in "The Wave," the chamber's bimonthly newsletter, along with a full-page description of TransAction's plan for Lincoln Place, although the word *description* doesn't quite capture what read like a full-throated sales pitch for the project. Sheila Bernard had been invited to the meeting to receive a plaque recognizing the LPTA as a new chamber member, and she was eager to hear what Coxeter might say about the tenant-purchase plan. At that point, his only response to the $47.7 million offer was, as quoted in a March LPTA newsletter, "The property is not for sale; we are not soliciting offers. However, we will consider an offer from the tenants if you prove you can raise the money." The Agora Group had sent him the feasibility study and a fifteen-year income and expense projection, but he hadn't further responded so it was impossible to know if he was seriously considering the offer. However, at the luncheon, he sounded dismissive of the whole idea, which reinforced Bernard's feeling that the only way to get TransAction to sell was to thwart their redevelopment plan. A reporter covering the meeting for the *Argonaut* quoted her as saying that Coxeter "basically said he would never sell to us at that price, so we have to make it clear to him that he's not going to get to do his development. Then maybe he'll sell to us."[26]

On the morning of the Chamber of Commerce meeting, the main headline on the first page of the *Los Angeles Times* Metro section was "Jury Told Video Proves the Case Against Officers." Prior to the closing arguments in the Rodney King beating trial, the prosecutors had repeatedly played the videotape of the officers kicking and beating King with their batons as he rolled about on the ground, and for most people who saw the grainy, black-and-white footage on TV, the only real question at this point was the sentences the officers would get, not whether they were guilty. There was some uneasiness about the fact that the judge had earlier ordered the trial moved to Simi Valley, a nearly all-white suburb northwest of Los Angeles, but hardly anyone expected what dominated the airwaves on the afternoon of April 29, the breaking news that the jury had acquitted three of the officers and failed to reach a verdict on the fourth. The shocking verdict got national attention, with even President Bush weighing in, saying he couldn't see how the jury decision could possibly square with what millions saw with their own eyes. But at that point, suspense was no longer a matter of the verdict, but how the Black community would react. John Singleton, the young movie director who had made a splash a year earlier with *Boyz n the Hood*, was in a crowd that had gathered outside the courthouse to await the verdicts. In a 2011 CNN documentary on the Rodney King saga, he perfectly summed up what would happen after the acquitted officers were hustled away and jurors were escorted to waiting buses. "By having this verdict," he said, "what these people done, they lit the fuse to a bomb."

The riot—or uprising, as many chose to call it—started in South L.A., a majority-Black part of the city long beset by substandard housing, unemployment, and what many saw as excessive use of force by the LAPD. In that regard, it had echoes of the 1965 Watts riot, which started in the same general area and was blamed on the same root causes. Unlike the Watts riot, however, the looting and burning in the aftermath of the Rodney King verdicts wasn't confined to that community but spread north into the midcity Koreatown area. Tensions between Black residents and the Asian immigrants who owned liquor stores, dry cleaning stores and other small businesses in South L.A. had been simmering over the perception that these business owners were often disrespectful to their Black customers and had no interest in the community beyond taking people's money. Just thirteen days after the Rodney King beating in 1991, this resentment had reached a high pitch when a Korean-born convenience store owner and a Black teenage customer named Latasha Harlins got into a dispute over a bottle of orange juice that ended with the owner pulling a pistol and shooting the girl in the back of the head. The owner, Soon Ja Du, was arrested, tried, and convicted of manslaughter, but instead of the prison sentence sought by the prosecution, the judge ordered her to serve five years' probation and pay a $500 fine. The district attorney appealed the sentence, but it was upheld by a state appeals court just a week before the Rodney King verdicts, a fact that further inflamed tensions between the Black and Korean communities.

Local television stations aired round-the-clock coverage of the unfolding unrest, including footage of Koreatown business owners standing guard over their properties with pistols and rifles. People in middle- and upper-class white communities who saw an eerie landscape of burning buildings on their TV screens and lived near enough to hear the wail of police and fire truck sirens when they stepped outside wondered how far the unrest would spread. *Will it happen here?*

In Venice, many considered that fear credible. The Oakwood neighborhood across Lincoln Boulevard from Lincoln Place suffered from the same issues that fueled the uprising, if not on the same scale. Two gangs, one Black and the other Latino, operated on the same turf, and violence was a constant for people who called the neighborhood home. Oakwood was already seen by many as an incubator for criminal activity in other parts of Venice, and it was easy for them to imagine young Black and Latino men deciding to join the party and start looting and burning. The 7-Eleven convenience store just a block from Lincoln Place boarded over its windows, and other liquor stores and small businesses in the community did the same. California National Guardsmen ordered to Los Angeles by Governor Pete Wilson could be seen on Venice's major commercial streets, which were unnaturally deserted, particularly at night because of Mayor Tom Bradley's declaration of a dusk-to-dawn curfew.

Rodney King appeared on TV to make his emotional "Can we all get along?" plea, and five days later, the fires were out, and jail cells were crowded with suspected looters and arsonists. Burned-out buildings were being boarded up, and the streets were being cleared of torched and overturned cars, broken glass, bricks and the other detritus of a rampage both senseless and entirely rational. Sixty-three persons were dead and thousands injured. Nearly four thousand buildings were set afire, with more than a quarter of those completely destroyed. Politicians were joining members of the Black community in demanding that the acquitted officers be fired. Sheila Bernard, who followed the appalling events with everyone else and whose awareness of racial injustice was amplified by having a mixed-race child, believed that the fate of Lincoln Place had elements in common with social justice issues arising from racism, poverty, and the failure of society to provide decent, affordable housing for all its citizens.

In the May LPTA newsletter, she wrote, "Deep injustices have given rise to our present crisis. We can understand desperate actions because so many legal routes to equity and justice are being closed down: jobs are scarce; our governor has cut social services; a great deal of affordable housing is being demolished in our city; and the final straw is that a jury has handed down a blatantly racist decision in the Rodney King case." And in an LPTA press release touting the tenant-purchase plan, she pointed a finger at James Coxeter, alluding to the uprising and accusing the landlord of "adding fuel to the fire" by pushing the redevelopment plan for Lincoln Place.

Bernard was also someone naturally inclined to imagine the positive things that could rise from the ashes of a disaster, and she thought it was a good time to write to Jack Kemp while Los Angeles was on the minds of so much of the nation. She didn't know exactly what the HUD secretary could do to help Lincoln Place tenants, but she thought he would at least be sympathetic to their plight. And, who knows? Given his avowed interest in helping lift people out of poverty by giving them ownership of their homes, he might have useful suggestions, or otherwise offer some kind of help in persuading TransAction to sell.

She sent the letter on May 7, and received a reply three weeks later from Margaret Milner, director of the Office of Resident Initiatives. Milner pointed out that Lincoln Place wasn't a HUD-owned or insured property, so the department had no control over its disposition. She wrote, "I commend you and the residents for empowering yourselves through the establishment of the Lincoln Place Tenants' Association and for your pursuit of ownership. Your diligence in exploring various legal and political options as you attempt to persuade the owner to resident ownership is indeed notable. However, as I am sure you are aware, without a willing owner, sale of the property to the residents cannot occur."

This splash of cold water with its reminder that the vast majority of renters in the country occupied their homes at the pleasure of private, profit-making entities was offset, at least to a degree, by a letter Bernard received that month from Public Counsel. The public interest law firm had sent inquiries to a hundred private firms in the Los Angeles area, explaining the LPTA's activities and its need for pro bono legal assistance. The single response came from Marcia Scully, a forty-four-year-old land-use attorney who worked for the large, well-known firm of Sheppard, Mullin, Richter & Hampton. Scully would represent the tenant group in its purchase efforts, as well as its ongoing fight against the Lincoln Place redevelopment. Bernard was thrilled. This, she hoped, would help level the playing field with TransAction, which in its quest to get its plans approved could afford the services of high-powered attorneys and lobbyists.

Although the signals sent thus far by Coxeter were less than encouraging, Bernard believed that having an experienced attorney from a prestigious law firm on board would give a definite boost to the tenants' purchase plan. But how to bring TransAction to the table? Just before Memorial Day, with the Rodney King episode still fresh in people's minds, the LPTA held a demonstration outside Coxeter's office in Marina Del Rey. An LPTA press release announced, "Tenants to Serve Eviction Notice on Their Landlord," and it went on to say, "The demonstration is an attempt to pressure TransAction into selling Lincoln Place to the tenants." A dozen mostly elderly tenants showed up for the midday demonstration, carrying signs that read Save Our Home; Housing for People, Not for Profit; and Seniors Lives Are Not A Toy. The tenants also brought a large yellow poster in the form of an official eviction notice. Formally issued to Coxeter and TransAction vice president Jim Merlino, it read:

<u>NOTICE TO QUIT</u>

TAKE NOTICE, that you are hereby required to:

QUIT planning to demolish these buildings!

QUIT insisting on maximum profits, instead of reasonable profits!

QUIT allowing units to stand vacant while people are homeless in Los Angeles!

THIS IS INTENDED as a notice to quit, for the purpose of terminating your stranglehold on this community.

Ingrid Mueller, who helped create the poster and joined the demonstrators that day, says that the plan was to present the notice directly to Coxeter. "He had tried to evict people," she says, "So we wanted to give him a sense of how it would feel to get the notice." But when they knocked on his office door nobody answered. Was he there? Mueller doesn't know, but she says the point was nevertheless made. "We had someone taking photographs. We were making our own history."

Bernard saw the demonstration as one piece of a strategy built around the premise that an overwhelming display of opposition by Lincoln Place residents and community members to the redevelopment plan would persuade Coxeter to sell. Was that a miscalculation? Did being repeatedly called callous and greedy make the landlord less likely to consider the tenant-purchase offer? While Bernard clearly holds strong opinions, she comes across as open-minded and willing to give others the benefit of the doubt. But in hindsight, she doesn't believe that the LPTA had any choice but to throw as many obstacles as possible in TransAction's path.

"Maybe some of the rhetoric got a little harsh," she says. "But we really believed that if things got difficult enough they'd see that their best course was to sell. After all, they had other properties so it wasn't like all their eggs were in the Lincoln Place basket. And it seemed that they were really interested in making money from selling condos, not running an apartment complex." She even appealed to Coxeter's better nature, pointing out that selling the complex to tenants would create good will by showing that a company could be socially conscious and care about more than just the millions it could pocket by selling luxury townhouses built on the graveyard of a diverse, affordable community.

While the LPTA awaited Coxeter's response, the company took actions that seemed to show its determination to push the redevelopment forward. One was alluded to in the "Notice to Quit" served on Coxeter and Merlino, the leaving of units vacant when tenants moved out, presumably so that there would be places to move seniors and others into when their buildings were ready to be demolished. Another was an addendum to new rental agreements stating that tenants would have no expectation of remaining in their units beyond September 1, 1993, the target date for the beginning of construction. The company also took actions the LPTA regarded as harassment of long-term tenants, the presumed objective being to force them out because of the need for temporary residences during construction. Or so it could be shown that the LPTA had overstated the numbers of lower-income tenants. Or simply because these tenants were LPTA supporters who likely opposed the redevelopment.

One of those actions concerned the subject of pets. From the very beginning, rental agreements had contained a clause prohibiting pets. This hadn't been strictly enforced, though, and by the time TransAction bought the property in 1986, the fact that a number of tenants had dogs or cats was widely known. But in July 1991, all tenants got a letter from management informing them that complaints from some residents about pets were being investigated and that further steps would be taken, if necessary, to enforce the no-pets policy. The letter ended with a list of organizations that would help tenants find shelter for their pets if they had to remove them. Bernard and the LPTA steering committee decided it was manifestly unfair to force those who had kept dogs or cats for years to give them up, and they paid a local attorney who specialized in animal rights law to write Coxeter a letter and to take further legal action, if needed, to defend pet owners from the threat of eviction. In the letter sent three weeks after the management notice, the attorney asserted that TransAction's failure to enforce the no-pets policy even when it was common knowledge that some tenants had pets constituted a waiver of the prohibition in rental agreements.

"Be aware," the attorney wrote, "that such notice has caused much heartache and grief to elderly tenants whose pet is the only living creature with which there is continuous contact of any kind. To insist that they be made to choose between affordable housing or a loved one is an unconscionable choice that LPTA will not abide."

Many thought the letter had put the matter to rest, because no immediate action was taken against any of the pet-owning tenants. But in February of 1992, a single mother living with two small children and a dog was given an eviction notice for violating the no-pets clause. At a court hearing, the tenant said she had heard someone trying to break into her apartment and didn't feel safe without her dog. She also brought up the legal argument advanced by the attorney, and a judge dismissed the case. But Sheila Bernard didn't believe that Coxeter and TransAction were ready to give up. In an LPTA newsletter, Bernard wrote, "The owner is not attacking pet owners because he cares about our homes. If he cared, why did he take no action on the many pets at Lincoln Place for five years? Why now? It is clear to us that this eviction is an attempt to uproot longtime tenants to weaken our movement to save our homes from being demolished."

Another issue seen as harassment was management's attempt to prohibit yard sales on the property. In the fall of 1991, the LPTA had organized a sale on the lawns outside the buildings on Lake Street, the thoroughfare that bordered the north side of Lincoln Place, and it had been considered a great success. Tenants spread blankets or set up card tables to sell household items, knickknacks, and used clothing, among other things. The LPTA had a table with newsletters and informational literature, and Bernard and others were on hand to answer questions about TransAction's redevelopment and the tenant-purchase plan. The aim was twofold, Bernard says. "It was a social event for tenants and people in the neighborhood, and it was a way to get the word out about who we were and what we were doing and hoped to do. We weren't soliciting money. Some people donated the money they made to the LPTA, but the whole idea was to bring people together."

Unbeknownst to Bernard and the yard sale participants, the event would trigger a long fight with the landlord that culminated in serious legal trouble for the LPTA president, but for the moment, it was seen as a good way to build support, along with LPTA-organized celebrations on the Fourth of July, Halloween, Thanksgiving, and Christmas. A second sale was scheduled for August of 1992, although residents who regularly perused the landlord's *Lincoln Place News* had seen a brief message from the manager to the effect that yard sales weren't permitted. Bernard didn't know of any specific prohibition in rental agreements, and decided the warning was just another attempt to harass the LPTA. But twelve days before the sale, every resident got a letter from the manager, Lucy Farber, stating that yard sales were a violation of Lincoln Place rules and regulations regarding use of lawns and other shared spaces. She claimed to have gotten numerous calls after the previous sale, both from tenants and nearby homeowners, complaining about noise, disruption of car and pedestrian traffic, and the fact that it was held on Sunday, when people wanted to sleep in or observe religious traditions. Pointing out the fact that the LPTA's notices for the latest event mentioned the sale of food and beverages, Farber said that would make the planned sale a commercial venture. She also warned that food sales unregulated by the county health department could pose a health risk.

Bernard got a similar letter from Jim Merlino. It made many of the same points as Farber's, but ended in a much more threatening tone. The yard sale, he wrote, had impacts that "infringe upon the property rights of tenants, apartment owners, and homeowners and may create significant liability for you and your organization." Merlino, a law school graduate, concluded with, "The owners and management of Lincoln Place Apartments shall have no responsibility for any causes of action brought against you or your organization as a result of any claims made by others, including but not limited to those for infringement upon private property rights or quiet enjoyment and all matters of safety and public health including but not limited to those relating to the sale or dispensing of food and beverages."

Bernard hadn't heard anything negative about the first sale, and there was no way to prove or disprove the claim that there had been many complaints. But if her inherently courteous demeanor had led Farber or Merlino or anyone else to believe that she could be easily intimidated, they would be guilty of a misjudgment. She responded to the management threats in an LPTA bulletin, beginning with this heading in bold type:

**Why Having a Yardsale
should be a
Constitutional Right,**
or,
We're Having It Anyway

She wrote, "What an uncharacteristically speedy and resolute response the owner has made to an alleged complaint! Why don't complaints about apartments needing paint jobs, maintenance problems, the need for better security get action like this?"

On the subject of food sales, she ridiculed the warning of potential health department violations, writing, "Who's ever been to a church bazaar where there wasn't a bake sale? And who's ever witnessed a 10-year-old handcuffed and dragged off to jail for setting up a lemonade stand on a hot day?

"Yard sales are harmless fun. They help people get to know one another and help the Planet Earth ecologically by recycling goods. It seems absurd to try to repress or prohibit them."

Bernard had learned that Farber and Merlino were alleging the violation of a regulation that stated, "Entrances, hallways, walks, lawns, and other public areas shall not be obstructed or used for any purpose other than entering and exiting." In the bulletin, she wrote "According to that, you only have a legal right to scurry back and forth in and out of your apartment. You don't legally have the right to walk on the grass far enough to smell a flower, much less play ball, barbecue, or sunbathe."

She never entertained serious thoughts of canceling what had proven to be highly popular with most tenants. But after discussing the matter with the LPTA steering committee, it was decided to move the site of the sale to Elkgrove Avenue, the major street through the interior of the complex. Hopefully, that would avoid complaints about traffic or parking from any homeowners on the north side of Lake Street. On the day of the sale, twenty-four residents staked out spots on the lawns to sell the usual items. Tenant-baked cookies and pastries were displayed on a table with a red-checkered cloth. Several tenants with musical skills played guitars and other instruments. At one end of the two block-long sale the LPTA booth dispensed information along with newsletters, bulletins, and "Let's Own It" window signs. At four o'clock, the blankets and tables were folded, and everyone pitched in to pack up unsold items to be donated to a local women's shelter and a homeless services center. Nobody from management showed up to warn the participants or try to stop the sale. Bernard hoped—mistakenly, as it turned out—that she would hear no more about the matter.

She suspected that the attack on yard sales wasn't only harassment of the LPTA, but part of the landlord's strategy of encouraging fear among some homeowners that a tenant-owned Lincoln Place would have a negative impact on the neighborhood. Yard sales were fairly innocuous, but what else might be in store? Music concerts? Events that would create noise and traffic problems and attract the wrong kind of people to the site? Homeowners had seen their property values rapidly increase through most of the 1980s, and although the recession that still lingered in California meant those values were actually dropping in many areas, dreams of home equity providing financial security or the means to a more affluent lifestyle were alive and well. Coxeter and Merlino had met with the Penmar Neighborhood Association to promote the redevelopment plan, and had mailed brochures describing the plan to residents in the blocks surrounding Lincoln Place. While nobody connected with the company publicly said that replacing apartments with new condominiums would bring a better class of citizen, the idea that homeowners were more desirable than renters was clearly implicit in objections to the LPTA purchase plan.

What to do? Bernard believed in the power of conversion, so to speak— that the minds of those who looked at Lincoln Place buildings and imagined apartments filled with criminals and drug addicts and other assorted lowlifes could be changed if renters and homeowners had more contact with each other. She got her hands on a Penmar Neighborhood Association membership form and printed it in the LPTA's monthly newsletter. She urged Lincoln Place residents to join, expressing the hope that "we can eventually break down some of the barriers that divide renters and homeowners in our neighborhood."

Ingrid Mueller, who spent much of her post–World War II childhood in a garden-style apartment complex in Hamburg, Germany, hadn't encountered antirenter attitudes until she came to the United States and eventually settled in Southern California. But she shared Bernard's belief that more contact with neighbors could only be beneficial, and she filled out the membership form and mailed it along with a ten-dollar check for the annual dues. But the uncashed check was returned, along with a less-than-welcoming response from Judith Pressman, whose letter to the editor in the *Argonaut* had warned of people with antisocial attitudes moving into Lincoln Place if it was owned by tenants.

While not directly saying that Mueller's presence would be unwelcome, Pressman pointed out that only homeowners could vote on association business. "As you know," she wrote, "there are several tenants' rights organizations dedicated to the interests of renters, and so there are also homeowners' groups which trouble-shoot the interests of property owners. Sometimes in certain cases, the interests of the two groups merge, but in general they do not, since the primary goals are different."

There was one issue that concerned both homeowners and renters, however, and that was crime. The fears aroused by the Rodney King uprising weren't new—crime had been steadily climbing in many areas of Los Angeles, including Venice. The crack epidemic that arose in South L.A. in the 1980s had spread to mostly white-and-affluent west-side communities like Culver City, Santa Monica, and Venice, where gangs operated in minority neighborhoods and periodically battled over the control of trade in the destructive drug. In Venice's Oakwood neighborhood, the Black members of the Shoreline Crips and the Latino members of Venice 13 engaged in periodic skirmishes over crack sales, and it wasn't uncommon for Lincoln Place and Penmar neighborhood residents to hear eruptions of gunfire from that area at night, often followed by the wail of sirens and turbulent beat of a police helicopter. And to the dismay of Bernard and other LPTA members, TransAction seemed to exploit this fear on the part of Lincoln Place tenants. Seniors would no longer have to feel vulnerable because their new apartments would be in a secured building. The condominiums would all have security gates and systems. Vandalism of cars wouldn't be a worry because the new parking garages would be accessible only to residents.

As the tumultuous year drew toward a close, the Rodney King beating and its aftermath were still on the minds of Lincoln Place residents and the rest of the Los Angeles citizenry. The four officers whose acquittal had triggered the costly and destructive uprising had been indicted by a federal grand jury on charges of using unreasonable force and were expected to go to trial in federal court early in 1993. Police chief Daryl Gates had resigned in the wake of scathing criticism of the LAPD's response to the disturbance as well as tactics perceived by many in minority communities as violent and overtly racist. Bill Clinton had overcome long odds and been elected president after winning the Democratic nomination over better-known candidates, including former California governor Jerry Brown, and housing activists were hoping that the new administration's policies would go beyond Jack Kemp's largely unfulfilled vow to give renters ownership of their homes.[27]

The LPTA threw a holiday party at the Penmar Park recreation center, with food, beverages, and a gift exchange. Volunteers decorated the community room and the atmosphere was festive. With an experienced attorney on board to handle negotiations, there was cautious optimism that Sheila Bernard's quixotic "Let's Own It" campaign might actually bear fruit in the coming year. There were also reasons for concern. James Coxeter hadn't shown an inclination to seriously consider the tenant offer and was still actively promoting the redevelopment plan. A draft of the project's EIR was expected to be publicly released sometime the following spring, which would mark the beginning of the process of getting the approvals needed to start demolishing buildings. Bernard told everyone who would listen that the LPTA was fully committed not only to pursuing the tenant purchase, but fighting to the bitter end against the redevelopment. Nobody who had seen her quiet determination firsthand doubted her, but it was still a David-versus-Goliath contest, and skeptics knew that Davids lose those battles against deep-pocketed corporate Goliaths more often than not.

7

BANKRUPTCY

We have worked successfully since 1987 to prevent unfair evictions, to call citywide attention to the danger of demolition of our housing, to drive forward a plan to prevent demolition, and to make an offer to purchase Lincoln Place, which could lead to the permanent afford-ability of our units. This has all happened because of the effort and persistence of many members of LPTA, and the financial support of hundreds of others.

—LPTA plea for member dues

People on the street or in the market ask me and other members of the Steering Committee, "So when are we gonna own the place?"
—Sheila Bernard

IN THE SPRING OF 1993, Sheila Bernard was teaching at the Business Industry School, a public adult education and vocational-training center in an area near Koreatown that was still marked with burned-out buildings and other scars of the Rodney King uprising that had paralyzed the city almost exactly a year earlier. She had sold her self-described "junky" 1980 Honda for practical reasons—saving money on repairs and other costs—and from the belief that people truly concerned about environmental problems like air pollution and fossil fuel use should demonstrate that concern in the way they lived their lives. With three children ranging in age from eight to seventeen, all in different schools, doing without a car was a serious challenge, and when she sold the car, Bernard described feeling as if she had "jumped off a cliff." In a *Los Angeles Times* article about people living without cars in Los Angeles, she was quoted as saying, "I felt really vulnerable. But I don't like it when people complain about how bad things are without getting out and becoming part of the bigger solution."[28]

There was also a silver lining that had nothing to do with the environment or car expenses. With a bus ride that could take as long as an hour in heavy traffic, she had plenty of time to think about Lincoln Place without having to concentrate on driving. And there was a lot to think about. Marcia Scully, the LPTA's pro bono attorney, had met several times over the past six months with an attorney representing TransAction and reported that the company seemed ready to negotiate over a specific price and other details of a tenant purchase. Final touches were being put on the EIR for TransAction's redevelopment plan and the city planning department was expected to make it public at any time. A city election campaign was underway, with a hotly contested mayoral contest that had implications for the future of Lincoln Place and other affordable-housing complexes.

But Lincoln Place wasn't the only thing on her mind as the bus rolled past liquor stores and other shops where Korean American owners had stood guard with guns while flames and smoke billowed from nearby buildings. The four police officers acquitted by a state court jury of King's videotaped beating had gone on trial in federal court in February, and by the beginning of April, prosecutors and defense attorneys were getting ready for final arguments. If the federal court jury also acquitted the officers, would history repeat itself? Would the city again erupt into destructive violence?

The answer wasn't long in coming. On April 16, the jury convicted the two officers most directly involved of violating King's civil rights, and although the two other officers were found not guilty of all charges, the city remained calm, and people breathed a little easier. The judge set a sentencing date in August, and while sentences deemed too light or mere slaps on the wrist could provoke further unrest, there was widespread feeling that an ugly chapter of Los Angeles history had come to a close. People like Bernard knew that racial and other issues exposed by the two-year-long episode hadn't magically disappeared, but she was nevertheless relieved, and when she stepped off the bus on Lincoln Boulevard at the end of her ride home from work and walked the short distance to Lincoln Place, she expected to relax a bit before her kids came home from school. She would talk to them about their studies and other things going on in their lives before turning to her near-daily routine of attending to LPTA business—making phone calls, working on newsletters and bulletins, writing notes about future plans, developing and refining strategy.

The first thing she did, though, was glance through her mail, and she saw amid the usual bills and pieces of junk mail an envelope bearing the logo and name of the Lincoln Place Apartments.

She set the other mail aside and opened the envelope. Getting a letter from the landlord was no surprise, but the contents of the single page were so surprising that she read the three brief paragraphs twice. Addressed to "Dear Lincoln Place Resident," the letter said that the TransAction subsidiary that legally owned Lincoln Place had filed for Chapter 11 bankruptcy protection in order to restructure certain debts. It promised that there would be no impact on Lincoln Place residents, neighbors, or employees, and concluded with the avowal that the company "will carry on its business as usual with no diminution of services and fully expects to proceed with all of its plans and programs for the redevelopment of the Lincoln Place Apartments."

As she digested this information, Bernard saw the future suddenly brighten. If TransAction was having serious financial problems, then James Coxeter would surely be more disposed to sell the property to the tenants. And despite the confident statement about moving ahead with the redevelopment, a bankruptcy proceeding couldn't possibly be anything other than cold water thrown upon those plans. She called Ingrid Mueller and other LPTA steering committee members, and most agreed with her assessment. Despite the doubts of some other LPTA members, she had always been optimistic that tenants would eventually prevail in their quest to own the property. But now, she remembers, she felt ecstatic. "Would they be more likely to sell? Yes! Could this kill their condo plan? Yes!"

She was eager to discuss the news with Marcia Scully, who had a meeting scheduled later in the month with TransAction's attorney. Just two weeks earlier, Scully had come to the LPTA's monthly meeting at the Penmar Park recreation center to brief tenants on the status of the purchase plan. The bankruptcy filing wasn't yet public knowledge then, but Scully told tenants that the current real estate market might be acting as an incentive for TransAction to sell. The Southern California economy was still in the doldrums, and median home prices and rents had actually fallen from their peaks at the beginning of the decade. Unemployment had soared, with the construction industry hit particularly hard. Even if TransAction got the financing to build those 654 market-rate condominiums, there was no guarantee that people would line up to buy them.

The gentrification of Venice that had picked up a full head of steam in the latter half of the 1980s had stalled, and with increased crime and gang activity, the community was seen by some as a place where they'd rather not put down roots. In fact, in the middle of March, a woman was robbed and sexually assaulted in a carport just a stone's throw from Bernard's apartment, and people were on edge because the perpetrator hadn't been caught. The crime intensified tenant demands for better security. It also fed the narrative of some Penmar neighborhood activists that Lincoln Place was crime infested and would become even worse if tenants owned the property.

Crime was a major issue in the citywide election campaign. Mayor Tom Bradley was retiring after twenty years, and the two main aspirants for the office, city Councilman Michael Woo and Richard Riordan, a well-to-do attorney and businessman, differed sharply in their views. Woo, a liberal Democrat, favored programs to address poverty and racism, while Riordan, a Republican and self-described conservative, supported stiffer sentences and swifter punishment of lawbreakers. Both promised to hire more police officers, but Woo's plan to pay for this with a property tax increase was harshly attacked by Riordan, who wanted to raise the money by leasing the Los Angeles International Airport to a private operator. Of most interest to Bernard and tenant advocates, however, were the candidates' views on housing. Woo had supported Lincoln Place tenants and others in their fight against major rehab evictions, and he wanted to strengthen rent control and require developers to include more affordable units in their projects. Riordan, on the other hand, considered such measures unwarranted intrusions into the free market. The answer to a shortage of affordable housing, he argued, was to encourage the private sector to build more by streamlining regulations and loosening other hindrances to development. He had long opposed rent control, and housing advocates feared that if elected he might push for its repeal. The LPTA joined other advocacy groups in publishing a "Mayoral Report Card" on housing issues. It gave Woo an A and Riordan an F.

As the campaign moved into the final six weeks before the June 8 election, the planning department released the long-awaited draft of the Lincoln Place EIR.[29] Members of the public would have sixty days to read and submit comments on the seven-hundred-page document, after which the consulting firm that prepared the report would publish a final version that incorporated those comments with responses. City planners would then decide whether to accept the report or send it back for revisions. As a practical matter, the latter was not uncommon, but outright rejection of an EIR was very rare, and almost everyone expected the city to eventually give its stamp of approval.

Although EIRs were prepared by independent consulting firms certified by the city, opponents of developments often cast a jaundiced eye on them. That was because the firms were hired and paid by developers, a fact that many felt compromised their objectivity and made an EIR read less like critical analysis than advocacy for a project. Fairly or not, this view held that developers spending upward of six figures on an EIR for a large project would expect a favorable report, and consultants who pointed out too many negative impacts might be informally blacklisted and find themselves without clients. The Lincoln Place EIR proved to be no exception. Opponents attacked the report's credibility, saying it ignored and minimized negative impacts and even twisted facts to make the project look more benign than it really was. Especially galling to Bernard and LPTA members was the EIR's findings regarding impacts on housing. Because TransAction was proposing to build a total of 850 new apartments and townhouses to replace 795 existing apartments, the EIR concluded that there would be a net gain of fifty-five housing units. But it was absurd, Bernard argued, to compare the existing apartments occupied by hundreds of low-income tenants to townhouses for sale to the well-to-do. She was also incensed by the report's conclusion that any negative impacts on the housing stock and housing affordability were social and economic in nature and therefore didn't fall under the purview of CEQA, which concerned a project's effects on the physical environment.

Marcia Scully disputed this conclusion in an EIR comment letter submitted on behalf of the LPTA. She quoted a CEQA section stating that a project could have "a significant effect on the environment if it will cause substantial adverse effects on human beings either directly or indirectly." To that point, she wrote, "The destruction of the existing Lincoln Place apartments will clearly have a significant detrimental effect on the tenants currently residing in the apartment project." She added a quote from city housing policy stating that the city "should encourage preservation of existing rental housing as an essential resource whose affordability cannot be matched by new construction."

A total of thirty-six persons submitted comment letters. They included city Councilwoman Ruth Galanter, State Senator Tom Hayden, and officials with state and local agencies concerned with transportation, water use, air quality and public safety. Both Galanter and Hayden questioned the adequacy of the EIR, particularly in regard to impacts on housing. Twenty-five comments came from members of the public, either individually or as representatives of organizations. Twelve of those were Lincoln Place tenants, and ten were residents of the surrounding Penmar neighborhood. Eight of the tenants expressed support for the redevelopment, while four, including Bernard, writing as LPTA president, opposed it. The comments from the Penmar neighborhood were evenly split between supporters and opponents.

Of the eight tenants who wrote letters supporting the TransAction plan, most were members of a newly formed tenant's group called Lincoln Place Tomorrow. The spokesperson for this group was Mary Roberts, a seventy-two-year-old retired nurse with a round face and snow-white hair who enthusiastically supported the redevelopment. In her EIR comment letter, she wrote, "The new apartments offer residents a secure apartment at the same rents that we pay now. This is of particular concern to seniors. Mr. Coxeter has assured us that all seniors, handicapped and single-parent residents will get a new apartment and I believe him." She concluded with, "I am looking forward to moving into a new apartment with all the new appliances and fixtures and I hope that you approve the plan to redevelop Lincoln Place." Others echoed these sentiments. A tenant named Lawrence Sherman wrote that he had to use crutches as a result of childhood polio, and was looking forward to moving into a building with the latest accessibility features, including an elevator. A retired aerospace worker named Henry Ricard wrote that the existing complex was poorly designed not only for the handicapped, but in terms of parking and security. On top of that, he wrote, his work experience showed him how systems wear out, and he knew that the plumbing and electrical systems at Lincoln Place were reaching that stage and bringing them up to modern standards would be prohibitively expensive.

Weighing in on behalf of the Penmar Neighborhood Association were cochairs Judith Pressman and Chris Williams, a realtor active in local affairs who was especially vocal on the subject of crime and policing. Pressman and Williams repeated many of TransAction's talking points. The forty-two-year-old complex had reached the end of its useful life, and pouring millions into repair and renovation would not be a sound business decision. They touted TransAction's promise that the 144 new rental units would remain permanently affordable, repeating the company's dubious claim that if the property wasn't redeveloped almost all low-income tenants would be gone in ten years, with vacancy decontrol meaning their units would be rented at market rates. Both Pressman and Williams had publicly warned that Lincoln Place would become a crime-ridden slum if it was owned by tenants, but they didn't repeat this grim prediction in their EIR comments.

Despite this letter and others from Penmar neighborhood residents who supported TransAction's plan, Sheila Bernard refused to believe that the comments represented the majority opinion of homeowners in the area. In fact, one of those homeowners, a woman named Sandy Moring, had recently organized a group called the Committee to Preserve Lincoln Place and had begun holding meetings at her home to build support and develop strategy on behalf of the LPTA. Moring and her husband David lived on Rose Avenue three blocks north of Lincoln Place, and David wrote an EIR comment letter opposing the redevelopment.

"My primary concern with the proposal outlined in this EIR," he wrote, "are the unknown impacts of the disruption and expulsion from our neighborhood of many longtime residents. My family has lived on Rose Avenue over eighteen years. During that entire time, we could only describe the residents of Lincoln Place as good neighbors. There has never been a time when our area was in turmoil over the overall conduct of the tenants living there." Like Bernard and Scully, Moring attacked the EIR's conclusion that the redevelopment's impact on affordable housing would be negligible. "As much as the EIR's housing section masks what will happen, it is very evident that hundreds of individuals and families are going to be driven out of their residences within a short time after this project is approved. Some will be shuttled from one phase to another over the years. But most will simply have no option but to leave."

It wasn't known how long it would take the EIR authors to prepare responses to the comments and produce a final report, although it wouldn't surprise anyone if it dragged on for a few months, especially given the fact that TransAction's bankruptcy filing was casting a long shadow over the project. According to the federal court filing, the company owed Bank of America $30 million, Admiral Insurance Company $5 million, and the City of Los Angeles $375,000, the latter a part of a loan made in 1989 to rehabilitate certain apartments for tenants with HUD Section 8 certificates. Bernard was hoping that these creditors would balk at TransAction's plan for repayment, in which case the court could then order the sale of the property to satisfy the debts. In such a scenario, the Lincoln Place tenants would make their purchase offer to the court, rather than TransAction, and thus bypass the stressful negotiations that had been dragging on for the past year and, despite Scully's optimistic appraisal, were showing little signs of bearing fruit.

In early summer, a TransAction bankruptcy hearing was scheduled on a day Sheila Bernard didn't have to work, and she and Ingrid Mueller decided to go downtown to the federal courthouse and see firsthand what was happening. James Coxeter and Jim Merlino had been the public face of TransAction in matters involving Lincoln Place, but Coxeter's partner, Robert Bisno, was at the hearing and Bernard and Mueller remember that he approached them during a recess. "He came up to us in a friendly, joking way and said that we should buy him lunch," Bernard recalls. "I responded, less friendly, and not joking, that we had been buying him lunch for years."

Despite Bisno's jocular manner, there were increasing signs of TransAction's hostility toward the LPTA. One arose from an unlikely source, the laundry rooms attached to carports behind each of the Lincoln Place buildings. These small rooms with coin-operated washers and dryers had bulletin boards where the management posted notices and tenants could post messages about things like items for sale. Mueller, who was in charge of getting LPTA newsletters and bulletins produced and distributed, had organized a small group of volunteers to help her pin these communications up on the bulletin boards, but she soon heard that they were disappearing after a day or two. Mueller, who had an earlier career in the hospitality industry, is normally affable, but she can also react with a "Don't mess with me!" attitude when feeling threatened or mistreated. It took her little time to decide that the proper response would be to replace the posted newsletters and bulletins as quickly as possible. If they were taken down again, she would just have to make sure they were put back up.

In the LPTA newsletter of May 1993, she wrote a short item titled "Laundry Rooms and Freedom of Speech." Calling herself the "Laundry Room Phantom," she wrote that she and her helpers had posted not only newsletters and bulletins, but also friendly hints about keeping those spaces cleaner and safer. "It's our ONLY ACCESSIBLE PUBLIC SPACE!" she wrote, adding what was widely believed by LPTA members, that the landlord wanted to silence criticism. "Understand that single-digit percentile of support for the so-called redevelopment of Lincoln Place will certainly not keep this phantom from posting the facts!"

Several weeks later, Bernard wrote a letter on the subject to Lucy Farber, the Lincoln Place manager. In her typically reasonable tone, Bernard wrote, "So far in the struggle between tenants and management over the future of Lincoln Place, both sides have been openly adversarial, but civil. We engage in public dialogue, trusting the people to make an informed choice and exert their will through the political process." She asked Farber if management had directed the property's maintenance workers to remove LPTA newsletters from the laundry-room bulletin boards. "We hope your response will confirm that the struggle between the LPTA and management will be resolved openly and publicly, without destruction of each other's materials."

Farber obviously showed this letter to Jim Merlino, because ten days later, Bernard got what could only be described as a hostile response from the TransAction vice president. Referring to Mueller's invocation of the First Amendment, Merlino pointed out that all of Lincoln Place, including the laundry rooms, was private property, and as such, the bulletin boards weren't subject to any constitutional guarantee of free speech. He denied that the LPTA materials were targeted for removal, saying that bulletin boards were cleared of posted notices when the laundry rooms were cleaned. "It is unfortunate," he wrote, "that you have chosen to deliberately misconstrue the simple removal of a few of your newsletters during routine cleaning as a constitutional issue. Such hyperbole is an insult to all members of the Lincoln Place community." But Merlino didn't confine himself to the subject of laundry-room bulletin boards. After writing that management had tried to encourage an atmosphere of cooperation through "evenhanded adherence" to rental agreements and other regulations governing Lincoln Place, he wrote, "Unfortunately, the LPTA has undermined this spirit of cooperation through many of its actions. By encouraging the violation of provisions of our rental agreements regarding the keeping of pets, the LPTA has shown a disregard for the rights of many of their fellow residents who are pestered by feral animals and flea infestations. By encouraging the violation of provisions of our rental agreements regarding the use of Lincoln Place property for commercial purposes such as yard sales, the LPTA has shown a disregard for the rights of many of their fellow residents who must now contend with non–Lincoln Place residents setting up yard sales."

These professions of concern for tenants struck Bernard and other LPTA members as hollow at best. Many believed that the proposed redevelopment would drive them out, with no guarantee that they could find another place in the community they could afford. TransAction had promised to build 144 units for seniors, people with disabilities, and single-parent families, but the LPTA's tenant survey two years earlier had identified more than two hundred residents in these categories. TransAction, in the LPTA's view, was not only making promises it might not be able to keep, but continued to act in callous ways, with no demonstrable concern for tenants' welfare.

An especially egregious example arose that summer of 1993. In a letter to the LPTA, an eighty-two-year-old tenant named Dolores Mitchell complained that for months she had been calling the management office to report problems like an inoperative garage door, broken glass in her kitchen door, and peeling paint around her wall heater. She hadn't gotten any response, she wrote, then added that she had recently been in the hospital and her doctor had told her, "No more stairs!" This had posed a serious problem because her apartment was on the second floor, but fortunately, while she was still in the hospital, her son had arranged to move her things to a first-floor unit that happened to be vacant. Problem resolved. Or so it seemed, until she discovered to her shock that the landlord intended to charge the going rate for the new apartment. "Imagine paying almost $350 a month more just to be in a first-floor apartment identical with my old one in which I had lived for over twenty years!"

While technically legal under the city's RSO, this outraged Bernard and other LPTA members, who saw the owners treating the struggles of an elderly tenant with health issues as an opportunity to pad their bottom line. Or perhaps their aim was to force a tenant who had repeatedly complained about maintenance problems to leave. For her part, Mitchell wrote, in seeming resignation, "Oh well, life plays some tricks on us as we get old."

LPTA members also believed that TransAction was playing dirty by putting out misinformation to both tenants and neighborhood residents about the redevelopment and the tenant-purchase effort. One of the more persistent claims was that the tenant group had been trying for more than two years without success to line up funding for the acquisition. Another was that tenants would have to use taxpayer money to buy the property. Yet another was that all tenants would lose their security deposits because that money, in total more than a half million dollars, would go toward the purchase price. If the tenants owned the property, another claim went, the city would require an increase in density, that is, the conversion of many two-bedroom apartments to three and even four bedrooms, which would bring large families and serious overcrowding. Finally, TransAction repeatedly pointed to the draft EIR as having given the redevelopment a clean bill of health with no negative impacts on either tenants or the surrounding neighborhoods.

Bernard refuted each of these claims in an LPTA bulletin.

Was there no source of funding for the tenant purchase? "No! The landlord and his friends try to say that the LPTA plan has no funding source, although we have stated for two years that the LPTA plan would be financed by a combination of tax-exempt municipal bonds and rehab loans."

Would the tenant plan be financed by government money? "No! A tax-exempt municipal bond is an investment sold by a bond company to private investors. This type of bond makes up the bulk of the financing of the LPTA plan."

Would tenant security deposits be part of the purchase price? "No! Your security deposit belongs to you, no matter who owns Lincoln Place."

Could the city require an increase in density? "No! The owner and his friends are trying to scare you into believing that the LPTA plan would crowd the apartments and the streets."

Did the draft EIR accurately assess the human and environmental costs of the landlord's plan? "No! The landlord's plan represents major harm to the East Venice community and is in flagrant violation of Los Angeles housing policy."

While the adversarial tone of pronouncements by both TransAction and the LPTA could be seen as boding poorly for the tenant-purchase plan, Scully and the Agora Group were diligently working to put together another offer, one they hoped, in light of the bankruptcy proceedings and the considerable opposition to the redevelopment, the owners would find impossible to refuse. There was little anyone could do to influence the course of the bankruptcy, but the redevelopment plan was another matter. If the city council could be persuaded to reject it, TransAction would be faced with the choice of continuing to operate Lincoln Place as is, which the company clearly didn't want to do, or selling. Scully, who had earned her law degree while working as a Los Angeles city planner, understood the importance of political support to both sides in fights over large projects, and she put the LPTA in touch with a government-relations consulting firm run by a former city planner named Donn Morey and his partner, Jeff Seymour. The men agreed to represent the LPTA on a pro bono basis; they would work with Ruth Galanter's office and lobby other city council members to defeat the redevelopment and build support for tenant ownership.

The city election proved a disappointment to those hoping for a mayor friendly to tenant interests. Richard Riordan, with his law and order campaign, beat Michael Woo by eight percentage points, which wasn't exactly a landslide but no doubt reflected concern among many people over crime and the lingering effects of the Rodney King uprising, which included the fact that four young Black men accused of dragging a white man from the cab of his truck and beating him nearly to death were scheduled to go to trial in just over a month. Would Riordan, whose major base of support came from the predominately white, middle-class San Fernando Valley, try to get rent control repealed? Would he push to make it easier for developers to tear down affordable-housing complexes and build luxury apartments and condominiums? Would tenant advocates be unwelcome in his office? The mayor had no direct power over matters like the Lincoln Place redevelopment or the tenant-purchase effort, but the LPTA had hoped that support from a sympathetic mayor like Woo could influence other decision-makers. Whether the election of Riordan was a minor bump in the road to hoped-for success, or a more serious impediment, was impossible to know.

In the meantime, further examples of what the LPTA considered TransActions's disregard of tenants were forthcoming. In early August, residents found a notice in their mail from a movie production company called Casual Pictures. According to the notice, the company would be on the property a week hence to film scenes for the movie *Ed Wood*, a Tim Burton–directed period piece starring Johnny Depp. Film crews on Venice streets were a common enough sight, but LPTA members were annoyed that nobody had sought the permission of the tenants whose building would be involved. The letter didn't mention any payment to those tenants, so it was assumed that the usual fee paid by film companies would go directly to the landlord. All cars on the street in the filming area would have to be removed for forty-eight hours, and twenty carports would have to be vacated to make way for period cars. Other disruptions to tenants' lives could be easily imagined.

Two days before the scheduled filming, crew members appeared with chainsaws and began cutting away the shrubbery alongside the building's deep, U-shaped courtyard. An alarmed tenant left a telephone message for Bernard, who confronted the workers shortly after she got home from work. To her consternation, she learned that the crew had orders not only to cut the shrubbery, but to remove the large, Brazilian pepper tree that had stood in the center of the courtyard for the past forty-two years. These trees with their rugged, twisting limbs, thick crowns of shiny leaves, and clusters of multicolored peppercorns were much beloved by most tenants, and Bernard's reaction to the news that management had given permission to chop one of them down for a movie was, "Over my dead body!"

She quickly recruited some other LPTA members, then sought out the person in charge, and told him that they were prepared to encircle the tree to protect it from destruction. Almost as appalling to her as the idea of chopping down a perfectly healthy tree was the fact that the landlord hadn't said a word to the building's tenants or anyone else in the complex. A spokesman for the film crew told her that the original plan had been to dig up the tree and replant it somewhere else on the property, but Lincoln Place gardeners had told them to go ahead and chop it down because pepper trees had limited lifespans, and the one in question would likely die within the next few years.

Bernard didn't believe this. In her mind, TransAction was planning to get rid of all the trees to make way for their new construction, and here was an opportunity to remove one without any cost. Or just as likely, the landlord simply didn't care about tenant comforts like shade and the visual pleasure the trees provided. Whatever the case, the tenants stood firm in their vow to protect the tree, and the film company finally agreed to hire a professional landscape company to dig up the tree, box the roots, move it aside, and replant it in its original place in the courtyard when the filming was over.

Despite the prediction of the tree's soon-to-be natural demise, it still stands green and lush in the courtyard twenty-eight years later. As for the movie based on the life of the director of such cult films as *Jail Bait* and *Plan 9 From Out Space*, it debuted in 1994 to generally good reviews, but didn't contain any scenes shot at Lincoln Place. After all the drama over the tree and the bad feelings aroused between tenants and landlord, the footage ended up on the cutting room floor. The opinions of many Lincoln Place tenants were summed up in a short article in the September 1993, LPTA newsletter, by a tenant named Michele Kort. A feminist writer who later published a biography of Laura Nyro and worked as a senior editor at *Ms.* magazine, Kort wrote, "This one-day shoot disrupted our lives for weeks. For four days before, we had to suffer through the frequent loud noise of heavy machinery (saws, generators, cranes) and the presence of crew members right below our windows. It was a very unrelaxing weekend, and that was nothing compared to the day of the shoot, when hundreds of people invaded our space and made us feel like we were living life in a fishbowl. Ah, the glamour."

That same newsletter announced an upcoming LPTA yard sale, an event almost certain to antagonize the management. The response, however, came indirectly, through a flyer distributed to tenants that bore the name of Lincoln Place Tomorrow. LPTA members viewed this tenant group that supported TransAction's redevelopment plan as a mouthpiece for the owners, and indeed the flyer repeated almost verbatim objections that management had made to previous yard sales. It listed Councilwoman Galanter's number and urged anyone who believed that the sale would adversely affect them to call her office and lodge a complaint. "Since the LPTA is making money through this yard sale at the cost of your peace of mind, parking spaces, and shared lawn space, we suggest that you request that the LPTA compensate you monetarily for the inconvenience." For anyone inclined to actually follow that suggestion, it listed both the LPTA and Sheila Bernard's home telephone numbers.

This dreary atmosphere of antagonism hung over Lincoln Place like the gray coastal clouds that often lingered on summer mornings before the sun burned them off. Bernard believed in civility, but didn't see any benefit in trying to make nice with owners who wanted to throw people out and tear down their homes. She was committed to her belief that keeping tenants engaged in social activities like the yard sales and holiday get-togethers was critical to sustaining opposition to the redevelopment and building support for the purchase plan. If the tenants stuck together, if they showed TransAction that nothing could shake their resolve, they would prevail.

With the court yet to approve a bankruptcy plan, Bernard felt the urgency of getting another, more detailed purchase offer ready. Thus far, the company had declined to counter the $47.7 million offer made at the beginning of 1992. Why? In a letter to Marcia Scully later that year, the attorney representing the landlord wrote, "Transaction has advised us that they will not enter into any further discussion regarding your client's desires for the future of Lincoln Place in the absence of evidence that your client has a commercially viable plan which can be funded or financed either through public agencies or private sources. Only after your client has passed this scrutiny will our client consider discussing any terms or conditions upon which an offer may be acceptable." In other words, show us the money and then we'll talk. But this, in Scully's words, created a catch-22 situation. TransAction would not discuss a purchase price until the LPTA had commitments from lenders and funders, but lenders and funders would not commit any money before the LPTA and TransAction agreed on a purchase price.

In an effort to break this impasse, Scully and Ed Kirshner of the Agora Group worked to show that specific loans and other forms of funding were available to nonprofit groups like the LPTA. Kirshner approached TRI Financial Corporation, a San Francisco–based company that provided government-insured loans for affordable-housing projects. The response was highly encouraging. The LPTA would likely be eligible for a federal mortgage insurance program that would cover most of the acquisition cost as well as provide money for rehabilitation work. In a December 17, 1993, letter to Kirshner, TRI vice president Robert Starr wrote, "This will be a unique chance for HUD to achieve affordable housing with its mortgage insurance tools and without direct federal subsidy." Starr made oblique reference to the fact that with the election of Bill Clinton as president, the post of HUD secretary had passed from Jack Kemp to Henry Cisneros, who was considered much friendlier to the idea of direct federal aid to affordable-housing projects. "I am hopeful," Starr wrote, "that the right attitude and the right people are now in place at HUD's headquarters' office to give impetus to this significant opportunity for resident ownership."

While Scully and Kirshner worked out the details of a formal offer, Bernard saw an article in the *Los Angeles Times* that gave her an idea. According to the piece, Bank of America had promised to invest $40 million in the construction and renovation of affordable-housing projects in California. Why not Lincoln Place, she thought, given the fact that $30 million of the bank's money was already at risk in TransAction's bankruptcy? She got the name of a vice president who supervised the bank's affordable-housing initiatives and wrote to him at his San Francisco office, explaining the LPTA's effort to buy Lincoln Place and suggesting that it would be in the bank's best interests to support it. "We are hoping that Bank of America will see its own interests as coincident with our own," she wrote. "That is, to refuse the owner of Lincoln Place the opportunity to extend his indebtedness while destroying hundreds of units of affordable housing during a severe housing crisis. The bank could play a major role in seeing that a nonprofit sale of the property to the tenants is examined as a superior alternative to the owner's reorganization plan, and in the best interests of all creditors and the 1,500 tenants."

On November 19, 1993, Scully sent a proposed purchase option to TransAction's attorney. The six-month option established a purchase price of $40 million, and could be renewed three times before expiring. The total funding package would be $55 million, with $52 million from a federally insured mortgage bond issued by TRI Financial and $3 million in housing rehabilitation funds from the city of Los Angeles. While Scully, Bernard, and others did not expect TransAction to immediately accept this offer, they hoped that it would at least produce a counteroffer or some other point to begin negotiations. But on December 16, the attorney responded to Scully by flatly calling the option agreement "unacceptable." The property was worth at least $50 million, he wrote, adding that "our client believes that it can successfully complete the entitlement and redevelopment process and cannot be expected to accept bulk sale-based pricing." He also objected to the option terms that called for a $2,500 refundable deposit, which was admittedly low but reflected the LPTA's lack of immediate funds. Any option payment would have to be at least two percent of an agreed-upon purchase price and nonrefundable, although it would be credited to that price in the event that TransAction and the LPTA reached a deal. Which meant that even if the company agreed to $40 million, the LPTA would have to come up with $800,000 in advance. And if purchase negotiations fell through, that money would go into TransAction's pockets. James Coxeter and Robert Bisno obviously knew that the LPTA could never agree to such terms, and once again the only conclusion to draw was that they just weren't interested in selling, at least not to the Lincoln Place tenants.

To that point, Sheila Bernard hadn't gotten any response from Bank of America. But a week after TransAction rejected the purchase offer, the judge presiding over TransAction's bankruptcy approved the company's plan for repayment of its debts to the bank and other creditors. That shut the door on any opportunity for the LPTA to present a purchase offer to the court. It also showed that Bank of America was interested in being repaid, not in getting involved in the tenants' effort to buy the property.

Could "Let's Own It" be kept alive? Or were Bernard and her most ardent supporters tilting at windmills? As they gathered for the LPTA's annual holiday celebration at Penmar Park, many tenants were turning their thoughts to the challenges the new year promised, most notably the hearings that would be held on TransAction's redevelopment plan. Could a company like TransAction with its high-powered lawyers and lobbyists be defeated by tenants whose only real power was their numbers and the righteousness of their cause? Or were they just whistling in the dark?

8

EARTHQUAKE

AT 4:31 A.M. ON January 17, 1994, Los Angles began to shake. The upper floors of a large apartment complex in the San Fernando Valley pancaked, fatally crushing sixteen occupants of units at ground level. A few miles away, a freeway overpass collapsed and an LAPD motorcycle officer speeding through the darkness on his way to work rode into the abyss and died in the forty-foot fall. A section of the heavily traveled I-10 freeway between the west side and downtown collapsed, although light traffic at that hour helped preclude death or injury. Fires erupted from broken gas mains and set homes ablaze. Buildings shifted on their foundations, and ominous cracks appeared in stucco walls. Bricks cascaded down from chimneys. People sound asleep just moments earlier were wide awake in the chilly darkness, with no electricity or gas, trying to find flashlights or candles and battery-powered radios to get some news of what had just happened.

Venice was seventeen miles from the earthquake's epicenter in the San Fernando Valley community of Northridge, and while Lincoln Place tenants and other neighborhood residents were jolted awake, most were shocked when they heard news of the deaths and the extent of the devastation, which included the collapse of parking structures and such severe damage to a major hospital that the patients had to be evacuated. Ingrid Mueller's experience was typical. Her living room bookshelves toppled, but there was no visible damage beyond a few new cracks in the plaster walls. And once daylight broke, it was apparent that none of the fifty-two buildings had sustained damage more serious than minor stucco cracks.

In contrast, several large apartment buildings in Santa Monica just a few miles north suffered such severe damage that occupants weren't allowed back in to get their possessions, although nobody was killed or seriously injured. The fact that Lincoln Place escaped this fate could be attributed to several facts, including the geology of the coastal plain on which Venice lies, with its deep layers of sediment that didn't magnify the seismic waves in the same way as the bedrock underlying Santa Monica and the San Fernando Valley. But the construction of the Lincoln Place buildings played a major role. They were built before it was common to design apartment buildings with open parking stalls beneath second-floor units, a style known as "tuck-under" parking that proved to be especially vulnerable to earthquakes and was deemed a major factor in the fatal collapse of the San Fernando Valley building.

Lincoln Place manager Lucy Farber sent a letter to tenants four days after the earthquake, reassuring them of what appeared obvious, that the buildings hadn't suffered any structural damage. It wasn't long, though, before Sheila Bernard and Mueller and other members of the LPTA steering committee noticed that supporters of TransAction's redevelopment plan were adding to their talking points the fact that Lincoln Place didn't meet current seismic construction standards. While this was literally true, LPTA supporters saw it as an attempt to frighten tenants into believing that their lives could be at risk in the next big earthquake. Nobody could guarantee that the so-called Big One that loomed in people's imaginations wouldn't level large swaths of the city, including Lincoln Place, but it was extraordinarily unlikely. Buildings like those at Lincoln Place escaped major damage even close to the earthquake's epicenter, and engineers considered its construction style—woodframe with no "tuck-under" parking—to be among the most resistant to the violent shaking that could wreak havoc on other structures. But preying on people's fears, LPTA leaders believed, was of a piece with TransAction's willingness to bend the truth to get tenants and community members to support the redevelopment.

A glaring example could be found in documents filed as part of TransAction's federal court bankruptcy proceedings. From the moment the redevelopment plan was first announced in 1990, the company contended that Lincoln Place needed so much work that it wasn't financially feasible to maintain it. This assertion found its way into pronouncements by the Penmar Neighborhood Association and Lincoln Place Tomorrow, the pro-landlord tenants group. TransAction also repeatedly cited a high rate of tenant turnover to support its contention that Lincoln Place was a largely transient complex, not the homey, deep-rooted community in pictures painted by the LPTA. The high turnover rate also fed a narrative, pushed in particular by the Penmar group, that the Lincoln Place population was unstable, with strangers of uncertain character constantly coming into the neighborhood. In contrast, the new condominiums would be occupied by people who wanted to put down roots, who shared the values of the homeowners in the surrounding community. The LPTA worked hard to counter this narrative, and they got unexpected help from James Coxeter, who made a statement in bankruptcy court that seemed to directly contradict what he and his supporters were saying publicly. Responding to a creditor's allegation that TransAction would have difficulty refinancing the property because of its poor condition, the landlord had the following to say in a declaration filed with the court in December 1993:

"The property is currently 98% occupied. The tenants pay their rent current and we have collections of over 97%. Our tenant turnovers are substantially less than the turnovers experienced by other apartments in West Los Angeles or Los Angeles in general. These high collection, low vacancy factors, and low tenant turnover factors demonstrate the good maintenance and condition of the property. If the property were not properly maintained, the tenants would probably move out and it would be difficult to obtain new tenants; additionally, if there were problems with maintenance and upkeep the tenants would potentially withhold rent to force us to repair their apartments. Neither of these is the case."

Putting aside the questionable nature of Coxeter's statement that Lincoln Place tenants would move out or withhold their rent if the property was poorly maintained, the claim of low tenant turnover appeared to show one of two things. If the landlord was telling the truth in court, then he wasn't telling the truth to tenants, members of the public, and government officials. But if he wasn't telling the truth in his court declaration, he could be flirting with legal trouble. In any event, the declaration showed what Bernard and LPTA supporters had long believed, that the landlord was not above duplicity to advance the redevelopment plan.

On April 22, 1994, the city planning department released the final version of the Lincoln Place EIR. Of greatest interest to the LPTA, of course, was the section dealing with impacts on housing, and the final EIR addressed critical comments made on the draft report by Bernard, Marcia Scully, and others. It acknowledged that under state law and the city's guidelines, the project could have a significant environmental impact if it displaced a large number of people. It also deleted the assertion that the project would result in a net gain of housing units. Of the 795 existing Lincoln Place units, the final report said, 469 were currently renting at levels affordable to people with incomes classified as low and very low, less than eighty percent and fifty percent of the area median, respectively. Since TransAction was proposing to build 144 new units affordable to people at those income levels, the project would therefore result in a net loss of 325 affordable units. While this was a significant acknowledgment, Scully believed that the calculations should have also included people with incomes classified as moderate—between 80 and 120 percent of the area median—which would have brought the total loss of affordable units close to 600.

However, the final report recycled TransAction's claim that the apartment turnover rate meant that if Lincoln Place was left as is, nearly all current residents, including seniors and low-income tenants, would be gone in ten years. Their units would be renting at market rates, which meant that TransAction's plan to build 144 new rent-restricted apartments would actually result in a net gain of affordable-housing units in the community. This caused Bernard and other LPTA members to literally shake their heads. Their 1991 tenant survey had shown that almost all low-income tenants had lived at Lincoln Place for at least five years and had no plans to move, not only because they liked the place but also because of the daunting task they would face in finding an apartment they could afford in Venice or nearby communities. The LPTA believed that wealthier tenants accounted for most of the turnover cited by TransAction, with the same apartments being repeatedly rented and vacated while lower-income residents stayed put. Otherwise, almost all the tenants who had lived at Lincoln Place for at least five years would already be gone.

Jan Book, who moved to Lincoln Place in 1984 and wrote the scathing letter to James Coxeter after attending one of his early meetings with tenants, said that the apartment upstairs from hers had turned over five times since TransAction bought the property in 1986. And many believed that TransAction was encouraging this rapid turnover by advertising to students and requiring all new tenants to sign disclaimers stating that redevelopment plans were underway and tenancies could be terminated any time after the start of construction. In light of this, the fact that available units were being rented by people who planned to stay for a short period of time shouldn't have come as any surprise.

Despite the EIR's reliance on TransAction's questionable reasoning, LPTA members firmly believed that the project would drive out many residents who didn't want to leave. One of those was Ingrid Mueller, who loved living at Lincoln Place and had no plans to move. She was in her fifties, and both of her daughters were grown and living on their own, which meant that she wouldn't have priority for one of the new apartments. If the redevelopment was approved, she fully expected that she would have to look for another place to live. And with the modest amount she earned doing German voice-overs and subtitles for American films, finding a comparable place in the community would be exceedingly difficult.

To nobody's surprise, TransAction's take was quite different. In the June 1994 issue of the *Lincoln Place News*, James Coxeter wrote, "I am particularly proud of the 144 rental replacement apartments. With these units we are able to guarantee new apartments at the same rents to all Lincoln Place seniors (over sixty-two), all single-parent households and all disabled residents at Lincoln Place. With the ten-year phasing of the redevelopment taking advantage of the 22% annual turnover, we believe the replacement rental apartments will be able to serve all Lincoln Place residents who wish to remain here before becoming permanently affordable housing available to the community." The landlord's newsletter made other statements that Mueller, Bernard, and others considered at best misleading and, at worst, patently false. In an article titled "Environmental Review Shows Broad

Support for Community Plan," the landlord repeated an earlier claim that a majority of comment letters on the draft EIR supported the redevelopment, or as TransAction had taken to calling it, the "Community Plan." This was blatantly deceptive, Bernard believed, because her letter written as president of the LPTA represented the views of hundreds of tenants who paid dues and did volunteer work for the organization. Even if the letters from members of the Penmar Neighborhood Association and Lincoln Place Tomorrow reflected the views of a significant number of people, which she seriously doubted, there was nothing on record to justify the claim of "broad support."

The issue of community sentiment would become more critical if and when the project reached the city council, but at the moment, the EIR was foremost in the minds of Scully and others who had carefully examined its dense verbiage. In their minds, its conclusions badly understated the negative impacts of the redevelopment in regard to housing affordability and the effect on tenants, and now that public hearings were on the horizon, they could start making the case that the EIR was so flawed it should be rejected. The first hearing was held by the Venice Community Planning Advisory Committee, or CPAC, the same group to which Bernard had presented the LPTA's tenant-purchase plan two years earlier. The latest meeting was held on the evening of July 7, 1994, at the old Venice police station on Venice Boulevard, a 1920s art deco building vacated in the 1970s and occupied later by the nonprofit Social and Public Arts Resource Center. Committee members sat behind folding tables set up at one end of a large high-ceilinged room at the rear of the building. Lincoln Place tenants, community members, and others filled rows of white plastic chairs, while those who arrived too late to get a seat stood at the rear of the drably institutional space. At one side, against a wall with tall, frosted glass windows, Jim Merlino of TransAction stood with easels holding renderings of the new Lincoln Place, while Sheila Bernard stood on the opposite side of the room with a display of posters filled with statistics and other facts supporting the preservation of Lincoln Place and disputing the landlord's claims.

Merlino, dressed in khaki pants and a white shirt with rolled-up sleeves, opened by explaining why TransAction had decided to redevelop Lincoln Place. All the reasons familiar to those who had gone to Coxeter's "planning forums" and read the landlord's newsletters were included—problems with maintenance, parking, and security, among others. He went over the plans for the 144 new apartments and the 706 townhouses, all of which would have up-to-date security, adequate parking, and the latest in modern conveniences. He said the apartments would be built and ready for occupancy before any other construction started, and that current tenants would have three choices—to rent one of the new apartments, to wait and buy one of the fifty-two townhouses set aside as affordable, or to receive a relocation payment and assistance in renting a new place in the area. But once again, he repeated the landlord's claim that phasing the construction over ten years ensured that almost everyone who wanted to stay at Lincoln Place would be able to do so. In direct contradiction of Coxeter's bankruptcy court declaration, he said, "We have a very high resident turnover."

When it was Bernard's turn to speak, she contested this assertion, and cited statistics compiled in the tenant survey. "Lincoln Place is an unusually stable community," she said. But rather than launch into a detailed critique of Merlino's presentation, which might be seen as part of a "he said/she said" dynamic, she called on selected tenants to speak of their feelings about living at Lincoln Place.

Frieda Marlin, a seventy-year-old native New Yorker who had lived at the complex with her husband for thirteen years, said that TransAction's plan for new apartments in one corner of the property would create "a 144-unit ghetto." Instead of enjoying the lawns and trees and singing birds that made Lincoln Place such a good place to live, residents would have to live with ten years of noise and dirt from construction of the condominiums. "We need to stay in our homes," she said, "and make a community where there is respect for low- and moderate-income families, not just those who are comfortably able to buy a condo."

Stan Dounn, a sixty-two-year-old single man and Lincoln Place tenant for sixteen years, told the committee that "to create a community is a blessing, to destroy a community is a tragedy."

A tenant named Martha Perez, a single mother, said she was afraid that if she had to move she would never find another place like Lincoln Place, which she particularly loved because it was so close to a park and schools.

Bill Ullett, a native Englishman who had worked as a butler for many years, said that he had lived in other people's houses almost all his adult life, and when he retired and moved to Lincoln Place, he intended to make his apartment his home for his remaining years. When he sat down, Bernard concluded the presentation by saying, to enthusiastic applause, "This project will have disastrous consequences not only for Lincoln Place but for Venice and the entire city of Los Angeles."

Committee chairman Jeff Lee then opened the meeting to any audience member who wished to speak. Karen Brodkin, a Venice resident and professor of anthropology at UCLA who had been filming meetings and other LPTA activities that would later be footage in a short film titled *Let's Own It!: The Struggle of the Lincoln Place Tenants Association*, said she had gone to federal court and read documents regarding TransAction's recent bankruptcy case. She questioned the company's financial ability to complete the Lincoln Place redevelopment, saying that TransAction owed more than it paid for the property, and had already lost other properties to foreclosure. Referring to the recent nationwide savings and loan crisis, she asked, "Do we want to trust our community to the kind of folks who brought us the S&L?"

Anne Murphy, president of the board of Venice Community Housing, a local nonprofit that developed and managed low-income housing, said that it was "unthinkable to me that we could just destroy eight hundred units of affordable housing."

A young woman who identified herself only as a Lincoln Place tenant spoke of the social interaction fostered by the complex. "This is the one community where I've ever, ever lived in where I've been able to talk and communicate with my neighbors." Gesturing at the renderings of the new apartments along the wall, she said, "I grew up in a neighborhood that looked like this and never spoke to any of my neighbors my entire life."

Sandy Moring, the homeowner who founded the Committee to Preserve Lincoln Place, challenged complaints by some TransAction supporters that Lincoln Place attracted the wrong sort of people to the neighborhood. "The residents have always been good neighbors," she said.

Vera Davis, an African American woman and longtime activist in Venice's Oakwood neighborhood, said, "I've never heard such a ridiculous thing, especially in this area and this time to destroy homes and apartments. You shouldn't tear anything down, you should improve."

But perhaps the most moving comments came from eighty-year-old Adolphe Griffith, a retired mail carrier and WWII veteran who had lived at Lincoln Place for seventeen years. He told the committee that his wife died in their apartment after a bout with cancer, surrounded by himself and other family members. This made the place deeply important to him, and he didn't want to watch it being torn down.

While a majority of the audience applauded the speakers who opposed the redevelopment, a handful stood to speak in its favor. Mary Roberts, the spokeswoman for Lincoln Place Tomorrow, said that anyone bent upon committing a crime could freely walk into the complex and up to her front door. In the time she had lived at Lincoln Place, she said, her car had been vandalized nine times. Alluding to a recent surge in gang activity in Venice, she said, "There's a security problem when we have police chasing people with AK-47s through the place."

A local architect named Michael King said he supported the project "wholeheartedly" because it would help create "a real urban city rather than little residential ghettos." Both Judith Pressman and Chris Williams, cochairs of the Penmar Neighborhood Association, spoke in favor of the redevelopment and accused LPTA members of trying to paint themselves as victims. "Being a renter doesn't make one an automatic victim," Williams said, provoking boos from the audience. Speakers had each been allotted two minutes, but when his time was up, Williams refused to stop, saying he should get more time because Lincoln Place supporters had exceeded their limits. This brought more booing and shouts for him to sit down, and for a few moments it seemed as if the meeting would devolve into chaos, but he eventually decided to stop or ran out of things to say and a semblance of order was restored.

More than two hours after Lee called the meeting to order, committee members began discussing what they had heard. Moe Stavnezer, a local pharmacist and one of the founders of Venice Community Housing, said he was confounded by Merlino's statement that any current tenant who didn't want to move into one of the 144 apartments could buy one of the fifty-two affordable condominiums. "How can anyone currently at Lincoln Place possibly buy a condo for $140,000 to $160,000?" he asked. He also wanted to know what Merlino meant when he said that tenants who didn't want to stay at Lincoln Place would be assisted in finding an apartment in the area. What defined the area? Was it Venice? West Los Angeles? The entire city? Merlino didn't have an answer.

Challis MacPherson, who lived in an upscale area of Venice called the Oxford Triangle, said she had mixed emotions about the project. She had lived at Lincoln Place for six years and raised a child there, but was also the victim of crime when her car was stolen from the property. "I love the way it is, but I realize there will probably have to be some changes."

Committee members David Moring and Carol Berman didn't share that view, both expressing strong opposition to the redevelopment. Moring asked Merlino if TransAction was doing anything to repair and upgrade the complex, to which the company vice president answered, "We think it's in great shape." That elicited boos from the audience, presumably because it conflicted with his earlier statements about deterioration as well as the experience of many tenants who had complained about poor maintenance. Berman, a longtime Venice activist, said, "I can't see any sense at all in tearing up something. If it ain't broke, don't fix it." In the end, a motion was made and the chairman asked for a show of hands. Of the thirteen committee members present, eight voted to oppose the project, three voted in favor of it, and two abstained. Tenants and their supporters in the audience broke into sustained applause.

While there was euphoria among some LPTA members, Bernard had a clear-eyed view of how much effort it would take to beat back the landlord's plan and, hopefully, revive the seemingly moribund "Let's Own It" effort. The CPAC had no official power, and some in the community dismissed it as a collection of antigrowth zealots who had never seen a development project they liked. And although Ruth Galanter had publicly supported preservation of Lincoln Place, some feared that she might vote for a modified redevelopment plan if it provided more affordable units and had an ironclad guarantee that existing tenants wouldn't be forced to move. For Bernard, though, the goal was nothing less than outright rejection by the city council, and she knew that getting to that point meant convincing the councilwoman that tenant and community opposition was not only wide but deep. The CPAC vote was a step in that direction. But the LPTA had to get people to write letters, make phone calls, sign petitions, attend meetings. And to vote with their pocketbooks, to help defray the considerable expenses involved in printing flyers and newsletters, chartering buses to take people to city hall, and hosting social events on the property to attract and build support. Despite its recent declaration of bankruptcy, TransAction had plenty of resources at its disposal to hire expensive lawyers and lobbyists and put out slick publicity materials.

"We knew we were still fighting an uphill battle," Bernard says, "We knew that we still had a lot of work to do."

9

AGING BUT NOT DEAD

MARCIA SCULLY'S OFFICE IS on the twelfth floor of the Metropolitan Water District building in downtown Los Angeles. A visitor getting off the elevator is greeted with an expanse of glass that frames a view of the red tile roofs of Union Station next door and the lantern-like cupolas of the Terminal Annex just down the block, a pair of Depression-era buildings that are considered among the city's architectural landmarks. Beyond are the hills of Elysian Park and Dodger Stadium, and on the horizon, the rugged outlines of the San Gabriel Mountains. Beyond that mountain range, some 240 miles due east, is Parker Dam on the Colorado River and the origin of the aqueduct that brings water to nineteen million people in Southern California.

In a conference room just steps from her office, Scully sits with her back to a wall with two large aerial photographs of the semicircular dam, which straddles the border between California and Arizona. A slightly built woman with short, blond hair, one could imagine from her pleasant, unassuming manner that she is a librarian or schoolteacher rather than the head of legal affairs for the largest supplier of treated water in the United States. She is wearing glasses and a lilac-colored jacket with a large March for Science pin displaying the message, "Science, Not Silence." Asked how she feels about her experience working with the Lincoln Place Tenants Association, she doesn't hesitate before responding. "It was a wonderful experience working with the tenants group because they were a wonderful group of people who had a righteous cause."

It's clear from reading documents and letters and talking to LPTA leaders that she put an extraordinary amount of effort into helping advance that cause. Does she know how much time she spent on that unpaid work, which went on for more than four years? "I didn't keep track of the time I spent," she says, "but I know it was hundreds of hours. It was a big commitment of time, but I thought it was the right thing to do. I thought they deserved support and that it was a very worthwhile thing to be involved in." She momentarily pauses, as if to reflect. "My guiding principle has been to have the work I do, whether it's work I get paid for or pro bono work, to be work I care about, work that is helpful as opposed to harmful to the world."

Looking back to the summer of 1994, she says she was optimistic about the chances of winning the battle to stop the redevelopment, but she wasn't as confident as Sheila Bernard that victory would push TransAction to sell the property to the tenants. Even if the company had decided to sell, it might have been to a deep-pocketed developer who had ready money and was willing to wait until a more propitious time to resurrect the condominium plan or propose something entirely new. As for the prospects of the TransAction plan, Lincoln Place tenants and others had differing opinions. One popular view held that the city council was so beholden to developers and real estate interests that it would rubber stamp the project. Others believed that council members feared public opinion more than anything else and didn't want to pick up their newspapers and read stories about the poor and elderly being forced out of their homes to make way for luxury condominiums. Some people thought business-friendly Mayor Richard Riordan would lean on council members to support a large developer like TransAction; others were convinced that if Councilwoman Galanter held to her promise and voted against the project, other members who might want her vote on projects in their own districts would go along.

There were bridges to cross, though, before the plan landed on the desks of the fifteen council members. A hearing would be held in the city planning department by an entity called the deputy advisory agency, which despite the name was a single planning-department employee designated by the department director. After the hearing this so-called agency would issue a letter of determination approving the project as presented, approving the project with conditions, or rejecting it. Either the LPTA or TransAction would then have ten days to appeal the decision to the city planning commission.

While the advisory agency and commission hearings were open to the public, and people could make the same kind of arguments they had made at the CPAC meeting, Scully knew that convincing a citizens group in one of the most liberal communities in the city was far different than demonstrating to city officials and commission members that the owner's plan violated specific provisions of state law and city ordinance. It would be her job to call attention to those violations and show that they were serious enough to warrant rejection of the plan. People could come and speak at the hearings, and indeed it was important to demonstrate public concern, but legal arguments, not emotional appeals, were likely to carry the day either for TransAction or the LPTA.

Ruth Galanter had previously asked the LPTA to provide her with specific arguments to justify voting against the project, and four days after the CPAC meeting, Scully sent the councilwoman a seven-page memorandum laying those out. Both Galanter and Scully knew from their respective experiences how important it was for the city council to have sound legal reasons for rejecting a project. That's because the only recourse for developers on the losing end of council votes was taking the city to court. Defending against such lawsuits fell to the city attorney's office, which would often be facing off against some of the highest-paid legal talent in the city, so having the requisite facts and figures in the legislative record was exceedingly important.

In view of this, Scully's memorandum outlined specific violations of state laws and city ordinances. The first concerned the EIR, which under CEQA had to identify instances of adverse impacts and then propose mitigations that made those impacts less than significant. Scully cited a number of unmitigated adverse impacts, any of which were sufficient grounds to reject the project. She contended that the redevelopment would violate the city's General Plan, in particular its housing element, and quoted a section that read, "The City shall discourage the demolition of affordable housing unless there is adequate assurance that suitable replacement units will be made available." There was no guarantee, she argued, that the new affordable apartments proposed by TransAction would be enough for qualified tenants, nor was the company's promise to help tenants find apartments elsewhere in the area likely to be fulfilled. "Therefore," she wrote, "the destruction of affordable housing of this magnitude is directly contrary to the primary goal of the housing element."

Scully also argued that violations of the city's General Plan led directly to a violation of California's Subdivision Map Act, which came into play because TransAction's plan for condominiums required the filing of a new subdivision plan called a Vesting Tentative Tract Map, or VTTM. Scully quoted a section of the Map Act that said an appropriate governmental body "shall deny" approval of a subdivision map if it is inconsistent with the city's General Plan. Since that was clearly the case, for the reasons she had already outlined, she concluded that "the City cannot legally approve the proposed project."

The deputy advisory agency hearing was scheduled for August 3 at city hall. Two weeks before the hearing, the LPTA steering committee met at Frieda and Dave Marlin's apartment to talk about strategy. Frieda, who was one of the most active and vocal LPTA members, had just been featured in an *L.A. Times* column about the fight to save Lincoln Place. Written by popular columnist Al Martinez, whose human interest stories ran in the newspaper for twenty-three years, the piece described the Bronx-born Marlin as "tough, angry and awesomely determined" not to let anyone "tear down her home and shovel her off to some old people's ghetto."[30] Her willingness to attend meetings almost anywhere and speak out made her a valuable member of a contingent Bernard feared was not only getting smaller, but also beginning to lose enthusiasm for the fight against a corporate landlord many believed to hold most of the cards. Tenants like Marlin and Ingrid Mueller and a handful of others could be counted on to go to the wall for the cause, but how many others would do the same?

Two charter buses had been reserved to take tenants and LPTA supporters to the upcoming hearing, and Bernard wanted to get at least fifty people, which was always a problem because many of the seniors who were the core of LPTA support had physical problems that made such a trip difficult, and younger people typically had jobs and couldn't easily take time off. But the steering committee members would each call a certain number of people on a list of supporters and explain the importance of refuting a claim being advanced by TransAction and Lincoln Place Tomorrow that the LPTA only represented a handful of disgruntled tenants. During the rehab eviction battles five years earlier, it had been easy to get a hundred people or more to a public meeting, but once that fight was over, it seemed that many of those same people didn't feel the need to stay active. There wasn't universal enthusiasm for the "Let's Own It" campaign and the fight against the redevelopment involved legal and technical issues that some found intimidating and hard to understand.

On the day of the hearing, some forty people gathered in Elkgrove Circle. Most wore yellow Preserve Lincoln Place tags, and they boarded the charter buses with printed signs in the windows that read, Lincoln Place Tenants Association Antidemolition Express. Others were going to city hall by car, so it looked as if attendance might reach the fifty Bernard had aimed for, an especially important goal because two blocks away charter buses hired by TransAction were lined up in front of the rental office to take members of Lincoln Place Tomorrow and other supporters downtown. Bernard was confident that opponents of the redevelopment far outnumbered its supporters. But how would it look if there were more of those TransAction supporters than LPTA members at the hearing?

As it turned out, that didn't happen, although the front rows on one side of the hearing room were filled with people wearing yellow Lincoln Place Tomorrow tags and holding signs with the messages, Approve the Project, and New Homes, New Jobs, a REAL Future. James Coxeter and Jim Merlino of TransAction were there, both dressed in dark suits with white shirts and ties, Merlino's appearance a contrast to his casual attire at the Venice CPAC meeting. Most of the LPTA contingent filled the benches on the opposite side of the center aisle. People from the neighborhood included Anne Murphy of Venice Community Housing, and Chris Williams, cochair of the Penmar Neighborhood Association. Every seat was taken and a dozen or so people stood in the back of the room, a smaller version of the city council chamber with a Byzantine interior of arches supported by marble columns topped by ornate capitals, marble floors with diamond-shaped inlays, and tall windows of opaque glass divided by triangular grids.

The hearing was called to order shortly after 1:30 p.m. by Darryl Fisher, a city zoning administrator. He first called on the city planner in charge of the TransAction project, who laid out the basic details of the plan displayed in architectural renderings on easels at one side of the room. He next called on the applicant. Coxeter came forward to make a general statement on behalf of the redevelopment, then turned the podium over to a consultant who went over project features that had been repeatedly aired over the past several years by Coxeter and Merlino and laid out in the EIR, including the assertions most in dispute—that all current tenants who wanted to stay at Lincoln Place would be able to do so, and that if the property was left as is all the units now considered affordable would eventually be renting at market rates. He briefly touched on the LPTA's tenant-purchase plan, dismissing it as infeasible for a variety of reasons, including the basic fact that the purchase offer was unacceptable to the owner. In direct contradiction of Scully's arguments, he said that the city had no comprehensive housing affordability strategy and no policy that mandated the replacement of affordable units in a project like Lincoln Place. He concluded by saying that "this project represents a reasonable balance of the property owner's rights, adopted city housing policy and the rights and needs of the existing Lincoln Place tenants."

Fisher next opened the hearing to public comment and announced that Ruth Galanter would be the first speaker. The councilwoman, whose voice was slightly hoarse as a result of the knife attack seven years earlier, began by noting that a large number of Lincoln Place residents were of low and moderate income, and that many of those were elderly. She said that rent rolls submitted by TransAction as part of their project application showed that 457 of the 795 Lincoln Place units were priced in a range the city considered affordable. The redevelopment, she said, would result in an irrevocable loss to the community of most of those units. She went on to lay out the objections listed in Scully's memorandum, the unmitigated environmental impacts and the violations of the city's General Plan. She concluded by saying that the complex was "aging but not dead," and added that "as a city, we ought to be looking for ways to preserve such housing." For that reason, she said, the application for the redevelopment of Lincoln Place should be denied.

That brought a wave of applause from LPTA supporters, who had counted her as an ally but had wanted her to explicitly say in a public forum such as this that the city should reject the project. It seemed to clearly mean that she would vote no when the time came, and hopefully, bring a majority of other council members along with her. When the applause died down, Fisher began calling on people who had filled out public comment cards. After everyone had their say at the microphone, he closed the hearing with the announcement that the public record would be kept open for two weeks for people wishing to submit written comments. After that, he would issue the letter of determination.

The hearing merited a four-paragraph article in the following day's *Los Angeles Times* with the headline "Galanter Urges City to Block Redevelopment Project."[31] Interviewed after the hearing, she told the reporter that the redevelopment "would change Lincoln Place from a mixed community to one that, by economic necessity, excludes the elderly on fixed incomes and younger families starting up." In the article's final paragraph, Jim Merlino was quoted as predicting eventual victory.

Despite Fisher's statement that led some to believe that his decision would come before the end of the month, September and then October came and went without any word. Hardly anyone expected outright rejection, and the LPTA was prepared to appeal to the city planning commission, but for the moment, there was little for Sheila Bernard to do in terms of rallying the troops for more letter writing, telephone calling, and another trip to city hall. But Scully was busy preparing for an appearance before the commission, and she had also persuaded an attorney who specialized in environmental law to join the team. That lawyer, Jan Chatten-Brown, had worked for the California attorney general and the Los Angeles city attorney before going into private practice, and Scully believed that her extensive knowledge of CEQA and experience litigating cases involving that law would be a definite asset to the cause.

Not all was quiet at Lincoln Place, though. The LPTA had announced a yard sale to be held on September 18, and the management had issued yet another warning that such sales were prohibited. In a letter to all tenants, manager Lucy Farber repeated the claim that numerous complaints had been received from both residents and neighbors who found the sales disruptive and resented the noise and traffic they created. Bernard and other LPTA members had never heard a single one of these alleged complaints, so they dismissed the warning as they had dismissed previous warnings, as a formality intended to shield the landlord from any liability. It would remain to be seen whether that conclusion was correct, or wise.

On an even less salubrious note, the month of September saw news that the man who broke into Ruth Galanter's Venice home in 1987 and stabbed her in the neck had been paroled after serving slightly more than half his fourteen-year sentence. The man, Mark Allen Olds, was required by terms of the parole to stay at least thirty-five miles away from the councilwoman's home, but some were concerned that she might be fearful and less inclined to say and do things that would raise her public profile. Olds had been a heroin addict and gang member who lived across the street from Galanter, and a probation report prepared after he was found guilty of burglary and second-degree attempted murder said that the newly elected councilwoman believed that Olds had definitely intended to kill her. The report went on to say that Galanter, who spent fifty-six days in a hospital recovering from the attack that left her vocal cords permanently damaged, wondered if her life "still may be in jeopardy from others and there remains some uncertainty as to whether the attack was planned." In an *Argonaut* article about the parole, Galanter said she was frustrated that Olds wasn't convicted of premeditated, first-degree attempted murder, which would have carried a much longer sentence. She said that his release made her anxious and nervous, but she was trying to live her life as best she could. She now had two dogs, she added, and had installed a sophisticated alarm system in her house.[32]

While everyone awaited the deputy advisory agency's report, the *Los Angeles Times* published an article on October 17 titled "Lincoln Place: A Classic Affordable Housing Battle." The article quoted two people who supported preservation—a fifteen-year tenant and active LPTA member named Ruth Holzgreen and Steve Cancian, lead organizer for the Coalition for Economic Survival—along with two people who favored the redevelopment—Mary Roberts of Lincoln Place Tomorrow and Mark Ryavec, from a local nonprofit organization called the Venice Action Committee.

Holzgreen called the redevelopment plan a product of "pure greed" while Cancion said the demolition of low-income units should not be allowed when Los Angeles had the worst affordable-housing crisis in the nation. Roberts repeated claims she made at the July CPAC meeting about faulty plumbing and electricity and Ryavec said that the answer to the affordable-housing problem was not to infringe on property rights by denying projects like TransAction's, but to give private developers incentives to build more of the kind of housing the city wanted.

In the photograph that accompanied the article, four tenants stood outside the Lincoln Place rental office, two opponents of the redevelopment on one side of the eight-foot tall Lincoln Place sign and two supporters on the other. This greatly annoyed Bernard, who believed that the article and photo promoted a false numerical equivalency that fed into the landlord's narrative of widespread tenant support for the new Lincoln Place. To her mind, this was an illustration of why the LPTA should push forward with a new survey to show that most tenants actually opposed the redevelopment plan.

After some spirited discussion, the LPTA steering committee settled on the idea of circulating a petition. Because those responding to the 1991 survey were anonymous, the landlord and his supporters could cast doubt on its veracity, but a petition would have actual names and signatures, making it much more difficult to disparage. LPTA building captains would gather signatures from tenants in their respective buildings, a task that could hopefully be done before the project got to the city council. If a majority of tenants signed the petition, the claim that only a small percentage opposed TransAction's plan would be laid to rest. And a strong showing of opposition could help sway city council members to support preserving the complex as it had existed for more than forty years. Or so the steering committee members hoped.

While Bernard had embraced the role of cheerleader, working to infect others with her optimism, she was realistic enough to know that the city council might approve the redevelopment. And what then? The last resort would be a lawsuit, an expensive and daunting proposition that she had mentioned but hadn't publicly wielded as a threat. Now, in the October issue of the LPTA newsletter, she directly addressed that subject with an announcement titled "The $Thirty Seven-Fifty Campaign." She wrote, "It is essential that we keep ourselves informed and that we provide strong evidence to all the members of the city council to prevent the need for a lawsuit." But if that became necessary, money would obviously have to be raised, and she wrote that if 800 people each gave $37.50—hence the "Thirty-Seven Fifty Campaign"—the LPTA could raise $30,000.

On November 9, the long-awaited report from the deputy advisory agency was released. To almost nobody's surprise, it approved the redevelopment. However, it also included a long list of conditions ranging from the arcane—that first-floor dwelling units be within three hundred feet of a fire hydrant—to the highly relevant—that the 144 rental units be restricted in perpetuity to very low and low-income households. And that all those units be ready for occupancy before the demolition of any buildings to make way for the condominiums. Those conditions and others germane to the contentious subject of tenant displacement essentially codified what TransAction had been promising in its various public presentations. Qualified tenants—seniors over sixty-two, single parents, and disabled people—would be offered one of the new apartments at their current rents, regardless of their incomes. Remaining units, if any, could only be rented to people with low and very low incomes, a restriction that also applied to future vacancies. All current tenants, no matter their age, income, or family status, would be given the option to accept the relocation payment set by the city's RSO plus assistance in finding a comparable unit in the Venice area. All tenants would also be given 180-day notices prior to demolition of their buildings. The list went on to cover such matters as allowed hours of construction, routes for hauling dirt and construction materials, water usage, area lighting, and signage, among others. At the end, the report concluded that the conditions made the adverse effects of the redevelopment less than significant, and therefore, the EIR could be certified and the subdivision map—the VTTM—approved.

Two days later, TransAction took what looked like a victory lap in a letter to tenants. After announcing the planning department's approval, the letter signed by Jim Merlino went on to detail the phases of construction, beginning with the demolition of six buildings at the southwest corner of the property to make way for the new apartments. The letter didn't mention that the LPTA was preparing to file an appeal that would require further public hearings, but tenants who hadn't followed the issue closely might well have concluded that the new Lincoln Place was on its way.

Without referring directly to this letter, Bernard sought to dispel the notion that the battle against TransAction was over. In a LPTA bulletin on November 18, beneath the bold headline, **So, is it over?**, she answered, "No, it has only just begun." In response to a second question, **What is our chance of winning in city council?**, she wrote, "Excellent! Councilwoman Galanter has strongly expressed her desire to see the owner's plan rejected. Supporting the councilwoman's stand are many individuals and organizations who want the city to live up to its policy of preserving desperately needed affordable housing." She made a plea for help circulating the new LPTA petition, and for donations to the $Thirty-seven Fifty Campaign. "LPTA is a rare opportunity to make a positive impact on social and economic conditions and public policy," she wrote, adding that "It's not all hard work. We also have fun." Following was evidence in the form of an announcement that the group would be hosting a Thanksgiving Day potluck at her apartment and backyard of her building.

Bernard was also quoted in a November 15 article in the *Santa Monica Outlook* about the project approval. After telling the reporter that the redevelopment would do "profound damage" to the community, she referred to future hearings by the city planning commission and city council, saying, "We feel so strongly that we are going to take this to the wall."

This article prompted a letter to the editor from Henry Ricard, a member of Lincoln Place Tomorrow, who claimed that the LPTA only represented "about 30" of Lincoln Place's fifteen hundred residents. He also echoed an assertion made by James Coxeter in the landlord's newsletter, saying that TransAction supporters at the planning-department hearing had "greatly outnumbered its opponents."

In a letter to the newspaper on December 2, Bernard counterattacked, saying that "Lincoln Place residents opposing demolition have vastly outnumbered tenants supporting it at both public hearings held so far." But the exchange emphasized the importance of getting the petition circulated and signed so that the issue of numbers could be put to rest.

Thus, the eventful year for Lincoln Place tenants, and indeed, for many Los Angeles residents, drew to a close without those tenants knowing what would happen to their homes. If they were somehow able to stay, what would it be like to live through ten years of construction? How would it be to live in apartments that looked like a kind of afterthought to row upon row of condominiums? If they couldn't stay, where would they go? An estimated nineteen thousand rental units throughout the city had been rendered uninhabitable by the Northridge earthquake, and nobody was under the illusion that any but a small number of these had been replaced. Rents had been stagnant since the beginning of the 1990 recession and had even dropped in some cases, but nobody expected that to last indefinitely. A typical winter chill was starting to permeate the air, and storms were poised to roll down from Alaska and the Pacific Northwest with their seasonal freight of rain. After months of sunlight and cloudless, blue skies, it was always a challenge to get used to the winter days of cold and gloom.

The December LPTA newsletter noted the fact of more hearings on the horizon and predicted that the battle would not be over until the middle or even end of 1995. Among announcements of holiday events like caroling and a New Year's potluck was a poem by the Mexican poet and playwright Xavier Villaurrutia that a note called "appropriate to this cold time of the year and this intense time in our history."

Prisoner of my mind,
The dream longs to escape,
And prove its innocence
To everyone on the outside.
I hear its impatient voice;
I see its furious, menacing state.
It does not know
That I am the dream of another;
That if I were its owner,
I would have set it free.

10

THE ELLIS ACT

AFTER TAKING OFFICE ON July 1, 1993, Los Angeles Mayor Richard Riordan set out to fulfill a major campaign promise—to make the city friendlier to business and development. Nobody could reasonably argue that outgoing Mayor Tom Bradley had been hostile to the business community, but his support for the passage of rent control in 1979 had angered apartment-house owners and other real estate interests. Riordan didn't inflame the highly charged issue by publicly siding with those calling for the repeal of the RSO, but he did take actions that furthered his business-friendly vows. One of those was the appointment of like-minded people to various city boards and commissions, including the five-member city planning commission that would consider the Lincoln Place redevelopment.

The city's major alternative newspaper, the *L.A. Weekly*, published an article in November 1994, headlined, "Planning out of Bounds: Riordan's new Planning Commission rejects community input, staff advice in scramble to spur new development." The article described several controversial megaprojects the commission had approved despite community opposition, and quoted Marna Schnabel, who was then commission president, saying, "Economic issues have not historically been part of the commission's decision making, and that has changed." This attitude heartened those who touted the positive economic impact of the Lincoln Place redevelopment, but it also helped convince those favoring preservation that they wouldn't get a sympathetic hearing. The resumes of Schnabel and the other commissioners, all appointed by Riordan, reinforced that view. Schnabel was an executive with a medical electronics firm, and she and her husband, a venture capitalist and former US ambassador, were prominent figures in the Republican Party. George Lefcoe, who assumed the commission's presidency at the beginning of 1995, was a professor of real estate law at USC. Robert Scott was a real estate attorney and head of a business alliance in the San Fernando Valley. Anthony Zamora had worked as an attorney with Riordan & McKinzie, the law firm founded by the mayor. Les Hamasaki was the head of a solar energy firm.

How would these people look upon a ragtag group of tenants fighting a property owner who was prepared to invest more than $100 million in one of the largest condominium projects in the city? One that would create construction jobs, bring new tax revenue to city coffers, and create housing for those who wanted to own their homes but either couldn't find a house in a perpetually tight market or didn't want the responsibilities that went with traditional home ownership. Many expected the commission to give its stamp of approval, but even if that was a foregone conclusion, Marcia Scully understood the importance of presenting a detailed list of reasons why the redevelopment should be rejected. For one thing, the hearing would be another opportunity to publicly air the issues and get the attention of city council members. For another, if the commission approved the project and the LPTA appealed that action to the city council, which it almost certainly would, the appeal would have to be limited to issues already raised before the commission. The same would apply if the city council sided with TransAction and the LPTA challenged the decision in court.

While Scully was putting together a comprehensive list of reasons why Lincoln Place should be preserved as it was conceived—a diverse community of working people and others of modest means living in a parklike setting—she was also looking ahead to the possibility that the city council would give the project a green light and TransAction would prevail in any subsequent lawsuits. In that case, it would be vitally important that the project conditions include an ironclad guarantee that none of the current tenants would be forced out if they didn't want to leave. The conditions imposed by the deputy advisory agency fell short of such a guarantee, she believed, and TransAction's promise that no Lincoln Place resident would be displaced was just that, a promise that like promises in general could be always be broken.

The planning commission hearing was scheduled for January 19, 1995. Sheila Bernard had been telling people that the game would be won or lost at the city council, and getting a large showing of people to city hall when the time came would be much more important than stirring the troops to turn out for the commission hearing. It wasn't that commissioners were deaf to opinions of members of the public, but their task would be to consider the findings of the deputy advisory agency, not the larger social issues involving housing and real estate development. Scully would attack those findings point by point, and TransAction's legal counsel would defend them, making the proceedings more like a hearing before a judge than one in the court of public opinion. And unlike the council members, the commissioners didn't have to run for office and were, as Bernard and others reminded people, appointed by the business-friendly mayor. Nevertheless, she had reserved a bus to take people downtown, and Ingrid Mueller had arranged for the printing of Preserve Lincoln Place tags for those able to make the trek to city hall.

The day of the hearing was the kind of midwinter day that tends to create a smug feeling of good fortune in people originally from the East or Midwest—sun brightly shining, temperature near seventy degrees, a scattering of clouds in the sky. But many who might have been at the beach or otherwise enjoying the outdoors were in front of their TV sets, watching the O. J. Simpson murder trial just getting underway in a downtown courtroom. The front page of that morning's *Los Angeles Times* had an article concerning arguments by attorneys over what jurors would be allowed to hear, although the major headline had to do with the disastrous effects of a Japanese earthquake that had struck two days earlier—and by eerie coincidence—exactly one year to the day after the Northridge earthquake that wreaked havoc on much of Los Angeles. The city had the country's largest population of Japanese Americans, which lent particular salience to the disaster that killed thousands of people and destroyed or damaged hundreds of thousands of buildings in and around Kobe, Japan's sixth-largest city. One of those Japanese Americans was planning commissioner Les Hamasaki, a native of Hawaii whose advocacy for renewable energy made him the closest thing to an outlier on a governmental body dominated by members with direct and indirect ties to the real estate industry.

Hearings were often held in a modest meeting room on the twelfth floor of city hall, but if large crowds were expected, they could be moved to the much more spacious council chamber. This was the case with the Lincoln Place project, although as it turned out only two dozen LPTA supporters showed up for the 9:30 a.m. meeting, along with a somewhat smaller number of people wearing Lincoln Place Tomorrow tags. When commission president George Lefcoe called the meeting to order, more than half the seats in the cathedral-like chamber were empty.

Lefcoe sat facing the audience on one side of a polished wooden table set between the half circle of council member's desks. He was flanked by Schnabel and Scott, while Hamasaki and Zamora sat at the ends of the table. On the opposite side, with their backs to the audience, were Scully, Jan Chatten-Brown, Darryl Fisher from the planning department; Paul Silvern, the consultant who had presented TransAction's case at the August 3 hearing conducted by Fisher, and Maria Hummer, an attorney representing the company. As was the case at the earlier hearing, architectural renderings of the new Lincoln Place were set on easels off to one side, with James Coxeter standing beside them as the meeting got underway.

Lefcoe, a large, bespectacled man with an oval face and thick, dark hair, called first on Fisher, who described the project and gave an account of his findings and proposed conditions. When he was finished, Lefcoe asked the question that Scully had been prepared to address. "What have you done to prevent displacement of a large number of people?"

Fisher repeated that seniors, single-parent families, and the disabled would have priority for the new apartments, but Lefcoe asked, "What if I don't have priority for a new apartment but live at Lincoln Place and want to stay there? Where is a condition that says I will not be displaced?"

Fisher attempted to answer by pointing out that all tenants would be given the option of relocation payments and assistance in finding new apartments in the community, but Lefcoe interrupted. "To avoid displacement, you have to relocate tenants at the same rent to a comparable unit on the site. Tenants develop connections. If you relocate them elsewhere, those connections are severed."

Fisher conceded that none of the conditions directly addressed that issue, but repeated TransAction's assertion that the normal rate of apartment turnover meant that virtually all tenants other than the seniors and others who qualified for the new apartments would voluntarily move before their buildings were torn down. There was an exceedingly small likelihood that anyone would be forced to leave.

Lefcoe responded with, "We're not going to entertain speculation about turnover." His questions and statements were something of a surprise, coming from the head of a commission widely viewed as development-friendly, although it didn't mean that he would vote against the project. He didn't pursue the displacement issue further, but gave the LPTA and TransAction twenty minutes each to make their competing cases. Marcia Scully laid out what was arguably the LPTA's strongest, or at least most readily understandable, point. The project would destroy hundreds of units now affordable to people of limited means when the city faced a severe shortage of such housing and had adopted policies to encourage its preservation.

To that, Lefcoe asked Scully, "You're not really suggesting that the burden of the Los Angeles housing problem be placed on this applicant?" She didn't try to answer what sounded like a rhetorical question, but said that if the project conflicted with the housing element of the city's General Plan—which she believed it clearly did—then the commission had no choice but to reject it.

When TransAction's turn came, Silvern addressed tenant displacement, the issue that appeared uppermost in Lefcoe's mind. Scully had argued that CEQA defined the displacement of people from their homes as a negative environmental impact requiring mitigation, but Silvern contended that the law was meant to protect people displaced by such things as freeway construction, not residential development like the Lincoln Place project. While he couldn't categorically state that no tenant at Lincoln Place would ever be displaced, it was highly improbable, because his consulting firm had done the turnover projections "very, very carefully."

This didn't satisfy Lefcoe. "Are you proposing to give any resident the choice of a vacant unit on site or a check for relocation? It isn't in the conditions. There's a loophole big enough for an elephant to go through." The commission president, who despite his pointed questions projected an air of good humor, added, "These people are going to call me at home at night if they get pushed out into the street."

After everyone had their say, including some of the LPTA and TransAction supporters in the audience, Lefcoe proposed that the applicant and opponents get together with planning department personnel to hammer out the language of a condition guaranteeing that residents wouldn't be involuntarily displaced. The commission would meet in a month to discuss that language along with several other project conditions that either Scully or TransAction wanted to modify. Without discussion, the commissioners voted for that course of action.

At one point during Lefcoe's remarks on the subject of displacement, tenant supporters in the audience had applauded, but now there was a feeling of deflation. If the only things to be resolved were the conditions imposed on the project, what had they won? TransAction's Jim Merlino was quoted in the next day's *Santa Monica Outlook*, saying, "We're two for two. We're very encouraged," even though the commission wouldn't vote on the project for another month.[33] And no doubt he was right to be optimistic. The February meeting would likely see a vote of approval, after which the LPTA would appeal to the city council and a swarm of lobbyists for TransAction and real estate interests would descend on city hall to buttonhole council members and their staffs. More letters would have to be written. More phone calls would have to be made. More trips would have to be made downtown, more speeches would have to be prepared to fit the two minutes typically allotted for public comment at committee and council meetings. When would it end? And how?

The second commission hearing was held on February 16. Again, the O. J. Simpson trial was on the front page of the *Los Angeles Times*, with one story about DNA testing of blood samples and the second about pampering of the sequestered jury. It was another notably mild day, with an overnight low of fifty degrees and a forecast high of seventy-two. The hearing was again held in the city council chamber, but given the fact that the commission's action was mostly a foregone conclusion, it wasn't a surprise that there was only a smattering of people in the audience wearing Preserve Lincoln Place and Lincoln Place Tomorrow tags.

After calling the meeting to order, Lefcoe got directly to the business of tenant displacement. Since the last meeting, Scully and TransAction representatives had agreed upon the language of a condition requiring the company to give everyone who wanted to stay at Lincoln Place an on-site unit without any rent increase. Even if there were no such units available—for example, if the 144 new apartments were all rented and the buildings awaiting demolition were fully occupied—tenants would still have the right to stay. Their buildings couldn't be torn down until they could be moved elsewhere on the property. Lastly, if a tenant in that category wanted to stay but didn't qualify for the new apartments by reason of age, disability, parental status, or income, the landlord would have to rent them one of the new townhouses intended for sale, again without any monthly increase. Of course, every tenant would still have the option of accepting a relocation payment and leaving Lincoln Place, but that would be completely voluntary.

While this was a major step in the right direction, Scully and Sheila Bernard still saw a problem, because in a worst-case scenario, a tenant might have to move multiple times before all the construction was complete. Even though the agreed-upon condition also required TransAction to pay moving expenses, being shuffled from building to building would be stressful and highly disruptive to a tenant's life. And suppose a tenant was the only occupant of a building awaiting demolition? That could create a security issue, to say nothing of the fact that the landlord would have little incentive to maintain a building that was ultimately going to be torn down.

But Lefcoe seemed satisfied and moved the discussion to other subjects, including the central issue in Scully's appeal, the loss of hundreds of affordable apartments in a community where the need for such housing far outweighed the supply. Anthony Zamora said he was "uneasy" about eliminating such a large number of rental units, but he supported the redevelopment because it was "unfair to put the burden of the affordable-housing problem on one development." Robert Scott echoed this view, adding that people buying Lincoln Place condominiums would be subsidizing the new rental units occupied by low-income tenants. The commission then unanimously voted to approve the project, the TransAction supporters applauded, and the LPTA contingent got up and silently trudged out of the chamber. Two weeks later, the *Outlook* published a letter from Mary Roberts, the public face of Lincoln Place Tomorrow, who wrote as if she believed that city council approval was inevitable. "As a longtime Lincoln Place resident, I am pleased to see this project moving forward and look forward to living in one of the new apartments as soon as they are built."

By this time, city election campaigns had built up a full head of steam in advance of the April 11 primary election. Ruth Galanter faced three opponents, but none came close to matching her in name recognition and fundraising. The district's only debate was held on March 23 at a Marina Del Rey hotel, and candidates were questioned about a number of local issues, including the redevelopment of Lincoln Place. Galanter repeated her opposition to tearing down the complex, while her opponents offered opinions ranging from support of TransAction's plan to expressions of concern for low-income tenants. A week after the debate, the *Argonaut*, which was generally pro-development, surprised some people by endorsing Galanter, and most political observers believed that she would handily defeat her lesser-known and underfunded opponents.

Ten days later, the councilwoman appeared at an LPTA meeting at Penmar Park. Addressing the redevelopment, she said, "This is going to be a fight all the way down to the last vote on the city council." Scully also put in an appearance before the assembly of forty some tenants and LPTA supporters, speaking briefly after being introduced by Bernard as "our hero." Plans were underway, she said, for winning the hearts and minds of city council members. This meant compiling a Lincoln Place "fact book" and sending it to all fifteen council members, as well as meeting directly with as many as possible. But, she added, "we need to flood the council chamber. Your presence, your voice, your letters count the most."

When she was finished, tenants were given a chance to speak. Dave Marlin said, "Young people who come after us need a place to start a life and raise families," and his wife Frieda said "many thousands" of people could live at Lincoln Place in the future if it was preserved. Ethel Shapiro-Bertolini, whose husband Angelo had been a regular companion with her at these meetings but had recently suffered a debilitating stroke, emphatically declared, "This is our home!" A young woman with a toddler in her lap spoke in Spanish, and Bernard followed by noting that, "the diversity of our community is one of our most important assets." In her typically upbeat style, she urged people to believe that they could defeat a landlord who had the deep pockets to put out slick publicity materials and hire the best legal talent. "We are making history here together," she said.

On April 11, Galanter breezed to a third four-year term with seventy-five percent of the vote. With incumbents traditionally enjoying a huge advantage in city elections that rarely saw a turnout above thirty percent of registered voters, all but one of the council races on the ballot was decided on that day. The exception was a west Los Angeles district adjacent to Galanter's, where the incumbent, Zev Yaroslavsky, had left the council to run for the county board of supervisors. None of the candidates to replace him got fifty percent of the vote, which meant that the top two finishers would go head-to-head in a runoff election on June 6. The contest was of particular interest to the LPTA and others looking ahead to a city council vote on the Lincoln Place project because one of the candidates, Mike Feuer, an attorney and director of a nonprofit that provided legal services to low-income people, was considered a strong supporter of tenants' rights and likely to side with the LPTA. His opponent was Zev Yaroslavsky's wife, Barbara, and while her husband had supported rent control and the protection of tenants from major rehab evictions, she had been endorsed by Mayor Riordan and was believed to be friendlier than Feuer to development interests. How she might vote on the Lincoln Place project was open to speculation.

The next stop for TransAction and the LPTA would be the city council's planning and land use management committee, commonly known by the acronym PLUM. Any action by the three-member committee could be rejected by the full council, but in practice, its recommendations carried significant weight. It was naive to assume that every council member would spend hours poring over the thousands of pages of plans and documents that typically accompanied a major building project, so that task fell to PLUM committee members, or more realistically, to those on their staffs assigned to such matters. The committee members would also listen to an airing of issues related to a development, including comments from the public, and for this reason, both the cheerleaders for a project and its detractors regarded the committee meetings as vital places to make their respective cases.

In addition, the two sides in the dispute over the Lincoln Place redevelopment would now be making their pitches to politicians, not bureaucrats and mayoral appointees, which meant that the LPTA needed to forcefully show the human cost of destroying a genuine community and displacing many of its residents. In an interview by Karen Brodkin, the UCLA professor filming the LPTA's activities, Bernard painted a graphic picture of what lay ahead and what would have to be overcome. "There's an attitude that you can't fight city hall, a cynicism toward the political process," she said, adding that there was ample reason for optimism because the council was "more liberal and human-minded than the bureaucracy." She believed that there was a chance of winning, but it would require an "enormous push" over the next few months to build more support. "Anything short of winning denial," she said, "will be a defeat."

The idea of tenant ownership still burned brightly in Bernard's mind, and she told Brodkin that "we're only fighting because we have a vision of what could be afterwards." She wasn't sure that Ruth Galanter had confidence in tenants being able to operate such a large apartment complex, but said she believed that "big, visionary stuff" would get the councilwoman's support. "But we have to first defeat the redevelopment and then make another offer at the right time. If we stop the redevelopment, the whole landscape is going to change." Some like Dave and Frieda Marlin, Ingrid Mueller, and other members of the LPTA steering committee were captivated by Bernard's vision and dreamed of the day they could call themselves owners of Lincoln Place, but others were fighting the redevelopment for the simple reason that they liked where they lived and wanted to stay without constant fear of what might be around the corner. But regardless of how residents felt about Bernard's vision, a significant number of them had to be mobilized for the battle ahead.

One of the LPTA's priorities was countering TransAction's claim that a large number of tenants and residents in the neighborhoods around Lincoln

Place supported the redevelopment. At the beginning of the summer of 1995, the petitions the tenant group had put together six months earlier had been circulated and the results compiled. The results were an emphatic rebuke of TransAction's claim. Of the Lincoln Place households contacted, a total of 539 favored preservation, while only eighteen favored demolition and redevelopment. Because the petitions bore actual names and signatures, TransAction supporters could hardly argue, as some had after the LPTA's 1991 survey, that the results didn't accurately reflect tenant sentiment. The same petitions were circulated to Lincoln Place neighbors. Because TransAction had been required by city ordinance to give property owners within a five-hundred-foot radius of Lincoln Place notice of impending hearings, the LPTA decided to canvass the same area. Ingrid Mueller went to the office of the county assessor and got a map of addresses within that radius and she and other volunteers went out knocking on doors. Of 323 households contacted, 205 favored preservation while thirty-eight favored TransAction's plan (eighty declined to offer an opinion). These petitions would hopefully assure Galanter that she wasn't taking a stand at odds with tenant and neighborhood sentiment, as TransAction and its allies like Lincoln Place Tomorrow and the Penmar Neighborhood Association were arguing.

At the same time, the tenants of Lincoln Place Tomorrow were ramping up their efforts in support of the landlord's plan. A slick, eight-page color brochure promoting the redevelopment appeared in the mailboxes of tenants and neighborhood residents, and while it only bore the Lincoln Place Tomorrow name, it was widely assumed that TransAction had designed and paid for it. The brochure made the familiar arguments—the buildings were old and deteriorated, units weren't handicapped accessible, parking was limited, the lack of security features made the place unsafe. The brochure featured photos of five tenants, all seniors, along with testimonials about how their lives would be greatly improved if the landlord's plan went forward. In one photo, Mary Roberts stood outside her kitchen window in front of an African daisy bush in full bloom and repeated the promise that would reverberate into the future in ways that nobody could have predicted. "Now everyone who wants to stay at Lincoln Place will be able to."

Lincoln Place Tomorrow also circulated its own petitions to tenants and community members. Conducted over a period of five days, this petition drive collected 2,477 signatures in favor of TransAction's plan, but it wasn't confined to Lincoln Place and the immediate neighborhood. There were signatures of people from such far-flung Los Angeles–area communities as Thousand Oaks, Huntington Beach, and Simi Valley. One signer listed his address as the Camp Pendleton Marine Corps Base, which was two hours south of Los Angeles, and another simply wrote, "Australia." Such signatures had likely been gathered at the Venice Beach boardwalk, one of the city's most popular tourist destinations, and to Sheila Bernard and LPTA supporters, this was just one of several reasons for Ruth Galanter and city council members to cast jaundiced eyes upon the petitions. For another, the wording was at best misleading. The redevelopment was called a "compromise plan" that would allow all tenants "to remain at Lincoln Place in a new or existing apartment on site at their same rent." While it was true that the city planning commission had imposed this condition, the petitions failed to disclose that all existing buildings with 795 apartments would be torn down to make way for 144 new apartments and 706 condominiums. But an even more serious issue involved the fact that the petitions bore the signatures of more than 250 Lincoln Place residents. How could that be, when the LPTA had surveyed 623 households and found that only eighteen favored redevelopment?

One thing was obvious. Lincoln Place Tomorrow volunteers couldn't have gathered almost 2,500 signatures in just five days, which meant that TransAction almost certainly hired workers for most, if not all, that work. Furthermore, a former Venice resident wrote a letter to the LPTA saying that he had been offered a job gathering those signatures. He would be paid eight dollars an hour plus one dollar per signature, but said he declined because he supported the LPTA. This in itself could be reason to question the results, but even as the petitions were being circulated, charges of outright deception arose. Outtakes of Karen Brodkin's film include an interview with a tenant who says she signed the Lincoln Place Tomorrow petition after being told that its purpose was to prevent the eviction of single-parent and elderly tenants. The name of Lincoln Place Tomorrow was nowhere on the petition, and the woman assumed it was being circulated by the LPTA, but to her great dismay, she had just found out that it wasn't. In subsequent footage, Brodkin approaches a young man going door-to-door with the petition forms. She questions him, but he refuses to say what he is telling tenants and answers, "It's none of your business," when she asks how much he is getting paid.

The PLUM committee was expected to hold a hearing on the project sometime in July. At the beginning of June, Marcia Scully told Bernard that she had been contacted by TransAction's attorney, Maria Hummer, who wanted to explore the possibility of common ground between the company and the LPTA. Specifically, could the project be modified or conditions added that would make the redevelopment acceptable to the tenant organization? Did this mean TransAction was afraid the city council would reverse the planning commission's approval? Whatever the reason, the olive branch, if that's what it could be called, bore the thorns of a threat. After meeting with Hummer to discuss ground rules for any negotiation, Scully reported that while the TransAction attorney wanted to discuss a possible compromise, she was also adamant that the landlord would not indefinitely continue to operate Lincoln Place in its current form. If the company couldn't win approval of the redevelopment, it would either sell off some or all of the thirty-five parcels into which the property was currently subdivided, or demolish buildings parcel by parcel and build smaller projects that wouldn't require EIR's and new subdivision maps. That would be possible because each of those parcels was owned by a separate legal entity under the TransAction corporate umbrella. What would happen to the tenants in such scenarios was anybody's guess.

But an even more ominous threat concerned a state law known as the Ellis Act, which permitted owners of rent-controlled apartments to evict tenants without cause if those landlords were going out of the rental business; for example, by demolishing their buildings or converting them to another use such as condominiums. This possibility was directly raised in a letter to Scully from another TransAction attorney, Allan Abshez, who wrote, "We hope you will agree that forcing TransAction to proceed under the Ellis Act would not be in the long-term interest of either the Lincoln Place

Tenants Association or the surrounding community." The attorney closed by writing, "Maria and I are looking forward to our tentatively scheduled meeting of Friday, June 16, during which we hope to hear your recommendations regarding the Redevelopment Project proposal (for example, your ideas for potential design alterations) which would help your clients settle their differences."

Most Lincoln Place tenants, including LPTA members, had either never heard of the Ellis Act or never considered its relevance to Lincoln Place. The few familiar with it found reason for concern, though. Did TransAction contemplate throwing out Lincoln Place residents even though the company had just agreed to the condition guaranteeing them the right to stay? If the city council rejected the project, would that condition no longer be relevant? Or would it still apply no matter what TransAction decided to do with the property, including selling it to another company? Once Bernard told other LPTA members what Scully had told her, these questions gathered like storm clouds in everybody's minds.

On June 15, the day before the tentatively scheduled meeting between Scully and the TransAction attorneys, the LPTA steering committee met to discuss the situation. Bernard forcefully argued that unless the preservation of Lincoln Place was one of the options on the table, there was no reason to sit down with TransAction. There were no "design alterations" that could make the destruction of Lincoln Place palatable. She had prepared a written resolution to this effect, and it was signed by all ten committee members. She informed Scully of this and the attorney relayed the news to Hummer and Abshez. The idea of so-called settlement discussions died, but the invocation of the Ellis Act by the TransAction attorney lived on. It was the dog that might start wildly barking in the middle of the night or the crazy uncle who might get drunk and wreak havoc at the family gathering. It was the Sword of Damocles that would hang over Lincoln Place far longer than anyone would have imagined.

11

THE HORSE RANCH AND THE FIFTH AMENDMENT

HARRY WARNER, THE OLDEST of four brothers who founded Warner Brothers Pictures, died in Los Angeles on July 25, 1958. The studio mogul was a horse racing enthusiast, and his estate included a thousand-acre San Fernando Valley ranch where he raised thoroughbreds to compete at racetracks in Southern California and other parts of the country. After his death, the property was sold to developers who transformed it over the next thirty years into a massive office-and-commercial complex called Warner Center. The change from open space to a major hub of business activity proceeded with relatively little controversy, but that changed in the 1980s when a developer announced plans to build almost one million square feet of office space on a twenty-one-acre part of the property known as Warner Ridge. Because this parcel at the edge of the former ranch abutted a neighborhood of single-family homes, residents there organized a protest, arguing that the development would create intolerable congestion and traffic problems. They wanted the site limited to homes and park space, and with support from the city council member then representing the area, they persuaded the council in 1990 to rezone the property from commercial to residential.

As often happens in Los Angeles with major real estate projects, the dispute then headed to court, with the developer contending that the council's action amounted to an unconstitutional taking of property without just compensation. A superior court judge and an appeals court panel both ruled in favor of the plaintiffs, and council members were told by legal counsel that the city could be on hook for at least $50 million. That prospect was so alarming that the council rezoned the property back to commercial and, in 1992, approved the construction of 690,000 square feet of office space and 125 apartments. Thus, they avoided paying out millions in damages, although by the time the saga ended, the city had spent hundreds of thousands in legal fees and other costs fighting the ultimately futile battle.[34]

What did any of this have to do with Lincoln Place and the dispute between TransAction and the LPTA? Nobody had brought up the Warner Ridge case at the city planning-commission meetings in January and February, but its ghost had made noises when a TransAction attorney alluded to unconstitutional "takings" if the city failed to approve the Lincoln Place project. Marcia Scully had addressed that issue in both written comments and oral testimony before the commission. Lincoln Place was a viable apartment complex, she had argued, and rejection of the redevelopment wouldn't deny TransAction the use of its property. She cited the bankruptcy court filing in which TransAction declared that the $4 million in annual rental income was sufficient to both maintain the property and pay off creditors. If this was true, city council denial could hardly be construed as the taking of private property without just compensation. The city would simply be exercising its legal right to control land use and zoning within its jurisdiction.

Sheila Bernard trusted Scully's legal acumen, but the attorney had earlier told her that if the project ended up in court, she wouldn't be able to represent the LPTA. She just didn't have the requisite experience in litigation. She would do all she could to help find a qualified lawyer willing to work on a pro bono basis, but it wouldn't be easy. At that moment her time and energy were invested in preparing for the upcoming PLUM committee hearing, where legal issues would take a back seat to the picture she hoped to paint for politicians, of the redevelopment as a train wreck with a devastating impact on tenants and on affordable housing in the community.

As LPTA members waited for the committee to set a definite date for a hearing, they got a bit of good news—Mike Feuer, who started his campaign as a decided underdog, swept to a landslide victory over Barbara Yaroslavsky in the runoff election. His record of defending tenants in disputes with landlords led to the hope he could be counted on to vote to preserve Lincoln Place. Of more immediate concern, though, were the three members of the PLUM committee—Hal Bernson, Laura Chick, and Richard Alatorre. Bernson, the chairman, was a Republican—city elections were nonpartisan—who represented a district in the northwest part of the San Fernando valley regarded as the most conservative in the city. Chick, whose district was in another part of the valley, and Alatorre, who represented a heavily Latino district on the east side of the city, were both Democrats and thought to be friendlier than Bernson to the concerns of renters. The chairman had been a strong backer of a controversial 1,300-acre residential-and-commercial development in his district called Porter Ranch, but he had also incurred the wrath of some commercial property owners by pushing for stricter earthquake safety standards for buildings, measures that were later credited for limiting damage in the Northridge earthquake.

The task of meeting with Bernson, Chick and Alatorre would be taken on by Donn Morey and Jeff Seymour, the consultants working for the LPTA, since they knew the committee members and had met with them on other development issues. Scully and Jan Chatten-Brown would put the finishing touches on the Lincoln Place Fact Book, which in its final draft ran to more than five hundred pages of details about the city's housing crisis, documents outlining housing policies, excerpts from the EIR, studies and statistics, articles, letters, partial excerpts of transcripts from public hearings, even a pro forma showing that rents from the new apartment units proposed by TransAction would fall short of the amount needed to sustain that part of the project. Whether any council member would read the entirety of this telephone-directory-sized tome was open to question, but no one could thumb through it and fail to be impressed by the sheer amount of material gathered in support of the LPTA's position. And perhaps that was the point. In any case, all those pages served as an exclamation mark for a simple message: the city should protect its most vulnerable citizens instead of allowing housing those people could afford to be torn down so that a property owner could make millions selling condominiums to the well-to-do.

The PLUM committee finally scheduled the hearing for July 18. An LPTA bulletin announcing the date included a short article by Sheila Bernard titled "The Landlord Shows His Fear." After references to threats made to evict tenants under the Ellis Act and sell off individual parcels if the project was rejected, she wrote, "On the Fourth of July we remember that although King George III of England had 'property rights' over the 13 colonies 200 years ago, the king's abuse of power led to his loss of ownership of the colonies. Similarly, the owner of Lincoln Place has stepped over the line: rather than achieving a reasonable return on his investment in Lincoln Place, he is recklessly insisting on maximum profits at the expense of an entire neighborhood. We make no threats, but we caution the landlord that he should heed the lessons of history, or one day he might wake up to find his tea spilled in the harbor."

A bus was reserved to take LPTA members and supporters downtown. Ingrid Mueller supervised the design and printing of posters for the meeting—one with an aerial view of Lincoln Place and two with the results of the tenant and neighborhood surveys. She made sure there were ample numbers of Preserve Lincoln Place tags. People rehearsed what they would say when their names were called for public comment. But the day before the meeting, Scully called Bernard to tell her that TransAction had asked for a postponement. The reason, she said, was that the company was considering a redesign of the project with at least some of the 144 new apartments scattered throughout the site, instead of being isolated from the condominiums. This, presumably, was meant to address the complaint that occupants of the apartments would be living in a kind of ghetto.

But Bernard was having none of it. In an LPTA bulletin announcing the postponement, she wrote, "The owner seems to think such an adjustment makes his plan more attractive. It doesn't." The last-minute change was a nuisance for everyone who had planned to go to city hall, and a particular inconvenience for anyone who had made plans to take time off work or arranged for child care. Speculation circulated through the tenant grapevine. Why would the landlord consider at such a late date a change that, in the overall scheme of things, was minor? Was the real reason for seeking a delay simply to harass LPTA members? And possibly affect turnout to the meeting in a negative way?

The PLUM committee agreed to a three-week delay and set a new date of August 8. The LPTA had already mailed copies of the fact book—at a cost of $363—to the committee members and the other city council offices. Morey and Seymour had met with Bernson, Chick, and Alatorre. Scully had prepared what she hoped were convincing arguments that Lincoln Place was not only a valuable community resource, but that allowing it be torn down would violate the city's fundamental principles. But she knew that the minds of council members would not be solely focused on the words of policies that expressed the city's aspirations and guided its decisions. They would be thinking about what might happen if they and a majority of their colleagues cast a no vote on the Lincoln Place project. Would TransAction simply turn and slowly walk away, like a ballplayer who has struck out with the bases loaded in the bottom of the ninth inning? No, it would start evicting tenants under the Ellis Act and redevelop the property parcel by parcel without being required to include a single low-income unit. Or—many considered this more likely—it would sue the city.

On the morning of August 8, headlines on the front page of the *Los Angeles Times* concerned the ongoing war in the Balkans, the congressional investigation into President Clinton's Whitewater dealings, and, of course, the O. J. Simpson trial, with speculation that LAPD detective Mark Fuhrman had lied on the witness stand. But none of this was foremost in the minds of LPTA members and supporters who boarded the chartered bus for the trip to city hall. Bernard and Mueller sat together, and in contrast to her usual cheerful manner, Bernard seemed somber, perhaps even distressed. Why? Warner Ridge had indeed risen from the shadows; she had just learned that council members were warned by the city attorney's office that turning down the Lincoln Place project could expose the city to a large financial liability. The Warner Ridge case, she was told, had been cited as the reason to fear that consequence.

Bernard told Mueller that Scully and Chatten-Brown didn't believe that the facts of the Warner Ridge project could be applied to Lincoln Place, because that case involved undeveloped land, not a viable apartment complex. Even if the city turned down the redevelopment, TransAction could still operate as it had since buying the property nine years earlier. But the specter of lawsuits and financial liability could influence city council members who struggled every year to find enough revenue to pay for city services. And the threat of legal action was obviously part of TransAction's strategy. Adding to the atmosphere of unease, Mueller told Bernard of a rumor that a staff member in the mayor's office had called TransAction's plan "a slam dunk." To which Bernard responded, "Here we are, these mere mortals, trying to tell the city they should take care of their residents." Sounding wistful, with an uncommon note of pessimism, she said, "This is for me a real learning experience. I'm really going to learn a lot more about the way the world works when this is all over with."

PLUM committee meetings convened every Tuesday afternoon at one o'clock, although they seldom started on time. Once again people gathered in the city council chamber, with the committee members sitting at the table between the arc of council members' desks. Hal Bernson, a stocky sixty-four-year-old who had been on the council for sixteen years, sat alongside Laura Chick, a fifty-one-year-old former social worker who was elected in 1993 from the district that encompassed Warner Ridge. She had made headlines two months earlier by giving a luncheon speech in which she described city hall as "the most sexist, good-old-boys work environment that I've ever been in." She accused some male colleagues of making condescending remarks, telling off-color jokes, and passing around dirty pictures during council meetings, and she proposed that all council members undergo gender-sensitivity training. She didn't call out anyone by name, and whether her fellow PLUM committee members had engaged in this frat house-style behavior wasn't known. But as might be imagined, reports of this speech didn't endear her to everyone in city hall.[35]

By the time Bernson called the meeting to order, Richard Alatorre hadn't appeared. The chairman, who looked out over glasses perched low on the bridge of his nose, told the audience of people wearing yellow "Preserve Lincoln Place" and green "Lincoln Place Tomorrow" tags that the committee would take testimony until three o'clock, then go into executive session to hear legal advice from the city attorney. The presence of a court reporter off to one side of the table lent even more credence to fears that the Lincoln

Place project would not be judged on its merits and effects on tenants, but on the legal peril the city might find itself in by voting it down.

Bernson then called on Darryl Fisher of the planning department, who described the basics of the redevelopment and the major conditions imposed by city planning commission. Next, attorney Maria Hummer spoke on behalf of TransAction, rejecting the LPTA's argument that the project would violate city housing policies. That argument, she said, had been repudiated both by Fisher in his advisory agency findings and by the city planning commission. Paul Silvern, the TransAction consultant, also addressed the alleged violation of city policies calling for the preservation of affordable housing, saying that "affordability, like beauty, is in the eye of beholder." Allan Abshez, who identified himself as TransAction's "litigation representative," repeated a claim that would likely be part of any future lawsuit—denial of the project would violate the company's right to due process and equal protection under the law. He brought up the Ellis Act threat, claiming that under that law TransAction could redevelop the property without providing a single unit of replacement rental housing. The opponents' agenda, he said, was plainly visible on the LPTA's letterhead in the form of the "Let's Own It" slogan. The LPTA was "seeking to embroil the city in an effort to force the sale of the property by driving down its value."

Bernson, who was eating from a bag of potato chips during the attorney's comments, then turned to Scully and Chatten-Brown. Scully called Abshez's statements inappropriate. "At no time has there been any discussion by any agency about forced taking of this property. Denial of the project would not force the applicant to sell to the city or anyone else." Chatten-Brown added that she had been brought in to review the project's EIR, and had concluded that it was vulnerable to a successful legal challenge.

Bernson then opened the meeting to public comment, warning speakers to be brief because the committee would retire to executive session in less than half an hour. The chairman was known both for occasional gruffness and for stumbling over the pronunciation of unfamiliar names, and he demonstrated the latter in calling on people who had filled out speaker cards. He alternated between supporters and opponents of the project. Steve Clare, the executive director of Venice Community Housing, said the redevelopment of Lincoln Place was the "biggest threat to affordable housing in Venice and the west side of Los Angeles." Larry Gross, executive director of the Coalition for Economic Survival, attacked the project as "a plan solely based on greed." But Chris Williams of the Penmar Neighborhood Association defended TransAction, saying the owner's plan should be applauded, and added the highly questionable claim that the project had "overwhelming support" in the community. Mary Roberts of Lincoln Place Tomorrow asserted that many people opposing the project didn't live at Lincoln Place and "just have an ax to grind." She alluded to widespread support of the redevelopment by current tenants, saying, "Nobody knows what's better for Lincoln Place than the people who live there."

Before closing the meeting to the public, Bernson said that the committee wouldn't be taking any action, but would consider the project again in two weeks and hopefully be prepared at that time to vote. Neither Bernson nor Chick discussed the substance of what they had just heard, and Alatorre still hadn't shown up. Ruth Galanter had been standing off to the side during the public comments, and when the committee members got up to go to another room behind the chamber, she spoke briefly to Bernard and a handful of other LPTA members. City Attorney James Hahn had met with Bernson, she told them, and she said she would work to get him to agree to defend the city against any TransAction lawsuit. Then she joined Bernson, Chick, and a representative from Hahn's office in the closed-door session. At the time, her presence in that session as a non-committee member didn't seem remarkable, but later events would prove it to be a serious problem.

The inconclusive hearing meant making more phone calls, putting out more bulletins, holding more strategy sessions, and organizing another bus trip to city hall. It was hard not to feel impatient with these delays, although Jim Merlino of TransAction was quoted in the following day's *Santa Monica Outlook* saying, "We've been at this for five years. We can wait another two weeks."[36] Later that week, the LPTA steering committee met at Frieda and Dave Marlin's apartment. Amid talk about strategy and the organizing of tasks, there was mention of an unsigned letter that had circulated in the complex, saying that eighty tenants had shown up at the PLUM committee meeting to support the redevelopment, a claim that was patently false. Sheila Bernard, who was deeply disturbed by those who didn't share her commitment to facts and fair play, seemed to feel at least a tug in the direction of fighting fire with fire. "Should we put brass knuckles on," she asked. "Not just bare knuckles?"

August 22 was sunny and warm, with a high of eighty-six degrees forecast for the downtown civic center. The second PLUM committee meeting saw a smaller turnout of LPTA members and TransAction supporters, although all the main actors—Scully, Chatten-Brown, Hummer, Silvern, James Coxeter, Jim Merlino, and Councilwoman Galanter—were in the chamber. Again, only Bernson and Chick were present, with no explanation offered for Alatorre's second absence. Bernson opened the meeting by announcing that the committee would adjourn to executive session for a briefing from both the planning department and city attorney, but advised people to stay in the council chamber because after reconvening in public the committee would likely vote on the Lincoln Place project.

Most of the LPTA contingent sat on the right side of the center aisle, while most TransAction supporters sat on the left. Others milled about, talking among themselves. Everyone wondered how long they would have to wait. But the closed-door session was mercifully brief, and after Bernson and Chick returned to their seats, the chairman called on Gordon Hamilton, the deputy director of the planning department. Hamilton said that the department had concluded that "there is an argument to be made for the need to preserve residential neighborhoods, the need to preserve affordable housing at a rental level, versus home ownership units. And there is also the need for preservation of existing character of a neighborhood." Hamilton didn't elaborate further, but this was clearly a change from the department's earlier position. Bernson then said that taking 795 units of rental housing off the market "flies in the face" of city policies and would destroy what was essentially an entire neighborhood. Addressing Chick, he said, "I was concerned about the fact of whether we had the legal findings to deny such an application. I am now convinced that we do, and I am prepared to entertain your motion if your motion is to deny." Chick then made that motion, she and Bernson voted to overturn the planning commission's approval, and the right side of the aisle erupted in applause.

Smiles and hugs displaced the gloom that had lingered since the specter of Warner Ridge had begun making its unwelcome sounds. Bernson wielded considerable influence in land-use matters, and with his unequivocal support for Lincoln Place preservation, along with Galanter's unwavering opposition to TransAction's plan, many believed that the city council was certain to affirm the PLUM committee's action. Others stuck to the famous Yogi Berra adage, "It ain't over 'til it's over." Galanter sounded this note when speaking to Bernard and other LPTA supporters after the committee adjourned. Calls should be made or letters sent to all fifteen city council offices. There wasn't much time, because the matter would be on the agenda the week after Labor Day, when the council returned from recess. People could be sure that Coxeter, Merlino, and the lawyers and lobbyists working for TransAction would now be busy pressing the case that the PLUM committee's finding regarding a violation of city housing policies was dead wrong, and if the council upheld the committee action, the city would find itself neck deep in legal hot water.

The days leading up to that council meeting saw a flurry of editorials and letters to the editor, both pro and con. In a letter to the *Outlook*, Judith Pressman, cochair of the Penmar Neighborhood Association, ripped into Galanter, writing that the councilwoman's opposition to the redevelopment amounted to "nothing short of confiscation of the Lincoln Place owner's property." A starkly different view was offered by Sheila Bernard in a letter published in the following day's issue. "A home is not just four walls," she wrote, after delivering a spirited defense of Galanter. "A home is a neighborhood, a support system, a social setting. Los Angeles needs more, not less, of what Lincoln Place offers socially."

However, the *Outlook* and *Argonaut* both editorialized in favor of TransAction's plan. The *Argonaut* piece, under the byline of the publisher, David Asper Johnson, consisted largely of an attack on Galanter for impeding a number of worthwhile projects in the community. Predicting that she would "kill off" the Lincoln Place plan at the upcoming city council meeting, he wrote, "We will be treated to a barrage of political banter about how democracy works, how much great public input there was and how wonderful the system is that keeps a forty-five-year-old apartment complex that is falling apart from being upgraded."

The *Outlook* editorial took a more temperate tone, warning that stopping the redevelopment would just result in the fulfillment of TransAction's threats—lawsuits against the city, and ultimately, a redevelopment that wouldn't include any affordable housing at all.

But the most impressive opinion on the subject didn't come from newspaper editorials. In a three-page letter to city council members, Peter Dreier, a professor at Occidental College and nationally known writer and commentator on housing and other urban issues, set out detailed reasons why Lincoln Place should be preserved. Dreier, who had worked as a consultant for the US Department of Housing and Urban Development, referred to an article he had written for the *Harvard Business Review*, in which he made the case that a stable and affordable-housing stock was a major factor in a city's business climate.

Los Angeles, he wrote, suffered from an acute shortage of such housing and the loss of Lincoln Place apartments would increase the demand for rental housing and contribute to "rising rents, more overcrowding, and increased homelessness. At the same time, it would destabilize a neighborhood and displace many long-term residents, leading to a number of serious psychological and emotional problems correlated with involuntary displacement and housing instability, especially among senior citizens."

The Lincoln Place project appeared on the council agenda for September 12. At eight-thirty that morning, when LPTA members and supporters began boarding a pair of buses with Antidemolition Express signs in the windows, the temperature was already climbing toward a predicted high in the low nineties. The front page of the *Los Angeles Times* featured two headlines about the O. J. Simpson trial and two about California Governor Pete Wilson's floundering quest for the Republican nomination for president in the 1996 election. There was an atmosphere of hopeful anticipation among those heading downtown to city hall, but there were also expressions of sadness over the fact that Ethel Shapiro-Bertolini's husband, Angelo, had passed away the day before. The two had been inseparable companions, coming together to LPTA meetings before Angelo fell prey to serious health problems. How would his death affect his eighty-five-year-old wife, who had health problems of her own? As almost everyone involved with the LPTA knew, the organization might never have come into existence without her tenacity, unflagging spirit, and passion for social justice.

The city council chamber was full, although Lincoln Place was just one in a list of agenda items and not everyone was there to show support for either the LPTA or TransAction. Once again, most of the LPTA supporters sat on the right side of the center aisle while tenants from Lincoln Place Tomorrow and others favoring redevelopment sat on the left. Tenants who had come on the buses wore Preserve Lincoln Place tags and some older women held bamboo fans imprinted with that slogan. The LPTA had set up a display on the side of the chamber, with an easel holding a large poster with a photo of Lincoln Place buildings amid trees and lawns juxtaposed against a rendering of one of the buildings being demolished. The photo and rendering were captioned, respectively, with the words "Don't Let This" and "Become This." On the opposite side of the aisle, a Lincoln Place Tomorrow contingent held signs that said "Approve the Plan" while others wore green tags with the name Penmar Neighborhood Association.

When council president John Ferraro called up the Lincoln Place agenda item, the Lincoln Place Tomorrow people held their signs above their heads, prompting Ferraro to ask them to keep them down so that people in the rows behind could see. The council president, who was serving his twelfth year in that position, then read the first of the names of people who had filled out request cards at the PLUM committee meeting but hadn't gotten the opportunity to speak.

Mary Roberts, of Lincoln Place Tomorrow, stepped to the public speakers' podium and began by saying, "I have a dream." The dream, she continued, was to live in one of the new, modern apartments promised by TransAction, and as she extolled the various features of the landlord's plan she kept repeating, "I have a dream," in the manner of Martin Luther King's famous 1963 speech in Washington, DC. This picture—a seventy-five-year-old white woman appropriating the iconic words of the civil rights leader—struck many as peculiar, if not downright offensive. A dream of shiny appliances, fresh paint and brand-new carpeting wasn't quite the same as a dream of an end to hundreds of years of oppression and injustice.

OUTSTANDING APARTMENT VALUES

Lincoln Place

1430 LINCOLN BLVD.
VENICE, CALIFORNIA
EXbrook 6-3117 • UPton 0-4805

**MODERN GARDEN
APARTMENTS**

Features

Introducing a new high in functional and decorative appointments, LINCOLN PLACE APARTMENTS have a more complete assortment of added values than any similar community.

Some of the many features · · ·

- SPACIOUS CABINETS & DRAWER SPACE
- BUILT-IN BREAKFAST NOOK & TABLE
- COVE BASE LINOLEUM KITCHEN FLOORS
- CORNICE BOXES WITH BUILT-IN DRAPERY RODS ABOVE EACH WINDOW
- GARBAGE DISPOSAL UNITS
- 30 GALLON GAS WATER HEATERS
- VENETIAN BLINDS ON ALL OPENINGS
- ALL ROOMS COMPLETELY DECORATED, WALLS & CEILINGS
- PLENTY OF CLOSET SPACE
- FINEST POLISHED OAK FLOORS
- MODERN SLAB DOORS THROUGHOUT
- TV OUTLETS IN EACH APARTMENT
- TILED KITCHENS AND BATHROOMS
- TILED PULLMAN SINKS IN BATHROOMS
- GARAGE WITH LARGE STORAGE SPACE INCLUDED WITH EACH APARTMENT
- LAUNDRY ROOMS WITH AUTOMATIC WASHERS & DRYERS
- MANY WITH PATIOS AND BALCONIES
- PHONE CABLES BUILT INTO EACH APT.
- GOLF COURSE AND PARK ADJACENT TO PROPERTY
- GROUNDS BEAUTIFULLY LANDSCAPED & MAINTAINED BY OUR STAFF
- SEPARATE BUILDINGS FOR FAMILIES WITHOUT CHILDREN
- COMPLETELY INSULATED WITH SPECIAL PARTITIONS BETWEEN APARTMENTS
- 24 HOUR MAINTENANCE SERVICE

Beautiful Interiors

No effort has been spared in making the LINCOLN PLACE APARTMENT interiors the ultimate in exquisite beauty and smart, modern appearance. The photographs portray typical furniture arrangements and built-in features.

TWO BEDROOM APARTMENTS Ideal for families with children or couples who want to furnish one bedroom as a den. Guest closet, Mr. and Mrs. closets in master bedroom and double-sized closet in second bedroom.

ONE BEDROOM APARTMENTS Completely new design in the apartment field emphasizing modern treatment and convenience. Unusually large bedroom with double-door closet for easy accessibility, and convenient guest closet.

Individualized Floor Plans

Architecturally perfect apartment designs that incorporate many desirable features, offer the perfect opportunity for gracious living and an organized household with its modern facilities and many spacious closets. Careful planning and consideration to every detail of room arrangement has resulted in highest praise for LINCOLN PLACE floor plans.

Southern California's Most Outstanding Apartment Values

A completely planned $8,000,000.00 community of 795 one and two-bedroom apartments.

Lincoln Place

1430 LINCOLN BLVD.
VENICE, CALIFORNIA
EXbrook 6-3117 • UPton 0-4805

**MODERN GARDEN
APARTMENTS**

1950 Lincoln Place rental brochure (collection of Gerald Bialac)

Lincoln Place architect Ralph Vaughn,
about 1940 (collection of Ronald Vaughn)

Lincoln Place architectural details
(courtesy of 20th Century Architectural Alliance)

Ethel Shapiro-Bertolini and Angelo Bertolini
outside their Lincoln Place apartment (photo by Bill Ullett)

LPTA president Sheila Bernard making presentation at Venice
Community Planning Advisory Committee (photo by Bill Ullett)

Los Angeles city hall (photo by the author)

Attorneys Jan Chatten-Brown and Marcia Scully at city hall hearing
on Lincoln Place redevelopment plan (photo by Bill Ullett)

Lincoln Place residents at Los Angeles
City Council meeting (photo by Bill Ullett)

Flier for screening of "Let's Own It!" film (collection of Sheila Bernard)

Lincoln Place building 18 being remodeled. Tenant Laura Ponce's unit, upper right, the only one occupied (photo by Ingrid Mueller)

When she had gone on for several minutes, Ferraro cautioned her that she was taking up time from other speakers and she began reading off people's names and asking them to stand to show their support for the redevelopment. Chris Williams of the Penmar Neighborhood Association and several others spoke in favor of the TransAction plan, repeating most of the landlord's talking points—the buildings were old and run-down, the new Lincoln Place would be a boon to the community, no current tenant would be forced out. And so forth. Ferraro then called on opponents of the project. Alan Heskin, the UCLA professor who had advised the LPTA in its early days, said that approval of the project would be "one of the great planning disasters" in the city's recent history. Anne Murphy and Steve Clare of Venice Community Housing spoke of how tearing down Lincoln Place would "devastate" the community. Frieda Marlin delivered a simple plea to council members. "Please don't destroy Lincoln Place."

Marcia Scully and Jan Chatten-Brown both addressed the thirteen council members present. Scully referred to a letter sent to council members the previous day by Allan Abshez, who cited the Warner Ridge case in support of a claim that rejecting the Lincoln Place redevelopment would violate the company's constitutional rights. Once again, Scully said that the facts of the Warner Ridge case didn't support the landlord's claim. In fact, she said, that court decision actually strengthened the argument for preserving Lincoln Place. Because the city's General Plan had called for the Warner Ridge property to be commercial, the court ruled that rezoning it to residential without first modifying the plan was illegal. And since the General Plan contained policies that called for the preservation of affordable housing, Scully said, tearing down Lincoln Place would likewise violate that legally enforceable document.

When all members of the public had aired their views, Bernson stood at his desk and told colleagues that the PLUM committee had sought the advice of the city attorney before taking a vote, and he was confident that the city would be on sound legal footing in rejecting the project. He spoke of the housing issue that was at the heart of the Lincoln Place debate. "Preserving affordable housing," he said, "is very important to the Venice community."

He was followed by Ruth Galanter, who said that opposing the redevelopment hadn't been an easy decision because she knew that some people's hopes and dreams were riding on a new Lincoln Place. "It has been an agonizing several years trying to resolve this," she said, but added that in the Venice community, "this project scares the living daylights out of us."

With that, Ferraro called for a roll call vote. Members voted electronically, so it was only a few seconds before the clerk announced the result, 13–0 to affirm the PLUM committee's rejection of the project. Applause and cheers swelled from the right side of the aisle; a scattering of boos and hisses was heard from the other, and a man with a Lincoln Place Tomorrow sign yelled, "We'll see you in court!" Ingrid Mueller had been sitting beside Sandy Moring, the homeowner who formed the Committee to Preserve Lincoln Place, and she was overcome, burying her face in Moring's shoulder. Others exchanged hugs, smiling and laughing. One tenant said that she had put off buying a new rug and furniture because of uncertainty over what would happen, but now she could. Major figures in the drama—Scully, Chatten-Brown, Sheila Bernard—were showered with congratulations. For a few minutes, the space was transformed from a solemn place where weighty business was conducted into a scene resembling that of a party. But the council had other business to conduct and people were asked to take their spirited conversations outside the chamber. As they began filing out, someone remarked about the inscription above the double wooden doors that opened into a corridor and the city hall rotunda. *Law Is Reason Without Passion.* What did it mean, exactly? It could be argued that law and reason had prevailed, but without passion would people be smiling, laughing, feeling that after years of living in fear they might finally be safe?

When the buses got back to Lincoln Place the impromptu celebration continued on the lawn at Elkgrove Circle. One of the tables used for yard sales was set up, several bottles of wine and champagne appeared, and a dozen or so persons who had made the trek downtown sat in a circle of chairs in the shade of a pepper tree, drinking, munching on chips, and sharing impressions of the miracle that had occurred just a few hours earlier. They had fought city hall and won! Tenants walking by stopped to learn the news and offer congratulations. Bernard sat in the circle beaming like a mother taking pride in her children, but despite what some regarded as her proclivity for flights of utopian fancy, there was a pragmatic side of her personality that didn't allow her to proclaim that the enemy—the avaricious landlord—had finally been vanquished. "We have to figure out what's next," she said to the others. Then, as if taking care not to rain on a feel-good parade, she added with a smile, "But we have some time to relax."

The following day's *Outlook* featured the city council action in a front-page article. An accompanying photograph showed Mueller, Bernard, and an unidentified third person sharing an embrace in the council chamber after the vote.[37] The article quoted Galanter as saying that she was "very pleased." She alluded to Venice's community plan, which was part of the city's General Plan and called for the city to preserve the low-density character of Venice and maintain the current housing stock. "This is a very important statement by the city that community plans really do matter. We do care." Asked about the possibility of TransAction suing the city, the councilwoman answered, "They've been threatening lawsuits since the beginning."

Jim Merlino of TransAction, to nobody's surprise, had a very different view. He pointed out the approval by the deputy advisory agency and the city planning commission, saying, "A change of direction at this late date is wrong and no way for Los Angeles to do business." He didn't directly threaten legal action, but questioned Galanter's attendance at the executive session of the PLUM committee. "It would have been helpful to hear what discussion took place behind closed doors to understand why, at the 11th hour, the committee would disregard all the other city agencies' opinions."

In the article, Bernard sounded a conciliatory note. "This proposal has made this community a war zone," she said. "Now we've got to come together." But Mary Roberts was not about to sign on to any movement toward reconciliation. "As far as I'm concerned, I'm not angry at anyone in this complex, I just don't want anything to do with them."

The *Los Angeles Times* ran a much shorter article the next day in the newspaper's Westside section, briefly quoting Merlino, and Ingrid Mueller, who said, "We're flying a little bit high right now."

But two days later, the weekly issue of the *Argonaut* published a three-column article headlined "Lincoln Place owners to sue city after Council denies condo project." Most of the article was given over to quotes from TransAction's James Coxeter and Merlino. The latter brought up the Warner Ridge case and called the similarities "glaring" between it and the Lincoln Place rejection. "For the City of Los Angeles to make such a costly mistake again is an inexcusable waste of taxpayer's money." Coxeter was quoted on the subject of the closed-door PLUM committee meeting that Merlino had complained about in the *Outlook* article. "You have to wonder why Los Angeles has an application procedure at all," he said.

The promise of a lawsuit didn't surprise many LPTA members, but it was nevertheless a substantial dash of cold water on the euphoria that had risen with the clerk's announcement of the council vote. For Bernard, dismay didn't just arise from the possibility of TransAction winning in court and tearing down the complex after all, but from the realization that the fate of all the homes and their occupants could be in hands of lawyers and judges. What need would there be to organize tenants, write letters, make phone calls, put out bulletins, go downtown to meetings? For more than six years, her passion and energy had been invested in a movement she deeply believed in, and now it seemed that she would have to take a seat on the sidelines.

She assumed that if the LPTA could somehow find an attorney it could join the city in defending against a TransAction lawsuit, but again, it would be lawyers making arguments, deciding on courses of action. It was, to say the least, a sobering moment. But as events were about to prove, it was also best, to borrow from an Oscar Wilde quote, to expect the unexpected.

12

HIGH HOPES

KEN MEDLOCK WAS BORN in Venice and grew up just a few blocks from Lincoln Place. An actor best known for his role as the baseball scout Grady Fuson in the 2011 film *Moneyball*, his childhood passion was sports, and he and other boys often walked through the apartment complex on their way to Penmar Park to play baseball in the summer and after school.

"I knew a lot of kids who lived there," he says. "It was great for them, with all the space, the grass and the trees." His mother, Dicie Meyers, worked at a Thrifty drugstore lunch counter in the shopping center on nearby Lincoln Boulevard, and he would stop there on his way home for a drink and bite to eat. The gentrification that would sweep into Venice in the seventies and eighties was just a distant gleam in real estate speculators' eyes, and Lincoln Place was still what its architect and builders had intended, a home to working people and families for whom comfort and security was a reality, not a luxury they could only dream about.

Medlock went on to become a star baseball and football player at Venice High School, and later signed a professional contract with the Los Angeles Dodgers. His mother was then living in a rented house on Superba Avenue in Venice and working as a waitress at a Ships Coffee Shop in Culver City, one of an iconic chain of twenty-four-hour restaurants built in a futuristic design known as "Googie" architecture. But in 1982, the owner of the house decided to sell, and she moved into a one-bedroom apartment at 964 Elkland Place, the building at the far southwest corner of Lincoln Place. It was a big change from living in a house, but Medlock says his mother grew to love her apartment.

"Those places were really well built," he says. "And the people there were friendly. She got to know her neighbors and really settled in."

Meyers wasn't active in the LPTA, but she signed the tenant petition in 1995 and otherwise expressed support for the efforts to keep the complex from being demolished. And she kept up with developments by reading the LPTA's newsletters and bulletins. She was pleased by the city council's unanimous vote against the redevelopment plan, but wasn't prepared for the shock she got two weeks later when she opened her mail and read an official letter from the City of Los Angeles notifying her that TransAction had applied for a permit to demolish her building. The city's RSO required such notice to tenants, but what did it mean? That after thirteen years in the apartment she had come to love, she was facing the prospect of finding a new place to live? She quickly learned that all sixteen tenants in her building had received the same notice, while nobody in Lincoln Place's other fifty-one buildings had gotten one. What was going on?

"It freaked her out," Medlock says of his mother, who was then seventy-two and retired from her waitressing job. She was one of four seniors living in that building. The oldest, eighty-year-old Donald Morrissey, had moved into his apartment a year earlier, while Doris Sweeney, sixty-five, and Barbara Callas, sixty-two, had both moved to Lincoln Place in 1985. These four would be entitled under the RSO to $5,000 relocation payments if evicted; the other twelve tenants would get $2,000. But even $5,000 wouldn't go very far, given that most landlords required first and last month's rent plus a security deposit. Besides, nobody wanted to move. For some younger tenants the prospect was especially jarring. Two had young children and three had moved in just that year, one man as recently as the first of September, meaning that if the landlord actually proceeded with tearing down the building, his tenancy at Lincoln Place would be very short.

All three newspapers that covered goings-on in the Venice area—the *Argonaut*, the *Santa Monica Outlook* and the *Los Angeles Times*—ran stories about the notices. The *Outlook* article quoted Dicie Meyers as saying, "This just knocked the breath out of us. Everybody's scared. I didn't sleep at all after I got this notice." In the same article, Ruth Galanter said, "There is no purpose to this except straightforward retaliation." She called the notices "every family's worst nightmare," and added, "We're talking about everyday people with everyday lives here." Jim Merlino of TransAction predictably disputed the councilwoman's view, calling attention to the fact that tenants had been warned that buildings on each of Lincoln Place's thirty-five parcels might be torn down one-by-one if the city rejected the redevelopment plan. "If people want to assign fault or blame, they should start with the city council," he said.

Galanter cranked up the rhetoric in the *Times* article, calling the notices "despicable and vindictive." She gave a longer statement to the *Argonaut*, saying, "The most distressing aspect of this situation is that the tenants have done nothing to deserve these evictions other than to oppose the plan to demolish their complex. I will do whatever I can to stop these evictions and am now speaking with the city attorney and other city officials about possible options."

The LPTA held an emergency meeting on October 1, 1995, at Penmar Park. On the Sunday morning of the meeting the *Los Angeles Times* had the latest in an almost daily stream of articles on the O. J. Simpson trial, this one about jury deliberations expected to begin the following day. The city was deeply divided, largely along racial lines, on the question of Simpson's guilt, and some feared unrest in the Black community if the ex-football player and celebrity was convicted. Not to be caught unprepared as it had been after the Rodney King verdicts, the LAPD had put all officers on twelve-hour shifts and arranged to post one hundred on horseback around the county courthouse to quell any disturbances there.

But Simpson's fate wasn't foremost on the minds of Lincoln Place tenants who walked the short distance to the park. Some sixty persons, many of them seniors, filled the rows of folding chairs set up in the community room. The gathering included Chris Williams from the Penmar Neighborhood Association, who was regarded by some LPTA members as a spy with nefarious motives, although the meeting was public and anyone could attend. Ruth Galanter stood with an aide at the back of the room as Sheila Bernard called the meeting to order and briefly explained what had happened, then invited the councilwoman to speak on the issue in greater detail and answer any questions.

Galanter's opposition to the redevelopment had made her a hero to many tenants, and there was applause and some cheers as she walked to the front. Casually dressed in jeans and a long-sleeve shirt, she began by describing her reaction to learning that TransAction had applied for a permit to tear down the building. "I was as close to speechless as I get," she said. "Everybody I told in city hall was just shocked. It was inconceivable that there was a constructive reason for filing for this demolition permit." She repeated her allegation made in the newspaper articles that the landlord was retaliating for the LPTA's opposition to the redevelopment. "There's the coincidence of timing," she told the audience, "after you had the nerve to exercise your constitutional rights to disagree."

She hadn't been able to speak with James Coxeter, she said, but had called his business partner, Robert Bisno, who lived in the San Francisco Bay area. Bisno denied that TransAction was retaliating against tenants, she said, and declared that he would "never put people out on the street." She said that she reminded him of TransAction's attempt to evict tenants in 1987, a year after buying the property, and he reacted by calling it a "terrible PR move." But if the company didn't actually intend to evict the sixteen tenants, what was the purpose of seeking a permit to demolish their building?

"He told me they wanted the demolition permit, but weren't planning to use it and resented the city alarming people," Galanter said. Did he really expect people *not* to be alarmed if they got those notices? None of it made sense. "He told me there wasn't any current market for condominiums, and that if the ones proposed for Lincoln Place were built, it wouldn't be in the near future." But if that was true, then why did the company expend so much money and effort to get the project approved by the city?

"Depending upon the day of the week it is," Galanter said, "The story is different." One possibility was that if TransAction was thinking of selling the property, the city approval would make it more valuable. But that still didn't explain why the company wanted the demolition permit for a single building, other than to make good on the threat to tear the place down piecemeal if the city rejected the plan for the 850 new apartments and condominiums.

Galanter then asked for questions, and Dicie Meyers, one of several tenants at the meeting who had gotten the notices, said she had gone to the

Lincoln Place office and been told "not to panic. They weren't going to do anything." But, she said, occupants of the building had been given forms to fill out for the required relocation payments, which seemed to indicate the opposite. Another tenant said he had been told by Jim Merlino that nothing was guaranteed. "If they tear it down, we're back to square one," he said. "We haven't won anything."

Galanter advised the tenants against doing anything before getting legal advice. And Bernard told the group that the LPTA steering committee was planning to meet with a lawyer to find out if eviction attempts could be fought on the grounds that they were retaliatory. She spoke of trying to revive the stalled tenant-purchase plan, saying the LPTA was willing to talk with TransAction at any time. As the meeting drew to a close, Ingrid Mueller weighed in, sounding an optimistic note that may or may not have been shared by most of the people in the room. "Lincoln Place will be preserved—we know it."

Two days later, the O. J. Simpson jury returned a verdict of not guilty. To many, this verdict wasn't as shocking as the fact that it came after only four hours of deliberation. How could that be, in a trial that had lasted more than eight months? News media showed some African Americans openly celebrating the verdict, while any number of white persons appeared willing to go on record with their belief that Simpson had gotten away with murder. Although the verdict dispelled the fear of protests and disturbances in the Black community, it did nothing positive for race relations throughout the city. And the trial's unearthing of blatant racism on the part of an LAPD detective badly damaged the always-fraught relations between that community and the police.

For the LPTA and the sixteen tenants threatened with eviction, this news took a back seat to uncertainty over the future. In October's LPTA newsletter, under the heading "Back to the Barricades," Bernard wrote, "It turns out that the owner does not really intend to evict or demolish at the present time. He just wants to have the permits in hand, in case the city changes its mind, and the condo market improves at some time in the future." However, she reminded people that the owner had the right under the Ellis Act to go out of the rental business, and might be able to legally demolish every building at Lincoln Place without putting up a single thing to replace them.

Although she didn't know it when she wrote those words, Bernard had put her finger on the central question in a lawsuit TransAction filed against the city in Los Angeles County Superior Court just a day after the O. J. Simpson verdict. But what exactly was the Ellis Act, the law that had become an existential threat to Lincoln Place tenants and would remain so for the foreseeable future? Named after its sponsor, State Senator Jim Ellis, the seeds of the 1986 law were sown in 1978 when Hannah Nash, an ex-travel agent turned real estate investor, gave her seventeen-year-old son Jerome a small apartment building in the seaside city of Santa Monica. Whether he ever wanted the responsibility of owning and managing the six-unit building is open to question, but a year later, he decided to evict the tenants, tear the building down, and hold the vacant land while it appreciated in value. It was 1979, near the end of a decade of rapidly rising property values in Santa Monica and other parts of Southern California, and his expectation of making a tidy profit on his—or his mother's—investment looked entirely reasonable.

There was only one thing standing in his way. Santa Monica voters had just approved one of the strictest rent control laws in California, a measure that not only limited the rents landlords could charge but also aimed to curb precisely what Nash wanted to do; that is, evict tenants, tear down a perfectly habitable building, and hold the land for later sale. The teenage landlord and other property owners wanting to follow this route to real estate riches—popularly dubbed the "demolition derby" in Santa Monica—could no longer walk into city hall and get a demolition permit, but had to apply to a rent control board and meet strict standards intended to prevent the loss of rental units, especially those affordable to people of low and moderate incomes. Nash would have to show that tearing down his building wouldn't affect such people or adversely impact the city's housing supply. He would also have to prove that income from the property failed to provide a reasonable return on his investment.

Nash was quoted in a later court document, saying, "There is only one thing I want to do, and that is to evict the group of ingrates inhabiting my units, tear down the building, and hold on to the land until I can sell it at a price which will not mean a ruinous loss on my investment." Other land-lords may or may not have shared his view of tenants who paid their rent on time and didn't cause trouble as "ingrates," but when Nash turned to the courts after it became obvious that he couldn't meet the rent control board's criteria, many cheered him on, eager for a legal challenge to what they saw as draconian limits on their rights to use their properties as they saw fit.

In a lawsuit against the city of Santa Monica, Nash's attorneys argued that the rent control provision deprived him of his right to due process of law and amounted to an unconstitutional taking of property without just compensation. The lawsuit further argued that Nash simply wanted to get out of the business of owning and operating an apartment house. How could the city legally tell someone, whether a landlord or car dealer or plumber, that they couldn't leave their business? It amounted to a violation of the Thirteenth Amendment's prohibition of involuntary servitude. But attorneys for the city rebutted that argument by saying that if Nash no longer wanted to be a landlord, he could stop renting the units once they become vacant. Or he could sell the building. The city was under no obligation to help further speculative visions of profit, but it did have a compelling interest in keeping badly needed housing from permanently disappearing.

In the bench trial that followed, Nash conceded that his units were affordable to low- and moderate-income tenants, and that he could earn a fair return on his investment. So the question before the judge wasn't whether the young landlord had met the city's criteria for getting a demolition permit, but whether the rent control board regulations violated his constitutional rights. The judge decided that they did, and ordered the city to issue the permit to demolish the building.

The city appealed, first to the state Court of Appeals, which upheld the trial court judge, and then to the California Supreme Court. To the dismay of apartment house owners and other real estate interests, a majority of justices ruled on October 25, 1984, that the lower court decisions should be reversed. They found that the city hadn't violated Nash's constitutional rights, saying, in part, that, "protecting existing tenants against eviction and the scarce supply of residential housing in Santa Monica against further erosion, clearly serves important public objectives."[38] Five months later, the

US Supreme Court declined to review the case, and tenants in Santa Monica and elsewhere breathed a huge sigh of relief. Making sure people had decent homes they could afford was more important than the right of individuals or companies to wring every possible cent from a piece of property.

Elation would prove to be short-lived, though, because Nash and his supporters found a sympathetic ear in Jim Ellis, who quickly introduced a bill that prohibited cities and other local government bodies from passing laws that interfered with a landlord's right to go out of the rental business. A San Diego-area Republican, Ellis found ready support among colleagues of both parties in a legislature widely regarded as being unduly influenced by real estate interests. The bill was passed by the Senate and Assembly and signed into law by Governor George Deukmejian on October 2, 1985. It took effect on July 1 of the following year, less than two months after TransAction expanded its operations from Northern California and bought Lincoln Place.

The rent control law in Los Angeles was considerably less stringent than Santa Monica's, but landlords still faced hurdles before demolishing rental housing. For instance, an owner wanting to build a condominium project in place of an apartment building had to get city approval of the plans before a demolition permit could be issued. In the alternative, the owner could get permission to tear down a building by waiving the right to build condominiums on the site for a period of ten years. The measures had a twofold purpose: slowing down the rush to convert apartments to condominiums, and deterring owners from demolishing buildings and letting the land sit idle. In any event, TransAction had failed to get city approval of the Lincoln Place redevelopment, and hadn't signed a waiver of the right to build new condominiums. Accordingly, the city had refused to issue a demolition permit for 964 Elkland Place.

While TransAction claimed in its lawsuit that the Ellis Act gave it the absolute right to evict the Elkland Place tenants and demolish their building, it wasn't clear that the law applied. For one thing, the company was proposing to demolish only one of Lincoln Place's fifty-two buildings. How could it be going out of the rental business if there were still 778 apartments in the complex? For another, the Ellis Act explicitly stated that its provisions didn't preclude a city from regulating land use and zoning within its jurisdiction. By rejecting TransAction's application to demolish the building, the city was complying with its own General Plan by making sure the property was preserved for rental housing. How these arguments would play out in court remained to be seen. In an *Outlook* article about the filing of the lawsuit, Jim Merlino asserted that the city was throwing illegal roadblocks in TransAction's path, while a deputy city attorney said the city was on firm legal ground and countered the claim that city ordinance conflicted with the Ellis Act by calling the comparison of the two "apples and oranges."[39]

Two weeks later, TransAction attorneys were back in superior court with another lawsuit, this one seeking to nullify the city council's rejection of the Lincoln Place redevelopment. The PLUM committee, this lawsuit argued, had violated the state's open-meetings law, commonly known as the Brown Act, by allowing Ruth Galanter to attend two closed-door sessions even though she wasn't a committee member. In some quarters, the lawsuit was considered frivolous, just another attempt by TransAction to make life hard for Galanter and the obstructionist LPTA. It wasn't uncommon for council members who didn't sit on a particular committee to attend that group's meetings, even those behind closed doors, if the business at hand affected his or her district. Besides, Galanter hadn't voted on anything, and PLUM committee chairman Hal Bernson and member Laura Chick had discussed and voted on the project in public session. But in TransAction's telling, Galanter's presence in those meetings was an example of backroom dealing at its worst, and the company was asking the court to overturn both the PLUM committee action and the subsequent city council vote.

Tenants would celebrate the holidays that year in a state of suspense, a familiar, if unwelcome feeling that for the past half-dozen years had seemed to intensify in that season, dampening the cheer the LPTA tried to provide with parties, caroling, and gift exchanges. As if tenant spirits needed further depression, the day before Thanksgiving a fire broke out in a second-floor apartment on Elkgrove Circle. Firefighters managed to confine the fire to one room of the unit, but its occupant, a sixty-eight-year-old disabled woman, died of smoke inhalation. Ingrid Mueller wrote in the December issue of the LPTA newsletter about being out on her balcony enjoying the afternoon sun when she saw fire engines coming up the street. She joined a small group of people watching black smoke billowing from broken windows and firefighters' hoses gushing. In the group was a woman who openly opposed the LPTA, and Mueller wrote that the woman remarked, "Isn't it strange that only in tragedy we come together?" Mueller asked, "Are we together?" and when the woman answered in the affirmative, Mueller didn't answer, writing that she could "only nod and hope."

Mueller, like Bernard, had an inherent propensity to view things in an optimistic light, but middle ground between the LPTA and tenants who supported the landlord's plans seemed to lie at a distance beyond rocky, inhospitable terrain. Despite her infelicitous borrowing from Martin Luther King's speech, Mary Roberts did have a sincere "dream" of living in a brand-new, fully secure apartment building with units that were handicapped accessible and equipped with all the latest conveniences. A place where she could live out her life in the comfort and security that everyone deserved despite their views about preserving Lincoln Place. A place that, best of all, wouldn't cost her a dime more in rent. Along with other Lincoln Place Tomorrow members, she was clearly angry that the LPTA had helped dash those dreams. In a bulletin sent by the group to Lincoln Place residents after the filing of the first TransAction lawsuit, Roberts wrote, "As we have seen over the last week, the owners, as they said they would, will proceed with redevelopment as permitted by state law. All the LPTA and Galanter have done is put all of us at risk of eviction and lost the benefits we all worked so hard to gain from the owner. Gone is the peace of mind gained by knowing we all had a place to live at our same rent."

Around that same time, Bernard got an anonymous handwritten letter signed "A Lincoln Place Tenant" that expressed the anger in even more graphic terms. "Dear Ms. Bernard," it said. "I wish that you would back off, and let the Lincoln Place apartments be rebuilt. I have lived in the apartments for eight-teen (sic) years and through the years I've seen the apartments fall apart. Rotting wood, bad plumbing, and faulty electrical wiring are just a few of the things wrong. You may want to live in a rathole, but a lot more don't. Your bully tactics are bullshit, and uncalled for. The apartments are going to be built no matter what you do, so face it!"

Lincoln Place Tomorrow also attacked the LPTA's regular fundraising appeals. In her letter to tenants, Roberts wrote, "Please think long and hard before you give the LPTA any money or your support. You have to ask yourself where all the money the LPTA collects is going. Something is not right and it's time we all demanded an end to the LPTA's tactics that misinform and frighten us all."

In fact, LPTA treasurer Stan Dounn compiled regular financial reports that any tenant could see. The latest, dated a week after the Roberts missive, showed $665 in assets and $13,307 in liabilities, most of the latter owed to Jan Chatten-Brown and the law firm she had worked for before opening her own firm earlier in the year. And now that the fate of Lincoln Place was likely to be in the hands of the courts for the foreseeable future, getting the right legal help was a high priority. Marcia Scully's work had shown how important, even critical, such counsel was to the LPTA cause. But she wouldn't be able to represent the group in court, and just before the September city council meeting, she had joined the legal staff of the Metropolitan Water District. That agency had agreed to let her continue her pro bono work for the LPTA, but with the battle now in the courts, her role would be greatly reduced. And a search for an experienced litigator willing to work on a pro bono basis had thus far turned up empty.

Three weeks after Thanksgiving the holiday mood took another hit when superior court judge Hiroshi Fujisaki ruled that Galanter's attendance at the closed-door PLUM committee meetings had indeed violated the Brown Act. "There is a particularly serious appearance of impropriety if partisans on one side of an issue are admitted to a closed session while the other side is shut out," the judge said in his ruling. Noting that the Lincoln Place project had been approved by the deputy advisory agency and the city planning commission, Fujisaki said the PLUM committee's reversal of those actions "supports an inference that the closed sessions have not been limited to receiving advice of counsel. Rather, the evidence indicates that the closed sessions were turning points in the process and that decisions may have been discussed and crystallized there."

Fujisaki, who in the coming year would be in the news as presiding judge in a wrongful death lawsuit brought against O. J. Simpson by the families of his alleged murder victims, ordered the PLUM committee and city council to rehear the Lincoln Place redevelopment within ninety days. The ruling and order pleased TransAction's Jim Merlino, who was quoted in the next day's *Outlook.* "A decades-old practice of the city council was struck down because of Galanter's inability to address a proposal on its merits in open public forums. This decision will cause the council to change the way it does business, much to the public's benefit." But in the same article, Galanter argued that the closed sessions were only necessary because TransAction had publicly threatened to sue the city if the project was denied. "I didn't ask for a closed session," Galanter said, alluding to the fact that the meeting's official purpose was to hear advice from the city attorney's office. "The committee asked for it because they heard the same threats we all heard." She predicted that a second vote would turn out the same as the first, and said that forcing the city to go through the hearings again was part of TransAction's "colossal temper tantrum."

There was widespread agreement with Galanter's prediction. Nobody could point to anything that might impel council members to change their minds, which raised the question of TransAction's motive in filing the lawsuit. Was Merlino's suggestion that the company acted out of an altruistic concern for the public credible? Or had TransAction simply lashed out in anger over being told that it couldn't do what it wanted with its property? If the intention was to reverse the council's action, the lawsuit was a likely failure. But if it aimed to make life harder for tenants fighting the redevelopment, it succeeded, because there would have to be more organizing, more time and money spent on flyers and other communications, more trips downtown to city hall. And perhaps most importantly, more unease and anxiety about the future.

Of much greater worry, however, was the first lawsuit, which would come to be known, in a list of future lawsuits involving the property, as "Lincoln Place I." If the courts ruled that the city's refusal to issue the demolition permit violated the Ellis Act, nothing could stop TransAction from evicting tenants and sending in bulldozers to knock down their buildings. But in order to build new condominiums the company would then have to get separate approvals for each of Lincoln Place's thirty-five parcels, a tedious, time-consuming process that would almost certainly arouse public opposition. TransAction could avoid that lengthy process by simply replacing the demolished apartments with new units that could be rented at market rates, but under neither scenario would the company be under any obligation to include units for existing tenants or other people with low and moderate incomes, as the plan rejected by the city council had promised. The Venice community, long known and valued for its diversity, might watch hundreds of units of affordable rental housing be displaced by a thirty-eight-acre island of luxury condominiums or apartments that working people, the elderly, and others of limited means could never hope to afford. What then would the LPTA have to show for all its years of hard work?

For tenants who wanted to see Lincoln Place preserved, the high spirits that followed the city council vote were mostly a distant memory, replaced for some by a feeling of dread, for others by a sense of resignation over what looked like the landlord gaining the upper hand, for yet others by a renewed determination to keep fighting no matter the obstacles. In the days leading to Christmas the temperature dropped, the skies clouded over, and rain fell for hours at a time, apt symbols of the gloom that pervaded much of the complex. But at the same time, many tenants had put lights and decorations in their windows, lending the place a festive air. Sheila Bernard's two oldest children were grown and living elsewhere, but for Hanukkah, she lighted a menorah and fried latkes for herself and her eleven-year-old son. On the evening of December 20, with a respite in the damp weather, a group gathered at Ingrid Mueller's apartment for a cup of the Scandinavian spiced wine called *glögg* before heading out with flashlights and songbooks to walk through the grounds singing carols. Bernard brought her guitar, and for the next two hours, spirits were lifted and camaraderie and neighborly cheer once more defined the Lincoln Place that residents had long loved.

The sun shone brightly on New Year's Day. As usual, thousands lined up for hours on the route of the Rose Parade in Pasadena, while Santa Ana winds blew from the desert and over the mountains, carrying dust and smog and an abrasive dryness all the way to the sea. The editorial writers of the *Los Angeles Times* published a wish list for the city that included a better criminal justice system, greater support by Mayor Richard Riordan for enforcement of the city's ethics rules, and a push by the city council's four female members and their colleagues to "discourage, shame, and punish top city officials who harass women."

But foremost on the minds of Sheila Bernard and the LPTA steering committee members were the wranglings in the court and the need to raise money to hire legal counsel. For the first LPTA newsletter of 1996, Bernard compiled a financial report covering the entire eight years from the group's origin in 1987. Over that period $59,735 had been raised and $58,767 spent, exclusive of outstanding legal bills of more than $12,000 and fees deferred by consultants in the tenant-purchase effort. Membership dues had brought in $25,000, grants $20,000, and donations from various sources, $12,000. The balance was income earned from yard sales and T-shirt sales. Outside of legal fees, the single biggest expense—$35,000—was for the printing and mailing of newsletters and bulletins. Odds and ends like bus transportation to hearings, office supplies, telephone, and refreshments for meetings and events made up the rest. The treasury still had a balance of less than $1,000. In a preface to this report, Bernard wrote, "Are we in great financial shape? Like most nonprofits, our answer is: we are hanging on by our fingernails and we need your continued support!"

On January 24, attorneys representing TransAction and the city of Los Angeles appeared before superior court judge Alan Haber to argue the merits of the lawsuit to compel the city to issue a demolition permit for the Lincoln Place building. The question posed for the judge was straightforward—did the city's refusal violate the landlord's right under the Ellis Act to leave the apartment rental business? TransAction's legal counsel argued that it clearly did, while attorneys for the city countered that even though the titles to Lincoln Place's thirty-five parcels were held by separate legal entities, the apartment complex as a whole was owned and operated by TransAction and the company would have to stop renting all 795 apartments in order to meet the Ellis Act definition of going out of business. After listening to these arguments, the judge took the matter under advisement, saying he expected to issue a ruling in the coming weeks.

The hearing and the possible aftermath was a major topic of comments and questions at the LPTA's regular monthly meeting on February 4 at Penmar Park. If TransAction won, would tenants throughout the complex be getting notices that their buildings might be demolished? If the landlord lost, would the threat of evictions be permanently lifted? Would the city appeal an adverse ruling? There were no definite answers. "We're in limbo," Sheila Bernard told the group. "We just have to wait and see."

At the end of the meeting, about twenty people stayed for what Bernard had earlier announced would be a walk to the Elkland Place building to form a "circle of protest, love, and solidarity." Carrying signs with such messages as Save Lincoln Place; Don't Demolish Our Homes; and We Need Low Cost Apartments, Not Luxury Condos, the group left the park and headed west on Lake Street. Led by Bernard with a Save Our Home sign, the procession walked three blocks to always-busy Lincoln Boulevard and turned south past the Ralphs Supermarket and Thrifty drugstore to California Avenue, the street that led back into Lincoln Place. There was a scattering of honks from passing cars as the group turned right on Frederick Street and walked another block to the building TransAction threatened to tear down. There weren't enough people to actually encircle the building, which consisted of four wings surrounding a deep courtyard, so people stood for a while on the sidewalk in front, displaying their signs to pedestrians and passing cars before finally dispersing as the sun sank into the horizon and a chill pervaded the air.

The city council's PLUM committee scheduled the court-ordered second vote on the Lincoln Place redevelopment for February 13. Bernard and other LPTA leaders were confident that the vote wouldn't change, but they decided to leave nothing to chance and sent out flyers asking people to call committee members' offices and, if possible, come to city hall. Marcia Scully sent a letter reiterating the LPTA's arguments that the TransAction project violated city housing policies. She also brought up the two lawsuits filed by TransAction, saying that neither challenged the substance of the city council's denial of the project and therefore shouldn't sway council members to change their original votes. But in a letter sent on the same date, TransAction attorney Allan Abshez raised the potential threat of the Ellis Act, saying that forcing TransAction to proceed under that law would result in the loss of the very housing the city council claimed it was trying to preserve. The attorney also wrote that Councilwoman Galanter had been unresponsive to overtures TransAction had made to reach a compromise acceptable to all parties. As a result, he said, "There will be no guarantee against tenant evictions, no guaranteed replacement housing at current rents, and no commitment to build new permanently affordable housing."

Once again, the PLUM committee met in the spacious council chamber, although the number of people who came for the Lincoln Place vote was smaller than the contingent at the August 1995 meetings. But the usual suspects were present. Mary Roberts of Lincoln Place Tomorrow and Chris Williams of the Penmar Neighborhood Association on one side of the aisle, along with a small group of their supporters, and Sheila Bernard, Ingrid Mueller, and a dozen LPTA members on the other. TransAction was represented by Abshez while Scully would present the LPTA case, as she had at every public hearing beginning with the city planning-commission meetings almost exactly a year earlier.

Hal Bernson and Laura Chick were still committee members, but Richard Alatorre had been replaced by Mark Ridley-Thomas, who represented a south Los Angeles district and was considered to hold pro-renter views. But since he wasn't on the committee when it originally voted on the Lincoln Place project, he wouldn't be casting a vote or taking part in the latest discussion. After calling the meeting to order, Bernson once again asked city planners to briefly describe TransAction's plan, then called on Allan Abshez. The dapper thirty-nine-year-old attorney began by noting what nobody in the audience had known until they reached city hall, which was the fact that Judge Haber had just that morning issued a ruling in TransAction's Ellis Act lawsuit. In the judge's opinion, Abshez told the committee, the law gave landlords the "unrestricted right" to go out of business and city ordinances impeding that right were invalid. As a consequence, the judge was ordering the city to issue the demolition permit for the Elkland Place building. Nevertheless, Abshez said, TransAction wasn't going to rush out and evict Dicie Meyers and the other tenants and knock it down. The company was still open to discussing compromises for an overall redevelopment plan that would be acceptable to the LPTA, Councilwoman Galanter, and the surrounding community.

Both Mary Roberts and Chris Williams echoed this theme, with the latter urging the parties to submit to mediation so a plan could move forward.

But Scully told the committee that the LPTA was adamantly opposed to any plan that didn't include the preservation of all existing apartments. As for the hot-off-the-press court ruling, she argued that it shouldn't influence the committee's decision because what TransAction was allowed to do under the Ellis Act was a separate issue. When Sheila Bernard's turn came, she confirmed Scully's statement that mediation was impossible unless TransAction was willing to consider preservation as an option. Ruth Galanter urged her colleagues, as she had at previous meetings, to protect a critically needed supply of affordable housing and stop the destruction of a genuine community.

After closing public comment, Bernson said that while a landlord did have the right to go out of business, as Abshez argued, the city still had the right to make land-use decisions based on guidelines set forth by the General Plan. Chick agreed, saying she hadn't heard anything that would cause her to alter her view, and with that, the committee voted to deny the project a second time.

The city council scheduled the matter for February 20. Most of those who had been at the PLUM committee meeting showed up, but since the committee had held the requisite public hearing the council didn't take comment from audience members, only hearing from Bernson, who repeated his earlier rationale for denying the project, and Galanter, who urged her colleagues to affirm the committee's action. In his distinctly deep voice, council president John Ferraro called, "Open the roll, tabulate the vote," and within seconds, the clerk announced the result—14–0 to once again reject the TransAction redevelopment plan.

There was applause from the right side of the aisle, but while LPTA members and supporters were happy with the outcome, the euphoria that had swelled after the September vote was notably muted. This latest vote wasn't simply anticlimactic—it did nothing to settle the larger question of TransAction's intentions. During the council meeting, Bernson had said he didn't think the company had any intention of demolishing and rebuilding parcel by parcel, and was just using the Ellis Act as a threat to sway the council to either approve the redevelopment or consider some compromise, but nobody could be sure. The uncertainty that had cast long shadows over Lincoln Place would remain a dreary fact of tenants' lives.

By the time the March LPTA newsletter was printed and mailed, the city hadn't announced whether it would appeal Judge Haber's ruling. Nevertheless, Ingrid Mueller struck a celebratory tone, writing under the headline "We All Did It!" that the city council "unanimously and whole-heartedly rejected TransAction's application AGAIN. You ask: that Ellis Act? We believe: Ellis Shmellis. TransAction went for the jugular of this com-munity—but we weren't sleeping!" In the newsletter, Sheila Bernard also applauded the council vote, calling it a "major milestone" for the LPTA. "We are especially grateful for the inspired and dedicated work of our attorney, Marcia Scully, and the strength and commitment of our councilwoman, Ruth Galanter." Because of that work and dedication, she wrote, the LPTA would host a "Thanksgiving in Spring" on March 24 in honor of those two women.

The affair was held at the Westminster Senior Center, a nondescript build-ing set in a small park of the same name a block from the beach in Venice. Food and drinks were set up on a table and a long banner that read, "Welcome Marcia, Thank You Forever, Fabulous Friend + Attorney," was hung across one wall. A group of five tenants calling themselves "The Too-Busy-For-Prime-Time Tenants" passed out printed lyrics for a musical toast to Galanter and Scully, who sat at a table with Frieda and Dave Marlin. The songs "High Hopes" and "Downtown" were paeans to Galanter, whose forcefulness at city hall had kept tenants feeling optimistic, while an adaption of the old standard "Sweet and Lovely" was an ode not only to Scully's efforts but to her notably gracious personality. Ingrid Mueller read a quote from the seventeenth-century Spanish poet Baltasar Gracián—"Wisdom and courage make mutual contributions to greatness"—and then presented Scully with a collection of potted plants and Galanter with a small eucalyptus tree, along with a promise that tenants would help the councilwoman plant the tree at her Venice home.

Both women spoke briefly. Galanter said that in the weeks following the city council's latest vote, TransAction representatives had been calling her office, wanting to discuss possible compromise plans, but as long as the plans didn't include preservation of Lincoln Place as it existed, she saw no reason to talk. "They still haven't gotten the message," she said. She concluded by urging tenants to keep up the fight against destruction of their homes. "They [TransAction] may have won a few battles, but still haven't won the war."

While Galanter would be involved in the Lincoln Place battle as long as she was a city council member, the shift from the political arena to the courts meant that Scully's work, for all practical purposes, was at an end, and her remarks had the tone of a farewell. Like Galanter, she had always encouraged the tenants to be optimistic, and she told the gathering that "High Hopes" was the most appropriate song, suggesting that it could become the LPTA's theme song. In her usual modest way, she gave credit for successes to the tenants, saying that "one of the most irritating things to the other side" was being thwarted by low-income tenants, a "bunch of women" who apparently didn't know their place.

As the afternoon light began to fade and some people dispersed while others stayed to clean up, Bernard reflected on her role as one of those women who wasn't willing to keep her mouth shut and accept what powerful men—James Coxeter, Jim Merlino, Robert Bisno—decided was good for her and other tenants. None of those active in the LPTA—not every one a woman, to be fair—were wealthy, none held positions of any particular authority, and none were adept at navigating the fraught seas of politics. Yet with a combination of hard work, tenacity, and an unwavering belief in their cause they had won the battle on those stormy seas. But now? Future arguments for preserving Lincoln Place would be made in the courts, by lawyers speaking a language as foreign as any one might hear on the streets of the city's many ethnic communities. It felt to her like handing over a child to a stranger, entrusting the future to people who wore suits and carried briefcases and didn't necessarily feel her passion for protecting the buildings and the trees and the lawns and everything that she and others truly felt was home.

She didn't know it then, but in just a few weeks the landlord would be filing yet another lawsuit seeking to overturn the city council's action. Years later, looking back, she had a wistful view of those moments, a view with just a slight tint of bitterness that was alien to her nature. When asked, she would put it as a kind of adage adapted from a popular country music song of the '70s: "Mamas, don't let your little movements grow up to be lawsuits."

13

WHY NOT LINCOLN PLACE?

"WE DO NOT WANT to be moved. These are our homes!"

This emphatic declaration by Ethel Shapiro-Bertolini opens the film *Let's Own It!: The Struggle of the Lincoln Place Tenants Association.*[40] Produced by UCLA professor Karen Brodkin, the thirty-two-minute video had its first public screening at the Penmar Park recreation center on October 4, 1998. Sadly, Shapiro-Bertolini wasn't in the audience of tenants and community members; the longtime social activist who convinced tenants to organize and resist TransAction's eviction attempts back in 1987 had died eight months earlier. Arguably, the LPTA would not have existed without this diminutive woman who wore thick-lensed glasses and spoke with a strong accent, and it seemed appropriate that she appeared both at the beginning of the film, and at its close, where she said, "If this place is to be demolished and fixed up for the rich after we are gone, after we are dead, the children of today and tomorrow will not forgive us!"

Brodkin became interested in the Lincoln Place struggle after moving to Los Angeles in 1986 to join the faculty of the UCLA anthropology department and direct the university's Women's Studies program. The battle between the tenants and their landlord had also attracted the attention of faculty members in the university's urban planning department, notably Allan Heskin, who had encouraged the LPTA to pursue tenant ownership, and Neal Richman, who lent his expertise in helping the LPTA conduct its 1991 demographic survey. But the deepest involvement in the Lincoln Place saga came from two women whose interests were both professional and personal—Brodkin, and a graduate student in urban planning named Gail Sansbury.

Before coming to UCLA, Brodkin had taught women's studies at Oberlin College in Ohio, where student protests against the college's investments in companies doing business with South Africa's apartheid regime had made national news. She took up residence in Venice, which is only seven miles from the UCLA campus, although notoriously heavy traffic in West Los Angeles could mean a slow rush hour drive. She was attracted to the community where she still lives, she says, because of its diversity—a mix of people differing in age, culture, race, and economic status. Lincoln Place was only a few blocks away, and it wasn't long before she learned of the tenants' fight against evictions. As a college student, she had gotten involved in the civil rights and women's liberation movements, and when she embarked upon an academic career, she focused on research and teaching about issues of gender, race, class, and activist movements arising from those issues. The Lincoln Place Tenants Association, with a leadership dominated by ordinary women fighting the forces of corporate power and gentrification, was a natural subject for both her academic interests and her personal commitment to positive social change.

In 1991, Brodkin interviewed Shapiro-Bertolini in the latter's Lincoln Place apartment. Then eighty-one years old and suffering from emphysema, the longtime labor organizer talked of various subjects, including her 1976 book *Through the Wall: Prison Correspondence*, a compilation of letters exchanged over a period of four years with hundreds of federal prison inmates. That book had indirectly led to an eviction threat, when the Lincoln Place management learned that after being paroled, one of those men had come to Los Angeles and stayed for a month in Shapiro-Bertolini's apartment. By that time—a dozen years after the CORE demonstration at the management office—a small number of African Americans lived at Lincoln Place, but Shapiro-Bertolini still believed that racism was involved because the man was Black and the issue of his presence had arisen from anonymous complaints by another tenant. But the eviction threat was withdrawn when she said the man was a short-term guest and wouldn't be living in the apartment permanently. At that time, the Yousem family still owned the property; how TransAction might have reacted is impossible to know.

In the interview, Shapiro-Bertolini also aired her views on grassroots organizations like the LPTA. Of critical importance, she argued, was maintaining a democratic structure and not allowing a single person or a few at the top to dictate policy for the entire group. Authoritarian organizations, she believed, were doomed to failure, and she pointed to the Communist Party as an example. This view, consciously or not, was embraced by Sheila Bernard, then in her second year as LPTA president. A common observation made by those who attended the group's meetings had to do with her diligence in not only keeping discussions organized and efficiently moving but making sure that everyone's voice was heard. Whether this commitment to democracy always worked to the group's advantage is another question.

Brodkin decided to make a film that documented the LPTA's fight to save the complex but also emphasized Bernard's dream of tenant ownership, which seemed an especially viable idea given that the landlord had recently declared bankruptcy. She got a grant from UCLA and enlisted the help of one of her graduate students, a woman named Mary Hardy who had studied both film and anthropology as an undergraduate at Hampshire College in Massachusetts. In the summer of 1994, Hardy went with Brodkin to an LPTA meeting, which marked the beginning of two years and untold hours of filming—Hardy usually wielded the camera and did much of the editing—of LPTA gatherings, city council and planning commission meetings, demonstrations at Lincoln Place, and interviews with Bernard, Shapiro-Bertolini, and other Lincoln Place tenants.

Brodkin's involvement with the LPTA wasn't just as an observer, though. When the draft EIR on TransAction's plan to tear down the complex and replace most of it with condominiums was released for public comment in the spring of 1993, she wrote a five-page letter detailing objections to the project that would end up, in her words, "reducing the diversity of Venice" and "destroying a functioning neighborly community in its heart." As noted earlier, she testified at the Venice CPAC meeting in July of 1994, raising questions about TransAction's solvency and the company's ability to build the project it was proposing, even if the city approved the plans.

Gail Sansbury also sent a comment letter attacking the findings of the EIR. The report had found the complex to be of "limited historical and architectural interest," when in fact it was, in Sansbury's words, "an important example of a successful interpretation and execution of federal design guidelines for multifamily housing." The EIR asserted that the design of Lincoln Place was loosely based on the bungalow court/garden apartments built in Los Angeles in the 1920s, while Sansbury argued that the architect followed federal guidelines based on international design precedents that strongly reflected the Bauhaus and garden city movements. In Sansbury's view, the report's most glaring omission was the failure to discuss those guidelines and the FHA program under which the complex was financed. If it had, she wrote, it would have been clear that Lincoln Place was intentionally built as low- and moderate-income housing and as such "has an important place in the social history of Venice and Los Angeles."

The final EIR included responses to these letters, but to put it bluntly, the objections were dismissed. However, two major points raised by Brodkin and Sansbury, the social significance of Lincoln Place as affordable housing and its place in architectural and cultural history, would prove to resonate long into the future, in the political arena and in the courts of law and public opinion. These issues would also draw new, significant figures into the long-running fray.

At the time she wrote her EIR comment letter, Sansbury was something of an expert on Lincoln Place history. But she lived far from Venice and knew nothing about the complex before a fellow UCLA graduate student who had worked on the LPTA's demographic survey invited her to an LPTA meeting in the fall of 1991. TransAction had recently unveiled its sweeping plan to redevelop the property and James Coxeter was meeting with small groups of tenants, while the LPTA leadership had gotten behind Sheila Bernard's "Let's Own It" idea and the consultants were studying the feasibility of a tenant purchase. Sansbury learned about this at the meeting, and because she was both interested in and sympathetic to the tenants' cause, she began attending the weekly LPTA steering committee meetings and the general meetings held once a month at Penmar Park. But when she asked how Lincoln Place happened to be built, nobody seemed to know with any degree of certainty. Some tenants thought it was built by Douglas Aircraft or Hughes Aircraft to house their workers. Some community members believed it had been built by the city as public housing, but a tenant assured Sansbury that it was the work of a private developer, although who that developer was seemed to be a mystery. She decided to research these and other questions and make Lincoln Place and the LPTA the subject of her master's degree thesis.

Sansbury finished that thesis in 1993. Her research into Lincoln Place history uncovered a wealth of detail about the original builders, the financing of the project, and the principles that went into its design, but one fact eluded her as well as others for another half-dozen years. The documents she examined listed only Heth Wharton as Lincoln Place's architect; Ralph Vaughn, the man who actually directed the design, was invisible. This fact, an unhappy consequence of the racism that suffused government agencies in the late 1940s and beyond, would come forth through the efforts of another person, one who wasn't from the academic world but had the same tireless drive to learn details of Lincoln Place's history. It was a fact that would prove invaluable to those fighting to save the apartment complex from being destroyed.

Laura Burns got her first look at Lincoln Place in the spring of 1996. She had grown up in Austin, Texas, but lived something of a peripatetic existence as an adult, spending extended periods of time in Germany and Mexico. But in 1990, she was back in Austin, newly divorced from her German husband, when she saw an ad for extras in a movie being shot in the area. She had long been interested in theater and film, having graduated from Catholic University in Washington, DC, with a degree in drama and later from the University of Texas with a master's degree in radio-TV-film. The movie was *The Ballad of the Sad Cafe*, starring Vanessa Redgrave and Keith Carradine, and at the cattle call for extras, she was offered a small speaking part. During the shoot, she became friendly with one of the main actors, a stand-up comedian from Los Angeles named Cork Hubbert, and it was this acquaintance that would eventually lead her to Lincoln Place.

After the film shoot, Burns went back to Germany, where she met Bernard Perroud, a Frenchman who would become her second husband.

The couple eventually decided to settle in Mexico City, but the peso devaluation of 1994 and the resulting economic crisis made everyday life there
too difficult, so they decided to move to Los Angeles to work in the film
business. They stayed with Hubbert while they looked for a place to rent. By
chance, he lived in the Penmar neighborhood that bordered Lincoln Place,
and even though Burns and Perroud looked at other apartments in the area,
nothing had the appeal of the complex with its abundantly landscaped
open space, modernist architecture, and feeling of a genuine community.
In May of 1996, they moved into a one-bedroom apartment on Elkgrove
Avenue, just around the corner from Ingrid Mueller, although it would be
several years before they got to know her and become friends and allies in
the cause of saving the Lincoln Place they came to love.

Burns didn't immediately get involved with the LPTA and its efforts.
She was doing freelance film editing, while Perroud was putting his skills
as a sculptor to work in making props for a film company. When the couple
moved in, they signed the standard disclaimer that redevelopment of the
property could put an end to their tenancy, but nothing appeared imminent,
so they didn't worry about having to soon pack up and move. Burns learned
of the LPTA through reading newsletters that came in the mail and were
posted on laundry room bulletin boards, but at that time, the final years
before the turn of the century, the landlord-tenant battle seemed muted,
and she didn't go to any LPTA meetings or otherwise involve herself in its
activities.

That quietude was deceptive, though. In May 1996, a month after the
LPTA honored Ruth Galanter and Marcia Scully in a celebration of the
city council's rejection of TransAction's plan, the company filed another
lawsuit against the city, this one charging that the council's denial violated
its right to redevelop the property. A ruling on TransAction's first lawsuit,
which claimed that the city's refusal to issue a demolition permit for the
building on Elkland Place violated the state's Ellis Act, was pending in the
state Court of Appeal, which meant that two lawsuits seeking the same
ultimate result—allowing TransAction to demolish Lincoln Place—were
hanging over tenants' heads. In the meantime, the LPTA was fighting
skirmishes over day-to-day issues, most prominently the lax maintenance

that prompted many complaints, although yard sales and the keeping of pets continued to be subjects of conflict. And to the extreme annoyance of LPTA members like Ingrid Mueller, newsletters were still being removed from laundry room bulletin boards.

On April 7, 1997, the appeals court upheld the lower court, ruling that the city's denial of the demolition permit indeed violated the Ellis Act. While the ruling was a clear victory for TransAction, it didn't raise as much alarm as might have been expected. TransAction hadn't made any further move to evict the building's tenants, and it was assumed that the landlord was awaiting the outcome of the lawsuit seeking to overturn the city council's vote on the redevelopment because it really didn't want to tear down buildings and put up new condominiums or apartments one parcel at a time. That outcome could be several years off, so tenants had some breathing room, although nobody who had been in the heat of the fray was inclined to relax.

Sheila Bernard still held out hope that the city would do something to support the tenant-purchase effort, but in the 1997 city election, Richard Riordan handily defeated Tom Hayden for a second term as mayor, dimming the prospects of help from that office. Both candidates had been invited to speak at an LPTA meeting before the election, but only Hayden had shown up, which indicated to many the opinion Riordan held of a tenants' group fighting his natural constituency of business and development interests. The outlook for a tenant purchase was further muddled by a notice tenants received in November instructing them to make rent checks out to both Lincoln Place Investors, the legal entity that owned the property under the TransAction corporate umbrella, and Deutsche Bank, the German-based global investment firm. There was no explanation for this change, but Bernard learned that TransAction had refinanced the property and Deutsche Bank was now the primary mortgage holder. In December's LPTA newsletter, she reported this fact, and added a segue to tenant ownership. "We are renting from an owner whose major motivation is to maximize profits. In spite of that, many of us continue to visualize Lincoln Place as a democratically controlled, environmentally sustainable community." As if taking a breath, she continued in a new paragraph: "We know it will take a miracle. Personally I have witnessed the modest miracle of a scraggly band of ragtag tenants and our many friends and supporters prevailing in a ten-year battle for our neighborhood. It is little miracles like this which continue to renew my faith and trust that all things work out as they are supposed to, if we only continue steadfastly to do what we know we must do."

The year 1998 was momentous both nationally and internationally, with a major financial crisis in Asia, the bombing of two US embassies in Africa, the reaching of a peace accord in Northern Ireland, and the impeachment of President Bill Clinton. A domestic event that made few waves at the time but would have far-reaching consequences was the introduction of the Google search engine. In Los Angeles, Mayor Riordan set into motion an overhaul of the city charter that would give his office significantly more power and establish a system of neighborhood councils that would—in theory, at least—give local communities like Venice a greater voice in city affairs. Up the coast, Oakland Athletics slugger Mark McGwire set the single season record for home runs, a milestone tainted by his later admission of steroid use. And 1998 saw smoking banned in all California bars and restaurants.

For the LPTA, the screening of *Let's Own It!: The Struggle of the Lincoln Place Tenant's Association* was undoubtedly the high point of a year that didn't see any hearings, court decisions, or notably provocative actions by the landlord. Sheila Bernard, one of a small number of persons to view the film before the screening, wrote about it in the August LPTA newsletter. "It's a wonderful thing to be on the silver screen. Our society bestows high honors on those with the talent, the drive, and the dedication to become well-known actors. And then there are the rest of us. Our lives are sometimes depicted in movies about 'ordinary' people struggling with 'ordinary' problems; people who manage to come through life's difficulties with greater wisdom and more love in their hearts than they had before; people who turn 'life isn't fair' into 'life is what we make it.'"

After the screening, the film was acquired by the University of California's Center for Media and Independent Learning, where copies were available for rental or purchase. The listing called the film an "outstanding teaching tool" for courses like sociology, anthropology, and urban studies and planning. It included a blurb by a professor of urban studies at the University of the District of Columbia, who described the reaction of her students when she showed the film in class. "They loved seeing renters fight back to claim their community and they immediately connected with the role of seniors, with more time, working to make a vital neighborhood which included the young families with children, but little time."

Ethel Shapiro-Bertolini certainly fit that role, as did others who made up the sea of white hair that Sheila Bernard saw a decade earlier when she walked into her first LPTA meeting. Those seniors were under personal threat, certainly, but also saw their place in the Lincoln Place battle the way the students did, as people working on behalf of those who were unable to come to meetings, distribute flyers, make phone calls, and attend to the myriad tasks inherent in a volunteer social movement. Two of the most faithful were Frieda and Dave Marlin, who hosted LPTA steering committee meetings at their apartment and almost always made the bus trips downtown to meetings and hearings. But three weeks before Christmas, the seventy-six-year-old World War II veteran who had worked as a driving instructor for disabled persons died suddenly of a heart attack. LPTA members who knew him would miss his good-humored presence at committee meetings and gatherings, but his death was also a portent for Bernard and other LPTA supporters; the seniors who were the beating heart of the organization could succumb to health problems at any time. Younger people had to be brought into the fold; otherwise, the organization would gradually wither and die.

Bernard was a thirty-nine-year-old single mother of three with a full-time job when she took the reins of the LPTA, but unlike her two predecessors who were also in their thirties but together served less than two years, she was willing to spend an enormous amount of time and energy leading the tenants' cause. But she was a rarity. Who would replace those like Ethel Shapiro-Bertolini and Dave Marlin? Frieda Marlin, who was seventy-four when her husband died, had medical issues, as did other active steering committee members like eighty-four-year-old Adolphe Griffith and seventy-two-year-old Ruth Holzgreen. Stan Dounn, a relative youngster at sixty-seven who impressed everyone with his diligence and attention to detail as LPTA treasurer, had finally realized a dream of owning his own home and bought a condominium in a nearby community. Younger persons like

Jan Book, Laura Burns, and several others would play important roles in Lincoln Place's future, but they hadn't yet become active in the LPTA's efforts.

The last year of the millennium began the way the previous year had ended, without anyone having a clear idea of the fate of Lincoln Place and its tenants. There were glimmers of hope, though. Democrat Gray Davis was inaugurated as California's thirty-seventh governor, following sixteen years of Republican incumbency, and while he was regarded as a moderate, he was expected to be decidedly more pro-renter than his predecessors. In fact, he soon signed into law several Ellis Act amendments designed to give tenants greater protection. One of those—increasing a landlord's required notice before evicting elderly and disabled tenants from sixty days to a full year—would later prove especially significant to Lincoln Place residents. Four years after taking office, Davis would become the second state governor in US history to be recalled by voters, but at the moment, tenant advocates looking to Sacramento to help staunch a steady flow of Ellis Act evictions in Los Angeles and other metropolitan areas had reason for cautious optimism.

Unfortunately, the desire to find ways to get rid of long-term tenants paying low rents was intensified by an apartment market that had shed its mid-decade torpor and turned red hot in popular areas like Venice and the west side of Los Angeles. In 1996, for example, the average Lincoln Place rent was $600 a month; three years later, the landlord was asking as much as $1,400 for a newly vacated, two-bedroom unit, a figure out of reach for most seniors and many working families. The Center on Budget and Policy Priorities, a Washington, DC, research institute, published a study showing that Los Angeles, of forty-five major metropolitan areas, had the worst affordable-housing problem. The term "housing crisis" showed up regularly in articles and editorials in the *Los Angeles Times* and other news outlets, a dismal echo of FHA administrator Wilson Wyatt's declaration on his visit to the city all the way back in 1946, when Lincoln Place was just the glow of an idea in Samuel Bialac's mind.

In the summer, though, Bernard and the LPTA got some good news. To the surprise of many, Shapiro-Bertolini's estate was relatively sizable, and her will made bequests to both the LPTA and Bernard. Other heirs contested the will, but when it was settled, Bernard and the LPTA both got

$19,000. Because LPTA expenses had regularly exceeded income, Bernard had been making up deficits from her own pocket, including those created by legal expenses. In a letter telling Marcia Scully about the unexpected bequest, she wrote, "I can finally worry about something other than where my next organic orange is coming from." She also imagined the money left to the LPTA being used to help re-energize the tenant ownership plan, which Shapiro-Bertolini had strongly supported. In the letter to Scully, she asked the attorney for her opinion about trying to meet with the landlord, saying she hoped that "you still think this project viable and its half-crazed activists still capable of rational thought."

The negotiations that failed to bear fruit five years earlier had been with James Coxeter and TransAction attorneys, but Coxeter seemed to have quietly faded from the Lincoln Place scene, replaced without any formal notice by Robert Bisno, TransAction's chairman and CEO. For tenants who had dealings with them, the two men's personalities seemed strikingly different. Most found Coxeter to be polite and affable, projecting an image of a benevolent landlord willing to listen to tenants' points of view, although he was clearly trying to convince those tenants to support the redevelopment project. By contrast, residents found Bisno to be much harder-edged, a businessman first and foremost who wasn't used to letting things stand in his way, although this quality did not fully manifest itself in the beginning of his tenure as the face of Lincoln Place ownership. In fact, when Sheila Bernard contacted him to broach the possibility of new negotiations for a tenant purchase, he readily agreed to an informal meeting to talk about it.

In a show of possible accommodation, he said he would come to her apartment. "He was friendly and candid," Bernard wrote in the August LPTA newsletter. But he clearly had no desire to sell, telling her that he regularly got offers for the property that were double what the LPTA had offered in 1992 and 1993. "He is not accepting any offers," she wrote, "because he still wants to create a condominium community on this property. His vision has not changed. He is waiting for an opportune time to propose his plan to the city again. He is every bit as clear and determined as we are."

She closed her description of the meeting on a mixed note of hope and resignation. "I am an optimist who believes in miracles and ironic twists of fate. Even so, the prospect of several more years of waiting and wondering is a bit daunting and we have to think this through." To that end, she offered practical suggestions. Tenants should avoid anything that might give the landlord cause to evict them, such as being late with their rent or getting into disputes with neighbors or management staff. Tenants should work with their neighbors on issues like poor maintenance that affected their buildings. They should always maintain a civil tone in their contacts with the management. She ended by writing, "I hope Lincoln Place can be for you, as it has been for me, a place of dreams both realized and as yet unrealized, a place of cozy social, political, and artistic connections, a place you can call home."

In the 1999 city election, Ruth Galanter easily won a third four-year term on the city council, but with matters in the hands of the courts, there wasn't much she could do on the political front. In that election, voters approved a new city charter that gave the mayor more authority over city departments and commissions, and established the neighborhood council system, but how significantly the change would alter the balance of power between the mayor and the city council wasn't totally clear. Just as unclear was the potential effect, if any, the changes would have on the future of Lincoln Place.

But as the year drew toward a close, Bernard got an idea. She had read Gail Sansbury's master's thesis and EIR comment letter arguing for the property's historical and cultural significance. She knew that the city had a cultural heritage commission empowered to designate notable houses, commercial buildings, and other properties as historic-cultural monuments, and she thought, "Why not Lincoln Place?" She wasn't interested in architectural preservation, per se, but saw the historic status as potential protection for tenants. While the designation wouldn't prohibit TransAction from demolishing everything, it would definitely make it more difficult. For one, it would trigger a CEQA provision requiring environmental review prior to the demolition of historically recognized properties. While the Lincoln Place owners had already conducted an EIR, the CEQA-mandated review would have to go further and study the feasibility of preserving the buildings. In addition, the city commission had the power to delay any demolitions for up to one year, a period in which, hopefully, a preservation plan acceptable to the landlord could be worked out. Monument status would also qualify the property for a tax break under a state law known as the Mills Act, which gave a property tax reduction to owners who agreed to preserve and maintain their property for a minimum of ten years, although signing up for it was voluntary, not required.

People were generally positive about Bernard's idea, although nobody had any idea of the work involved in preparing an application. She contacted an architectural firm in Hollywood that specialized in historical preservation, and on a warm, sunny day just after Christmas, she and Ingrid Mueller gave one of the firm's partners a brief tour of Lincoln Place. He agreed to write up a proposal with a fee for preparing an application and presenting it to cultural heritage commission.

On January 1, 2000, the banner headline on the front page of the *Los Angeles Times* announced that Russian president Boris Yeltsin had stepped down and handed the reins of power to Vladimir Putin, an act with far-reaching significance that few likely grasped at the time. Other articles concerned the hand-over of the Panama Canal, the end of an airline hijacking standoff in Afghanistan, and the annual Tournament of Roses Parade in Pasadena. A small, one-column headline read, "Dark Worries: Despite worry of a possible disaster, the world economy took Y2K in stride." Other articles evinced an air of optimism about the beginning of the twenty-first century—smart appliances were on the way to people's homes, and it would soon be possible to sit at a computer and create a custom menu and have the meal delivered to the door. The change from Yeltsin to Putin boded well for Russia and its relations with the rest of the world. Columnist John Balzar wrote of how the past century brought advances unimaginable at the beginning—television, computers, airliners—as well as catastrophes like the world wars and the Jewish Holocaust. "New Year's Day reminds us that tomorrow beckons from beyond our imagination. Toward this unknown, hope travels along with our apprehension. It always has."

That mixture of hope and apprehension pervaded the feelings of Lincoln Place tenants, especially those who had been at the barricades fighting to save the complex. Sheila Bernard and Ingrid Mueller still dreamed of an ideal community of tenant-owners, while others just wanted to live in peace and quiet, pay their monthly rent, and not worry about being forced to move. Aside from signs of neglected maintenance, Lincoln Place appeared as it did in 1950 when the first units were advertised for rent, in 1972 when the owners made an abortive attempt to convert it to condominiums, and in 1987 after TransAction began trying to evict longtime tenants. A stranger driving down its streets wouldn't have any inkling of its history or its possible future as something completely different.

Perhaps this aura of permanence lulled some tenants and others into thinking that the Lincoln Place battle was, to quote Macbeth, "full of sound and fury, signifying nothing." If so, the new year would soon prove them wrong. Bernard and Mueller and those who lent material and moral support to the LPTA would be confronted by events they couldn't have foreseen, that would test them in ways they couldn't have imagined when they first signed on to the fight to save their homes.

14

THE SAGA OF BUILDING 18

IN JEWISH TRADITION, THE number eighteen corresponds with the Hebrew word *chai,* which means "life." Those observant of the tradition consider the number good luck; for example, monetary gifts and charitable contributions are given in multiples of eighteen. The builders of Lincoln Place—Samuel Bialac and Philip Yousem—were Jewish, but whether they observed this tradition or believed in its power to bring good luck isn't known. Each of Lincoln Place's fifty-two buildings had multiple entrances and street addresses, so for identification purposes the buildings were assigned a number. Few outside the ownership and management had reason to know these numbers, but in the first year of the new millennium tenants throughout the complex became aware of number 18, the large, U-shaped building at the corner of Lake and Frederick Streets. It would become the site of high drama, and nobody would be able to say that the occupants of its twenty-eight units were blessed with anything resembling good luck.

Sheila Bernard, who grew up in a Jewish family, knew the significance of the number eighteen, although the irony of the tenants of Building 18 suffering misfortune was tenuous enough that it didn't occur to her until later. "The Saga of Building 18," as she called it in LPTA newsletters, began on February 22, 2000, when residents found a memorandum from Transaction CEO Robert Bisno on their doors. It read, "Please be advised that the building containing your apartment has been sold, effective immediately. All maintenance requests or other matters will go through the new owner's representative, Mr. Elly Nesis." Following this unexpected news was an address and telephone number for Nesis, a Venice realtor and owner of a property-management company. There was no further elucidation.

What did it mean? Was TransAction finally following through on its threat to redevelop or sell off the property parcel by parcel? And what did that bode for the fifty-odd residents of the building? Would they soon be facing eviction and the disheartening prospect of trying to find new homes? Finally, who was the new owner? A check of records at the Los Angeles County Recorder's office showed that title to the building's parcel had been transferred to a limited liability company named Pfeiffer Venice Properties. A further check of public records revealed that this company was owned by TransAction, which meant that the building hadn't been "sold" in the commonly understood sense of the word but put in the name of a new legal entity. All of Lincoln Place still belonged to TransAction. Why Bisno would want tenants to think otherwise was a mystery, as was the reason for hiring an outside manager for just one of Lincoln Place's fifty-two buildings.

The residents of Building 18 felt varying degrees of trepidation. Lincoln Place tenants had long been given a grace period of five days after the first of the month to pay their rent, but under the new management, those who didn't get their rent checks to the office on the first were served with three-day notices to pay or quit. As long as the rent was paid within the three days, nothing would happen, but if there was so much as a single day beyond that period, the landlord could legally initiate eviction proceedings. This posed a particular problem for tenants who had been in habit of taking their checks or money orders to the manager's office on the property, because now they were directed to mail or deliver that money to Elly Nesis's office near the beach, a mile away. An attempt was also made to evict a Building 18 tenant on the grounds that his cluttered apartment created a nuisance, and while ultimately unsuccessful, others wondered if some pretext might be found to try to evict them as well. Finally, residents noticed two things that further aroused fears that the landlord wanted them out of the building so that it could be torn down, or perhaps remodeled to attract higher-paying tenants. One, vacated apartments that had always been quickly re-rented were standing empty. And two, maintenance was clearly being neglected. Lawn sprinklers, for example, hadn't been turned on since the announcement that

Nesis would be the new manager, the result being that grass soon turned yellow and other plants began to wither and die.

Sheila Bernard kept a close eye on these developments, but her immediate focus was on getting Lincoln Place designated as a city historic-cultural monument. The consultant who toured the property the previous December had submitted a bid of $5,500 to prepare an application to the cultural heritage commission, plus $95 an hour to shepherd it through public hearings. While those amounts didn't seem unreasonable, Bernard decided to do the work herself, with help from Gail Sansbury, who was well-versed on Lincoln Place's history, and a tenant named Michael Palumbo, who was chair of the modern committee of the Los Angeles Conservancy, the city's major nonprofit advocacy group for historic preservation. She sensed—correctly, as it turned out—that the LPTA would need that money to defend tenants against a landlord determined to get rid of them. What she didn't know was how thoroughly the perils of Building 18 tenants would occupy her time and attention, and how eventful the year 2000 would prove to be after the relative lull that had settled over Lincoln Place following the city council's 1995 rejection of the redevelopment plan.

At that point, she and Laura Burns hadn't met even though they lived within a few minutes' walk of each other's apartments. But that was about to change. One evening in early July, Burns was watching a public affairs program on TV when she saw a piece about an apartment complex in the San Fernando Valley called Chase Knolls. The 260-unit complex in the community of Sherman Oaks had been nominated as an historic-cultural monument, and the city council would be taking up that nomination the very next day. Although her father had been a builder, Burns hadn't grown up with any particular interest in architecture, but her husband had friends who were architects and had collaborated with several on art projects. And she had lived in Europe where there were highly visible examples of the kind of garden city design that distinguished Lincoln Place. Council meetings were broadcast live on the city's public cable channel, and she decided to tune in.

Although Chase Knolls was less than a third the size of Lincoln Place, the two complexes had much in common. Besides the garden city–inspired design, with abundant open space, courtyards, and buildings that differed in size and orientation, both were built after World War II to house returning veterans and working families. Both were financed by FHA-guaranteed loans and owned by the same families for years before being sold to developers who didn't envision themselves as landlords of elderly and working-class tenants paying below-market rents. In the case of Chase Knolls, which took its name from the dairy farm that once occupied the site, the new owners bought the property in early 2000 and almost immediately announced plans to demolish everything and build a much larger luxury apartment complex. Depending upon age and parental status, tenants were offered up to $15,000 to move out; those who declined faced the very real prospect of eviction.

But just as Lincoln Place tenants did thirteen years earlier, the residents of Chase Knolls fought back. They formed a residents' association and campaigned for public support to preserve their homes, an effort that bore fruit when their city councilman, Mike Feuer, nominated the complex for historic-cultural monument status. On the morning of July 11, 2000, Burns watched on her living room TV as the city council took up the matter. More than one hundred tenants and their supporters filled the chamber; among the speakers urging the council to approve the designation were neighborhood residents, historic preservationists, and ninety-two-year-old Penny Singleton, a Chase Knolls tenant who won fame playing the comic-strip heroine Blondie Bumstead in numerous motion pictures. Despite strenuous objections from the owners and speakers representing real estate interests, the council unanimously voted for approval.[41] It wasn't an ironclad guarantee against demolition, but the immediate threat of tenants being forced to leave was lifted.

Photographs of the apartment complex were displayed in the council chamber, and Burns was struck by the similarity of the buildings to those at Lincoln Place. "It has to be the same architect," she remembers saying to her husband, who was home that morning. "If that place gets historic status, then Lincoln Place should too." At that moment a road appeared in her mind, although she didn't know exactly where it would lead or how winding it might prove to be. In the afternoon she got in her car and took the I-405 freeway over the Sepulveda pass to the San Fernando Valley and then the 101 freeway to Sherman Oaks, a journey of seventeen miles. Chase Knolls occupied a nine-acre site on Riverside Drive, just a block from the freeway, and when she parked her car and walked around, the resemblance to Lincoln Place—the architecture, the placement of the buildings, the landscaping—was even more striking.

The next day, she walked the short distance to Sheila Bernard's apartment and knocked on the door. She introduced herself and explained her interest in Lincoln Place's history, and in turn, Bernard told her about the effort underway for historic designation and showed her what Sansbury had written, including the fact that Heth Wharton was the architect of both Lincoln Place and Chase Knolls. This confirmed Burns's instinct, but she was disappointed by the sparseness of detail about Wharton. Lincoln Place was too beautifully designed, she thought, to have so little publicly known about its architect. When she had the time, she decided, she would try to find out more.

Burns had seen news of the management change at Building 18 in an LPTA newsletter, and Bernard told her that TransAction undoubtedly had plans to do something, not only with that building, but with others in the complex. In fact, a month before the city council voted to grant historic status to Chase Knolls, concrete evidence of that intention had come in the form of the following notice from Elly Nesis to Building 18 tenants: "Your parking privilege on the premises is being suspended effective 7/8/2000. Do not park your vehicle in the parking area. Accordingly, your rental amount is being lowered at the rate of $50.00 per month effective 7/8/2000." The parking area in question consisted of two banks of carports between the north and south wings of the building, but the tenants were given no reason why they could no longer park there.

When one of them showed Sheila Bernard the notice, she immediately had questions. First and foremost, what exactly was TransAction planning? And could the landlord just unilaterally take away parking privileges? Would that somehow run afoul of the RSO? The curt tone of the notice struck her as offensive, and the absence of any explanation for the change that would force building residents—some of whom were elderly or had disabilities—to find scarce parking on the street showed a striking indifference to tenant welfare. Generally polite and congenial, Bernard was anything but meek and complaisant when she believed that tenant rights were under threat. She would do everything in her power to help the tenants of Building 18 resist the loss of their parking privileges as well as whatever else was coming.

She began by contacting an attorney she had met in the early 1990s when both served on the board of directors of the California Mutual Housing Association, a nonprofit group that worked to preserve and expand low-income housing. The lawyer, David Etezadi, who also did work for the ACLU, told her that when Lincoln Place was built, the city required one on-site parking space per unit. Hence, the twenty-eight spaces in Building 18's carports. But unless a landlord had a valid reason to temporarily put those spaces off-limits, such as repaving the parking area or doing some other construction work, the tenants couldn't be legally forced to give up those spaces in exchange for a rent reduction.

Bernard sent the tenants a letter informing them of these facts and inviting them to a meeting at her apartment. She checked with the city's department of building and safety to see if permits had been recently issued for work at Lincoln Place, but there weren't any on file under any of the seven addresses associated with the building—two on Lake Street, three on Frederick Street, and two on Elkhart Place, the street that ran along the south side. Still, those who came to the meeting at Bernard's apartment were deeply concerned. The tenant grapevine had been buzzing with a rumor that the landlord planned to turn the building into luxury housing, and putting the carports off-limits might be connected to that plan. Given the unfriendly tone of communications from Elly Nesis and the clearly neglected maintenance, this rumor seemed plausible. But Bernard reminded those gathered in her apartment that a decade had passed since James Coxeter first announced TransAction's plan to tear down all of Lincoln Place, and every building in the complex was still standing. She urged the tenants to resist. Just because they got a notice or were threatened with eviction, they didn't have to immediately pull up roots and bid goodbye to the place they called home.

She composed a form letter that tenants could sign and send to Elly Nesis. It began: "You have contacted me saying that my parking location is to change. This letter is to notify you that I will not be changing my parking location." The letter stated that the landlord had to go through a legal process in order to change tenant parking privileges. It also went on to make a number of maintenance requests, and complained about the lack of a resident manager whom tenants could call or physically contact in the case of an after-hours emergency such as a serious plumbing leak or electrical outage. If the residents called the main Lincoln Place office, they were told that Building 18 was managed by Elly Nesis and all maintenance requests, emergency or otherwise, had to be directed to his office. While TransAction still owned the building, the company had apparently divested itself of responsibility for the well-being of its occupants.

Finally, Bernard made a formal complaint to the code enforcement unit of the city housing department about the threatened loss of parking spaces. That complaint elicited an unexpected response—the city *had* issued a building permit, but the address the owner provided wasn't one of the seven associated with Building 18. This permit called for the construction of new carports with fifty-six parking spaces, double the existing number. That was bad news in two respects. One, the landlord might have legal grounds to force tenants to temporarily give up their parking spaces, and two, it added credence to the rumor that TransAction was going to do work designed to attract higher-paying tenants, ones who would expect the two off-street parking spaces per unit that had become standard for new apartment complexes.

Up to that point, neither Nesis nor anyone associated with TransAction had attempted to explain to residents what was going on. However, tenants began getting a new communication from Nesis that acknowledged the plan to build new carports. But instead of being forced to park on the street, they would be assigned a temporary space elsewhere on the property and given a $100 reduction in their monthly rent. Again, this was presented as a *fait accompli*, not a matter of tenant discretion. And again, Bernard urged resistance, even though the $100 was a meaningful amount for many of the working-class tenants. Where would these spaces be? Close by, or in some far corner of the thirty-eight-acre complex? She also thought the permit to build the new carports might be invalid because it had an incorrect address, although getting it voided on those grounds was likely a long shot. More significantly, the existing carports couldn't be legally torn down without a demolition permit, and there didn't seem to be any such permit on file with the city.

At the beginning of August, Bernard wrote another letter to Building 18 tenants telling them "to watch for anyone with a big truck. You need to listen for any noise that sounds like demolition." If they saw or heard such things, they were to call Bernard or one of several other LPTA members whose numbers were listed. "After you call us, some of us will come and do our best to stop the demolition of the garage by talking to the workers who are there. We will explain to them that we will not permit them to destroy the garage illegally. If you can, please join us."

Not long after sending this letter, she got word that a chain-link fence had been put up to block access to the carports, with a security guard posted to direct tenants away. At the same time, she was approached by a resident who told her that Elly Nesis had offered $4,000 and sixty days' notice to leave if the tenant signed a waiver of all rights under the city's Rent Stabilization Ordinance. The landlord's intention, the tenant told her, was to completely remodel all the units and turn the open lawns around the building into private yards with fences and locked gates. The units would rent for at least $2,000 a month, more than double what any current tenant in the building was paying.

In the next few days she heard from others who had gotten the same offer. In response, she would explain that the LPTA was exploring legal avenues to protect everyone from eviction, but she couldn't blame anyone who chose the money over the uncertainty and grief that could come from doing battle with a company like TransAction, even though the rental market was such that finding a decent apartment in the area for the rent they were paying at Lincoln Place was highly unlikely. They would face the choice of straining their budgets to pay higher rents, or moving to a less desirable area farther from jobs and schools. In either case, the $4,000 could quickly disappear.

The city's twenty-one-year-old rent control ordinance had always allowed landlords to evict tenants in order to do major rehabilitation work on their units, and TransAction had cited this provision when it attempted to evict Lincoln Place tenants in 1987. While the city council had subsequently amended the provision to make these evictions more difficult, the LPTA and other tenant groups had always advocated for getting rid of it altogether. While rents were stagnant or even falling through much of the 1990s, the provision mostly gathered dust, but when property values and demand for apartments began to soar toward the end of the decade, owners of rent-controlled properties turned again to major rehab work as justification for evicting tenants and renting their vacated units at significantly higher rates.

Landlords had to show that the rehab work wasn't just cosmetic and would render a unit uninhabitable for at least forty-five days. Evicted tenants had a right of first refusal to return to their units when the work was done, and twenty-five percent of the rehabbed units had to be rented at rates the city classified as affordable. But if the tenants in those units moved out voluntarily, the requirements wouldn't apply, a fact that appeared to underlie TransAction's strategy of enticing Building 18 tenants to leave with "relocation" payments above and beyond those required by the city. The company, it was presumed, didn't want to put serious money into remodeling the building and then be forced to rent up to seven of the apartments for less than half what it could get for the other units. Tenants taking the enhanced payments would have to sign away their rights under the RSO, including the right to return, but if everyone accepted, nothing stood in the way of turning the property into a building of twenty-eight luxury apartments generating well over $50,000 a month. Nothing, that is, except any tenants who refused the offers and forced the landlord to evict them.

But even if tenants rejected the TransAction offers and were evicted, how many would want to go through the time and expense of finding a new place to live just to pull up stakes a few months later and move back to Lincoln Place? In Sheila Bernard's view, the best protection for tenants was resistance—just saying no to TransAction's offers and staying put. After all, nobody knew exactly what work the landlord was planning and whether it rose to the level required by the major rehab provision. In the worst case, tenants who were legally evicted would have the right to return if they chose to. And even if none did, the fact they were evicted would trigger the requirement to preserve seven of the rehabbed units for people without the means to pay luxury-level rents.

While this drama unfolded, Bernard and Gail Sansbury, who had since graduated from UCLA and was teaching at California State Polytechnic University in Pomona, were putting the finishing touches on the application to the city's cultural heritage commission. It relied heavily on Sansbury's research into the garden city movement and the intersection of modernist design with postwar housing policy. "The architecture and history of Lincoln Place exemplify the profound effect of postwar national housing policy not only on neighborhoods, but on the entire building industry," the application stated.

It took an indirect swipe at TransAction's efforts to create a community of fenced and gated buildings by noting that the complex was only a short distance from a heavily trafficked commercial street. "Yet, traveling the half-block to Lincoln Place from Lincoln Boulevard, one of the busiest streets in Los Angeles, one experiences a sudden, striking transition to a quiet neighborhood which feels insulated, in spite of the lack of gates, fences, berms, or any other physical barrier."

The application stated that architect Heth Wharton was active in designing houses and commercial buildings in the 1920s and '30s, but added that he was "something of a shadowy figure" where Lincoln Place was concerned. Ralph Vaughn's role as principal designer of the complex was still unknown to tenants and others involved in historic preservation; when Sheila Bernard signed and dated the application on September 9, 2000, he was ninety-three-years-old and living in obscurity in Stockton, California, a San Joaquin Valley city east of San Francisco. He would die just six weeks later, an important figure in the city's social and architectural history, but invisible to people living in one of his most significant achievements.

That September would prove to be one of the most eventful—and harrowing—months in the saga of Lincoln Place. Three days after submitting the application to the cultural heritage commission, Bernard learned that Pfeiffer Venice Properties, the legal entity that owned Building 18, had gotten permits to remodel all the units. Wiring and plumbing pipes were to be replaced, new fixtures installed, and square footage added to the second story to create four three-bedroom apartments.

At the same time, a crew showed up to tear down the carports. Bernard attempted to talk to the workers but was kept away by security guards; calls to the city and even the police to complain about this work proceeding without a demolition permit seemed to fall on deaf ears. By then, only fifteen units were occupied; a number of tenants had taken the $4,000 offer and moved out, and several others were considering it. Bernard hoped that ten or eleven would hold out, but conditions were becoming increasingly intolerable. Crews had shown up to begin the electrical and plumbing work in vacant apartments, and people at home had to endure noise, dust, and the other disruptions that come from living in the middle of a construction zone. Bernard found herself sending emails to Elly Nesis complaining of problems—workers leaving the laundry rooms filthy; workers and security guards using the bathroom in a vacant upstairs unit, tromping up and down the stairs all hours of the day and night; water being shut off and not turned back on; holes being knocked through the walls of still-occupied apartments.

But unlike James Coxeter, who had usually been friendly and seemingly willing to listen to tenants' concerns even as he promoted the TransAction redevelopment, Robert Bisno took a harder line with those who opposed the company's plans. On September 20, Bernard and the LPTA, along with eleven other tenants, were served notices that they were being sued in Los Angeles County Superior Court by Pfeiffer Venice Properties. The formal charges were intentional interference with economic advantage, negligent interference with economic advantage, intentional destruction of personal property, civil conspiracy, and unfair competition. The lawsuit asked for a minimum of $25,000 in damages from each defendant who, in addition to Bernard, were LPTA steering committee members Ingrid Mueller, Frieda Marlin, Rosemary Murphy, and Ruth Holzgreen; four other tenants who were LPTA supporters; one tenant of Building 18; and former LPTA treasurer Stan Dounn, who had moved away from Lincoln Place almost three years earlier.

What had these tenants—for whom legal fees and judgments would almost certainly be financially devastating —done to incur the wrath of their well-to-do corporate landlord? The lawsuit claimed that they had conspired to "frustrate and delay renovations and improvements" in order to lower the value of the property and prevent the owner from receiving fair market rents. This conspiracy, the lawsuit alleged, was part of a scheme to coerce the owner into selling the property to the tenants at a below-market price. And exactly how had the defendants advanced their nefarious conspiracy? For one, they had encouraged tenants of Building 18 to refuse to vacate their parking spaces, which constituted a breach of rental agreements. Sheila Bernard, the lawsuit alleged, had gone so far as to try to block a tow truck called to remove a car belonging to a noncompliant tenant. One of the defendants, the lawsuit claimed, had forged a signature on the form letter Bernard had given to the building tenants to inform the landlord of refusal to give up parking spaces. The lawsuit also accused the defendants of engaging in "numerous" acts of vandalism for the purpose of raising the owner's operating costs. These included the removal and destruction of signs put up to inform tenants that they could no longer park in the carports, and the deliberate opening of water valves and breaking of sprinkler pipes in an attempt to flood the grounds. The only Building 18 tenant named in the lawsuit, a woman named Laura Ponce, was accused of putting foreign objects in the door locks of the unit with the bathroom used by security guards and workers, rendering those locks unusable and necessitating replacement.

To many, the Lincoln Place story had always looked like a David-versus-Goliath struggle, but without the biblical climax. Now, it seemed, Goliath was throwing the full force of his army against David because the latter had heaved a pebble in the giant's direction. The vandalism claims, even if true, were minor and surely didn't merit a full-blown lawsuit. As for the allegations regarding the devaluation of the property, weren't the tenants just exercising their constitutional rights in opposing the landlord's plans? Even if their ultimate goal was tenant ownership? In any event, the tenants would be forced to defend themselves, and Bernard again called David Etezadi to ask if he could help. Despite the fact that the LPTA had very little money to pay legal fees, the attorney readily promised to do what he could.

But as the old adage goes, "When it rains, it pours," Almost before Bernard and the others could draw their breaths, they got news that a superior court judge had issued a ruling in TransAction's 1996 lawsuit seeking to overturn the city's rejection of the Lincoln Place redevelopment plan. And it was jarring news indeed. The judge, Dzintra Janavs, found that the city's primary rationale for denying the project—that it would result in a permanent loss of affordable housing—conflicted with the state's Ellis Act guarantee of a landlord's right to leave the rental business. Janavs, a Latvian native who would make news in her own right six years later when she lost an election to retain her judicial office, did not immediately order the city to approve the project but scheduled an October hearing to hear arguments on the question of how her ruling should be implemented.[42]

Did this mean that TransAction would soon start tearing down buildings? Councilwoman Ruth Galanter reacted with a statement obviously meant to palliate those fears. The court decision, she said, "did not order the city of Los Angeles to allow the developer to tear down Lincoln Place and build condominiums. What it did say is that if the city is going to deny the developer condominiums, it has to be on grounds other than preservation of affordable housing." She went on to accuse TransAction of what had long seemed obvious—looking for ways to get rid of low-paying tenants in order to raise rents. "The developer is trying to threaten the elderly low-income residents of Lincoln Place in order to scare them into moving so that they can avoid the city's Rent Stabilization Ordinance and rent the units at market rates." She concluded with the caveat "Don't be fooled by their tactics."

Unsurprisingly, Robert Bisno objected to the councilwoman's statement, telling an *Argonaut* reporter that the company was definitely not using the decision as a scare tactic. He noted that the city was likely to appeal the decision, which made any action on the redevelopment project premature. He also reiterated what TransAction had first promised in response to a demand by the city planning commission back in 1995, that no tenant would be forcibly evicted in the course of the redevelopment and whoever wanted to stay at Lincoln Place without any rent increase would be able to do so.[43]

At this point, the company still hadn't made any formal announcement regarding Building 18, but rumors circulated widely that its plan was to eventually remodel all fifty-two Lincoln Place buildings and turn each into a luxury premises surrounded by fences with locked gates. But if those rumors were accurate, how would that plan be affected by the lawsuit ruling? If

TransAction still wanted to tear everything down to build condominiums, would the work on Building 18 be suspended? In the absence of any word from the owner, tenants could only guess.

But the month of September wasn't finished throwing curves at the LPTA. It had distributed notices of its semiannual yard sale to be held November 19, and just as it had since the first sale nine years earlier, management warned that the event would violate Lincoln Place regulations. The LPTA's response had always been that renters had the same rights as homeowners to hold garage and yard sales, so the matter had turned into a kind of dance, with the LPTA scheduling spring and fall sales and the landlord issuing warnings. While Lincoln Place Tomorrow had taken the landlord's side and a few tenants had grumbled about increased traffic and strangers coming on the property, most had embraced the opportunity to sell unwanted items and see what their neighbors had to sell, which had come to include such things as baked goods, crafts, and artworks.

Nobody was surprised that the latest sale announcement elicited another warning. It came in the landlord's September newsletter, among notices of such mundane matters as management office hours and garage inspections. But this warning had a more ominous tone. In all caps that contrasted markedly with the lowercase text of the rest of the newsletter, it read, "YARD SALES ARE NOT ALLOWED. IF OUR SECURITY PEOPLE OR OFFICE STAFF SEE A YARD SALE FLYER THE VIOLATOR WILL BE NOTIFIED THAT THE SALE CANNOT TAKE PLACE. IF A SALE IS IN PROGRESS THE RESIDENT WILL BE TOLD STOP IMMEDIATELY. THERE ARE NO EXCEPTIONS."

Despite all the past threats, management had never physically disrupted a sale, and Sheila Bernard had no reason to believe that this time would be different. It was just more saber-rattling meant to intimidate tenants. But she and eleven of those tenants were being sued for what, in her view, was the exercise of their constitutional rights, so she couldn't be sure that the landlord wouldn't escalate the ongoing yard sale dispute. She had no intention of canceling the sale, but she would need to warn participants that they might be harassed. And it seemed to her that harassment of the LPTA had indeed become a major element of TransAction's strategy to break down tenant opposition to its plans, whatever those plans ultimately proved to be.

15

SCROOGE IN VENICE

LAURA PONCE'S CEMETERY MARKER is engraved with the dates of her birth and death—January 23, 1947, and October 28, 2003—in both English and Hebrew, along with the inscription, "Our Love Follows You Beyond the Stars." The black granite stone is one of thousands set in the verdant slopes of Sholom Memorial Park, a Jewish cemetery at the foot of the San Gabriel Mountains in the far northeast corner of Los Angeles's San Fernando Valley. Less than a half-dozen miles from a freeway and the bustle of a major metropolis, the site is notably quiet and bucolic, a fitting place of repose for a woman who vainly sought respite from the troubles that marked the final years of her life.

Ponce moved to Lincoln Place in October 1987, not long after separating from her husband of fourteen years. The rent for her one-bedroom apartment at 1012 Frederick Street was $695 a month, more than double what some long-term residents were paying, although she didn't know it at the time. She also didn't know that just three months earlier the landlord had served eviction notices on ten of those tenants—the opening act of the drama that would pit landlord against tenants for the foreseeable future. She was just happy to settle into the second-floor apartment with its sunny balcony and west-facing living room window that looked out onto a row of Mexican fan palms along the back wall of the shopping center across the street.

By the time TransAction announced plans in 1990 to demolish Lincoln Place and build upscale condominiums, she was very much aware of the LPTA and its opposition to those plans. She wasn't part of the faithful who marched in demonstrations and piled into buses to go to city hall hearings, but she supported the group's efforts and signed the 1995 tenants' petition that overwhelmingly opposed redevelopment. Both Sheila Bernard and Ingrid Mueller knew her as a friendly but private person who seldom talked about herself. They also sensed that she was a kindred spirit, a woman who would stand up for her beliefs and not let herself be pushed around. Mueller paid visits to her apartment, which had an upright piano in the living room, and a garden of carefully tended potted plants on the balcony. A spry, compact woman, she could regularly be seen riding a bicycle in the direction of the beach, where she would take a refreshing plunge in the cold ocean water.

Unfortunately, by the time she was one of the tenants sued by Pfeiffer Venice Properties, she had been diagnosed with lupus, an autoimmune disorder that caused her to suffer chronic pain and fatigue. She didn't want to move from Lincoln Place, and wasn't tempted by the landlord's $4,000 offer, which would mean finding a new apartment, packing up everything she had surrounded herself with to make a genuine home, and enduring the considerable labors of moving. Anxiety and stress exacerbated her physical symptoms, and without knowing exactly how her condition would progress, she just wanted to live the years she had left in peace and quiet. But this entirely reasonable desire was in direct conflict with the landlord's desire to create a building of luxury apartments for people willing and able to pay $2,000 a month or more in rent. It also conflicted with a view of rental housing as a commodity subject to the laws of supply and demand, a product allocated, not according to need, but to the consumer's ability to pay. In this view, Laura Ponce's apartment was her home only in the sense of a temporary shelter. It belonged to Robert Bisno and his corporate creation, and any alternate conception clashed with the sanctity of his right to make as much money as possible from his property.

By the middle of October 2000, everyone but Ponce and four other tenants had taken the landlord's $4,000 offer and moved out. The building had turned into a construction zone, with workers gutting vacant apartments, uprooting trees and shrubbery and digging trenches in the lawns. Work began early, and those still in the building would get up some mornings to find that the water had been shut off, or that there was no gas for cooking.

One of those mornings, without any notice to the residents, workers began taping plastic sheeting over apartment windows. A truck pulled up in the street, a large hose was unfurled and a man aimed a high-pressure blast of sand at the building's stucco walls. For those inside their units, the roar of the operation was nearly unbearable, but even more alarming was the cloud of dust that rose and settled in a fine layer on windowsills and door thresholds and seeped through the smallest gaps and cracks.

Sheila Bernard knew that Building 18 and others had been repainted over the years, and it was probable that lead-based paint had been used. The substance wasn't harmful if undisturbed, but if the dust raised by the sandblasting contained fine lead particles, it would clearly pose a health hazard for tenants and anyone else in the vicinity of the building. Workers were also stripping the roof and gutting vacant apartments, although vinyl floor tiles, window glazing, heater flues, and roof flashing commonly contained asbestos. Bernard knew that a section of the 1993 EIR for the redevelopment had called for an asbestos survey prior to any demolition or major renovation work, with abatement to be done by a professional contractor following strict procedures, including the sealing off of areas from which asbestos would be removed. She decided to call the South Coast Air Quality Management District (AQMD), the agency that regulated stationary sources of air pollution in the Los Angeles area. She also called the Los Angeles Fire Department, which had jurisdiction over the handling and disposal of hazardous materials.

Both agencies sent inspectors to the site. They told Bernard that proper procedures weren't being followed—for one, the sandblasting operation should be using water to keep down dust. They agreed that there was a high probability of lead in the old layers of paint. The AQMD inspector told workers that they should stop, but the agency took no formal action, and the sandblasting continued for a number of days, with windows left taped over at night, making it impossible for tenants to get outside ventilation. By this time, sand and dust had accumulated in hallways, stairwells, and balconies. Laura Ponce was furious that the plants she so lovingly tended on her balcony were coated with the gritty dust and had to be laboriously washed. The tenants in another unit had to take a child with asthma to the doctor when the condition worsened; they suspected the sandblasting as the cause, although that would be hard to prove.

Bernard also complained to the city's building and housing departments that the construction activity not only put tenants at risk, but represented a "diminishment of services" that violated their rental agreements. Ingrid Mueller took photographs of the building as work progressed, and some of those, as the adage goes, are "worth a thousand words." One, from the vantage point of Frederick Street, shows Laura Ponce's balcony filled with potted plants and her living room windows covered with curtains while the stucco on the wall of the unit directly below is mostly broken off, showing bare studs and gaping holes that were once windows. On the ground, wooden forms await the concrete foundation for the addition that will convert her one-bedroom apartment to three bedrooms. There is no fencing to keep people from wandering onto the property, just yellow security tape strung between wooden stakes, some of it drooping to the ground. The bare earth that was once a lawn is littered with pieces of lumber, concrete, and other debris.

In the apparent view of some city officials, though, the LPTA complaints were just part of the ongoing dispute with TransAction over redevelopment. According to Bernard, a building inspector told her that "you can't use the Department of Building and Safety as a weapon against the developer." It seemed that the city had come to regard her and the LPTA as nuisances, chronic complainers about every little thing, and she was afraid that even the steadfast support of Councilwoman Ruth Galanter might reach a limit, leaving tenants completely on their own to fight an implacable force that wanted them gone.

But all wasn't cause for despair. Good news came when the ACLU agreed to represent Bernard, Ponce, and the other defendants in the Pfeiffer lawsuit. In a public announcement on November 2, ACLU attorney Dan Tokaji said, "Scrooge came early to Venice this year. This lawsuit is a blatant attempt to intimidate tenants of limited means from exercising rights protected by the Constitution. We will not allow these tenants to be bullied or brow-beaten into silence through a frivolous, unfounded lawsuit." Tokaji said that he intended to file a motion to dismiss the lawsuit under

California's anti-SLAPP statute, the acronym standing for Strategic Lawsuit Against Public Participation.[44] Enacted in 1992, this law was meant to deter lawsuits filed for the purpose of quelling the public's right to free speech; for example, in cases of individuals or community groups finding themselves hauled into court and accused of inflicting financial harm because of their opposition to a real estate development or other private project.

"The Lincoln Place tenants gather signatures," Tokaji said. "They picket. They attend city council meetings. They educate their neighbors. That's why they've been slapped with this lawsuit, and those activities are all protected by the Constitution."

Predictably, the landlord took a different view. Attorney Allan Abshez told the *Los Angeles Times* that the defendants had destroyed locks, torn down posted notices, and flooded the property from outdoor faucets. "This lawsuit has nothing to do with the tenants' rights to speech," he said. "It's about vandalism and it's about people refusing to honor their leases and encouraging others to breach their leases."[45] Robert Bisno's reaction was publicly aired several days later, in an article in the weekly *Argonaut*. "There is no legal privilege for defacing my property," he said. "It is uncontested that tenants have damaged my property. The tenant association is living outside the law."[46]

One of the first orders of business for Tokaji was getting everyone but Sheila Bernard and Laura Ponce dismissed from the case, since there was no evidence that any were involved with the acts alleged by the lawsuit. The attorney solicited written declarations from some of these tenants, including seventy-six-year-old Frieda Marlin, who said, "When I got the summons in this case, I got sick because it was very traumatic for me." Marlin didn't live in Building 18, but her declaration painted a vivid picture of the precarious nature of her life and those of other elderly, long-term tenants who had been living for years in fear of being forced from their homes. Her rent, she said, was $740 a month, but her only income was $940 a month from Social Security. She listed some of her infirmities, including a heart condition, a knee replacement that made walking difficult, and macular degeneration that degraded her vision. In conclusion, she said, "Lincoln Place is my home. It is where most of my friends live. Other than my neighbors here at Lincoln Place, I have nobody except my son and my brother-in-law. We want our neighborhood and our community to be beautiful. We would never do anything to diminish the beauty of Lincoln Place."[47]

Abshez agreed to Tokaji's request, and Marlin and nine others were dropped from the lawsuit. A court hearing in the case wasn't expected before the end of the year, so Bernard and Gail Sansbury, with help from Laura Burns, turned their attention to the application for city historic-cultural monument status. Considering the fact that there were almost seven hundred such designations throughout the city, among them a former jail, a water-and-power-distribution station, and the famous Hollywood sign, it didn't seem a stretch to include a large garden apartment complex built under an innovative and historically significant federal housing program. But Bernard and Sansbury also knew that the cultural heritage commission would give considerable weight to the architecture, and therein lay a problem. Ralph Vaughn had died on October 20, but an obituary wouldn't appear in the *Los Angeles Times* and the *Los Angeles Sentinel* until the following April. His role as principal designer was still unknown to anyone involved with Lincoln Place and the LPTA.

The commission had scheduled the Lincoln Place matter for November 15, but the meeting was postponed to December 6 at the request of Robert Chattel, an architect hired by TransAction to analyze the nomination. This was worrisome, because Chattel, who specialized in historic preservation, had spoken against the Chase Knolls nomination when it came before the commission that past summer. In a *Los Angeles Times* report of the meeting, he made a notably dismissive comment about that complex with many similarities in terms of architecture and landscaping to Lincoln Place. Prefacing his remarks with the fact that he lived close to Chase Knolls and often drove past it, he said, "I have never felt compelled to stop and take a look at it. I do not find it interesting."[48]

TransAction had already submitted a letter of comment to the commission. Written by Andrew Fogg, a law firm colleague of Allan Abshez, it accused Sheila Bernard of "bad faith" in submitting the application for historic status. She wasn't concerned with historic values, he wrote, but was merely trying to "frustrate and delay implementation" of the court decision overturning the city's rejection of the plan. He concluded with a thinly veiled threat that TransAction would sue the city for damages if the historic status was approved.

It wasn't clear how Bernard's widely known efforts to stop the redevelopment would influence the commission. After all, many movements to give properties historic status, including the one started by Chase Knolls tenants, were motivated by the desire to save those properties from demolition and redevelopment. More concerning was the fact that commissioners were likely to give significant weight to the reputation of the architect, wanting to bestow historic status on works that were part of an architect's body of achievement in particular styles and genres. A building designed by Frank Lloyd Wright, for instance, would be considered more important historically than one designed by an architect almost nobody had heard of, even if those buildings had similar features. And while Heth Wharton wasn't totally unknown, there was almost no record of his activities after World War II, the period when Lincoln Place and other FHA-sponsored garden apartment projects were built.

In an effort to find out more, Laura Burns had volunteered to dig through newspaper archives and old magazines in local libraries. After hours of scrolling through microfilm and poring over magazines and other materials, she came across a reference to a Mary Oakley of Santa Barbara, California, who was identified as Heth Wharton's daughter. Burns found a Mary Oakley listed in the Santa Barbara phone book and called the number. The woman who answered was indeed Heth Wharton's daughter, and while she didn't remember anything specific about Lincoln Place, she was able to provide more details about his work, which included the design of houses for actors and others involved in the film business.

Her father had died in the late 1950s, she said, but even though he had grown up in a conservative Southern family he was very liberal and had been involved throughout his adult life in pro-union and antidiscrimination causes. Sansbury also talked to her, and the woman expressed great interest when told that the tenant's association was seeking historic status for Lincoln Place. Burns and Sansbury hoped that Oakley might be persuaded to make the hundred-mile trip to Los Angeles for the hearing, but the sixty-nine-year-old woman said she had health problems that would make such a trip impossible. But she would gladly write a supporting letter to the commission.

How these details about Wharton might help the cause of historic preservation was open to question, but Sansbury, Bernard and others believed that they certainly couldn't hurt. Then, just after the Thanksgiving Day weekend, excellent news came in the form of a commission staff report recommending approval. It called Lincoln Place "a good, unusually large site of mid-twentieth century affordable, Modern, garden apartment housing in Los Angeles and is one of a small group of examples of this scale." But optimism was tempered by a letter submitted at almost the same time by Robert Chattel. The letter opened with Chattel's conclusion that Lincoln Place didn't deserve historic status. It wasn't typical of the garden city movement, he wrote, and had no unique design features. Heth Wharton wasn't a master of his craft; his designs of Chase Knolls and Lincoln Place "derive from what he saw around him, rather than what a creative imagination could envision and his competency could implement." Despite his earlier dismissal of Chase Knolls as not worth stopping to look at, Chattel wrote that the San Fernando Valley complex did a better job of integrating buildings into the landscape. Raising the eyebrows of those who loved Lincoln Place for its ample lawns, trees and shrubbery, Chattel wrote that "Lincoln Place pales in comparison to Chase Knolls for the quality of its landscape planning, design and maintenance."

On December 6, as people were finding seats in the commission's meeting room on the tenth floor of city hall, much of the city's attention was focused on the disputed presidential election results in Florida, where George W. Bush had come out ahead of Al Gore in the November 7 election by fewer than two thousand votes. That dispute would officially end when the US Supreme Court stopped a manual recount of the votes, but on the day of the city hall hearing, the question of how the commission would vote on Lincoln Place was as open to speculation as how the Supreme Court was going to rule. The Chase Knolls vote didn't provide any clarity. The commission had deadlocked 2–2, with one member absent. Commissioners Kaye Beckham and Catherine Shick had supported the designation, while current commission president Holly Wyman and commissioner Robert Nizich had opposed it.

However, Shick and Nizich had since left the commission, and in their place, Mayor Richard Riordan had appointed Mary Klaus-Martin and Michael Cornwell. Lincoln Place supporters hoped that Beckham's affirmative vote for Chase Knolls was a positive sign, but where two more votes would come from was a matter of guesswork. Klaus-Martin was a founding member of the Los Angeles Museum of Contemporary Art and wife of a principal in one of the city's largest architecture firms; Cornwell was an entertainment insurance broker and member of the Los Angeles Conservancy. Since all members of the commission were appointed by a mayor widely regarded as pro-development, cynics believed that commissioners were certain to side with TransAction. Others hoped that the members would see the historic and cultural significance of an honest-to-goodness community with a diverse population in the middle of an area that was gradually turning into an enclave of the upper middle class and rich.

As the applicant, Sheila Bernard was the first public speaker. She was feeling a degree of dread because she had seen Abshez talking to several commissioners in the hallway outside the room before the meeting was called to order. It might have meant nothing, or it might have been a sign of which side the commission would take. She began by noting the remarks about hidden agendas and ulterior motives, but implored the commission to ignore those accusations and base its decision on the question of Lincoln Place's historic and cultural importance.

"I submit to you that Lincoln Place falls within the guidelines. I say this because Heth Wharton designed housing for people who were not rich and not famous: ordinary people. And this housing for ordinary people was actually extraordinary. Fifty years later, it still affords ordinary people an extraordinary degree of comfort and aesthetic pleasure on a modest income. In our view, providing not merely adequate but beautiful housing to working and retired renters, as the FHA purposefully did after World War II, is a cultural value worth preserving, a value worth emulating."

Also speaking in favor of the designation were Gail Sansbury and Michael Palumbo. "It's the best community I've ever lived in," Palumbo said. "Heth Wharton understood what community was about." But when Robert Chattel's turn at the microphone came, he characterized the architect in starkly different terms. "It's a nice place to live, but what does this educate us about?" He dismissed Wharton as "not a creative thinker."

After listening to these comments and discussing the application, the commission voted 4–1 against the designation. Klaus-Martin seemed to express the sense of the majority when she said that while she hoped that the integrity of the community would be preserved, she didn't believe that Lincoln Place was "a significant piece of architecture." Commissioner Cornwell cast the only vote in favor.

The Chase Knolls bid for historic designation had gone on to the city council even though the commission's vote had ended in a tie. But that was only because it was initiated by a city council member, not a private citizen, as in the case of Lincoln Place. Ever reluctant to give up despite disappointments and setbacks, Sheila Bernard wondered if Ruth Galanter might be persuaded to pluck it from the commission's reject pile. But that was a long shot. TransAction had already shown a willingness to follow through on threats of legal action, and this could make council members wary of getting embroiled in yet another Lincoln Place lawsuit. And because the designation had already been turned down by the commission, the council would need a two-thirds vote in favor, rather than a simple majority.

As the holidays approached, the future looked as unsettled as it ever had before, certainly more than the past several years. For one thing, TransAction had further escalated the long-running dispute over LPTA-sponsored yard sales by going to court to stop the sale scheduled the Sunday before Thanksgiving. The judge had refused to issue a temporary restraining order, ruling that the owner hadn't taken legal steps to stop the sales even though they'd been held every year since 1991. The judge also concluded that TransAction had failed to show that the sale would cause the company irreparable harm. But that wasn't the end of the landlord's threats. Ingrid Mueller, who had always been busy on sale days, putting out things of her own as well as helping with organization, found a menacing notice on her door five days before the sale. Titled "Notice to Perform Covenant of Rental Agreement or Quit," it was essentially a threat that if she participated in the upcoming yard sale, the landlord would start eviction proceedings against her.

Mueller soon learned that other tenants had gotten the same notice. In response, the LPTA distributed a bulletin written by Sheila Bernard that encouraged people wanting to participate in the sale to resist intimidation. The chances that the landlord could successfully follow through on the eviction threat were very small, she wrote, but if such an attempt was made, the LPTA would arrange for the tenant's legal defense. At the end, she posed a question, "Is the yard sale worth all this hassle?" and then proceeded to answer: "In our view, the owner is trying through intimidation to curtail our right to assemble, as well as our right to free speech. If we value our liberty, we will sometimes be called upon to fight for it. Even if an itty bitty yard sale seems like a small thing, it is a powerful symbol that democracy is for everyone, owners and renters alike."

The morning of November 19 was mild and sunny, perfect weather for an outdoor gathering. As in past years, tenants laid out blankets or set up tables and portable canopies on the lawns along a three-block stretch of Elkgrove Avenue. In a letter written that same day to ACLU attorney Daniel Tokaji, a tenant named Charles Kruger said he wasn't an LPTA member and had never participated in past yard sales, but had decided to check this one out because he was "outraged" by the landlord's threatening notice to tenants. He wrote that he had stopped at the LPTA table and was talking to Sheila Bernard when armed security guards appeared and began ordering everyone in the vicinity to disperse. Bernard, he said, told the guards that if they believed laws were being broken they should call the police, which they apparently did, because an LAPD patrol car soon appeared. The officers spoke to Bernard, who briefly filled them in on the ongoing dispute, but since there were no obvious law violations, they got back in their car and left. Shortly thereafter, Kruger wrote, the property manager showed up with a camera and notepad and began taking photographs and writing down the names of the participating tenants.

The landlord didn't follow through on the eviction threat, but shortly before Christmas, another notice to tenants added fuel to the uncertainty and anxiety. Signed by Robert Bisno, it announced that Elly Nesis would be taking over management of five buildings on Lake Street. While the notice gave no reason for the change, it was widely assumed that those buildings, with a total of fifty-nine apartments, were destined for the same fate as Building 18; that is, transformation into gated, luxury rentals. In fact, attorney David Etezadi, who was negotiating terms for the relocation of the five tenants still living in Building 18, sent a fax to Bisno in which he referred to the landlord's statement of intention to complete a "down-to-the-studs" remodel of every Lincoln Place building over the next two years. Unless, of course, the legal restraints to demolishing the entire complex and building new condominiums were finally banished for good. In any event, residents of those Lake Street buildings could expect to be told soon that they would have to move out. And any who refused could find themselves, like Laura Ponce and the other holdouts in Building 18, facing the threat of eviction while trying to carry on their lives in the middle of a construction zone.

The first day of 2001 saw more of the warm, sunny weather that had long made Southern California a magnet for migrants and tourists from the cold, snowy regions of the Midwest and East. The front page of the *Los Angeles Times* featured an article on violent clashes between Israelis and Palestinians, which threatened to sink former President Bill Clinton's attempts to revive peace talks, but there was little inkling that terrorist acts provoked by that conflict would visit the United States later in the year and lead to profound changes not only domestically but in much of the Middle East. Locally, eyes were on the upcoming city elections. Because of term limits, Mayor Richard Riordan was retiring after eight years, and a competitive race was developing between City Attorney James Hahn and Antonio Villaraigosa, the former speaker of the California State Assembly. The latter was seen as the stronger advocate for affordable housing and other progressive causes, and thus the campaign was being closely watched by the LPTA and tenant advocacy groups throughout the city.

The LPTA had also lent its support to calls for a citywide moratorium on evictions for major rehabilitation. Advocates asked why the city should allow people to be forced out of their rent-controlled apartments just because landlords believed they could get much higher rents. The intent of the provision, they argued, was to allow owners to do needed repair work, not to add amenities for renters willing to pay for luxury accommodations.

While Lincoln Place's Building 18 was an especially glaring example of this, a rising demand for rental housing was prompting landlords all over the city to once again invoke the major rehab provision to force lower-income renters out of their apartments.

Sheila Bernard and David Etezadi discussed this subject in a meeting in early January with Robert Bisno. According to an account by Bernard in the January LPTA newsletter, Bisno told them that if the city enacted a major rehab moratorium he would simply exercise his rights under the Ellis Act, evict every tenant, and tear down the entire complex. However, if the LPTA agreed to cooperate with his remodeling plan, he would include sixty units for low-income seniors.

Bernard wasn't tempted. In the newsletter, she wrote, "Unless we take a strong stand against destructive attacks such as Bisno's, such attacks will continue, with stable neighborhoods disappearing in the interest of increased wealth for the very few at the expense of quality of life for the many. In addition, even if sixty units were enough to take care of the remaining seniors and disabled residents at Lincoln Place (and sixty is not enough), what would happen to the neighbors and friends (the support system) of those seniors? The seniors would be isolated from neighbors who help them continue living independently. It is better to continue fighting for our rights and our community, even if we lose, rather than to cooperate with an owner who is harming our neighborhood and will go on to harm others." She concluded with the announcement that the subject would be discussed in depth at the LPTA's monthly meeting on January 13 at the Penmar Park recreation center.

By that time, Etezadi had negotiated a settlement for the five remaining tenants of Building 18. Each would get a relocation payment of $8,000, and, as compensation for the disruption caused by the construction work, reimbursement of the rent they paid the last four months of 2000. They would have ninety days to move out and wouldn't be charged any rent during that time. Depending upon the rent they currently paid and the date they moved out, the total value of the offer would be $12,000–14,000. In return, the tenants would sign agreements waiving their rights under the RSO, including the right to return when the transformation of the building was complete. They would also promise not to lend their names to any lawsuit against the landlord.

The rents the tenants paid ranged from $591 to $848 a month. The average rent for apartments in the Los Angeles metropolitan area was then approximately $1,200 a month, but significantly higher in the west-side area that included Venice. While $14,000 was a lot of money to the working-class tenants at Lincoln Place, the expense of moving, added to what would almost certainly be higher monthly rent, suggested that the money would have little long-term impact. Still, all the tenants but Laura Ponce accepted the offers. She sent a fax and letter by certified mail with a straightforward message to Elly Nesis and Robert Bisno.

"Gentlemen," it said, "This is to inform you that I do not intend to 'voluntarily vacate' my home at 1012 Frederick St., #3. In the event that an eviction action is filed against me, it will be contested. Should you prevail in such an action, I will exercise my rights under any and all applicable law, including but not limited to those enumerated in the Rent Stabilization Ordinance."

Once the four other tenants agreed to move, Ponce's eviction was presumed to be a matter of when, not if. She and Bernard also faced a rapidly approaching court date in the Pfeiffer Venice Properties lawsuit, scheduled for hearing on February 26 before superior court judge Gregory O'Brien. As usual in such cases, there was speculation about how the judge might view the antagonists—a corporate property owner represented by lawyers from one of the city's large, prestigious law firms and a pair of tenants of no particular stature defended by the ACLU. Would he sympathize with the tenants, or with a company trying to protect its economic interests against lawless interference? Judge O'Brien was a Republican who had been on the bench for fourteen years, but other than being known for having something of a dry wit, there wasn't a lot to indicate how he might rule on the matter at hand, which was a motion by ACLU attorney Daniel Tokaji to dismiss the case under the state's anti-SLAPP law.

The morning of the hearing was chilly, with gray skies portending rain. Bernard made the trip downtown, but Laura Ponce stayed in her apartment since the judge would just be hearing from the attorneys and not taking testimony from any witnesses. Tokaji and another lawyer from a private firm who did pro bono work for the ACLU were there on behalf of Bernard and Ponce, while Allan Abshez represented the landlord. The judge had issued a tentative ruling, but only the lawyers had read it. When the judge invited Abshez to respond to this ruling, the attorney began by alluding to the central allegations of the lawsuit, that the locks to the apartment used by security guards as a bathroom had been jammed, that outside faucets had been turned on and allowed to run, that signs put up by the landlord had been torn down, and that a tenant's signature had been forged to one of the form letters Bernard had composed for tenants to use to inform the landlord of their refusal to vacate assigned parking spaces. The landlord, Abshez said, had been subjected "to an escalating campaign of vandalism and submission of fraudulent documents that not just, my client says, disrupted his tenant relationships, but individual tenants said it disrupted the tenants' relationships."

In response, the judge said that a security guard's declaration that Ponce was guilty of jamming the locks because she was the only one living on that floor wasn't proof that she did it. "But beyond that, assuming that you could prove that Ms. Ponce jammed two keys into a lock of a door of an apartment house is a very petty small claims case of the twenty-five-dollar variety. I don't know why your client chose to come to superior court to litigate a very petty small claims case."

Abshez responded by referring to a handwritten note that Ponce admitted putting on the apartment door telling security guards to use a bathroom elsewhere. In turn, the judge said, "Fine. Ms. Ponce wrote a note. You're going to sue Ms. Ponce even in small claims court for writing a note saying 'Don't Relieve Yourselves On These Premises'? That's an actionable claim?"

Abshez answered, "Your Honor, and the next day the lock was broken. The next day, the locks were broken again." To which the judge responded, "Then evict her if you don't like her." After some back-and-forth on the subject of grounds for eviction, he added, "Why are you here in superior court? Why would the landlord go to a silk-stocking law firm to bring this case in the Superior Court for two broken locks and a sign?"

Abshez asked the judge to let him explain, saying the reason was related to tenant interference with the demolition of the building's carports, but the judge said, "Your case has nothing to do with the parking structure. Maybe it did at one time, but all we're left with is two broken locks, a sign, and someone turning on the water. And you expect the L.A. Superior Court to entertain this case while you do what? Put these people through discovery, take their depositions, send out interrogatories, send out requests for admissions, require that they be present at mandatory settlement conferences, require that they be present for what, a jury trial? Excuse me?"

When Abshez attempted to speak, the judge interrupted. "You're going to put them through thousands upon thousands of dollars in expense in order to litigate two broken locks? Counsel, this is offensive. It's outrageous."

Abshez gamely continued, bringing up the removal and destruction of posted signs and the turning on of water faucets. The judge dismissed this by saying that no evidence had been put forward that either Bernard or Ponce was responsible. As to the issue of the water faucets, he said, "You haven't indicated there was any damage, let alone major damage, created by turning on the water faucets, simply that she turned them on. In the language of the law, big deal." The judge was equally dismissive of the claim that the tenant-landlord relationship had been disrupted when a tenant's signature was forged to one of the form letters Bernard had composed that said the landlord had to go through a legal process with the city to eliminate or change parking privileges.

"So what?" he said. "I don't care if it was signed by the pope. It says 'go through the legal process.' How does that interfere with anything?" He then concluded the hearing by saying, "Upstairs, counsel. Next stop, 300 Spring Street." Upstairs meant the Small Claims Court and 300 Spring Street was the address of the state office building where appeals to superior court rulings were filed.

When the hearing was adjourned, Tokaji showed Bernard the judge's tentative ruling, which would be the official order dismissing the case. The judge likened the lawsuit to "using a blunderbuss to kill a gnat" and wrote that it was "sufficiently offensive to cause the court to invoke its inherent powers to strike the complaint under the doctrine of *de minimis non curat lex*, and as improper, frivolous and abusive." That bit of Latin was a common-law principle whereby judges will not sit in judgment of extremely minor transgressions of the law. It has sometimes been restated as "the law does not concern itself with trifles."

In a public statement released the same day by the ACLU, Tokaji said, "This lawsuit was an abuse of the legal process. It was brought by a well-financed neighborhood bully to intimidate tenants brave enough to stand up for their rights. Today's ruling sends a loud and clear message that companies will pay a heavy price if they attempt to bludgeon community advocates through litigation."[49]

Bernard was happy and relieved, but didn't really expect Bisno to be permanently chastened. Too much was at stake. In order to realize the vision of a luxury building at the corner of Frederick and Lake Streets, he had to get Laura Ponce out of her apartment. In order to realize the vision of a 795-unit luxury apartment complex, he had to ultimately get all the tenants out of their apartments. And she knew he had the resources to file more lawsuits and do whatever was needed to achieve that goal, which meant that she and the LPTA were going to have to double their efforts to resist. Which in turn meant raising money, because not every legal action would involve constitutional issues falling within the purview of the ACLU, although the state's anti-SLAPP law allowed defendants like Bernard, Ponce. and the LPTA to seek attorney fees. And while the LPTA had agreed to assign such fees to the ACLU, the group would get a percentage of any money above and beyond the ACLU's costs.

By the middle of March, Ponce's apartment was the only one of the twenty-eight units still occupied, and a photograph taken at that time shows some of the plants flowering on her balcony. The roof had been stripped and covered with a tarp, but it had leaked in recent rains. and another photograph taken inside Ponce's unit shows a sheet of plastic on the floor, containers set to catch leaks, and damage the water caused to an upholstered chair. Why would anyone want to live under such conditions? In a formal declaration made as part of her fight to resist eviction, she put it this way. "I have refused to accept the landlord's offer and move because I do not want to leave my home. I have a debilitating disease, Lupus, and the symptoms are exacerbated by stress. I believe a move would be detrimental to my health. Additionally, I have limited income and do not want to give up the benefits of the controlled rent that I am presently paying."

Still, it was to the landlord's interest that she accept the offer made to the other tenants and voluntarily move, because eviction proceedings could delay the completion of the remodeling work and the renting of the building. But she kept making her intention to stay put abundantly clear, and on June 8, 2001, she was handed a thirty-day notice to vacate her unit, along with a $5,000 check, the relocation payment mandated by the RSO for elderly or disabled tenants. Her response was to fight back by enlisting the LPTA's help to hire Sonya Molho, the attorney who had represented the ten residents who faced eviction back in 1987.

Shortly before that, Councilwoman Galanter had submitted a motion to place a moratorium on major rehab evictions. Because the number of such evictions had nearly doubled from 1999 to 2000, the measure had considerable support on the council, but before it could be enacted it would have to be vetted by the city housing department, drawn up by the city attorney's office and go through committee and council hearings. At best, that would take months. And the measure wouldn't save Ponce, since moratoriums almost always exempted actions like evictions that were already underway.

Molho appealed Ponce's eviction on the grounds that it didn't meet the requirements of the major-rehabilitation provision. A hearing was held on October 8, 2001 in Los Angeles County Superior Court, where the attorney argued that the work, which included the demolition and reconstruction of the unit's kitchen and bathroom, the installation of new plumbing and electrical fixtures, the replacement of doors and windows, the addition of two bedrooms and a bathroom, and the raising of ceilings, was not the kind of rehabilitation work intended by the law even though it required permits. None of it was needed to bring the unit up to code, or to make repairs ordered by health or fire departments. In addition, the law required that the work render a unit uninhabitable for forty-five days, and she presented a declaration from a licensed contractor that necessary rehabilitation work on the unit wouldn't take that long.

The landlord's attorney countered these arguments by saying that the major rehabilitation provision didn't require the work to be mandated for health or safety reasons, and presented evidence that the remodeling would take longer than forty-five days. The judge, Debra Wong Yang, accepted the landlord's arguments, and ruled that the eviction was lawful. On October 22, that judgment was formally entered, and Ponce was faced with the choice of moving or being locked out of her apartment by county sheriff's deputies. She chose to move, leaving the place she had called home for fourteen years to live in the home of an acquaintance in the San Fernando Valley, almost thirty miles and a world away from Lincoln Place.

Her long, often lonely, often harrowing fight with the landlord was over. And almost exactly two years later, her body was laid to rest in a grave on a grassy hillside at Sholom Memorial Park.

16

THE VILLAGE AT VENEZIA

ON THE SATURDAY AFTER Labor Day in 2001, TransAction CEO Robert Bisno stood at a podium in front of an audience of more than fifty Lincoln Place residents gathered outside the management office that occupied a ground-floor apartment in a Frederick Street building. Some sat on rows of folding chairs on the lawn between the two wings of the building; others stood behind. With Bisno were Allan Abshez, TransAction's attorney, Elly Nesis, manager of nearby Building 18 and the five Lake Street buildings now slated to undergo major remodeling, and a pair of security guards. A large poster with an aerial view of Lincoln Place was set on an easel, with groups of buildings colored in bright hues—orange, magenta, purple, and green.

Laura Burns had to work that day, but she sent her husband, Bernard Perroud, with a tape recorder. As small planes taking off from the nearby Santa Monica airport regularly buzzed overhead, Bisno explained that the colors represented phases that would culminate in the complete remodeling of Lincoln Place, transforming it into a modern, vibrant complex called the Village at Venezia. The building that housed the management office and the one directly behind it, with a total of forty-four apartments, would be demolished and replaced by a recreational facility with a swimming pool and other amenities. A new building with forty-four units would also be built on the site, he said, but instead of rentals these would be condominiums. As the construction work progressed, all tenants would eventually have to move out, but they would be given ample notice and the relocation assistance mandated by the RSO.

The model for this new, improved Lincoln Place—or Village at Venezia—was Building 18, now completely remodeled except for the unit that would be occupied by Laura Ponce for another two months. Sheila Bernard had taken to calling it the "Frankenbuilding." To add more interior space to second-floor apartments, balconies had been enclosed and new balconies supported by wooden columns now jutted from the building's face. For Burns and others with a keen interest in Lincoln Place's architecture, this was a travesty, because the original design, with balconies set within building planes, had given the exteriors their sleek, modernist appearance. Decorative elements unique to each building, like wood motifs and glass inserts above the entries, had been removed. But even more distressing to those who valued Lincoln Place for the way its design promoted a mingling of tenants, Building 18 was now enclosed by a six-foot-high wrought iron fence with security gates at each of the seven entries. Fences also created private yards for each of those entries so that four units shared a private outdoor space. The only remaining public area was a narrow verge of lawn between the sidewalks and the perimeter fence. When all buildings were transformed this way, residents would no longer be able to wander freely, bump into their neighbors, gather on the lawns for birthday parties, barbecues, and the other social occasions. Lincoln Place would cease to be an honest-to-goodness community and become a large collection of individual apartment buildings.

Unlike Lincoln Place builders Samuel Bialac and Philip Yousem, who certainly wanted to make money but embraced a social purpose for their creation, Robert Bisno and those who worked for him appeared to see Lincoln Place through the eyes of investors intent on maximizing their returns, whether that be from stocks, commodities, or real estate. And to achieve their goal, they had to appeal to people with a degree of affluence, not seniors on fixed incomes or the kind of working-class families that Bialac and Yousem deliberately set out to attract. In a *Los Angeles Times* article three weeks after the September meeting with tenants, Bisno put it bluntly. "Affordable housing is not a profitable venture." The article described the plight of Wanda Wolski, a ninety-year-old Lincoln Place tenant living on Social Security who was in danger of losing her apartment because

TransAction had stopped accepting the federal government's Section 8 rental subsidy vouchers. She had lived at Lincoln Place almost thirty years, but she and others faced the same dire questions posed by the landlord's plans and actions. Where would they go? What would become of them?[50]

By the time of the meeting, classified ads for Village at Venezia apartments had begun to appear in the *Los Angeles Times* and local newspapers. Monthly rents for one-, two-, and three-bedroom units were listed from $1,679 to $3,119, which graphically illustrated the dilemma of tenants like Wolski, whose monthly income was $732. A display ad that appeared around the same time painted an even more vivid picture of the chasm between many existing tenants and those TransAction wanted to attract. The Village at Venezia was labeled as "West Los Angeles Luxury Apartments" and "The Beginning of Something Beautiful." The ad also offered "Free Rent & $1,500 Shopping Spree," which may have been an indication of softness in the upscale rental market, related to the recent bursting of the dot-com bubble and attendant economic recession.

Most of the tenants in the Lake Street buildings that comprised the second Village at Venezia phase had moved out, some telling friends and neighbors that watching what had happened at Building 18 had convinced them of the futility of resistance. The landlord was no longer negotiating or trying to cajole anyone into leaving with increased relocation money. In a letter to tenants in phase three, which included the buildings where Sheila Bernard and Laura Burns lived, the company offered the legally required payments—$5,000 to the elderly, disabled, and parents with dependent children, and $2,000 to all others. In return for leaving and waiving their rights under the RSO, including the right to return, tenants would be given two months' free rent. Otherwise, they would be served notices of eviction for major rehabilitation. And the letter contained a not-so-veiled threat that if the company had to go court to enforce eviction orders, it would seek substantial attorneys' fees and monetary damages.

Bisno told people at the September meeting that TransAction had all the permits needed to remodel the five Lake Street buildings and was applying for permits for the buildings in phase three. However, it hadn't escaped the notice of some, including Bernard, that while many vacated apartments on

Lake Street had been gutted, there hadn't been any sign of further work. Which hadn't been the case at Building 18, where vacant units had been remodeled—new plumbing and wiring, new fixtures, new cabinets and flooring—even while Laura Ponce and other holdout tenants still lived there. So why were gutted units in the Lake Street buildings just sitting empty, some for months? LPTA members speculated that TransAction's Village at Venezia plan was a red herring, meant to distract people from the fact that the owner's intention was still to tear the whole place down and build condominiums. Others thought the company might be in financial trouble, a plausible idea given that it had recently been in bankruptcy and had large projects underway in both the Los Angeles area and Northern California. Still others believed that TransAction's ultimate goal was to sell the property to another developer, and getting all the tenants out would make that easier.

That last speculation gained currency earlier in the summer when it was learned that TransAction had sold a fifty percent interest in Lincoln Place to a Colorado-based real estate investment trust. No announcement was made to tenants, but the news appeared in a short article in the business section of the *Los Angeles Times*.[51] According to the article, the buyer, Apartment Investment and Management Company, or Aimco, had paid $57.5 million for its half share of the property, a sobering fact for Bernard and others who still harbored dreams of tenant ownership. The article gave no further details about Aimco, a company none of the LPTA members had heard of, but Laura Burns, who had assumed the unofficial role of the group's researcher, looked online and found a press release about the sale that proved to be an eye-opener. It said that Aimco owned and managed approximately 1,640 properties with 313,000 apartments in forty-seven states, the District of Columbia, and Puerto Rico, which made it one of the largest landlords in the country. The release also said that redevelopment of Lincoln Place was underway and expected to be completed over the next four years.[52]

Further research uncovered facts about Aimco's founder and CEO, Terry Considine. He wasn't a faceless corporate executive, but a former Republican politician and highly visible advocate for such conservative causes as cutting taxes, reducing regulation, and privatizing social security. In Colorado, where he had served as a state senator and made an unsuccessful run for the US Senate, he had stirred up a tempest by publicly calling Latin American immigrants "wetbacks."[53] To some people at Lincoln Place and elsewhere in Venice, this was jarring, since the community had long been one of the most liberal of the many that make up Los Angeles. It was Southern California's beatnik haven in the 1950s and a center of hippie culture in 1960s. A local chapter of the Peace and Freedom Party was established in Venice during that era and is still active. While gentrification has tempered its reputation as a hotbed of social and political activism, its population still tilts heavily leftward. In the 2016 presidential election, for instance, fewer than ten percent of voters in its precincts cast their ballots for Donald Trump.

Of course, there is nothing especially notable about business owners and the communities in which they operate being on widely divergent poles of the political scale. But for some, the irony of a company run by a prominent conservative acquiring a large stake in an apartment complex that had been the scene of so much grassroots activism on behalf of people without wealth and power was too strong to ignore. A company getting a large foothold in a community that over the years had food co-ops, alternative art spaces and bookstores, a long-running alternative monthly newspaper, even—for a short time—a nude beach.

But the big question was what this meant for the future of Lincoln Place and its tenants. After Bisno explained the phases of the Village at Venezia plan, he took questions from the assembled residents, and one asked why there wasn't an Aimco representative at the meeting. Bisno indicated that Aimco's role was strictly limited to that of an investor. "Our firm is in charge of the rehab," he declared.

Four days after that meeting, the front page of the *Los Angeles Times* was taken up by a photograph of smoke billowing from New York City's World Trade Center towers and the bold, eighty-point headline, TERRORISTS ATTACK NEW YORK, PENTAGON. The fact that the two hijacked airliners that crashed into the towers were en route to Los Angeles and had many residents of the city on board brought the tragedy even closer to home. Like millions elsewhere that day, Lincoln Place residents were staring in disbelief, fear, and profound sadness at their TVs. Sara Sakuma, who lived in a Lake Street building that had been partially gutted, was one of them, and she remembers the dissonant sound of workers banging away inside nearby units while the TV screen showed the astonishing sight of one the towers collapsing in a massive cloud of debris-filled dust. There were only three other tenants left in her building, and she hadn't decided whether she would move or wait until the landlord tried to evict her. But the sound of demolition work going on around her seemed not only disrespectful of the grave moment, but somehow emblematic of how TransAction viewed the tenants of its buildings, or indeed, anything that might interfere with its money-making plans.

Classified ads for Village at Venezia apartments continued to regularly appear in the *Los Angeles Times*, and in October 2001, shortly after the judge upheld Laura Ponce's eviction, Sheila Bernard and Ingrid Mueller decided they would try to deter potential renters by picketing Building 18. That might have seemed rash, given that TransAction had already sued—albeit unsuccessfully—over tenant activities it claimed were causing the company financial harm, but Bernard strongly believed that potential renters should know that the landlord's pursuit of profit had driven elderly and working-class tenants out of the building. So on a Sunday morning, Bernard, Mueller, and a handful of others set out chairs on the sidewalk beneath a Mexican fan palm on the west side of Frederick Street and propped up signs with messages displayed to cars passing on the street and any people going in and out of the building. Among the messages were Boycott Village Venezia, Don't Rent Here, and Bisno + Aimco Must Go!

Mueller wrote an account of that morning in an email to friends and neighbors. Shortly after they sat down, she wrote, Bisno pulled up to the curb in his blue Jaguar and warned them against any picketing or demonstrating on the Lincoln Place property across the street. He then drove off, but soon returned and began taking photos of the group and the signs, one of which displayed a poison symbol and the words "Asbestos" and "Lead," a reference to the improper abatement of hazardous materials during construction work on the building. "These accusations aren't true," she quoted the landlord as saying. "My lawyer will be in touch." She ended her account by saying that while she and the others were sitting across the street, not a single prospective tenant entered the Village at Venezia office and model apartment on the ground floor of Building 18. She obviously regarded the demonstration as a success.

Bisno ratcheted up the war of words in a letter to tenants in November. Directly attacking Bernard's motives, he alluded to the fact that she had publicly expressed an interest in running for the Los Angeles City Council. Was the real agenda behind LPTA appeals for money, he asked, the funding of such a campaign? He also warned tenants against the LPTA leader's exhortations that they fight eviction, noting that this could have an adverse effect on credit ratings and the ability to rent in the future. "Do you want Sheila to foul up your credit and possibly cause you to incur thousands of dollars in legal fees, so Sheila can stay where she is now, in her below-market rate apartment? Don't throw away your credit on Sheila's agenda."

Elly Nesis sent a letter in the same vein to tenants in the buildings slated for remodeling under phase three of the Village at Venezia plan. While the only Lincoln Place resident mentioned by name was Laura Ponce, who he said was facing significant attorney fees and damages because of her refusal to vacate her unit, he issued a warning to others "not to be misled by the LPTA." The landlord didn't wish to litigate with any tenant, he wrote, but added that "if you fail to comply with our notice to vacate, you will delay our rehabilitation work and cause us additional foreseeable damages which we will be entitled to recover. In addition to liability for attorneys' fees and monetary damages, you should be aware that an eviction may adversely affect your personal credit." The warning letter was followed two weeks later by a letter with the names of fifteen property-management companies in Los Angeles that offered free rental lists. Although the intent was apparently to help tenants looking for new apartments, it felt to those threatened like rubbing salt into their wounds.

These communications made no mention of the RSO's provision requiring twenty-five percent of rehabilitated units to be affordable, with the first right of refusal to tenants who had moved out after eviction orders. But at Bisno's September meeting with residents, several questions were raised about this, and the landlord said that TransAction intended to comply with the provision. Tenants required to move would be given priority for the remodeled units, based on the length of time they'd lived at Lincoln Place. If the units were among the twenty-five percent, the tenants would pay their former rent, plus an increase allowed by the city for recovery of the rehab costs. Bisno didn't say that TransAction had been offering incentives in the form of free rent to tenants who agreed to waive these rights. But as the later communications from Bisno and Nesis made amply clear, tenants were advised to sign those waivers, take what was offered, and get out. If they didn't, they'd be facing worry, hassles, and financial problems that could hound them far into the future.

But even if a tenant refused to sign away the right to return and just took what was legally required in relocation money, Bernard knew that TransAction's legal counsel and other attorneys representing real estate interests considered the twenty-five percent set aside to be a possible violation of the state's 1996 Costa-Hawkins Act, which forbade cities from limiting the rents on newly vacated apartments. It might be only a matter of time before it was challenged in court. She could only hope that the city would approve a moratorium on major rehab evictions before the elderly tenants and working families that she and the LPTA had fought so long for were all forced out.

The broken record of uncertainty and anxiety played its discordant sound as background for yet another holiday season. But at the same time, there were embers of hope in the cold ashes of the failed attempt to have Lincoln Place designated a city historic-cultural monument. Bernard and those involved in that effort—most notably Gail Sansbury, Laura Burns and Michael Palumbo—had been talking about other avenues of historic preservation. Bernard hoped that Ruth Galanter might be persuaded to renominate Lincoln Place so that the matter would go to the city council regardless of how the cultural heritage commission voted. Others believed that a more fruitful approach might be to nominate Lincoln Place to the California Register of Historical Resources, or even to the National Register of Historic Places. However, either process would be more detailed and time-consuming than the city's, and require more research into Lincoln Place history, particularly as it related to architect Heth Wharton, and the ideas and principles that guided his design. Fortunately, there was a person willing and even eager to take that on.

Laura Burns had been making regular trips from Los Angeles to Texas to deal with the aftermath of her mother's death following a long bout with cancer, as well as an older sister's suicide. But she kept thinking that a project as large as Lincoln Place would have generated news articles that could shed more light on Wharton. His daughter, Mary Oakley, had been of some help in this regard, but her memories about Lincoln Place were vague, and she didn't have any relevant articles or documents. In order to rescue Wharton from the portrait painted at the city hearing, as a competent architect but not any sort of creative genius, more had to be unearthed about his work.

In research for her thesis and other writings about Lincoln Place, Gail Sansbury had gotten details about the building permits and opening dates, and Burns used these as a starting point for looking once again at newspaper archives on microfilm in the Los Angeles and Santa Monica public libraries. She found several articles she hadn't already seen, but none mentioned Wharton. However, these articles included the name of Samuel Bialac, and a week before Robert Bisno's meeting with tenants, she decided to look for that name in a Los Angeles telephone directory. There were several Bialacs listed, and she called the first one. A man answered, and she asked, "Are you related to the famous developer Sam Bialac?" She didn't know it at that moment, but his answer would lead to many hours of further research and, ultimately, to a new chapter in the ongoing saga of Lincoln Place.

He told Burns that he was Jerry Bialac, Samuel's son, and had begun working in his father's real estate development business after leaving the air force at the end of World War II. He clearly remembered Lincoln Place and said he and his father had been quite proud of what they'd built. But when Burns asked him about Heth Wharton, he dropped what she later described as a "bombshell." Wharton, he told her, wasn't responsible for the design of the complex. That was an African American architect whose name he unfortunately couldn't remember, although the first name might have been Ralph. Because the man hadn't been licensed in California, he had formed a partnership with Wharton so that the project could be approved by the FHA. But he wasn't a nobody—he had designed other garden apartment projects that Bialac and his father had actually gone to look at before hiring him for Lincoln Place.

As soon as she could, Burns told Sansbury about this unexpected and potentially exciting new information. Exciting because they both thought the African American architect could have been Paul Williams, far and away the best-known Black architect in the city. Bialac was almost eighty years old, and his memory had some obvious holes, so he could have been confused about the name "Ralph." But as they considered that possibility, it seemed more and more unlikely. Williams had been licensed at the time and wouldn't have had to partner with somebody like Wharton. And his projects had been prominently featured in newspaper articles and magazines. If he had designed Lincoln Place, the fact surely wouldn't have lain under wraps all this time.

When Sansbury was doing research for her thesis in the early 1990s, she had gone to Washington, DC, to look in the National Archives for records pertaining to Lincoln Place, among them the builders' application for Section 608 mortgage insurance. She had taken extensive notes, and when she looked back at those notes, she saw that under the section listing architects there had actually been two names in addition to Heth Wharton—Ralph Vaughn and Will G. Norris. She knew nothing about either man, but Burns had arranged to go with Michael Palumbo to Jerry Bialac's Beverly Hills apartment to look at Lincoln Place documents he had, and Sansbury suggested that she ask him if the "Ralph" he mentioned might be this Ralph Vaughn.

Bialac told Burns that Ralph Vaughn was indeed the architect whose name he had forgotten. But he hadn't had any contact with the man for years and had no idea if he was still alive, or if he was, where he might be living. But Burns had her sleuth's hat on, and in the library, she found a listing for a Ralph Vaughn in a 1949 telephone directory. The number wasn't any good, but the listing included an address in Jefferson Park, a neighborhood near downtown Los Angeles that was once home to some of the city's wealthiest white citizens and later to upper-middle-class African Americans. Could Vaughn still live at that address? Unlikely maybe, but not impossible. Burns didn't know when he was born, but if he was alive he would definitely be quite old. With no idea who or what she would find, she decided to drive to the address.

Much of the neighborhood is distinguished by large Victorian and Craftsman-style houses, but the street she found herself on was lined with unimposing one-story houses and small apartment buildings. The house Vaughn had apparently lived in was no different—single story with a garage and carport facing the street, an umbrella tree in the small front yard and one of the city's ubiquitous ficus trees in the parkway between the sidewalk and street.

Burns, who has a disarmingly friendly manner, knocked on the front door and asked the woman who answered if she was related to Ralph Vaughn, the architect. No, the woman told her, then added, "You know he passed, don't you?" He had lived in the house, she said, but had sold it and moved to Northern California. When Burns explained her interest in finding out more about him, the woman invited her in and showed Burns a clipping of Vaughn's obituary that had appeared that past April in the *Los Angeles Sentinel*.[54] She had looked at it just the other day, she said, and meant to throw it out, but in what had proven to be a serendipitous act, she had put it back in a desk drawer.

As Burns read the lines below the headline, "Ralph Vaughn Succumbs," the first thing that struck her was the date of death: October 20, 2000. Which meant that he was still alive when she was trying to find more details about Heth Wharton for the city historic-cultural monument application. If she had dug just a little deeper, maybe she would have come across Vaughn's name and been able to actually talk to him. It was a very large if, but she still felt disappointed in herself, that she had in some way failed. The obituary mentioned his work with Paul Williams designing commercial buildings and homes, his stint as an MGM set designer during World War II, and his partnership with Warton (sic) in the design of Chase Knolls, North Hollywood Manor, and Lincoln Village. The names of survivors also caught her eye, in particular a son, Ronald F. Vaughn, identified as an architect in Sacramento, California. If she could contact him, he might be able to fill in details about Vaughn's work in designing Lincoln Place, which she assumed was the "Lincoln Village" of the obituary.

She was also struck by the house's interior, which had nothing of the bland, suburban look of the outside, but displayed many elements of modernist design, with liberal use of glass and an open, airy floor plan. Although she didn't know it at the time, the house had been featured in a 1947 *Los Angeles Times* article titled "Brilliant Design Makes a Little House Big." But perhaps tellingly for that era, the article included a two-page spread of photos of the house without mentioning its locale in a majority-Black neighborhood. And while Ralph Vaughn was identified as the owner and designer, neither he nor his wife and son were shown in any of the photos.[55]

The woman told Burns she could have the clipping. In addition to Vaughn's son, Ronald, it listed a daughter, two stepchildren, and four grand-children, but Burns decided to start with the son. If he was a practicing architect, she thought, he shouldn't be too hard to locate, and after searching through public records and directories, she found a telephone number and address for an architect with that name in Los Angeles. This led to a telephone conversation and then a meeting with the sixty-one-year-old who had not only followed in his father's footsteps by becoming an architect, but also kept copies of letters, magazine articles, resumes, and other documents that painted a picture of Ralph Vaughn's career both before and after the design of Lincoln Place. He also gave Burns the names of people who had worked for his father on Lincoln Place, and the recollections of one of them, a Chinese American architect who had been a draftsman at the time, would prove especially valuable to Burns's quest. His name was Allen Mock, and when she interviewed him, he told her how Vaughn had directed the design in conformance with modernist and garden city principles while applying unique elements of his own, many inspired by his work in movie set design. This belied the gist of the argument put forward by the opponents of historic designation, that Lincoln Place's architecture didn't display any original ideas but had been designed in a kind of cookie-cutter fashion.

The conversation with Mock took place in October 2001, a month after Robert Bisno outlined the phases of remodeling that would transform Lincoln Place into the Village at Venezia. Several weeks later, with Laura Ponce finally gone and workers tearing out flooring, cabinets, and fixtures from her unit in Building 18, TransAction asked the court to levy $95,000 in attorney fees in her eviction case. Since there wasn't the remotest possibility that Ponce could pay such an amount, the court request was widely seen as a message to tenants in the Lake Street buildings and elsewhere who were balking at the prospect of moving out. "Take our offer and sign the waiver of right to return; if we're forced to evict you, this is what you could be facing."

TransAction had also applied for permits to demolish the building on Frederick Street and the one behind it on Doreen Place, where Bisno said a recreation center and condominiums would be built. But there still hadn't been any signs of new work on the vacant, gutted Lake Street buildings, and suspicions were growing that the landlord intended to tear them down so that condominiums could be built there as well. If another historic preservation effort were to be mounted, either with the city or state, time was of the essence.

As 2001 faded into history, things were unsettled politically, socially, and economically, both on a global and local level. The government's answer to the 9/11 attacks was an invasion of Afghanistan, and many who had lived through inconclusive wars in Korea and Vietnam feared a repeat of those experiences, although few likely imagined that US troops would still be engaged in hostilities in two Middle East countries almost twenty years later. Adding to fears of further terrorist attacks on US soil, an American Airlines passenger had tried to detonate explosives hidden in his shoe, and another American Airlines jet had crashed just after takeoff from Kennedy International airport in New York City. The so-called shoe bomber was thwarted and the New York crash that killed 260 persons proved to have been caused by turbulence from a preceding flight, but along with much stricter security at airports the incidents increased travelers' jitters. On the economic front, Enron Corporation, a huge Texas energy conglomerate, became the largest company in US history to go bankrupt, an event that exposed a web of questionable dealings and fraudulent accounting practices that shook public confidence in Wall Street and the country's financial system.

Locally, the future envisioned by renters and tenants' groups like the LPTA was equally uncertain. Those groups had hoped that Antonio Villaraigosa would win the mayor's office in the 2001 election, but he lost to James Hahn, who was regarded as more friendly to the interests of property owners although he was a Democrat and certainly more liberal than outgoing Mayor Richard Riordan. As city attorney, Hahn had defended the city against TransAction's various lawsuits, although how much of that stemmed from concern for Lincoln Place tenants and how much from city council pressure was open to question. Also disappointing to LPTA members was city Councilman Mike Feuer's loss to political newcomer Rocky Delgadillo in the contest to succeed Hahn as city attorney. Feuer, who had spent the early years of his legal career representing low-income tenants and others of limited means and had supported rent control and other pro-tenant measures during his six years as a council member, was considered an ally by the LPTA and other renter groups. Delgadillo, the grandson of Mexican immigrants, had gone to Harvard and Columbia law school before joining a large corporate law firm and later working for Riordan as head of the mayor's economic development efforts. He won a strong majority of a growing Latino vote, but he also benefited from the support of big-money interests, in particular the billboard industry that had chafed at Feuer's highly vocal support for curbing the spread of outdoor advertising. Would he be friendly to tenants fighting a corporation like TransAction that was actively developing real estate and generating jobs and tax revenue for the city?

But most alarming to Lincoln Place tenants worried about the future was the fact that Ruth Galanter, a staunch ally for thirteen years, might no longer represent them on the city council. Galanter's term wouldn't end until 2003, but the city was required to redraw council districts after the 2000 census. Because population had grown more slowly on the west side than other parts of the city, the commission charged with drawing new boundaries had come up with a tentative plan to merge adjacent districts represented by Galanter and Cindy Miscikowski and create a brand-new district in the heavily Latino eastern San Fernando Valley. This would require either Galanter or Miscikowski to be moved from the districts where they lived to one some thirty miles away. This struck many as bizarre, but it was looking like a distinct possibility. Miscikowski was an unknown quantity to most in Venice, including Lincoln Place tenants, but the fact that she was married to a real estate developer was one reason to suspect that she wouldn't be as sympathetic as Galanter. Some assumed that because Galanter had been on the council ten years longer than Miscikowski, she would stay put, but Galanter was also a part of what was considered the old guard and had clashed with some of the younger council members who would vote on whatever redistricting plan the commission ultimately put forward.

As 2002 got underway, Laura Burns was working hard to put the fruits of her research—hours of interviews, notes, documents—into a form that could be used to create a coherent narrative of the creation of Lincoln Place as a genuine community that would be home to working people and families. The centerpiece of that narrative would be Ralph Vaughn's design, which not only aimed to incorporate principles of modernist architecture, but to create a sense of well-being for tenants through interior and exterior elements more associated at the time with housing for the upper classes. It was clear to Burns after talking to Jerry Bialac, Ronald Vaughn, and Allen Mock, that Ralph Vaughn believed in architecture as an art form that could also serve a social purpose—promoting communal activity, increasing aspiration, giving people a sense of permanence and ownership, conferring dignity on their lives by surrounding them with aesthetic beauty—and she wanted both tenants and the public at large to understand that. At the same time, she was juggling her film-editing career and dealing with ongoing family matters in Texas.

That winter, while she was in Austin taking care of an issue related to her mother's estate, she got an unexpected telephone call from a stranger that would prove critical to her Lincoln Place research and ultimately to the very existence of the complex, although she had no inkling of that when the woman on the line introduced herself. Her name was Amanda Seward, and she told Burns that she was a member of the Los Angeles Conservancy's modern committee, along with Michael Palumbo. He had told her about the LPTA and the ongoing drama at Lincoln Place, including the fact that Burns had been digging deeply into Lincoln Place's history. Seward said she wanted to nominate the complex for the National Register of Historic Places, and would Burns be willing to share her research for that effort?

17

FRANKENBUILDINGS

AMANDA SEWARD CLEARLY REMEMBERS the moment in 1971 that set her on the path to eventually becoming a lawyer. She was a fifteen-year-old student at Santa Monica High School, bright and capable of getting top grades, but more interested in cutting classes and hanging out with friends than pursuing academic excellence. She lived with her mother and four younger sisters in a Santa Monica apartment, but when she and friends went in search of diversion, it was usually to Venice, because that beach community directly to the south had a looser, more anything-goes atmosphere that appealed to teenagers on the prowl for fun and adventure. It also had drugs, gangs, and racial tensions centered in the Oakwood neighborhood, once an exclusive African American enclave but more recently home to growing numbers of Latinos.

A favorite hangout for Seward and her friends was the Fox Venice theater on Lincoln Boulevard, directly across the street from the east edge of Oakwood, and just three blocks from Lincoln Place. The theater, which hosted live music concerts and showed double-feature movies for two dollars' admission, had an unofficial section for marijuana smokers and conversation among audience members wasn't discouraged as long as it didn't get overly loud. The theater had also been the scene of fights and disturbances involving Black and Latino youths. Thus it was, when she and a few friends went there on a winter Sunday, that an argument broke out between other young audience members and escalated into fights, with the throwing of bottles and the inevitable calling of the police.

"We weren't part of that," Seward says. "But when the police showed up, they told everybody to stay in their seats. I wanted some popcorn, so I got up and went out to the refreshment stand, and this policeman grabbed me and said, 'You were supposed to stay in your seat.' I didn't like being grabbed, and I guess I said something he didn't like, and he put me in a headlock. I kept struggling, and they got me into their car and took me to the Venice police station. After they parked the car, they walked me down this dark alley, and I was sure they were going to beat me up. I remember thinking it just wasn't right—they could manhandle you but you had to stay passive."

She was charged with resisting arrest and disturbing the peace by using profanity in public. She had no prior record and was released to her mother's custody, but the two had to meet with the probation department and then go before a judge, who sternly told her that she shouldn't have resisted the police. She remembers thinking, "Are you fucking crazy? If somebody grabs you, you ought to have the right to grab back, to hit back." It was undoubtedly fortunate that she didn't say this aloud, because the judge agreed with the probation department's recommendation, to expunge the record of her arrest if she didn't get into further trouble.

"My mother was very proper," she says. "She was educated and had lived in England for a while and had a kind of accent, and she sometimes embarrassed me by the formal way she talked. But I could tell that she impressed the probation people, she knew how to talk to people like that, and I was impressed too, even though I still didn't feel like I did anything wrong. She told me afterward that I had to straighten out, and I did. My grades went up. I went to college and was able to get into law school."

The incident was the subject of an article in the *Los Angeles Times*.[56] It wouldn't have been newsworthy enough to merit the attention of the city's major newspaper if not for the fact that a boy who had tried to come to Seward's aid at the theater was allegedly beaten and subjected to racial slurs by the white police officers. Police harassment had long been a complaint in the Oakwood community and the reports of white police officers roughing up Black youths, including a fifteen-year-old girl, led to community meetings and promises of investigations, although many African Americans in Venice and other parts of Los Angeles expected little from such promises, believing that the police department under Chief Ed Davis was suffused with racism from the top on down. As for Seward, living in a majority white middle-class neighborhood in Santa Monica had spared her most of the experiences of Black youths in Venice's Oakwood neighborhood, but her outlook on issues of racial injustice and social inequality and the legal system was sharply focused by that experience and would come to affect her involvement thirty years later with Lincoln Place and its tenants.

When she picked up the phone and called Laura Burns in Austin, Texas, she and her husband, Hans Adamson, lived in a house in Mar Vista, a middle-class, mostly residential community east of Venice. The house was one of fifty-two in a nine-square block tract, all designed in a midcentury modern style by architect Gregory Ain, a Los Angeles native who had apprenticed with Richard Neutra, one of the city's most famous modern architects. The nearly identical houses, built in the late 1940s, featured open, flexible floor plans, a de-emphasis of the distinction between interior and outdoors, and generous landscaping, elements that appealed to both Seward and Adamson, a musician and music software developer who grew up in Sweden and had become interested there in midcentury modern design.

Seward had gone to Spelman College in Atlanta, then to Georgetown University Law School before working for an Atlanta law firm and then as an in-house attorney for Ted Turner's media empire. She met Adamson while working in the company's London office, but the job eventually brought her back to Los Angeles, where she and her husband lived for a time in Park La Brea, the largest garden apartment complex in the city. After buying their house in the Mar Vista tract, they began going to Los Angeles Conservancy meetings and soon joined some of their neighbors in organizing an ultimately successful effort to have their tract designated a historic district. At meetings of the conservancy's modern committee, they met Michael Palumbo, an encounter that would prove to be especially fateful when Seward learned about Lincoln Place and decided that it definitely merited historic recognition.

"I was very interested," she says, "And I had been told that a woman who lived there had done all this fantastic research, so it didn't seem like it would be too hard."

When she first spoke to Laura Burns by telephone, her sense was that Burns was wary about sharing her research with a stranger. For her part, Burns says her immediate inclination was to say yes, but she first wanted to speak to Sheila Bernard and Michael Palumbo. Bernard's reaction, Burns says, was skeptical. Who was this person and why would she just call out of the blue like that? When Burns got back to Los Angeles, she and Bernard met with Seward in Bernard's Lincoln Place apartment. Seward, who has a measured way of speaking that can quickly rise in intensity and passion without becoming loud or shrill, convinced the others that she was sincere and wanted to do what she could to protect Lincoln Place from the ravages of TransAction's plans, whether those were to turn every building into a "Frankenbuilding," as Bernard called the newly remodeled Building 18, or to bring in the wrecking ball and level everything to the ground.

"But the thing that really gave me incentive to do something," she says in reflecting on that meeting, "was finding out about Ralph Vaughn, about the fact that this place had been designed by an African American architect hardly anybody knew anything about."

Seward's enthusiasm and solid legal background gave heart to Burns, Bernard, and others who had worked to save Lincoln Place, but bad news was soon to follow, especially for Bernard. Although TransAction had failed to get a temporary injunction against the LPTA yard sale in the fall of 2000, the company hadn't dropped the matter, and in February 2002, a judge approved a permanent injunction against any future sales.

This struck many as a surprise since the order was issued by Gregory O'Brien, the same judge who had used such scathing language in throwing out TransAction's lawsuit against Bernard and Laura Ponce almost exactly a year earlier. The action would prove to have dire consequences, because three months later the judge awarded TransAction $50,000 in attorney fees. Neither Bernard nor the LPTA had that kind of money, and besides, she didn't feel it would be right to use money from the LPTA treasury when she had urged tenants to defy the landlord's warnings. She also expected TransAction to make every effort to collect, because, unlike Ponce, she had a job and regular income.

She had been certain that tenants had the right to hold sales on the property, notwithstanding anything the landlord could cite in rental agreements.

But she had been wrong. In the eyes of the law, it appeared, every square inch of the property was under the absolute control of the owner, and her refusal to recognize that fact had put her in serious financial jeopardy. It wasn't long before the company got an order to seize the money in her bank account and garnish her teacher's wages. Suddenly broke, with a big hole in her monthly paycheck, the essentials of life, like paying rent and putting food on the table would become an ongoing struggle.

Despite attacks of weariness and pessimism, she banished thoughts of giving up the fight to preserve Lincoln Place. She had been LPTA president for fourteen years, organizing tenants to resist the landlord's efforts, first to evict them in order to charge higher rents, then to tear down the place and redevelop it with mostly upscale condominiums. The evictions were happening again, and the redevelopment plan was still alive despite the fact the city had rejected it. Still, not a single building had been demolished, and only one had been radically remodeled and rented to people who were much more affluent than the long-term tenants who had lent their voices and money in support of the LPTA. She felt that she couldn't abandon these tenants. She would keep writing newsletters and bulletins, she would keep sending letters to public officials and going to meetings, and she would keep taking every opportunity to speak to media outlets about the Lincoln Place cause. Despite being sued, excoriated by the landlord, and pushed toward poverty, she wouldn't stop, because to do that would be saying to the landlord, "You win."

She was fifty-two years old and healthy, her three children were grown and living independently, and she was giving more thought to how she might work in the political system as more than a constituent who had to go hat in hand to city council members and other public officials and beg for attention. She had thought about running for city council when term limits would force Ruth Galanter to step down in 2003, but that idea was complicated by the fact that in April of 2002, the city redistricting commission approved the plan that made Galanter the representative of an east San Fernando Valley district and installed Cindy Miscikowski as councilperson for the district that encompassed Venice. There were grumblings and even some howls of protest from people who had come to count on Galanter to represent their interests, including Lincoln Place tenants, but the city council was expected to—and did—approve the plan. Miscikowski's term wouldn't end until 2005, though, which meant that Bernard's first opportunity to make a run for the council seat wouldn't come for another three years.

Miscikowski and her husband, Douglas Ring, lived in Brentwood, one of the wealthiest communities in Los Angeles and home over the years to many celebrities, including Marilyn Monroe, Steve McQueen, Arnold Schwarzenegger, and O. J. Simpson. The contrast to Galanter's neighborhood, a middle-class area of Venice dominated by one-story Craftsman- and Spanish-style bungalows on small lots, was too stark for some, who openly questioned whether Miscikowski could empathize with the working people, the elderly, the renters and members of racial and ethnic minorities who had long made the community stand out from the overwhelmingly white, affluent west side of Los Angeles. Before running for the city council in 1997, she had worked for Councilman Marvin Braude, a longtime advocate for environmental causes like preserving open space, establishing bike trails, and banning smoking in restaurants and government buildings. But unlike Galanter, neither Braude nor Miscikowski were especially vocal about affordable housing and the social issues that had always percolated in Venice and other communities with sizable low-income and minority populations. Finally, Bernard and others who had spent time in city hall and seen lobbyists bending the ears of council members were troubled by the fact that the man who had managed Miscikowski's 1997 campaign was a registered lobbyist whose clientele included TransAction.

Bernard ultimately decided against running for the city council. But she also didn't share the enthusiasm of those like Seward, Burns, and Palumbo for historic preservation. She would certainly support the efforts of others, but her failed attempt at the city level had left her with the feeling that it was possibly futile and that her energies were best spent, first in pushing the city council to enact a moratorium on major rehab evictions, and then in helping to advance initiatives that would make it impossible, or at least more difficult, to redevelop or demolish properties like Lincoln Place. As the saying goes, that would be a heavy lift, but if she hadn't believed such things were possible she would have long ago given up her role as head of the LPTA and just quietly gone about her life.

On July 16, 2002, the city council took up the moratorium. It was a typical summer day downtown—sunny, temperature in the eighties—and the council chamber was filled with tenants and their advocates, along with a contingent of lobbyists and members of landlord groups. Bernard had come with a group of Lincoln Place tenants; across the aisle was TransAction's attorney, Allan Abshez. In public comment, she asked council members to remember 1987, when landlords were evicting tenants, making cosmetic repairs and then charging much higher rents. The council had acted then to make such evictions more difficult, but now history was repeating itself, and economic incentives were prompting owners to once again take advantage of the law to get rid of long-term tenants. But Abshez and others representing landlords and real estate interests repeated the warning that properties would fall into disrepair if owners couldn't evict tenants to do needed work on their units. Abshez also argued that the call for a moratorium was really about the long-running dispute between TransAction and the LPTA over the fate of Lincoln Place and had little relevance to the city at large.

After hearing both sides, the council voted unanimously to impose a six-month moratorium on the evictions while the city studied ways to both protect tenants and accommodate landlords who had a legitimate need to fix up their properties. It was the first public test that might show where Councilwoman Miscikowski's sentiments lay, and Bernard and the Lincoln Place tenants were happy that she not only voted with the rest of the council, but expressed unequivocal support for the measure.

For the moment, then, tenants who had been pressured to leave to make way for the Village at Venezia project were safe, although several facts suggested that the plan laid out in great detail by Bisno almost a year earlier was either being abandoned or indefinitely postponed. All five Lake Street buildings with their fifty-nine apartments were vacant and fenced off in a sea of weeds, interiors gutted and windows broken by vandals. There were no signs of any remodeling work. Likewise, all forty-four units in the two buildings slated for replacement by a recreation facility and condominiums were vacant, but no move had been made to tear them down. Bernard,

Laura Burns, and others who lived in phase three of the Village at Venezia project hadn't gotten any communications since the initial notices in the fall of 2001 telling them they would eventually have to move. Yet another sign of a change in TransAction's plans was a notice tenants got in May 2002, informing them that Elly Nesis would no longer be managing any Lincoln Place buildings. Naturally enough, all this stimulated rumors, including conjecture that the company was in financial difficulty again and was looking to sell its fifty-percent share of the complex.

But the good news/bad news seesaw for tenants continued. No sooner had the ink dried on the major rehab moratorium than the state appeals court upheld the superior court judge's ruling that the city's rejection of TransAction's redevelopment plan violated the Ellis Act. To comply with the appeals court decision, the judge ordered the city to reconsider the plan and threatened to hold it in contempt if it failed to do so by a December deadline. This raised two possibilities. The city would approve the redevelopment, giving TransAction the green light to start tearing buildings down and putting up what it had originally proposed all the way back in 1991—706 condominiums and 144 apartments. Or it could reject the project a second time, in which case it would have to find some way around the judge's ruling. Any such action would almost certainly lead to further litigation, though, and it was far from clear that the city council had any appetite for continuing down that time-consuming and expensive path.

While the council met privately with City Attorney Rocky Delgadillo to discuss how to proceed, Amanda Seward finished work on the Lincoln Place nomination to the National Register of Historic Places. Getting on the list of more than sixty thousand properties as diverse as log cabins, churches, mansions, lighthouses, and parks was anything but simple. An appointed official called the Keeper of the National Register would make the final decision, but nominations had to be first recommended by individual states. In California, the responsible agency was the Office of Historic Preservation, operating under the aegis of a nine-member state historic resources commission. That agency's staff would analyze Seward's application and then send it to the commission with a recommendation for either approval or denial. If the staff recommended approval and the commission concurred, the nomination would go to the Keeper in Washington, DC. After a forty-five-day period for public comment, that official, then a woman named Carol Shull, would make a final decision. If she agreed with the state commission, Lincoln Place could be added to the national register, an action that would also automatically add the complex to the California Register of Historical Resources.

But as might be expected in this kind of bureaucratic process, there were some conspicuous caveats. The major one was that a property couldn't be listed on either the state or national register if the owner objected. And nobody would be surprised if Robert Bisno did just that. However, such an objection didn't necessarily sound the death knell for the Lincoln Place application. The state commission could still approve it and forward the nomination to the Keeper, who had the power to declare the apartment complex eligible for the register without actually putting it on the list. This had been done in other cases, for various reasons, one being that owners could change their minds or sell their properties to buyers amenable to historic designation and the tax advantages that often followed. Then, the properties could simply be added to the register.

The national register didn't confer any protections upon a property. Even if Lincoln Place was listed, Bisno could tear the whole place down without running afoul of any federal statute. One might then have asked, what's the point? The answer was to be found in CEQA, the California Environmental Quality Act. A provision known as a "trigger" required an environmental impact report prior to the demolition of any building listed or found to be eligible for either the national or state register. That requirement was also codified in a Los Angeles city ordinance. In other words, even if Bisno lodged a formal objection to historic designation, he could still be forced to submit a new EIR or at least an addendum to the existing one before demolishing any Lincoln Place buildings. That would not only take time, but the EIR would be required to examine the question of whether the preservation of the buildings was feasible. If the report answered this question in the affirmative, it could allow the city to impose a requirement for at least partial preservation. It would also give the city or the LPTA another hammer to swing in any future court fight.

Ideally, though, the owners would cooperate. The California law known as the Mills Act gave property tax breaks to those who agreed to preserve and maintain historically designated properties, and for an apartment complex the size of Lincoln Place this could amount to a sizable savings. There were potential federal tax advantages as well. While Seward knew there was a good chance that Lincoln Place owners would object to the nomination, she decided to send letters to both Bisno and Aimco CEO Terry Considine, telling them of her effort and inviting their support. She wrote that members of the Los Angeles Conservancy were interested in working with the property owners "on a preservation plan that would serve as a model partnership between owners, residents, and preservationists in preserving this wonderful historic resource."

She got no replies. But she, Burns and Palumbo had solicited an impressive number of endorsements from preservation experts and organizations like the National Trust for Historic Preservation and the National Organization of Minority Architects. They had also gotten expressions of support from California's US senators, Barbara Boxer and Dianne Feinstein; and from US Representative Jane Harman, whose district included Venice. And unlike members of the city's cultural heritage commission, who could be anybody the mayor chose to appoint, those serving on the state historical resources commission had to have recognized credentials in such fields as history, archaeology, and architectural preservation. Seward, who had a natural air of confidence that had undoubtedly been an asset in her legal career, was certain that Lincoln Place would get a more knowledgeable and sympathetic hearing by the state commission than it had from the city, where Bernard and others suspected that pressure on that commission's political appointees had influenced its negative vote.

The state commission scheduled a hearing on the nomination for October 30, 2002. In the meantime, the LPTA turned its attention to Aimco, which had operated thus far as a silent partner in Lincoln Place ownership. But with the Village at Venezia project either delayed or abandoned and Robert Bisno rumored to be negotiating with a buyer for TransAction's ownership share, the LPTA wanted to find out more about Aimco's intentions. Attempts by Sheila Bernard to communicate with Terry Considine and others at the company's Colorado headquarters had been fruitless. However, Laura Burns, the redoubtable researcher, was able to put together a picture of the company. And for Lincoln Place tenants and advocates for affordable housing, it wasn't pretty.

Aimco, it seemed, had been pursuing the same business model embraced on a much smaller scale by TransAction, which was to buy housing complexes with low-income tenants and then find ways to get rid of them in order to raise the rents. According to an article in the Sacramento Bee, the daily newspaper in California's capitol, Aimco regularly bought properties built with federal subsidies and then paid off the mortgages as soon as legally possible in order to lift restrictions on the rents.[57] The company would either manage those properties, or make millions by flipping them to buyers willing to pay a premium for complexes with unrestricted rents. When TransAction bought Lincoln Place in 1986, the mortgage had already been paid off and there weren't any rent restrictions beyond those imposed by the city's RSO, but by 2002, it had stopped accepting rental subsidies under the federal government's Section 8 program. According to the *Bee* article, Aimco had done the same at a number of properties, thus forcing many low-income tenants to move in search of cheaper places to rent or landlords willing to accept the subsidies. For the elderly and working-class families who were the main beneficiaries of the Section 8 program, that imposed an enormous burden. Research also uncovered the fact that the US Department of Housing and Urban Development had sued the company in 1999 for alleged mismanagement of subsidized properties, including failure to properly maintain a large complex occupied by minority and low-income tenants in San Francisco. In another court case, a federal judge found that Aimco had violated a requirement that owners seeking to pay off mortgages of HUD-subsidized properties first offer those properties to nonprofits or other purchasers that would agree to maintain them as low-income housing.

In September 2002, an opportunity arose to bring some of this to the attention of a wider public. An announcement in the July issue of *Apartment Age Magazine* listed Peter Kompaniez, vice chairman of Aimco, as a keynote speaker at an apartment industry conference on September 19 in Beverly Hills. When Bernard saw the notice, she decided that the LPTA should organize a demonstration at the site of the conference, the Beverly Hilton Hotel. In a press release three days before the conference, she accused Aimco of "raiding" subsidized housing, with devastating effects on local communities trying to provide affordable rental housing. "Investors naively hope to make good returns on their real estate investments. They don't realize that by investing in Aimco they are fundamentally undoing any public good their tax dollars could accomplish." Noting that Lincoln Place tenants had tried without success to engage the company in dialogue, she promised that those tenants "will fight tooth and nail to save our neighborhood, as we have for the past 15 years. We don't care how big and bad a corporation Aimco is."

The *Santa Monica Mirror* ran a story about the demonstration, featuring a photo of seventy-eight-year-old Frieda Marlin on the sidewalk outside the luxury hotel on Wilshire Boulevard, holding a large sign with the message DON'T MAKE GRANDMAS HOMELESS.[58] The entrance to the hotel is set back from the street, and the group of two dozen demonstrators on the sidewalk weren't able to confront any conference attendees. Kompaniez declined the newspaper's request for comment, but Bernard still considered the demonstration a success because it showed tenants and other housing advocates that the LPTA was willing to carry the fight to a rich and powerful corporation. Setting that example, she thought, was especially important given the fact that Aimco had recently bought out another company that owned several thousand HUD-subsidized apartment complexes in Los Angeles and elsewhere in California. She wanted those tenants to hear that they didn't need to meekly accept whatever the landlord wanted to do to pad the bottom line, but could assert their own interests. In other words, organize and fight!

On the preservation front, Amanda Seward was busy preparing for the state commission meeting in November. As the applicant, she was required to provide the commission staff with addresses and mailing labels for all owners of the property, and as far as anyone knew, Lincoln Place was owned only by TransAction and Aimco. But titles to individual parcels were held in the names of various limited partnerships, and she got the names and addresses of each one from county tax records. In all, there were only two separate addresses, but in an abundance of caution she filled out a mailing label for each of the parcel owners. She sent these to the commission staff, which would then mail copies of the Lincoln Place nomination and formal notice of the upcoming commission meeting.

Not long before that meeting, she was extremely disappointed to learn from the staff member handling the nomination that TransAction attorney Allan Abshez had objected on the grounds that the ownership entities hadn't been properly notified. The staff member told her that the attorney had also said that the owners weren't necessarily opposed to the historic designation, but needed more time to study it. This raised her hopes just slightly that TransAction and Aimco wouldn't lodge a formal objection. But the Lincoln Place nomination would have to be taken off the agenda, and because the commission met quarterly, the earliest it could be rescheduled was in February 2003. This struck Seward and the LPTA as a delaying tactic, and Bernard and some other tenants believed it was related to the fact that City Attorney Rocky Delgadillo had advised the city council to take up TransAction's original redevelopment plan before the December deadline set by the judge. Some theorized that Bisno believed that the city had no choice but to approve the project, at which time demolition of buildings could get underway. That would be easy, since seven were vacant and boarded up, and the city had already issued demolition permits for the two buildings on Frederick Street and Doreen Place. If buildings no longer existed when the state commission met, then the description of the complex would be inaccurate and the commission would have no choice but to reject the Lincoln Place nomination.

It was impossible to know how much credence to give this theory, although it sounded plausible. And it was consistent with Bisno's reputation among activist tenants as a schemer who wasn't above dirty tricks to get what he wanted. In any event, the city moved ahead, and the council's PLUM committee scheduled a new hearing on the redevelopment for November 19.

The LPTA built its successful line of attack in 1995 on the fact that the community would lose a significant amount of affordable housing, but since the judge had explicitly rejected that argument, another approach had to be found. The group could no longer rely on the expert and tireless help of Marcia Scully, the attorney they had dubbed their "angel," but Bernard,

Seward, and others put their heads together and decided that a vulnerability might lie in the original EIR. The authors of the report had concluded that Lincoln Place wasn't historically or culturally significant. It didn't have unique or ground-breaking architectural features and its designer—then believed to be Heth Wharton—wasn't renowned for his work. When the draft of the EIR was circulated for public comment prior to certification, only Gail Sansbury had taken issue with those conclusions. But now, thanks to the persistent research of Laura Burns, it was known that the actual designer was Ralph Vaughn. That in itself was significant at a time when African American architects were a rarity, but even more noteworthy given his connection to noted Black architects like Hilyard Robinson and Paul Williams and his design of other garden apartment complexes like Chase Knolls and North Hollywood Manor. And Burns's interviews with Jerry Bialac, Ronald Vaughn, and Allen Mock had revealed how central the idea of creating a real community of people and not just a collection of apartment houses was to Vaughn's conception of Lincoln Place.

In a letter to PLUM committee members prior to the hearing, Sheila Bernard wrote that this new information meant that the EIR's findings were out of date. She argued that any action on the redevelopment should be postponed until after the state historical resources commission meeting in February. If Lincoln Place was found to be eligible for the national register, surely that would call into question the EIR's conclusions and argue for a new environmental review. Anticipating objections that a delay would conflict with the judge's deadline, she wrote that in the six years since the original filing of the lawsuit the plaintiff had caused serious delays; surely the judge would agree to waiting a few months longer so that the city council could take into account the commission's action, whatever that proved to be.

On the morning of November 19, the temperature was heading for the upper eighties in downtown Los Angeles, with gusts of hot, dry Santa Ana winds. To some superstitious folk, the winds that rose in the desert and swept down mountain canyons into the city were a bad omen, but for Bernard, Burns, Seward, and a contingent of Lincoln Place tenants, they were just a backdrop to the tough sell they had on their hands. Hal Bernson, whose support for preserving Lincoln Place had been invaluable back in 1995, was still on the committee although no longer chairman. The two other members who had voted with Bernson seven years earlier were gone, replaced by Ed Reyes, the chairman, who represented mostly Latino neighborhoods west and north of downtown, and Wendy Greuel, from a relatively affluent part of the San Fernando Valley. Bernard and other Lincoln Place supporters hoped Bernson would once again take the side of tenants, and the fact that Reyes was one of the council's more vocal proponents of affordable housing gave them some confidence.

They also hoped that Councilwoman Cindy Miscikowski might make the kind of full-throated defense of Lincoln Place they had learned to expect from Ruth Galanter, but when she addressed the committee, she just laid out the questions committee members would have to answer. First, was the new information about Ralph Vaughn and his design enough to justify delaying a decision until after the February meeting of the state commission, and second, would a delay pass muster with the judge who had ordered the council to reconsider the project?

Following Miscikowski, a staff member from the city planning department told the committee that the information about Ralph Vaughn wasn't deemed significant enough to call into question the conclusions of the original EIR. Reyes then opened the meeting to public comment. Sheila Bernard summarized what she had written in her letter and urged the committee to postpone action, and Ingrid Mueller said that if Los Angeles allowed the destruction of Lincoln Place, it "would not be a City of Angels, believe me." Also addressing the committee was a single mother evicted from Lincoln Place when TransAction opted out of the federal government's Section 8 program. She and her children, she said, were now living in a homeless shelter.

Committee members appeared to have some sympathy for tenants, but a lawyer from the city attorney's office argued that in light of the judge's decision the city couldn't legally justify denying the redevelopment a second time. All three members then voted to approve the project the committee had unanimously rejected seven years earlier.

The full council took up the matter the following day. Amanda Seward was at the meeting, and she raised the issue of the new information about

Ralph Vaughn and the significance of his design of Lincoln Place as a park-like setting that would encourage interaction and political involvement. She also urged the council members to fight for the public interest and not be deterred by fears of litigation. Alluding to Robert Bisno, she said, "This man is litigious. But I think that if the City is going to stand for anything, it's just one of those cases where you can't bow to a litigious person who is going to make you do something against the public interest."

Following public comment, Councilwoman Miscikowski took the floor, saying, "This is not a good day or a happy day, because I think the Council very much tried to establish a principle. But we also know that we are governed by a set of laws and rules as they are written today and interpreted by the courts." With that, President Alex Padilla called for a vote. Ruth Galanter was absent, which raised a few eyebrows, even though Lincoln Place was no longer part of her district. Three members who had voted against the redevelopment in 1996—Hal Bernson, Nate Holden, and Mark Ridley-Thomas—voted this time in the affirmative and those elected after that followed suit. Padilla announced that the long-stalled and contentious project was unanimously approved.

What next? In the December 5 issue of the *Argonaut*, Robert Bisno was quoted as saying that he was ready to hire architects to complete the design process and move forward with the redevelopment.[59] He also threatened to sue the city for between $30 and $40 million in damages, claiming that the city council's denial of the project and subsequent seven-year delay cost the company $100 million in projected earnings.

Sheila Bernard had a much different view, of course. In the December issue of Venice's alternative monthly, the *Beachhead*, she wrote an article titled "Lincoln Place—a Test of Perseverance" that displayed her signature optimism in the opening line. "A lost battle does not mean a lost war." After an account of the PLUM and city council meetings, she wrote, "It is startling to watch an entire city litigated into submission by a private speculative developer and his legal staff. It is sobering to see that no matter how serious our housing crisis gets, the right of developers to make more profit seems to supersede the right of tenants in our workforce to contract for homes for their families in stable neighborhoods." But concluding on an upbeat note, she wrote, "The battle for Lincoln Place continues to be educational and inspirational to those of us who hang in there year after year because of all it has taught us about law, democracy, land use, and above all, perseverance."

Despite a distaste for legal action as a way to resolve disputes, she got in touch with Jan Chatten-Brown, the attorney who had helped Marcia Scully when the redevelopment first came before the city planning commission. Chatten-Brown believed that the council's latest approval was ripe for a court challenge on the grounds that the original EIR not only failed to account for significant new information such as Ralph Vaughn's role, but didn't include the fact that one of the buildings had been extensively remodeled and seven others completely gutted. So-called CEQA lawsuits were often filed by opponents of large developments, either to stop them or to get more conditions imposed, but the legal actions didn't guarantee long-term success because a city could just require a developer to revise or update an EIR to pass muster. At best, that might delay a large project like the Lincoln Place redevelopment for a couple of years. But any delay was deemed worthwhile by those fighting to preserve the complex. There was the ongoing historic nomination process, and most importantly to Bernard, there was still the chance, the flame in her being that had flared and then flickered but had never gone completely out, that the owners would sell to the tenants.

With donations and what remained of the bequest from Ethel Shapiro-Bertolini, the LPTA scraped together $5,000 to retain Chatten-Brown and Susan Brandt-Hawley, a northern California attorney who specialized in historic preservation cases. Five payments of $3,000 would be due in each of the next five months, for a total of $20,000, a bargain-basement price for such a lawsuit but a daunting challenge for Lincoln Place tenants. In the December 2002, LPTA newsletter, Bernard asked for a pledge of ten dollars a month for ten months. She wrote, "We know that $10 per month is not easy for some households. But we ask you to consider the alternative. There is no better apartment out there, and they aren't building 'em like this anymore."

On December 20, the two attorneys filed a lawsuit in Los Angeles County Superior Court, asking a judge to void the city council's November action.

As in past years, the holiday season had arrived without tenants having a clear view of the future, although as long as Bernard and other active LPTA members hadn't given up, there was reason for hope. But Bisno and TransAction were tenacious foes, having spent a decade and an untold amount of money on high-priced legal counsel to pursue the vision of Lincoln Place as condominium complex for the well-to-do. With the newly filed lawsuit, the looming fight over historic designation, and the behemoth of Aimco lurking in the background with unknown plans, the coming year promised to be eventful and filled with suspense. And as the year unfolded, that promise would be more than fulfilled in a dramatic and sometimes dizzying array of episodes.

18

SHOW THOSE
BUILDINGS SOME LOVE

ON THE MORNING OF February 7, 2003, the sky above Sacramento, California, was cloudless and sunny, but the overnight temperature had dipped to the freezing point, and there was a lingering chill in the air. For many who followed the news, there was also apprehension—that morning's *Sacramento Bee* featured headlines about the imminent waging of war with Iraq and threats of retaliation from North Korea if the United States attacked its nuclear facilities. But inside the state resources building, a bland 1960s office tower a block from the capitol, people who had gathered in the first-floor auditorium had other matters on their minds. They were there for a meeting of the historical resources commission to consider the nominations of four properties to the National Register of Historic Places, one of which was Lincoln Place.

The nine commissioners took their places at a table in the front of the auditorium, and shortly after nine a.m., Chairperson Anthea Hartig called the meeting to order. The day's agenda included, in addition to Lincoln Place, a county jail in Monterey County, a historic naval training center in San Diego, and a 1901 Craftsman-style house in Los Angeles. The last, fittingly, in a neighborhood only a few miles from the place where Ralph Vaughn built a house for himself and family and spent fifty years of his life. In the audience were TransAction attorneys Allan Abshez and Andrew Fogg, who were expected to oppose the nomination, and Amanda Seward, Laura Burns, Sheila Bernard and Gail Sansbury, all of whom had made the trip to Sacramento at their own expense to testify on behalf of the Lincoln Place nomination.

Each side was given twenty minutes to make its case, with five minutes for rebuttal. With one exception, the arguments both pro and con had been aired before the city cultural heritage commission two years earlier. As the author of the nomination, Amanda Seward spoke first, and she quickly got to that exception, the fact that Ralph Vaughn and not Heth Wharton had been the principal designer of Lincoln Place. She noted his association with acclaimed African American architects Hilyard Robinson and Paul Williams and the fact, revealed through the interviews Laura Burns conducted with his son Ronald and draftsman Allan Mock, that he was strongly influenced by the garden city movement. Also speaking on behalf of the nomination were Burns, Bernard, Sansbury, and Catherine Barrier, who represented the Los Angeles Conservancy. Burns gave a detailed account of her research and what she had learned about the history and design of Lincoln Place, and Sansbury enlarged on some of the points in her master's thesis about the building of Lincoln Place during a critical housing shortage and how that made it such an important part of the city's social history. Bernard spoke very briefly, saying that as head of the Lincoln Place Tenant's Association for the past fourteen years, she fully supported the nomination.

When Abshez took the floor he argued, as he had before, that Lincoln Place lacked architectural distinction and cultural and social significance. He noted that a report written by a historic preservation expert for the 1994 environmental impact report and another for the cultural heritage commission hearing had reached that conclusion. "Lincoln Place is not an example of the garden city movement," he said. "It is simply a garden apartment project of a type that was already common when it was built and which remains common today." He also repeated his accusation that the push for historic status was just another facet of the LPTA's long-running fight against the owner's redevelopment plans. The National Register of Historic Places, he said, was "not intended to be misused as a tool to frustrate economic development activities such as reinvestment in the aging housing stock."

But when Hartig opened the floor for discussion by the commissioners, it quickly became clear that those arguments hadn't been persuasive. Three of them said they had visited Lincoln Place and had observed significant architectural details, the amount of open space and landscaping, and the sense felt by so many tenants and others—that the apartment complex was not just a collection of buildings but a real community. Two commissioners said that the fact that Ralph Vaughn designed Lincoln Place was an important piece of social history that added to its significance. When everyone had their say, a motion was made and seconded, and the commission voted 7–1 to declare Lincoln Place eligible for the National Register of Historic Places. [60]

While the Lincoln Place supporters were all smiles and ready to move to the corridor outside to exchange congratulations, commissioner Lauren Bricker put in a final word. She had visited the site, she said, and couldn't help seeing the gutted and derelict Lake Street buildings. In a pointed statement directed at Abshez and his colleagues, she said, "It's tragic really to see those buildings in that condition, so I would strongly encourage them [the property owners] to fix them up."

But the question in the minds of Seward, Bernard and the others wasn't when the owners would fix up those buildings, but whether they would find a way, despite the commission's action, to tear them down. The finding of eligibility would now go to Carol Shull, the Keeper of the National Register of Historic Places, who would render a decision at the close of the forty-five-day public comment period. She couldn't add Lincoln Place to the register over the owner's objection, but if she found it eligible, that would be enough to trigger the state and city requirement for a new environmental impact study before any buildings could be demolished. Despite Robert Bisno's statements to the press after the city council gave the go-ahead to the redevelopment project, neither he nor anyone connected with Aimco had publicly stated that the Village at Venezia remodeling plan was permanently off the table. In the eyes of Bernard and other LPTA members, keeping tenants guessing about the future was part of a strategy of harassment meant to convince them that they'd be better off living elsewhere. And she couldn't blame those who decided to move, because she knew the strain and anxiety could take a real toll on mental and physical well-being. It was a major reason she wouldn't give up on the "Let's Own It" ideal, which would give residents the sense of security they deserved but were denied just because they rented their homes.

Seward and the others felt confident, because approval by a state typically meant approval on the federal level as well. Or so they believed. In reality, Bisno, with the obvious though silent support of Aimco, wasn't about to let a noisy band of ungrateful tenants and meddling historic preservationists get the upper hand. Not long after the state commission meeting, he complained to a US congressman named George Radanovich that the process of historic designation had unfairly trampled on his private property rights. Radanovich was chairman of the House Subcommittee on National Parks, Recreation, and Public Lands, which oversaw the National Park Service, the agency responsible for the National Register of Historic Places. The Fresno, California, Republican was also solidly conservative, and clearly sympathetic to Bisno's complaint. In early March, he wrote a letter to Shull, alluding to an earlier meeting with her in which he had shared details of the dispute between Bisno and Lincoln Place tenants. It was clear, he wrote, that "the process is being exploited and may need statutory reform."

This only came to light because Gail Sansbury happened to be in Washington, DC, after the state commission meeting and went to the keeper's office to take a look at the Lincoln Place file. Along with the application and other documents, she saw the letter from Radanovich. The tone of it was ominous enough that Seward immediately wrote to the congressman, saying she feared that he might have been misled by the landlord's characterization of the nomination as a last-ditch effort by tenants to stop the redevelopment. She pointed out that she had authored the nomination but wasn't a Lincoln Place tenant and wasn't working on the LPTA's behalf. "This application is about architecture, the nation's historic efforts to address the severe housing shortage in this country in the period immediately after World War II, and the distinctive design of early low- and moderate-income housing during World War II and the housing shortage that followed. It is not about a landlord-tenant dispute."

She invited Radanovich to read her application if he hadn't already, and to visit Lincoln Place to see it for himself. She would be happy to meet with him, she wrote, or provide any further information he might need to decide whether Lincoln Place was worthy of historic designation. He didn't respond. But the matter became especially urgent when Susan Brandt-Hawley, one of the attorneys representing the LPTA in its lawsuit against the city, was told by

TransAction's legal counsel that the company intended to proceed with the demolition of the two buildings slated for replacement by a recreation facility and condominiums as part of the Village at Venezia project. The landlord had already invoked the Ellis Act to evict all forty tenants of those buildings, and the city had issued the requisite demolition permits more than a year earlier.

Seward got in touch with Councilwoman Cindy Miscikowski's office to complain that it would be a travesty to allow any buildings to be demolished while the state-approved nomination to the National Register was pending. In response, the councilwoman's planning deputy, Kristen Montet, said there was nothing the city could do because any local laws that might stop or delay the demolitions were trumped by the Ellis Act. This didn't sit well with Seward. In a *Santa Monica Mirror* article about the pending demolitions, she was quoted as saying, "The point is that a historic resource is going to be torn down. It somehow survived and now that we know it is historic, is the city just going to allow it to be torn down?"[61]

Less than a week later a chain-link fence went up around the vacant buildings, a sign of what was coming. Then, just three days after the fence appeared, TransAction applied to the city for permits to demolish the five vacant buildings on Lake Street. Did this mean that the company was now proceeding with the original redevelopment plan? If so there were some glaring problems. For one, the plan approved by the city required TransAction to build the 144 low-income apartments and have them ready for occupancy before proceeding with the 706 condominiums. Moreover, the rental units were to be in a new building at the southwest corner of the property, not on Lake Street, which marked Lincoln Place's northern border. The city had also imposed a condition that required buildings slated for demolition to be photographically documented, both inside and out, and offered for sale to anyone who would agree to move them to another site. In light of these facts, the city could hardly give TransAction the green light to start tearing them down. Or so some people believed.

TransAction claimed that the demolitions weren't part of the redevelopment approved by the city council, so none of the conditions applied. Before the city building department could issue the demolition permits, the applications had to be reviewed by the city planning department, and Seward and others expected city planners to ask, "Well, if these demolitions aren't part of the approved redevelopment project, what project are they part of?" The only other Lincoln Place project then approved related to the Village at Venezia, which involved remodeling, not demolition, but to everyone's dismay the planning department never asked the question but simply accepted TransAction's dubious claim.

At the end of March, an asbestos-abatement crew showed up at the Frederick Street and Doreen Place buildings and tore out roofing materials, flooring tiles, and heating ducts. Another crew followed, breaking the stucco and piling the joists and beams and other wood framing members onto flatbed trucks, presumably to be shipped to Mexico, where used lumber was in demand for new construction. Ingrid Mueller was away from home until late afternoon, and she recalls returning to the shock, though not surprise, of seeing the buildings replaced by a "gaping, bare grass hole." She thought about Bill Ullett, a longtime LPTA steering committee member and faithful supporter who had lived in the Doreen Place building before falling ill and dying in a hospital. He was gone before the tenants were evicted, and she was glad he didn't have to see his home of many years reduced to rubble. To Sheila Bernard, who lived a five-minute walk away, the Frederick Street building in direct line of sight of anyone turning toward Lincoln Place from Lincoln Boulevard was the face of the apartment complex. Seeing it and the building behind it gone, she says, was "like seeing somebody with their front teeth knocked out."

To add insult to injury, the demolitions meant that the description in the pending national register nomination was now inaccurate. There were no longer fifty-two buildings and 795 apartments. That fact was brought to Carol Shull's attention by TransAction attorney Allan Abshez, who submitted an extensive list of reasons why the nomination should be rejected. According to an April 24 letter from Shull's office to the California Office of Historic Preservation, those reasons included the two demolished buildings, the gutted Lake Street buildings awaiting demolition, and the removal of much of the original landscaping. Seward was infuriated that the landlord had deliberately set out to torpedo the historic nomination this way, rather than let it rise or fall on its own merits.

"I couldn't believe it," Seward says. "I couldn't believe you could get away with that." In her five years working for a major law firm after graduation from Georgetown, she says she never experienced anything so underhanded. "The people I worked with were decent, trustworthy people. I never once saw anything like this."

But Shull didn't reject the nomination. Instead, her office asked for an up-to-date description of the property as well as additional information about Lincoln Place's design and answers to questions related to the garden city movement and the role of the FHA. The keeper could still deem Lincoln Place eligible for the national register and help protect it from destruction. But nobody knew when that might happen, which made stopping demolition of the five Lake Street buildings critically important.

At the time, Seward was working as a senior vice president in the animation division of Warner Brothers, and her career had been spent in the field of entertainment law. But Brandt-Hawley and Jan Chatten-Brown were experts in CEQA, land-use laws, and historic preservation. In their opinion, the city's apparent belief that the Ellis Act superseded any local ordinances relevant to the demolition of Lincoln Place buildings was flatly wrong. Even though the national register nomination had been returned, they believed that the state commission's finding that Lincoln Place met the criteria for listing was enough to trigger state and city laws requiring environmental review—including a study of the feasibility of preservation—before any buildings could be demolished.

Despite the okay from the planning department, the building department had sought advice from the city attorney before handing TransAction the Lake Street demolition permits, and the city attorney's office had asked the state office of historic preservation about the official status of the Lincoln Place nomination. Apparently tiring of these bureaucratic delays, the company filed a lawsuit in Los Angeles County Superior Court on April 28, asking a judge to order the city to issue the permits. On April 29, the state's historic preservation officer sent a fax to the city attorney's office saying that although Lincoln Place met the criteria for the national register, it hadn't been "officially" listed as eligible for either the national or state registers. Whether this was an exercise in semantics, or a sign that state officials didn't want to wade into the muddy waters of a tenant-landlord dispute, the city attorney's office took it to mean that the city didn't have legal grounds to withhold the permits. It so advised the building department, and with the permits in hand, the company dropped the lawsuit.

Some thought that the city was just trying to avoid being embroiled in yet another lawsuit that could drag on for years and end up the same way as earlier ones, in unfavorable rulings. Others thought the city had a good case and should have fought back against what they regarded as a litigious corporate bully. Seward was firmly in the latter camp. She and her husband formed an entity they named the 20th Century Architectural Alliance and retained Chatten-Brown and Susan Brandt-Hawley to file a lawsuit in superior court asking for an order to revoke the permits. She also recruited a statewide nonprofit organization called the California Preservation Foundation as second plaintiff, and asked the Los Angeles Conservancy and the National Organization of Minority Architects to join the effort, which they later did.

The courts typically required plaintiffs in such cases to exhaust all administrative remedies, so Seward filed an appeal with the city's Board of Building and Safety Commissioners, an appointed body empowered to review and, if necessary, modify or reverse building department actions. Seward and Chatten-Brown prepared an extensive presentation for the board hearing scheduled for June 3. This included photographs, other visual aids, and the documents submitted with the nomination to the National Register of Historic Places. There were also letters of support from a number of people, including California senators Dianne Feinstein and Barbara Boxer, famous architectural photographer Julius Shulman, and an architect named Dan Peterson, who had been hired by TransAction in 1992 to conduct the architectural and historical evaluation required for the Lincoln Place EIR.

In his letter, Peterson supported the argument that Lincoln Place was historically and architecturally significant and should be preserved. This came as a surprise, because TransAction had repeatedly pointed to conclusions from his earlier study as showing the very opposite, that Lincoln Place wasn't worthy of any special recognition. Company representatives had argued this before the city council, the city cultural heritage commission, and the state historical resources commission. It was a central point in the city's defense against the LPTA lawsuit—the EIR hadn't shown that the redevelopment would cause any adverse cultural and historic impacts and the only new fact that had come to light—Ralph Vaughn's role as designer—wasn't significant enough to require a new review.

What had happened? Had Peterson, a recognized authority in his field, changed his mind in the intervening eleven years? Had TransAction mischaracterized his study without anyone noticing the fact?

These questions arose because of yet another tenacious research effort by Laura Burns. She had been rereading the materials submitted in 2001 to the city cultural heritage commission, including the report by architect Robert Chattel rejecting claims that Lincoln Place merited historic status. She didn't find anything new in his dismissive observations, but at the bottom of one page, she saw a footnote with a reference to Peterson's 1992 report. Neither Sheila Bernard nor Gail Sansbury knew anything about it, since the full report hadn't been included in the EIR. There had only been a summary without any attribution. But internet research led Burns to a Dan Peterson in the San Francisco bay area who specialized in historic preservation; she called him, and he told her that he remembered Lincoln Place well and believed it was worthy of listing on the national register. However, properties could be listed only if they were more than fifty years old, and at the time of his evaluation, Lincoln Place was eight years short of that standard. He told Burns that he believed at the time that Lincoln Place would definitely qualify once it reached the fifty-year mark.

Peterson agreed to mail a complete copy of his sixty-six-page report to Susan Brandt-Hawley, and to send a letter to the Board of Building and Safety Commissioners. In that letter, he repeated what he had told Burns about the national register's fifty-year requirement. He went on to write, "This [Lincoln Place] is a very significant low-income housing project in the context of the vast growth of housing in the Los Angeles area after World War II. It is also one of the few significant low-income projects remaining in the Los Angeles area with this kind of architectural integrity."

The Peterson report would later be at issue in the LPTA's lawsuit against the city, and attorneys would argue the question of whether the architect's sentiments about Lincoln Place in his 2003 letter were more favorable than those expressed in his 1992 report. But to Burns, getting the report with its discussion of the fifty-year eligibility standard was "like finding gold," and she and Seward hoped that it and Peterson's letter would have a positive effect, if not on the building and safety commissioners, then on the legal system that appeared likely to hold Lincoln Place's ultimate fate in its hands.

By coincidence, the same day the board met in downtown Los Angeles to hear the appeal, the House Subcommittee on National Parks, Recreation, and Public Lands was convening a hearing in Washington, DC, for the purpose, according to chairman George Radanovich, of conducting oversight on "private property protection" under the National Historic Preservation Act. One of the witnesses scheduled to testify was TransAction CEO Robert Bisno.

In an opening statement, Radanovich explained his reasons for calling the hearing. "Recently, a case was brought to my attention where an application for eligibility was submitted by a third party for an apartment complex in Los Angeles, California. What concerns me with this case is twofold. First, the owner of the apartment complex furiously objected to the application, yet it appears his pleas were largely ignored by the state historic preservation office; and, second, what will be the effects from the case on the integrity of the National Historic Preservation Act."

Radanovich went on to summarize a major objection by Bisno and TransAction; that the city planning department, planning commission, cultural heritage commission, and the city council had all rejected the claims of historic significance. "Today," he said, "I am very concerned that this important act, one that I support very much, will now become a tool used by preservationists and activists in State historic preservation offices to halt development or redevelopment of communities across the country."

When Radanovich called on Bisno, the TransAction CEO got directly to his complaint against the LPTA. The group's agenda, he told committee members, was to block redevelopment so tenants wouldn't have to move.

"I see the abuse of the National Register Process as the number one tool today to stop economic development unless you take steps to stop it." He said that the Village at Venezia project would have preserved Lincoln Place and accused tenants of opposing it because they didn't want to pay higher rents. "I am being told that the National Register does not have an impact on our property rights. I am living proof that it does. Our rights are being trampled by this process.

"Those who oppose property rights have carefully designed the system to strangle development activities by the mere filing of an application," he said, and he called for changing federal law to preclude a state from even considering an application to the national register without the property owner's consent.

Responding to Bisno's testimony, Radanovich said he had reviewed the Lincoln Place application and concluded that the state should never have approved it. Without mentioning Seward by name, he took a swipe at both her and the state historic preservation staff by asking "how could they expect something like that [the application] that was so poorly done and had so many holes in it could have been possibly approved."

Radanovich concluded the hearing by asking the chairman of the federal government's Advisory Council on Historic Preservation to take up the issues that had been raised and "at least review the Bisno situation to see if there were changes that could be made."

Historic preservationists were alarmed. There were reasons why getting consent or even notifying owners of pending applications to list properties as eligible for the national register was far from ideal. For planning purposes, the federal government and states would sometimes want to identify entire areas or districts with historic qualities, but getting hundreds and possibly thousands of property owners to consent before even considering such a matter would be, at best, cumbersome, and at worst, impossible. Even in cases of individual properties, the need to get an owner's consent before analyzing historic qualities could have a chilling effect. New legislation in response to alleged abuse in the isolated case of Lincoln Place could end up being a detriment to the cause of historic preservation throughout the country. Furthermore, as more than one witness pointed out, Bisno's argument wasn't really with federal law that didn't restrict the use of private property deemed historic, but with the State of California and City of Los Angeles and their requirements for environmental review before buildings could be demolished. Even then, as Bisno himself acknowledged in his testimony, neither the state nor city was trying to impose that requirement.

The claim that an EIR was required was being made by the 20th Century Architectural Alliance in its lawsuit.

While Bisno was airing his grievance in Washington, DC, Seward and others were telling the building and safety commissioners why the demolition permits should be revoked. The city ordinance requiring a study of the feasibility of preserving historic properties prior to any redevelopment clearly applied to Lincoln Place. Even though the Keeper of the National Register of Historic Places hadn't officially accepted or rejected the nomination, the members of the state historical resources commission, all with expertise in fields related to history and architecture, had found that the apartment complex met the national register's criteria. But the city attorney disagreed. Unless the keeper officially listed Lincoln Place as eligible for the register, the ordinance was irrelevant.

Seward and other Lincoln Place supporters testified about Lincoln Place's architecture, the work of Ralph Vaughn, and the social and cultural role of the complex in the community. TransAction, in turn, displayed photographs of the vacant Lake Street buildings showing weeds, dead landscaping, and broken windows to support its claim that Lincoln Place had no historic significance. This got the attention of commissioner Barbara Boudreaux, who said, "There's nothing there now to preserve, there's nothing there now to restore. You can't be proud of what we see in these photographs. No one took any time to show love to the buildings. There's no love there...somebody erred when they didn't keep this property up." If Boudreaux, a Black woman, was especially disturbed because the buildings were designed by a Black architect, she didn't say. But her comments constituted the entirety of board discussion before she joined the other commissioners in adopting the building department findings and voting to deny the appeal.

The cursory discussion and dismissal was discouraging but not especially surprising, given the opinions from City Attorney Rocky Delgadillo, seen by many as a friend of real estate developers. But the board decision didn't mean that the Lake Street buildings would immediately be reduced to rubble. Chatten-Brown hoped that a superior court judge could be convinced to order a stay of the demolition permits pending a ruling on the merits of the 20th Century Architectural Alliance lawsuit. She filed a motion to that effect, with a hearing scheduled for June 23. Until then, everyone would be holding their breath.

Sheila Bernard had planned to drive downtown to the county courthouse for the 8:30 a.m. hearing, but she was awakened shortly after six a.m. by voices outside her apartment window. Her building was separated from the vacant Lake Street buildings by an alley and bank of carports, and by the time she got up and stepped outside to see what was going on, she saw the claw of a heavy-duty excavator ripping chunks out of one of the buildings. It was unbelievable that the owner would start this on the very morning of the court hearing. Generally calm and imperturbable, she was nearly shaking with rage as she hurried back inside her apartment to call Chatten-Brown and tell the attorney what was going on.

In her Elkgrove Avenue apartment two buildings away, Ingrid Mueller was also rudely awakened by what she described as an "incredible, unusual, thunderous, blitzkrieg-like noise." She quickly got dressed and went outside, where she joined some of her neighbors to watch the yellow excavator rip into the buildings, bringing the roofs and walls crashing down as if they were no more substantial than dollhouses or other childhood constructions. Unlike the earlier demolitions of the buildings on Frederick Street and Doreen Place, with salvaged lumber being sorted and stacked on trucks, this looked like an effort to reduce the buildings to rubble as quickly as possible. She asked a worker standing nearby if he knew about the court hearing scheduled to convene in a little more than an hour. He didn't respond. "Whoever ordered this should go to jail!" she declared to all within earshot.

Bernard left for downtown at seven thirty. She now felt heartsick, the scene of the excavator claw ripping through the building like the appendage of some science fiction monster playing in her head. She still had a glimmer of hope that a favorable ruling by the judge would mean the demolitions could be stopped before everything was gone, but that hope was dashed when she got to the courthouse and learned that the judge, David Yaffe, was delayed and wouldn't start the hearing until after nine o'clock. By then, she was all but certain, it would be too late.

At the courthouse, Chatten-Brown told Bernard that she was ethically obligated to tell Judge Yaffe about the demolitions. As expected, the judge ruled that the motion to stay the permits was now moot. Bernard wondered afterward what might have happened if she hadn't told Chatten-Brown, and the judge had ruled in their favor. Could they have pursued damages or taken some other action against TransAction? It was just speculation and, in any case, wouldn't have saved the buildings, which were all down by the time the judge gaveled the hearing to order. When she got back to Lincoln Place late that morning, the shambles of wood and stucco that had resembled the aftermath of a tornado or hurricane had been loaded onto dump trucks and hauled off to a landfill. A gas company crew was digging in the bits of concrete and debris that remained, and one of the workers told her that they were trying to locate gas lines, because the demolition crew had apparently been in such a hurry that they hadn't called the gas company to shut them off.

A tenant named Carol Beck wrote about the demolitions in the July issue of the Venice *Beachhead*. The sixty-year-old woman was a good friend of Laura Ponce and had become a stalwart LPTA supporter during the losing battle over Building 18. In her article, she described the scene, with dust and grit in the air, beeping and roaring from the excavators and bulldozers, and the odor of diesel fumes and natural gas. "Shouldn't they have notified us that this demolition was going to take place so we, the people (the residents and the surrounding neighborhood) could protect ourselves from the toxic materials spewed out into the air? Was this an illegal stealth attack with no due process?"

It certainly appeared to be a stealth attack, although the question of due process could only be settled by the courts. And nobody knew how long that might grind on, and what the ultimate outcome might be. Four days after the demolitions, Chatten-Brown sent a fax to the city attorney's office about scheduling and other technical matters in the 20th Century Architectural Alliance case, but she ended with an unambiguous statement of the lawsuit's ultimate goal. It would seek, she wrote, "to have the buildings rebuilt in a manner compatible with the remaining Lincoln Place buildings, and according to historical plans."

Could Ralph Vaughn's vision actually arise from the rubble of the destruction? Could a fifty-two-year-old building be replicated in all its details? Depending upon a person's perspective, it was either a wonderful prospect or a pipe dream. But one thing was certain. The apartment complex was facing its most existential threat since 1991, when TransAction first began drumming up support for its redevelopment plan. The reality of the threat was emphasized by the fact that the landlord was letting vacated apartments sit empty instead of re-renting them. Normal attrition accounted for some of these vacancies, but it was widely believed that most were a consequence of people moving because of the threat of eviction for the Village at Venezia project, and fears aroused by the demolitions. While it was difficult to get an exact count, in the summer of 2003 the LPTA estimated that only about four hundred tenants occupied the 696 units that remained after the five buildings on Lake Street and the two on Frederick Street and Doreen Place were torn down.

The economic doldrums of the first half of the 1990s had slowed Venice gentrification, but it had gathered momentum later in the decade. The recession of 2001 had provided a respite, but by 2003, houses were going on the market at prices that shocked longtime residents, and the community's population was clearly shifting toward a younger and more affluent demographic. This caused particular tension in the Oakwood neighborhood, where longtime Black and Latino residents felt the pressure of displacement. When plans were announced in 2002 for a radical makeover of the Lincoln Center shopping complex on Lincoln Boulevard, it was widely seen as part of a change that would threaten low-income residents of Oakwood to the west, and Lincoln Place, just to the east. The 440,000-square-foot commercial property was still owned by the heirs of Philip Yousem, and it had long served a working- and middle-class clientele, with a chain supermarket, a drug store, and a variety store that was later a home improvement store and then a discount clothing outlet. The new plans called for demolishing everything on the site to make way for a mixed-use commercial-and-residential development. According to the developer, there would be a large upscale anchor store on the ground level, complemented by smaller boutiques, restaurants, and other businesses. Above the stores would be 280 luxury apartments, rising in tiers to eight stories at the back of the property where it abutted Lincoln Place.

Demolition of Lincoln Place buildings on Lake Street
(photo by Lydia Ponce)

Demonstration by Lincoln Place residents (photo by Margaret Molloy)

Los Angeles County sheriff's cars at Lincoln Place on
day of mass evictions (photo by Hans Adamson)

Amanda Seward, left, talking to Laura Burns at Lincoln Place
on day of mass evictions (photo by Hans Adamson)

Bill Rosendahl speaking to media at Lincoln Place
on day of mass evictions (Photo by Hans Adamson)

Lincoln Place tenant Patricia Martinez speaking to a TV
news reporter after being locked out of her apartment by
sheriff's deputies (photo by Hans Adamson)

Bill Rosendahl outside locked Lincoln Place office on day
of mass evictions, trying to call manager. Note peeling paint
and cracked stucco (photo by Hans Adamson)

Carol Beck, tenant and LPTA activist (photo by Hans Adamson)

Gwyn Gorg, who led 1964 CORE protest of Lincoln Place
rental policy, speaking at Lincoln Place rally on Martin Luther King Day.
Amanda Seward at right (photo by Margaret Molloy)

LPTA fundraiser hosted by Stanley Sheinbaum, August, 2006. From left,
Gloria Morales, Ingrid Mueller, Stanley Sheinbaum, Amanda Seward, Jane
Fonda, Don Geagan, Sheila Bernard, Sara Sakuma, Suzanne Thompson,
Laura Burns, Ruth Holzgreen (photo by Douglas Eisenstark)

LPTA fundraiser. From left, Lincoln place tenants Sheila Bernard, Frieda Marlin and Ingrid Mueller, attorney John Murdock, Stanley Sheinbaum (photo by Douglas Eisenstark)

Tenant attorney Jan Book, right, with tenant Susan Ostanek at LPTA meeting (photo by Ingrid Mueller)

Bill Rosendahl presenting Sheila Bernard with city
Certificate of Appreciation, 2010 (photo by Ingrid Mueller)

Many Lincoln Place tenants saw this as a threat. The shopping center had been originally developed to serve the needs of Lincoln Place's working-class renters, with the supermarket and drugstore within easy walking distance, but where would those people, many now elderly, go to buy their groceries and fill their prescriptions? Along with longtime residents in Oakwood, they were hearing the message that they were no longer welcome in the community they had long called home. Even younger and more affluent people in other parts of Venice worried that gentrification was destroying one of the things that had attracted them to the community, its diverse mixture of people in terms of age, ethnicity, and economic class.

Some homeowners in the vicinity of Lincoln Place formed a group called the Venice Community Coalition and began organizing opposition to the project. Ingrid Mueller, Carol Beck and several other tenants started attending the group's meetings, where they not only volunteered to help stop the Lincoln Center project, but also talked to neighborhood people about the threat to Lincoln Place. The relationships they formed with some of those people would prove critical to the very future of the apartment complex.

Early in August 2003, while the LPTA awaited a date for a hearing in its lawsuit against the city, tenants got news that Aimco had bought TransAction's share of the property and was now the sole owner of Lincoln Place. Robert Bisno, the LPTA's *bête noire* for the past half-dozen years, was apparently gone for good, but beyond that, nobody could really guess what the ownership change meant for the future. Would Aimco, a company that owned and managed more than three hundred thousand apartment units, continue to pursue TransAction's redevelopment plan, which was predominately condominiums? Would it put forth an entirely new plan involving the demolition of existing buildings and construction of new apartment houses? Would it resurrect the widely despised Village at Venezia project? Or would it—the most optimistic tenants hoped this might be the case—keep Lincoln Place as is and just fix up the buildings and landscaping that had fallen into such depressing disrepair?

There was yet another possibility, which was that Aimco would try to flip the property and walk away with a profit. Whatever the likelihood of that might be, Sheila Bernard glimpsed an opportunity to revisit her never-abandoned dream of tenant ownership, or at the least, of seeing the property in the hands of a nonprofit that would maintain it as affordable housing and not cede it to condominium buyers or renters looking for luxury apartments. She decided to try to talk to someone at Aimco about the company's plans. The LPTA hadn't had any communications during the two years of Aimco's part ownership, and despite demonstrating against the company and publicizing its less-than-savory practices, she hoped to get off on a good foot with the new owner and put the often-poisonous dealings with Bisno and TransAction in the past.

She called Aimco's Denver headquarters and was connected to a woman named Patti Shwayder, the senior vice president in charge of government and community relations. In the August 2003 issue of the LPTA newsletter, Bernard wrote that after she expressed the LPTA's desire to have better relations with Aimco, Shwayder assured her that this would be the case. Bernard said she invited Shwayder to one of the LPTA's monthly meetings at Penmar Park whenever the Aimco executive was in Los Angeles. She also asked Shwayder how Aimco's purchase would affect the LPTA and 20th Century Architectural Alliance lawsuits, and what plans Aimco had for the future of Lincoln Place. The woman didn't know the answer to the first question, Bernard wrote, but promised to find out. As for Aimco's future plans, the executive said they weren't firm yet. Bernard concluded by writing that she was encouraged by this conversation. "I hope we are embarking on a calmer chapter in the stormy history of Lincoln Place."

That certainly was a sentiment shared by everyone involved in the tenant struggle. But there were still storm clouds overhead, and nobody could predict whether those clouds would break and let in a flood of sunlight, or darken and unleash a fury of wind and rain. If anyone had been able to peer into a crystal ball, though, they would have seen that Lincoln Place tenants would soon find out which of those possibilities was fantasy, and which was very real.

19

ROASTED CHESTNUTS AND STUFFED GRAPE LEAVES

A verguenca en usted!

—Written on the stump of a tree cut down
during Lincoln Place demolitions

ON NOVEMBER 17, 2003, Arnold Schwarzenegger was sworn in as the thirty-eighth governor of California. The bodybuilder and former Mr. Universe, who gained fame playing movie action heroes like the Terminator and Conan the Barbarian, had surprised many people that past summer by telling host Jay Leno on *The Tonight Show* that he would be a candidate in a special election to recall incumbent Governor Gray Davis. Some people had trouble taking him seriously, with his pronounced Germanic accent and cartoonish film persona, but his celebrity and the deep unpopularity of Davis helped propel him to an easy win over 134 other candidates, a field that included such luminaries as Gary Coleman, widely known as a child actor in the TV sitcom *Diff'rent Strokes*; Larry Flynt, the controversial publisher of *Hustler* and other X-rated magazines; and Angelyne, a busty, blond model and minor actress known for scantily clad images of herself displayed on billboards on some of Los Angeles's busiest streets.

Tenant advocates in Los Angeles and elsewhere took a lively interest in the election, because Davis, a moderate Democrat, had supported and signed into law measures promoted by groups working to correct what they saw as a serious imbalance between the rights of renters and property owners. But the single biggest item on advocates' wish list, the repeal or extensive revision of the despised Ellis Act, had run up against the real estate interests that wielded abundant influence in the state legislature, and nothing had gotten anywhere near his desk.

Without any record in public office, Schwarzenegger's views on this area of legislation were unknown. But he was a Republican who touted the long-standing tenets of the party—low taxes, limited regulation, support for business interests and property rights—so renters didn't hold out hope that he might be their friend in Sacramento. But if his election was disagreeable news for Lincoln Place tenants, they had gotten worse just four days before his inauguration. Los Angeles County Superior Court judge Dzintra Janavs had ruled against the LPTA in its lawsuit challenging the city's 2002 approval of the Lincoln Place redevelopment project. The LPTA was expected to appeal, but the ruling was one less obstacle to a vision of a new Lincoln Place that would no longer be home to large numbers of working-class and elderly renters but to owners of luxury condominiums.

The lawsuit claimed that the city should have ordered an updated EIR that considered new facts such as Ralph Vaughn's role as Lincoln Place's principal designer. But Janavs, the same judge who ruled that the city's rejection of the project in 1995 violated the Ellis Act, didn't agree. The original EIR, she wrote in her three-page ruling, was sufficient because these new facts, including the action of the state historical resources commission, didn't constitute "significant new information."

In the December issue of the LPTA newsletter, Sheila Bernard wrote that the group's lawyers regarded the judge's decision as "a bad call" and believed that chances were good that it could be reversed on appeal. As for Aimco, she wrote, the company hadn't rushed downtown to apply for new demolition permits so for the immediate future Lincoln Place appeared to be safe. The landlord hadn't made any public announcement about future plans, either, but she referred to a quarterly conference call for shareholders in which a spokesperson said the company might be interested in building 1,300 new units on the property, or in the alternative, selling it to another developer. Building those 1,300 units would require a completely new EIR, she observed, and selling the property might open the door for an offer from a nonprofit or other developer willing to preserve the complex as affordable housing. "Either of these possibilities," she wrote, "offers us new opportunities to protect Lincoln Place. As always, we will explore all our options and 'never say die.'"

As an antidote to bad news from the court and uncertainty about the future, the month of December brought news from city hall that lifted the holiday spirits of tenants who had lived for years in dread of finding eviction notices on their doors. Eighteen months after directing the city's housing department to study the problem of landlords evicting tenants under the major-rehabilitation provision of the RSO, the city council approved new regulations designed to stop this abuse. No longer would landlords be able to evict a tenant of a rent-controlled apartment, do the legal minimum amount of repair work on the unit and then rent it at the going market rate to somebody new. Instead, landlords would have to pay to relocate that tenant to comparable accommodations while the apartment was undergoing rehabilitation work. If those accommodations cost more than the tenant's rent, the landlord had to pay the difference. When the work was done, the tenant had the right to return at the same rent plus an increase of no more than ten percent.

The major rehabilitation provision had been invoked to evict the tenants of Lincoln Place's Building 18, although all but Laura Ponce had taken financial inducements to leave voluntarily. Most of the tenants in the fifty-nine Lake Street units had done the same. After Aimco became sole owner, there were fears that the company might decide to revive the Village at Venezia project and crank up the eviction machinery, so the council's action brought a definite measure of relief to the four hundred or so tenants who still called Lincoln Place home. Back in 1995, during the initial hearings on the redevelopment project, city planning commission president George Lefcoe had demanded a guarantee that no current tenant be forced to leave Lincoln Place, but one of the claims of the 20th Century Architectural Alliance lawsuit was that the city had flouted that guarantee by approving the demolition of the Lake Street buildings.

Now it appeared, at least to the most optimistic, that the law protected tenants from displacement no matter what kind of redevelopment Aimco or a successive developer pursued. But if, as the saying goes, a pessimist is a well-informed optimist, facts indicated otherwise, and most of them pointed at every California renter's nightmare, the Ellis Act.

As promised, LPTA lawyers appealed Judge Janav's ruling to the California Court of Appeal. Two weeks later, superior court judge David Yaffe rejected the 20th Century Architectural Alliance's challenge to the Lake Street demolitions, ruling that the city had lawfully issued the permits to tear down the buildings. In March, the alliance followed the LPTA's lead and appealed that decision to the state's higher court.

At that time, Sheila Bernard was still considering a run for the city council. But she had also cast her eye on something brand new, a system of neighborhood councils formed to act as advisory groups to the city. Conceived by Mayor Richard Riordan as an element of a revised city charter approved by voters in 1999, the councils were organized on a neighborhood and community level without definite structures and rules imposed by the city. The head of a Venice group dominated by home-owners led an effort to organize the Grass Roots Venice Neighborhood Council—the "Grass Roots" was dropped from the name a few years later—and held an inaugural governing board election in June 2002. But in the following year's election, a group calling itself the "Progressives" put up a slate of candidates that advocated, among other things, for the interests of renters. Bernard was one of those candidates, and she soon came under criticism stemming from her outspoken advocacy for the preservation of Lincoln Place.

The opposition slate, which called itself "Team Venice," claimed that if Bernard and the other "Progressives" were elected, Venice would become a "BANANA Republic." The "BANANA" standing for "Build Absolutely Nothing Anywhere Near Anyone." Also on the Team Venice slate was Chris Williams, the cochair of the Penmar Neighborhood Association and persistent critic of Bernard and the LPTA. Both Bernard and Williams were elected, but when it became clear that the Progressives would be in the majority, Williams and several other Team Venice members resigned. As people sometimes remarked in reference to a history of contention between different groups in the community, "Welcome to Venice."

As originally conceived, neighborhood councils would have had actual decision-making powers, but opposition by entrenched political interests meant that in the final iteration the bodies would only play an advisory role. Views ranged from the cynical—politicians would give lip service to this expression of grassroots democracy but feel free to ignore it—to the sunnily optimistic—neighborhood councils would become rallying points and voices for their communities that politicians could only ignore at their electoral peril. Bernard, whose natural predilection was to hope for the best, wanted to use her position to advocate for the cause of affordable housing throughout the community, not just the preservation of Lincoln Place. But by virtue of its size, Lincoln Place loomed large as a community issue, and when the neighborhood council board appointed Laura Burns as one of nine members of its land use and planning committee, the apartment complex had another passionate voice that tenants hoped would be heard by their city council representative and other elected officials.

At the urging of Burns, the committee sponsored a community forum on the future of Lincoln Place. In announcing the forum to be held on March 16, 2004, at the Penmar Park recreation center, Burns said, "Part of the empowerment of neighborhood councils is to give stakeholders a voice and genuine input on how developments shape their future. Since it appears the condo project is dead and some other project will shape the future of Lincoln Place, we'd like to give the community the opportunity to speak out before, rather than after, a submission to the planning department."

Before the start of the forum, the LPTA invited attendees to what it called "strolling buffet tours" of the complex. In the public announcement of the forum, Bernard described the purpose of the tours. "People in Venice have been hearing about Lincoln Place for years, but many have never really walked through it to discover all the unique gardens and courtyard spaces, the fabulous modernist architecture, and the exceptional floor plans." Led by selected tenants, these tours included foodstuffs like roasted chestnuts and stuffed grape leaves for participants to eat while they "strolled" through the property.

The forum attracted more than a hundred persons. Aimco had been invited to send a representative to talk about future plans, but the company declined. Speakers who did appear included Lisa Bialac, granddaughter of Samuel Bialac; Ronald Vaughn, the architect son of Ralph Vaughn; Drake Dillard, vice president of the National Organization of Minority Architects; and Amanda Seward, who showed slides to illustrate how Lincoln Place was designed to be a community where neighbors would unite and form powerful bonds. Also attending and briefly speaking were representatives from the offices of Congresswoman Jane Harman, city Councilwoman Cindy Miscikowski, and the city housing department.

In the question-and-answer period that followed the presentations, one person pointed out the irony of several hundred Lincoln Place apartments sitting vacant while Venice had one of the largest homeless populations in Los Angeles. Another drew applause by suggesting that people without housing in some other countries would simply squat in those vacant apartments. Several elderly tenants in the audience wanted to know, as they had for years, if and when they'd be forced to leave their homes. One longtime resident posed a poignant question: "Why don't they just shoot us?"

When a community member brought up the subject of someone buying Lincoln Place—the tenants, a nonprofit housing developer, even the city—Sheila Bernard mentioned the Aimco stockholders' conference call and said she believed that the company might be open to some kind of offer. The LPTA, she said, was forming a committee to explore this possibility. A purchase would likely require $100 million, if not more, and raising such an amount would be a daunting challenge. Of course, there was the question of whether Aimco was truly interested in selling, rather than developing the property with new apartments, condominiums, or a combination of the two. Whenever that question was put to Aimco representatives or anyone connected with the company, the answer was always that final decisions were yet to be made.

What Bernard and audience members didn't know then was that the company's actions would speak louder than words, and almost immediately bring its intentions into much sharper focus. Two days after the community forum, on a foggy, chilly morning, a truck stacked with sections of chain-link fencing pulled up to the corner of Doreen Place and Elkgrove Avenue. Workers quickly began erecting the six-foot high fencing around the two vacant buildings on opposite sides of that corner and draping it with black canvas. Laura Burns, who lived next door to one of the buildings and usually worked at home, walked to the Lincoln Place office, then located in a building at the corner of Elkgrove Avenue and Lake Street, and asked the manager why the fencing was being put up. To keep out vagrants, she was told. That might have been true in the strictest sense, but to Burns, the black-draped fencing was more than just a sign of Aimco's desire to protect its property from vandalism and other damage.

Across the street to the west of those fenced-off buildings was the site where Robert Bisno had stood at a podium three years earlier and told tenants that they would eventually have to leave because all of Lincoln Place was going to be turned into the Village at Venezia. Bisno was now out of the picture, the buildings where he stood had been torn down, but the only thing that had risen on the site was a lush, green carpet of weeds. To Burns, Bernard, and others, it was a kind of wasteland, an insult to the designer and builders of Lincoln Place, a slap in the face to a community that needed housing. Now, they feared, that wasteland would soon extend even deeper into the complex unless the destruction could be stopped.

Burns, the LPTA's resident sleuth, had been checking city records almost daily, and two days later she saw that Aimco had applied for demolition permits for the two vacant buildings. She alerted Amanda Seward and the attorneys representing the LPTA and the 20th Century Architectural Alliance, who quickly made plans to petition the state appeals court for what was called a writ of supersedeas. If granted, such a writ would stop any demolitions pending a decision on the appeal of Judge Yaffe's February ruling that the Lake Street demolitions had been lawful. Burns had a fax machine in her apartment, and sensing that a race for time might be in the offing, she asked the attorneys to send her a copy of any court order as soon as one appeared.

Early the next morning, she saw workers taping plastic over the windows of one of the buildings. A few minutes later, a white van towing a large yellow generator pulled into the alley behind it. From the name on the van, Spectrum Abatement, Burns surmised that a crew had come to remove asbestos, a required step preceding demolition. It typically involved removing parts of the roofing, ripping up flooring, and breaking into walls to get at asbestos-bearing heating vents. Which meant that serious damage would be done even if the building could be saved from total destruction.

Word quickly spread, and Sheila Bernard and Ingrid Mueller spoke on the phone about organizing an impromptu protest. Access to the building site was through a gate in the temporary fencing at the rear, and Mueller and Carol Beck decided to try to block the workers from getting inside. There were two rows of carports behind the building, and Beck pulled her thirty-year-old Dodge Dart across the space between them so that the crew couldn't reach the gate with their van and a truck that had shown up shortly after. Mueller fortified this blockade with her little white Scion. Bernard called Frieda Marlin and others likely to be home and asked them to bring lawn chairs or whatever they had and come to the site. Altogether, including Mueller and Beck, seven women and one man sat on chairs in a row in front of the gate. The workers asked them to move so they could bring in their equipment, but the tenants, who were all over sixty, politely declined. The workers acted more baffled than angry at the sight of gray- and white-haired seniors blocking their entry. Having herself and others who looked like they could be the crew members' grandparents was good strategy, Mueller says, because it inclined them to be respectful.

The standoff continued while the crew's foreman called his supervisor. The tenants were prepared to sit as long as necessary, but later in the morning, they heard a shout and saw Burns running toward them—literally—with a piece of paper in her hand. Just out of her fax machine, it was a court-issued temporary stay that read, "Pending further order of this court, real parties [Aimco] shall conduct no physical activity (including without limitation asbestos abatement or removal or other predemolition activities) on the properties located at 1018–1022 Doreen Place and 1003 Elkgrove Avenue, and 1032–1036 Doreen Place and 1002 Elkgrove Avenue in the City of Los Angeles. The order signed by Presiding Justice Dennis Perluss and Associate Justice Laurie Zelon directed Aimco to file its opposition to the petition for a writ of supersedeas by April 1.

Bernard had joined the gathering, and she and Burns tried to find the crew's foreman and show him the order. Even though the brigade of seniors had successfully blocked the gate so the van and truck couldn't get in, workers had been going into the building carrying sledgehammers and other tools, raising fears that serious damage would be done. Bernard called the police and the city building department, because the demolition permits hadn't been officially issued. When an officer arrived, she showed him the court order, and he advised the crew's foreman to stop any work, although he didn't threaten to arrest anyone. Later in the day, a building department inspector showed up and taped an "Order to Stop Work" to the wall beside the building entry.

In the immortal words of Yogi Berra, it had seemed like "déjà vu all over again"—workers ready to tear up parts of buildings at the same time attorneys were in a courtroom trying to get an order to stop them. It wasn't as dire as the excavator claw ripping apart the Lake Street buildings while attorneys cooled their heels in the county courthouse, and it had a happier outcome, at least temporarily. It was also a lesson in vigilance—if Burns hadn't seen Aimco's application for demolition permits when she did, the subsequent court order could have come too late to stop the asbestos abatement and potentially irreversible damage. That was especially important because Amanda Seward was thinking of renewing her effort for historic recognition, although she would bypass the National Register of Historic Places this time and make a formal application just for listing on the California Register of Historical Resources. In one sense, that might have appeared to be a slam dunk, given that the state historical resources commission had already deemed Lincoln Place historically significant, but Governor Schwarzenegger had appointed new members to the commission, so there was a definite element of uncertainly. What was critical, though, was to avoid a repeat of 2003, when the landlord tore two buildings down while the Keeper of the National Register was considering the Lincoln Place nomination and then lodged an objection on the grounds that the site description was inaccurate.

In its opposition to a writ of supersedeas, Aimco pointed to the fact, as did TransAction so many times before, that no agency of the city, state, or federal government had officially deemed Lincoln Place to be a historic property. Aimco attorneys argued that because Amanda Seward's nomination to the national register had been returned, the action of the state commission was a "dead letter." They also raised the new and possibly novel argument that because one building had been extensively remodeled and seven others demolished, whatever historic integrity Lincoln Place might have had was already impaired. But the court didn't agree. On April 8, a three-judge panel issued an order prohibiting any demolition permits or asbestos-abatement activity on any Lincoln Place building until the appeals court could rule in the 20th Century Architectural Alliance lawsuit against the city.

Any ruling in that case was likely to be at least a year away. For Bernard, that meant time to try to persuade Aimco to sell Lincoln Place, given the possibility of an adverse court decision and the uncertainty of prospects for redevelopment. She began meeting with Amanda Seward, Laura Burns, and Jan Book to discuss ways to proceed. Seward's role was obvious—making certain that any deal included the preservation of Lincoln Place buildings. Burns had done considerable research into Aimco and its operations throughout the country and Book was a certified public accountant with a law degree, which made her especially valuable when it came to the vital task of crunching numbers. Up to that time she hadn't been active in LPTA affairs beyond giving the organization money and writing several supportive letters, but she had always had a strong interest in the architecture and history of the complex and had actively supported Seward's preservation efforts.

Bernard's ideal was still the "Let's Own It" model, where a tenant-run Lincoln Place Housing Corporation would buy and manage the complex. But it had taken the assistance of a paid consultant and many months of work to find sources of funding for the $47 million purchase offer TransAction rebuffed in 1992, and the prospect of raising more than $100 million to make an offer to Aimco before the company proceeded with demolitions looked overwhelmingly difficult. The former head of the city housing department introduced Bernard to an attorney who represented buyers and sellers of apartment and condominium complexes, and with his help, the committee set to work on alternatives, which included a mix of ownership by for-profit and nonprofit developers, the conversion of some of the units to condominiums, and the sale of the land where the seven demolished buildings had stood.

Book collected and organized the relevant financial data and put together a detailed proposal. The vacant lots would be sold to the highest bidder. The extensively remodeled units of Building 18 would be converted to condominiums and sold at market rates. Another 366 apartments would also be converted, with 286 sold at market rates and the other fifty at discounted rates to Lincoln Place tenants. The remaining buildings would be sold to a nonprofit entity that would maintain the 330 units as rentals for existing tenants and others of low and moderate incomes. All this was projected to bring in $163 million, which meant that if Aimco would accept an offer of $130 million, which was above the appraised value, there would be $33 million left over.

In one sense, it was an audacious plan. Every single building then standing at Lincoln Place would be preserved. No tenant who wanted to stay would have to move. Some with the wherewithal could even buy their own units and keep living in the place they had grown to love. But there were obvious and even glaring difficulties. Aimco couldn't be handed a check for $130 million and bid goodbye and good riddance; the company would have to agree to some kind of extended payment plan or the money would have to be borrowed against expected proceeds. And nobody could guarantee that all the condominiums would sell, or that a ready buyer for the vacant land could be found. The plan also included $13 million to rehab all the units except those of Building 18, and given the fact that Lincoln Place had suffered from a lack of maintenance for years while owners plotted to tear it down, that figure could prove to be seriously low.

Paul DeSantis, the attorney advising Bernard, had approached Aimco and reported getting signals that the company might be open to an offer, but at the end of September, every tenant got a letter from the landlord that seemed to imply the opposite. Addressed to "Dear Resident," the letter opened with this paragraph:

"We know you are anxious to learn about the future of Lincoln Place Apartments. As you may know, the owner has been considering a number of options to change the land use of the property and redevelop a major portion of it. As part of this plan, it will be necessary to relocate residents. We are pleased that many residents enjoy living at Lincoln Place, and it is our goal to make the relocation process as easy as possible for everyone."

It was what tenants had been hearing in one form or another ever since TransAction began eviction proceedings after buying Lincoln Place eighteen years earlier—you may love living here, you may have lived here a long time, you may be elderly and not have much money, but you're going to have to get out.

The letter referred to the provision of the city's RSO that required landlords wanting to evict tenants to give notice and pay relocation assistance. "However," the letter went on, "we prefer to meet with you personally to discuss your options and many residents have indicated that they want to relocate in advance of any formal notice. Therefore, we are currently offering a variety of relocation and personalized services for you to consider." Those services, the letter added, would be more generous than required under the rent control law, and would be handled by a professional relocation firm.

That firm was Shober-Livas Relocation, one of a number of companies in the business of helping property owners relocate tenants, typically when large rental complexes were being converted to condominiums. Shortly thereafter, tenants got another mailing from Aimco, a slick four-page brochure extolling the benefits of the relocation program. The landlord had already begun offering $10,000 to tenants who agreed to move, which was considerably more than the $3,200 payment the law then required for nondisabled tenants under the age of sixty-two, although only modestly more generous to the disabled and elderly, who were entitled by law to $8,000. The colorful brochure featured testimonials to Aimco's benevolence, which included an offer to help Lincoln Place tenants move to one of Aimco's fifty other apartment complexes in the Los Angeles area or to one of sixteen hundred in other parts of the state and country. A woman named "Gabriela" spoke of moving to a "beautifully built" Aimco building in nearby Culver City with amenities like a gym and swimming pool. A man named "Doug" said he was the father of a newborn and appreciated Aimco's generosity because the family needed more space. There was a photograph of a middle-aged couple broadly smiling as they held what was presumably a relocation check in their hands.

But the sales pitch for the relocation program wasn't just aimed at those who intended to keep renting; it touted the program as a way to help tenants buy their own homes. Bob Shober, head of the relocation firm, was quoted in the brochure. "Oftentimes, one of the major hurdles of home ownership is the lack of a sizable down payment. But the relocation program given to Lincoln Place residents right now can help pave the way for first-time home buyers to finally move into a home of their own." For emphasis, the brochure included a testimonial from ex-tenant "Jeff" who said he had just closed escrow on a house in Westchester, a community south of Venice. "I'm a satisfied customer," he said.

At that time, in the fall of 2004, the median sales price of a single-family house in Los Angeles was more than $400,000; for a condominium, well over $300,000. For working-class tenants in apartment complexes like Lincoln Place, the $10,000 in relocation assistance wasn't likely to mean they could suddenly afford to buy a home. Many lived paycheck to paycheck, with little savings; even if they could scrape together a down payment, qualifying for a loan could be next to impossible, although the subprime mortgages that led to the financial crisis of 2008 were beginning to proliferate. And for the sizable numbers of Lincoln Place seniors living on Social Security, the rosy pictures painted by the brochure were pure fantasy.

These upbeat messages from Aimco were silent on significant issues. One was that tenants taking the enhanced relocation payments would have to sign away their rights under the RSO, including the right to return to Lincoln Place at their old rents if their units were put back on the market within a certain period of time. Another was that tenants who declined Aimco's relocation offers faced the threat of formal eviction under the Ellis Act, and it was a known fact, bluntly aired by Robert Bisno and others, that an eviction could damage a tenant's credit record and make it much more difficult to rent an apartment in the future. That would be manifestly unfair to those who had done nothing to merit being thrown out of their homes, but it was nonetheless a fact of renters' lives. And it undoubtedly convinced some tenants that they were better off taking whatever Aimco dangled in front of them, signing away their legal rights, and getting out.

The LPTA's response was contained in a bulletin titled, *Just Say 'NO'
to Aimco*. It began with these declarations:

NO: I don't want to move out of my apartment.

NO: I don't want to talk to a relocation specialist.

NO: I don't want my phone number or any personal information
given out without my permission.

That last NO was a reference to complaints that Shober-Livas employees
had been making unsolicited calls to tenants to convince them to sign up for
the program. The bulletin continued, "But they [Aimco] have *no* approved
project. Not even an application, *and* the lawsuits on whether Lincoln Place
already has historic preservation protections don't even go to trial till 2005.
That's what stopped the demolitions on Doreen Place." The "lawsuits" were
the two cases pending before the state appeals court, and the "demolitions
on Doreen Place" referred to the pair of vacant buildings that Ingrid Mueller,
Carol Beck and the rest of the tenant cohort had successfully blockaded that
past spring. The bulletin ended with an invitation to the LPTA's monthly
meeting at Penmar Park, where tenants could learn "how and why Aimco
is trying to trick you" into leaving Lincoln Place.

Shober-Livas posted notices of weekend sign-up sessions at the Lincoln
Place manager's office. The company also distributed a "Relocation Report"
that expanded upon the benefits listed in the Aimco brochure. The two-page
report included a notice that Aimco was sponsoring a tenant yard sale at
the corner of Penmar Avenue and Lake Street in December. This was a rich
bit of irony, given that TransAction had regularly threatened tenants who
participated in a decade's worth of LPTA yard sales in the 1990s, and finally
made good on that threat by suing Sheila Bernard, who was still paying a
hefty price for having stubbornly defended what she believed was one of
the tenants' fundamental rights.

Despite the evidence that Aimco was pushing forward with its own
redevelopment plans, the four women who called themselves the "acquisitions

committee"—Bernard, Seward, Burns, and Book—kept up their pursuit of a deal that would result in the company selling Lincoln Place. They knew that many developers with the financial wherewithal for such a purchase would be put off by the ongoing litigation and the organized tenant opposition, so a potential buyer had to be found who would pledge to preserve the buildings and allow all current tenants to remain. The pool of such buyers was likely to be small, but at the end of October, Paul DeSantis told the women he had found someone who was amenable to historic designation and the protection of tenants. In an email to the attorney, Book proclaimed the news "very exciting" and said she looked forward to meeting this person who owned other apartment buildings in the area and was serious about adding Lincoln Place to his real estate portfolio.

Aimco's "Dear Resident" letter had mentioned redevelopment and a change in land use, but the landlord hadn't revealed any specifics about what it intended once all forty-five buildings then still standing were empty. It seemed unlikely that the company would pursue TransAction's original plan even if the city's approval was upheld by the appeals court, since Aimco had never built and sold condominiums; its sole business was owning and managing apartment complexes. There were the thirteen hundred new apartments mentioned in the stockholder's conference call, but if the company evicted tenants who declined to sign up for relocation assistance, it would need to invoke the Ellis Act. And the explicit intent of the Ellis Act was to allow no-fault evictions by owners of rent-controlled properties who were going out of the landlord business. If a company like Aimco evicted tenants and demolished their buildings but then built new rental units on the same site, state law allowed a city like Los Angeles to reimpose rent control if units were offered to the public within five years. That presented a difficulty if Aimco actually contemplated new apartments, although possibly not an insurmountable one for a deep-pocketed company that could afford to let land sit idle for a few years. No matter what Aimco was planning, though, it was to the company's advantage to get tenants to leave voluntarily and thus avoid these legal issues altogether. Hence, the hiring of a professional relocation firm and the slickly produced brochure pitching the benefits of the relocation packages.

In trying to divine Aimco's larger intentions, Laura Burns had been keeping an eye on its corporate activities, and she discovered that the company had taken out a loan for $72.5 million, with Lincoln Place as collateral. At the Los Angeles County Recorder's office she looked at a Deed of Trust filed on October 1, 2004, which included statements about the use of the property. One that greatly piqued her interest declared that Lincoln Place "may only be used as a residential apartment complex and *for no other purpose*. The Real Property may not be converted to a cooperative or condominium without Beneficiary's prior written consent." Another set forth Aimco's agreement "to maintain in good repair the improvements, including structures, roofs, mechanical systems, parking lots or garages, and other components of the Real Property." This, she thought, was highly relevant, because tenants had long been complaining about lax maintenance. These complaints to management had mostly fallen on deaf ears, and as a result city officials and ultimately the Los Angeles County Health Department had gotten involved. The same month Burns looked at the deed of trust, a health department inspector came to Lincoln Place and noted a variety of health code violations. These included mold on apartment walls, peeling paint on walls and ceilings, missing window screens, and accumulations of trash and refuse in common areas.

Complaints had also been made about the condition of the two vacant buildings Aimco had sought to tear down at the corner of Elkgrove Avenue and Doreen Place. The appeals court justices who issued the order forbidding that demolition had directed Aimco to protect the buildings from damage and deterioration. But complaints from nearby tenants indicated that this directive was being ignored. Burns sent an email to Jan Chatten-Brown enumerating these complaints—people were regularly entering the properties through holes in the security fencing; windows and doors hadn't been boarded up and people were going into the buildings at night; apartments were full of trash, including food waste, condoms and drug paraphernalia. There was standing water in one building, and debris and defecation in hallways and on the surrounding grounds.

What was behind Aimco's apparent willingness to let the property deteriorate despite legal provisions, court orders, and citations by city and county agencies? One common surmise was that the company wanted the property to become so blighted that officials would declare it uninhabitable, and thus, all the stubborn tenants would finally be forced to leave. A simpler and probably more reasonable explanation was that Aimco didn't want to spend any more money than it absolutely had to on a property it planned to demolish and redevelop. In either case, tenants suffered, with the landlord's neglect especially jarring to those who moved to Lincoln Place when it was still owned and managed by the family of one of the original builders. Those tenants could remember prompt responses to service requests, regular painting and upkeep, and careful tending of the grounds. When they talked about what had attracted them to Lincoln Place, they often pointed out the landscaping that created a sense of living in the midst of a garden, and it was disheartening to see grass turned yellow, plants and shrubbery dry and withered and in some cases even dead.

Sheila Bernard and the LPTA leadership saw their best strategy as the one that Ethel Shapiro-Bertolini had urged when the curtain rose on the Lincoln Place drama back in 1987. Stay and fight. In a Venice *Beachhead* article, Bernard wrote, "After seventeen years of battles with various landlords, the tenants of Lincoln Place are weary but resolute." Those tenants, she wrote, "are encouraging one another to 'dig in and stay put,' for a bright tomorrow in which our community is preserved." In the LPTA newsletter, she addressed them directly, pointing out that leaving would almost certainly mean paying higher monthly rent, which could quickly eat up the $10,000 being offered by Aimco.

As the holidays approached with everyone yet again in a state of suspense about the future, LPTA supporters set up a picket across the street from the rental office, where a large sign announced relocation sign-ups. Carol Beck parked her Dodge Dart at the curb, opened the trunk, and propped up a three-by-four poster that read, Honk if U (heart) Affordable Rent. Others held signs saying Don't Demolish Lincoln Place, and Lies + Cheats = Bad Faith. Always ready to lend whatever help she could to the cause, Ingrid Mueller joined the pickets. Management personnel and a few tenants came and went from the rental office, but nobody spoke to the women with the signs. An occasional car honked.

At that point, only a small number of tenants had taken the relocation money and moved out; most seemed to be heeding the LPTA's call to remain stalwart. As usual, Bernard lit the candles of her menorah and other tenants put holiday decorations in their apartment windows, but with so many places vacant, the mood was less festive and more somber than it had been in the past. Jan Book had been forced to temper her excitement because discussions between Aimco and the possibly interested buyer hadn't yet gone anywhere. Prospects on that front were, at the very best, uncertain. And the dark cloud of the Ellis Act and eviction still hung low over the rooftops.

But the spirit of Lincoln Place and the qualities that had drawn people to it and kept them there despite so much uncertainty and disruption still prevailed. A *Santa Monica Mirror* article about the ongoing tenant struggle against eviction and the demolition of their homes featured an elderly couple named Donald and Caroline Akins, who had moved to Lincoln Place in 1953 and had raised a daughter who had left home as an adult but had later returned and rented her own apartment in a nearby building.[62] The World War II veteran and his wife spoke of tenants who hung a sheet on a fence and showed home movies for themselves and neighbors, of residents caroling at Christmas time, of a place filled with families and kids who would play whiffle ball and badminton on the lawns, of people who left their doors open in hot weather. If it sounded like an idealized scene scrubbed clean of big city realities like racism and poverty, in one sense it was, but in another it was just what its designer, a Black man who surely knew that people like himself might not be welcome, had intended. A place where people could make themselves into a community, be neighbors on a very basic level that was difficult and even impossible in places with high fences and locked gates. The corporate owners who arrived thirty-six years after Ralph Vaughn's vision became reality saw a different scene, a large piece of real estate that was failing to generate its highest and best profit. There was no room in such a scene for people like Donald and Caroline Akins and for the others who continued, despite the disruptions and anxieties, to regard Lincoln Place as their home.

20

REASONABLE ACCOMMODATION

Lincoln Place is part of the soul of Venice. If we destroy the middle-class complex, we're really destroying the soul of who we are.
— Bill Rosendahl, Los Angeles
City Council candidate

WHEN CITY COUNCILWOMAN RUTH Galanter's district was uprooted from the west side of Los Angeles in 2002 and moved lock, stock, and barrel to the San Fernando Valley, many Lincoln Place tenants felt they'd lost an old friend. She had come to their defense when the first shots were fired in the eviction wars back in 1987, and stayed alongside them in the trenches of the ongoing battle against what they regarded as corporate avarice and indifference to the plight of the working people and elderly who called Lincoln Place home. Her successor, Cindy Miscikowski, had expressed sympathy for those people, but unlike Galanter she wasn't a vocal advocate of preserving the complex. Because her husband came from a family of well-to-do real estate developers, some even speculated that her sympathies actually lay with the owners, not the tenants. Galanter lived just a few minutes walking distance from Lincoln Place and could be counted on to occasionally show up in casual dress at monthly LPTA meetings and mingle with tenants, although her normally sober demeanor was far from that of a glad-handing politician. By contrast, Miscikowski kept her distance, seldom appearing in Venice and giving the impression—fairly or not—of being disinterested in issues like affordable housing that burned hotly at Lincoln Place and much of the rest of the community.

Term limits meant that both Galanter and Miscikowski would leave office at the end of June 2005. The primary election was scheduled for March 8, and at the beginning of the year, a close and often contentious race had developed between the two favorites—Bill Rosendahl, a former cable TV executive from middle-class Mar Vista, and Flora Gil Krisiloff, a former planning commissioner and neighborhood activist from the well-heeled community of Brentwood. The two couldn't have been more different. Rosendahl was a large man, both in stature and personality, who clearly relished the rituals of campaigning, vigorously shaking hands and deploying a broad smile and voice that could easily carry over a din of conversation. Krisiloff, the wife of a doctor and mother of three sons, had a low-key manner but a reputation for being hardworking and well-informed. She and Rosendahl were both generally aligned with the liberal political leanings of the district, and both promised that if elected they would address the issues—real estate development and traffic congestion foremost among them—that voters seemed to care most fervently about.

Sheila Bernard had met Rosendahl the year before and talked to him about Lincoln Place and other community concerns. At the time, she was still thinking of running for the city council, but when the candidate filing deadline came, she decided against it. Rosendahl had lived at one time in Venice, and she believed that he understood the importance of affordable housing and genuinely sympathized with the plight of Lincoln Place tenants. She hadn't met Krisiloff, but the fact that the candidate had been endorsed by Miscikowski and conducted most of her activist work on behalf of well-to-do homeowners led her to conclude that Rosendahl would better represent the interests of Lincoln Place and the rest of Venice. And Galanter had endorsed Rosendahl, which added an exclamation point to Bernard's decision.

The race veered off the high road early on, with Krisiloff's campaign filing a formal challenge to the primary ballot description of Rosendahl as a university professor. While working for Century Cable and Adelphia Communications, Rosendahl had produced and hosted hundreds of public affairs programs, and that in turn had led to a part-time job teaching classes in media-related topics at one of the seven California State University campuses in the Los Angeles area. Krisiloff claimed that Rosendahl was deceiving voters by calling himself a professor when he was just a nontenured instructor, a charge to which Rosendahl responded by pointing out that the university itself had bestowed the title of "distinguished visiting professor." He accused Krisiloff of sleazy tactics and demanded an apology, which wasn't forthcoming although her campaign didn't push the matter further. But accusations from both candidates' camps would continue to taint the campaign, most memorably those related to Rosendahl's sexual orientation and the fact that, if elected, he would be the first openly gay man to run successfully for that office.[63] Some of his supporters accused the Krisiloff campaign of pandering to antigay sentiment, while her supporters suggested that the Rosendahl campaign was trying to create—without any evidence—the impression that she was a bigot and thus harm her prospects in the predominately liberal district.[64]

The *Los Angeles Times* endorsed Krisiloff, citing her experience as a community activist and her style of quietly building consensus. By contrast, the endorsement said, Rosendahl came across as "bombastic, divisive and ill-informed."[65] The LPTA decided to give tenants a close-up view of the candidates by inviting them to its monthly meeting at Penmar Park. For those tenants and the handful of community people who usually showed up, it was a definite contrast of style, though not substance. Both candidates pledged to support the preservation of Lincoln Place. Both said they were opposed to any zoning change that would allow Aimco to build a denser development. Both assured tenants that they were in their corner and would fight against any attempts to force them from their homes. In a letter to the editor published shortly afterward in the *Argonaut*, Sheila Bernard praised the candidates for what she called their "job interview." But she called Rosendahl a "mover and a shaker" with an enormous web of contacts he wouldn't hesitate to call upon on behalf of his constituents. Both candidates gave "excellent interviews," she said, "But for my money, I'll hire Bill as the public servant needed by CD11."

The March 8 primary turned into a nail-biter. When the votes had all been tallied the next day, Rosendahl led with forty-four percent, followed closely by Krisiloff with forty-two percent. A third candidate, labor attorney Angela Reddock, got fourteen percent. This meant that Rosendahl and Krisiloff were headed for a May 17 runoff, and voters could expect the next two months to be filled with more speeches, mailers, and the din of campaigning, not all of which promised to be uplifting and illuminating.

At Lincoln Place, of course, tenants had more on their minds than local politics. Just after New Year's, Aimco sent out another brochure about relocation, using the same colors and graphics as the first one but with the urgent title, *Last Chance!* The two-page brochure announced that January 10 would be the last day to sign up for the program—$10,000 in relocation payments, $1,500 for moving expenses, and free rent for the last month. It was impossible to know exactly how many tenants had already taken the offers and moved, but Bernard and other active LPTA members were certain it was small. That belief was supported by the fact that January 10 came and went and Shober-Livas was still on the scene, holding its weekend sign-up sessions at the rental office. But just how long was Aimco prepared to wait for several hundred obstinate tenants to see the writing on the wall and take the money and get out? That was the question that had everyone on edge.

The answer wasn't long in coming. On March 18, 2005, a rainy Los Angeles day on which news headlines were dominated by Congress members grilling baseball players about steroid use and others debating the fate of a comatose Florida woman whose husband was in a legal battle over his right to let her die, all the tenants found a letter from Aimco in their mailboxes. Few, if any, expected it to contain good news.

One of them, eighty-one-year-old Frieda Marlin, had moved with her husband to Lincoln Place in 1981. Even after developing serious health problems, she attended LPTA meetings and joined in demonstrations and could always be counted on to write letters opposing redevelopment and supporting historic preservation. When her husband suddenly died in 1998, her only family member, a fifty-three-year-old son with a disabling heart condition, moved in with her. The rent for the two-bedroom apartment was $858 a month, which took a large share of their income, but she loved Lincoln Place and knew that she could never find a place like it that she could afford. She had withstood the threats of Robert Bisno and TransAction, had resisted the cajolery of Shober-Livas Relocation, and expected to spend the years she had left in her apartment on Elkgrove Avenue with its living room window that looked onto a deep courtyard shaded by a pair of Brazilian pepper trees and a jacaranda that burst with purple blossoms every spring.

She opened the letter from Aimco and read, "Dear Tenant: This letter is formal notification that Aimco Venezia, LLC, owner of your apartment unit at 1034 East Elkgrove Avenue, Apt. #2, is withdrawing your apartment unit, as well as all of the apartment units in the Lincoln Place Garden apartment complex, from the rental-housing market. You must vacate your unit on or before July 18, 2005, unless you meet certain eligibility requirements that entitle you to an extension, as described below." For those at least sixty-two years old or disabled, the letter explained, the law required tenancies to be extended a full year to March 20, 2006. This clearly applied to Marlin, although the letter further stated that a written request for the time extension would have to be made within sixty days. The letter noted that tenants evicted under the Ellis Act had to be paid $3,200 unless they met one of the criteria for an extension, in which case they would get $8,000. This amount would be placed in an escrow account and released when Marlin vacated her apartment. And finally, the letter said, Shober-Livas Relocation would be available "to assist you in your relocation and in your search for a new home."

Marlin was one of 242 Lincoln Place tenants who got the notices. Of those, the LPTA estimated that at least a hundred were over the age of sixty-two, which would give them a year before they had to get out. Perhaps anticipating a business opportunity, Aimco distributed a list of fifty-seven other rental properties it owned and managed that were dedicated retirement complexes or offered affordable rents to seniors. Of twenty-eight in California, the closest was near the University of Southern California campus south of downtown Los Angeles. Others were in far-flung Southern California cities such as Anaheim, Bakersfield, and Palm Springs. The rest of the complexes were in Arizona, Nevada, and Florida. Rents ranged from $352 to $1,400 a month, the cheapest in Las Vegas and the most expensive in Saugus, a suburban community north of Los Angeles. Shober-Livas would help facilitate moving to these other Aimco complexes, and a flyer the firm distributed to tenants promised, in addition to the enhanced monetary benefits earlier offered, a free refrigerator if a new apartment didn't include one. The tenants only had to sign a piece of paper that said they were giving up all rights under the city rent control law, including the right to return if the landlord decided to put their apartments back on the rental market.

For Frieda Marlin and tenants like her, the idea of moving twenty miles across town was highly disagreeable, to say nothing of moving hundreds of miles or even all the way across the country. Some had lived at Lincoln Place more than thirty years and almost all had developed networks of people in the community—family members, friends, neighbors—who helped them navigate their daily lives. Those with health problems depended on others for aid in shopping, getting to doctors' appointments, and taking care of the demands of everyday life made more difficult and daunting by advancing age. And there was the fact that many of the seniors had lost spouses and siblings, which meant they depended upon neighbors they had known for years as a palliative to loneliness. Even if they could cope with the logistics of moving after being so long in one place, how would it be to live where they didn't know anybody, where they couldn't see old friends, where they couldn't pick up the telephone and call a neighbor to run an errand or just stop by for a chat? The rhetorical question posed by the elderly tenant at the 2004 forum at Penmar Park felt depressingly apt: "Why don't they just shoot us?"

For younger tenants, the outlook might not have been as bleak, but it was far from benign. They would have four months to find a new apartment and arrange to move, and rapidly rising rents in Venice and surrounding communities meant they would probably have to go some distance to find a place they could afford. For those with young children, this meant finding new day care facilities, enrolling in new schools and living in neighborhoods where allowing kids outside to play, as they freely had at Lincoln Place, wouldn't necessarily be safe. Commutes to jobs could be much longer, which meant more car and public transit expense, as well as complications to daily schedules.

The alternative—to stay and fight the landlord—was clearly a gamble. When the 120 days passed—or even the full year—people might still be faced with the need to pack up and get out. Finding a new apartment would then constitute an emergency, and they wouldn't have extra relocation money to make it easier. But the LPTA had been steadfast in its advocacy for tenants, it had lawyers, it had cases in court, and for many, the gamble was one they were willing to take.

While this slow-rolling drama—or disaster—had been unfolding over the past decade, Sheila Bernard's personal life had been almost totally occupied with her teaching job and the raising of her children, but now it had taken a turn in a new direction. She had met a divorced father and environmental consultant named Arrie Bachrach who shared her interest in progressive politics and social justice issues, and while he lived an hour's drive away in Camarillo, a small city north of Los Angeles, they had seen each other frequently enough to begin thinking of making a life together. She could even imagine the elusive day when Lincoln Place would be a safe haven rather than a threat to tenants, the day when she could step aside from the all-consuming business of the LPTA. But that day hadn't come, and her personal life would have to take second place to the unfinished work of protecting her fellow tenants and neighbors, many of whom had become close friends. Her life was also complicated by the fact that her twenty-three-year-old daughter had developed a disability and was now sharing the apartment on Doreen Place, which meant that the immediate future held no promise of respite from the hectic and harrowing moments likely to come.

When she first moved to Venice in 1987, Bernard had done volunteer work with the Venice Renters Canvass, a group of community activists who went door-to-door trying to organize renters to support issues of particular relevance like strengthening rent control and preserving affordable housing. There she had met a woman named Elena Popp, a Mexican immigrant who had gotten a law degree at UCLA, worked as a legal aid attorney and later founded a nonprofit legal services organization called the Eviction Defense Network. Now that Aimco had taken formal steps to evict everyone at Lincoln Place, Bernard knew it was critical to get legal help; she got in touch with Popp, who agreed to represent tenants willing to fight their evictions.

The LPTA held a meeting for tenants at Penmar Park on April 17 to hear Popp explain the eviction process. More than a hundred persons filled the meeting room that Sunday morning, with a table covered by informational materials and a large cardboard box with a slot for checks and cash donations to the LPTA. Before the meeting got formally underway, a petition titled NOTICE TO QUIT was passed around for signatures. It was identical to the notice issued to TransAction's James Coxeter and Jim Merlino back in 1992. Now addressed to Aimco, it read:

TAKE NOTICE, that you are hereby required to:

QUIT planning to demolish these buildings!

QUIT insisting on maximum profits, instead of reasonable profits!

QUIT allowing units to stand vacant while people are homeless in Los Angeles!

THIS IS INTENDED as a notice to quit, for the purpose of terminating your stranglehold on this community.

It was doubtful that this petition would have much, if any, effect on Aimco, but the LPTA was looking to boost lagging spirits as well as create publicity for the tenant cause. But the essence of the meeting came when Bernard introduced Popp. A short, dark-haired woman with a squarish face who would later tell an interviewer that she wanted her epitaph to read, "Latina lesbian activist who fought for peace and justice through nonviolence," she informed the tenants about the workings of the eviction process and the steps they would have to take if they wanted to contest it.[66] The forty-seven-year-old attorney didn't come across as a fiery orator, but her activist resume was impressive, beginning with volunteer work for the United Farm Workers while still in high school, continuing through legal battles with slumlords and advocacy for immigrants, working people, and women and children. Bernard believed that if tenants had any chance to win the fight against eviction, Popp would leave no stone unturned to help make it happen.

On the flip side of that coin, many remembered Laura Ponce's long and ultimately futile fight to keep her Building 18 apartment. And that eviction was for major rehabilitation under the RSO, while Aimco was invoking the Ellis Act, which, in the eyes of many legal experts and public officials, gave landlords an absolute right to leave the rental business. If Aimco was declaring its intention to do just that, then what legal arguments could tenants raise in claiming the right to stay? Tenant advocates could argue that the law had been intended to allow so-called mom-and-pop landlords to get out of the rental business without running afoul of local rent control laws, not to enable a huge company like Aimco to boost its profits by evicting hundreds of tenants and redeveloping the property. But the 1997 appeals court ruling involving the Lincoln Place building on Elkland Place had come down squarely on the side of the landlord, even though TransAction had never followed through on its threat to tear down the building, and ten years later eighty-two year-old Dicie Meyers and a number of others still occupied their apartments.

Popp had never approached such situations with a defeatist attitude, and she got unexpected help that would prove invaluable from Jan Book, who had left her auditing job and renewed her law license. Book's time was no longer consumed by the work of putting together proposals for a change of Lincoln Place ownership, because that effort appeared to have reached a dead end. But she still felt committed to the cause of preserving the complex and protecting the tenants, so she volunteered to assist Popp, even though she knew little about the legalities of eviction and would have to get a crash course in landlord-tenant law.

When she moved to Marina Del Rey in 1989 to live with her future husband, Book kept her apartment in a building on Elkgrove Avenue to use as a studio to pursue her growing passion for painting. When the apartment above became available, she rented it as well, turning it into a kind of gallery to display the colorful oil paintings she described as abstract realism. After volunteering to help Popp, she began hosting twice-weekly open houses in that upstairs apartment, on Monday nights for English-speaking tenants and Thursday nights for the considerable number who spoke only Spanish or had limited English skills. The fifty-year-old attorney, who had short red hair and bore a mild resemblance to the actress Annette Bening, sat with tenants at a table and explained the eviction process, signing up anyone who wanted to be represented by the Eviction Defense Network. A woman fluent in both English and Spanish came to the Thursday night sessions and helped with translation and filling out forms. The eviction defense would cost $300 per tenant, plus any added fees for court filings, and Book collected the payments and requisite forms to deliver to Popp. Although the cost was very reasonable, it was still a financial strain for some seniors and working people, and if any wanted to contest their evictions but didn't have the money, Book paid it out of her own pocket.

Most of the information that went into the forms was routine—names, ages, addresses, length of tenancies, number of persons in the households. But the form that Aimco required of tenants requesting a full year extension of their occupancy because they were over sixty-two or had a disability gave rise to an intense controversy. For elderly tenants, the landlord asked for a copy of a driver's license, birth certificate, passport, or other government-issued identification with a birth date. That was relatively straightforward, since nearly everyone had one or more of those documents. But for those requesting the extension on the grounds of disability, Aimco required proof in the form of a document from the Social Security Administration or other state or federal agency showing that a person was receiving some form of disability benefits. That was a problem for a number of tenants who were either under medical care or had been diagnosed with a disabling condition but had never applied for government benefits and didn't have the proof the landlord was demanding.

A case in point was Sheila Bernard's adult daughter. She didn't receive any state or federal disability benefits, but was under the care of medical professionals who could attest to the fact that she was unable to live independently and needed her mother's care. However, Bernard thought every tenant should request the one-year extension regardless of age or any disabling condition. Just as her daughter depended upon her, other disabled and elderly tenants depended upon their younger and more physically and mentally capable neighbors, and how would they cope if they were the only ones left after July 18, when the 120-day notice period expired? It was highly doubtful that Aimco would agree with this reasoning, and in fact, the landlord's responses to some of the first requests showed no inclination to flexibility.

One couple was denied an extension even though they had submitted a letter from the wife's doctor confirming that she suffered from a disabling heart condition. In an email to Jan Book, the woman's husband complained that the stress caused by Aimco's intransigence had triggered a cardiac incident that sent his wife to the hospital. The man characterized this as a "potentially fatal advance in her illness. It is also costing us money we can ill afford." Another tenant denied the one-year extension was a forty-eight-year-old woman who submitted letters from two doctors stating that she was being treated for clinical depression and migraine headaches. She also argued that all tenants should be granted the extension, describing an incident in which she had discovered an elderly neighbor who apparently fell and was lying semiconscious at the foot of the apartment-house stairs. Another neighbor was alerted and called 911, but what might have happened if that elderly tenant had been living completely alone in the building? "People truly care about each other at Lincoln Place," the younger woman wrote. "I could go on and on with many other incidents of neighbors here who are more like family."

Others denied the extension were a man with carpal tunnel syndrome, and a Vietnam veteran being treated at a VA hospital for PTSD. Because they couldn't show the kind of proof demanded by Aimco, they would have to be out by July 18 or face legal action that could end with them being locked out of their apartments, or in the worst case, being forcibly removed by deputies from the county sheriff's office.

Book agreed with Bernard that all tenants should request one year extensions. She also believed that Aimco was plainly wrong in requiring tenants to show they were getting federal or state disability benefits. In a letter to Aimco, she pointed to the Ellis Act's reference to the state law that defined disability as, in her words, "any mental or physical disorder or condition that limits a major life activity." Laura Burns had dug through public records to find specific conditions that had been deemed by courts or public agencies to fit this definition, and had compiled a long list that included depression, dyslexia, panic disorder, asthma, glaucoma, the afore-mentioned carpal tunnel syndrome and migraine headaches. Since any number of persons with these and other conditions wouldn't necessarily have the documents Aimco was demanding, the company, in Book's view, needed to drop that requirement.

In the same letter, she wrote that the statute defining disabilities also required landlords to make "reasonable accommodations" for disabled persons. This, she argued, should include a one-year extension for all Lincoln Place tenants. "A *reasonable accommodation* to a disabled tenant who has lived at Lincoln Place for many years, who has created interdependent relationships with their fellow tenants, who has enjoyed the peace and tranquility of having other apartments around them occupied, and whose peace of mind and physical security may be endangered if more tenants are asked to leave, would be for Aimco to extend the date of withdrawal on all rental units to March 20, 2006."

One of the things behind this furious resistance to what the landlord—and to be fair, many others—considered a property owner's lawful right—was the glimmering hope for historic preservation. Amanda Seward had updated her 2002 nomination to the National Register of Historic Places and sent it off to be considered for the California Register of Historical Resources. Everyone knew that it couldn't be formally listed if Aimco objected, but the historical resources commission could deem it eligible for the register, and that, Seward and other preservationists believed, would trigger the requirement for environmental review, including a study of the feasibility of preserving the buildings. The landlord clearly regarded that as a threat, because the state commission had scheduled hearings on the Lincoln Place application in February and again in May but had postponed both when Aimco attorneys raised procedural objections. The latest hearing date was August 5, and Seward and Lincoln Place tenants and their supporters had their fingers crossed that there wouldn't be any further delay.

At that same time, Sheila Bernard and others who believed that tenants needed a strong advocate on the city council were keeping a close watch on the heated battle between Bill Rosendahl and Flora Gil Krisiloff in the lead-up to the May 17 election. Shortly after Aimco mailed the 242 notices in March, Rosendahl issued a press release calling on the landlord to immediately halt its effort to remove the tenants. "For more than a decade," he said, "the various owners of Lincoln Place have attempted to destroy this affordable family living community. In addition to numerous redevelopment plans, the low-income tenants have been bought off, intimidated, and threatened by developers determined to eliminate one of the last lower tax bracket communities west of the 405 freeway." He also voiced support for historic preservation and for the move led by Jan Book to force Aimco to allow all tenants to remain on the property for a full year. If only elderly and disabled tenants remained, he said, they would be living in "virtual ghost towns susceptible to crime."

Both candidates showed up at the LPTA's monthly meeting in April, where Krisiloff joined Rosendahl in opposing the evictions and asking that all tenants be granted a one-year extension. But as the campaign headed into its final weeks, Rosendahl hammered his opponent for being beholden to development interests, pointing out, among other things, that a major campaign contributor was the Apartment Association of Greater Los Angeles, a pro-landlord group that opposed rent control and any watering down of the Ellis Act. Rosendahl supporters also continued to accuse the Krisiloff campaign of trying to make his sexual orientation an issue. For her part, Krisiloff painted the loquacious Rosendahl as a man who loved to talk but had very little to show in the way of accomplishments, while she had rolled up her sleeves as a community activist and planning commissioner and done the kind of work that showed she would be an effective member of the city council.

Rosendahl held his election night party at a supporter's house near the beach in Venice. The large crowd hoping to celebrate a victory included Sheila Bernard, Laura Burns, and Jan Book from Lincoln Place, who had pinned their hopes on the man they believed best able to advocate for tenants in the manner of their former representative, Ruth Galanter. But until the results began coming in they were left to elbow their way through the house that was undoubtedly one of the most unusual in Venice, if not in all of Los Angeles. The home of a marketing entrepreneur named Gary Shafner, the exterior was that of a nondescript 1950s apartment building, but the interior had been transformed into a fanciful space of wonders—a foyer with two classic cars, a hallway with dozens of wall-mounted musical instruments that played samples at the push of buttons, a kitchen and breakfast room that exactly replicated a 1950s diner, a bathroom fashioned from the cab of a Peterbilt truck, a campground on the building's roof complete with an Airstream trailer. And much more, all embellished with visual puns—an ottoman with "EMPIRE" stitched on its surface, a ceiling composed entirely of wineglasses, a curtain made of iron mesh. And in one of the most popular rooms, two ATM machines that dispensed, instead of cash, artworks one could choose and view on wall-mounted screens.

Shortly before midnight, when it appeared that Rosendahl had built an insurmountable lead, the would-be councilman appeared, moving through the crowded space, vigorously shaking hands and exchanging hugs. He gave a short speech of thanks to his supporters, and people began to disperse. The next day's *Los Angeles Times* declared him the winner, with fifty-five percent of the vote in reporting precincts. Venice went overwhelmingly for Rosendahl, giving him sixty-seven percent of the vote to Krisiloff's thirty-three percent. His outspoken support for Lincoln Place tenants had undoubtedly contributed to that large plurality, and everyone hoped that his words would translate into action once he was installed as a council member on July 1, although exactly what that action might be would remain to be seen.

The LPTA leadership and many Lincoln Place tenants had also kept an eye on the mayor's race, and were pleased that Antonio Villaraigosa's second try for the office was successful, with a solid victory over the incumbent, James Hahn. The election was a milestone, with the former labor organizer and California State Assemblyman becoming the first Latino mayor in Los Angeles history. But it was his progressive views and the fact he had written a letter in support of the Lincoln Place application to the California Register of Historical Resources that stirred hope he would actively support the tenant cause.

While Elena Popp and Jan Book pushed forward with the eviction defense effort and the LPTA worked on strategies to draw media attention to the situation, Shober-Livas Relocation was still on the scene with offers of enhanced relocation benefits. By the beginning of June, only 177 units were still occupied, the majority of them households with seniors or persons claiming disabilities. Perhaps sensing a public relations disaster if those people were thrown out of their apartments, Aimco proposed a settlement that would ostensibly remove the threat. In a June 15 letter to attorneys Jan Chatten-Brown and Susan Brandt-Hawley, the Aimco attorney, William Delvac, wrote that the company was offering to preserve 240 existing units for a period of twenty-five years. Of those units, 144 would be set aside for current tenants without any rent increase. Aimco would then seek city approval to demolish the remaining structures and put up new buildings with 704 units, either to be rented or sold as condominiums. The company would also seek permission to exceed the property's existing height limit of thirty feet, which would allow the new complex to have buildings of three or more stories.

In return, the LPTA and 20th Century Architectural Alliance would have to drop their lawsuits against the city and agree not to file any future suits. Amanda Seward would have to withdraw her application for listing with the state historical register, and the LPTA and tenants would have to agree to actively support Aimco's efforts to get city permits for its redevelopment. The letter ended by giving the parties until June 23, or a single week, to accept or reject this settlement. The question of whether the offer was made in good faith, or was merely intended to show that Aimco cared about tenant welfare, was open to speculation. In any case, nobody on the tenant side of the metaphorical negotiating table found it palatable.

Bill Rosendahl hadn't yet been sworn into office, but because he had offered his assistance in brokering a deal to keep tenants in their apartments, Sheila Bernard sent him a message saying that the LPTA and others were "more than willing" to negotiate a settlement. But not, she added, "with a gun at our heads." She repeated Jan Book's assertions about the law requiring "reasonable accommodation" to disabled tenants, and told the soon-to-be councilman that the LPTA wouldn't negotiate with Aimco until the landlord granted all 177 tenants remaining on the property the one-year extension.

Aimco didn't respond, but went directly to the tenants with a letter touting what it called the "extraordinary" settlement offer. It said, in part:

"We wanted to express to you our sincere disappointment that a few people with the LPTA rejected our proposed written settlement offer—within just a few hours! We can't imagine there was any discussion with the people most affected by the offer—you.

"The decision by a few individuals at LPTA can only achieve one thing—everyone loses. Rather than allowing current tenants to remain in preserved units at existing rents, it is clear that a few within LPTA prefer to continue this legal battle."

This line—that a handful of self-interested tenants were jeopardizing the welfare of the majority—went all the way back to the early 1990s, when Transaction unveiled its plan to completely demolish Lincoln Place and build a new condominium complex. While the accusation ignored the reality that the LPTA had always enjoyed widespread, though not universal, tenant support, anything Aimco could do to weaken that support could work to the landlord's advantage. With more than three-quarters of the units vacant, the company had to be losing a significant amount of money, so the sooner it could get its new building plans underway, the better. Company officials may have believed that the enhanced relocation benefits would entice everyone to leave, but nine months after Shober-Livas appeared like Santa Claus with a bagful of goodies, there were still 177 households showing no inclination to do so, even as the perennial eviction threat had become grimly real.

Sheila Bernard and the LPTA had always recognized the importance of drawing media attention to their efforts, and the eviction drama seemed ready-made for Los Angeles newspapers and the TV and radio stations that covered current events. With her inherent energy and enthusiasm, Laura Burns was the right person to take a leading role in raising media awareness. She compiled a list of news directors, editors, and producers of public affairs programs throughout Southern California and then faxed each a summary of the state of affairs at Lincoln Place. She even contacted the *Denver Post*, the major newspaper in Aimco's hometown, hoping a reporter or editor might be interested in the controversy swirling around the company's apartment complex in Venice, California.

In mid-June of 2005, she was invited as a guest on *Which Way, L.A.?* a highly respected public affairs program on KCRW in Santa Monica, one of Southern California's most listened-to public radio stations. Hosted by Warren Olney, a former TV news anchor and reporter, the half-hour program also featured Aimco vice president Patti Shwayder; Mark Haefele, an editor and columnist for the *L.A. Alternative Press*; and Carol Schatz, head of a downtown business association. Burns, who had a wealth of facts about Lincoln Place at her fingertips, talked about the garden city movement and Ralph Vaughn's design, which embraced the idea that the architecture of a place could create a closer-knit, healthier and more civically engaged community. The kind of design that distinguished Lincoln Place, she said, "creates better people, and with that, we will have a better city." The threat of eviction, she said, had seriously disrupted this dynamic, but had also brought the Lincoln Place community even closer together and strengthened the desire of its residents to stay in their homes.

Shwayder countered with the argument advanced when TransAction first unveiled its redevelopment plan fifteen years earlier—the buildings were old and falling into disrepair and fixing them up would be prohibitively expensive. In her words, Lincoln Place was "not aging gracefully," an observation that may have been superficially true but ignored the fact that lack of maintenance by successive landlords had greatly contributed to its present state. She disputed the contention that the complex had historic value and merited preservation. It was "cookie-cutter FHA housing," she said, nearly identical to thousands of other complexes in Southern California. She repeated a statement made in other venues, that Aimco's redevelopment plans weren't definite. But she promised that what was ultimately built would be "a wonderful, wonderful community that residents love to come home to."

Haefele disputed the claim that the buildings were old and needed replacement, pointing to the quality of their construction and the fact that apartment buildings in other cities like New York and Chicago were a hundred years old and nobody was clamoring to tear them down because of their age. But Schatz, whose organization represented some of the city's most powerful real estate interests, said it was unrealistic to maintain low-rise complexes with copious open space like Lincoln Place when the growing population of Los Angeles called for greater density and taller buildings to accommodate rental housing needs.

The program may have been informative for those who knew nothing of Lincoln Place, and Olney lived up to his reputation for even-handedness, but whether the discussion was enlightening or changed anyone's minds about the Lincoln Place situation was a question that couldn't be immediately answered. It wasn't lost on Sheila Bernard and others that Lincoln Place tenants had undoubtedly won the public relations battle in the 1990s but had ultimately tasted bitter defeat in the courts. Despite a general distaste for legal action, she had spent untold time and energy raising money and pursuing legal help, beginning with Marcia Scully, who longtime LPTA members still called their "angel." Now that role was split among Amanda Seward and Jan Book, who were donating their services, and Jan Chatten-Brown, Susan Brandt-Hawley, and Elena Popp, whose belief in the tenant cause meant their fees were much lower, say, than the fees charged by attorneys representing Aimco. But Bernard believed this legal team had an ineffable advantage, a commitment to social and environmental justice that vested their arguments with passion and power unmatched in the arguments of corporate attorneys whose aim wasn't to paint a picture of ordinary human beings in peril but of a rich corporation facing a threat to its profits.

A probable, and perhaps major, reason Aimco put forward the settlement offer was to rid itself of the lawsuits pending in the state appeals court. Although these lawsuits by the LPTA and the 20th Century Architectural Alliance raised different issues, they had been combined by the court, and oral arguments were held on July 7. At that hearing before a three-judge panel, the plaintiff's attorneys repeated the argument that the Lincoln Place EIR should have been revised to reflect new facts like Ralph Vaughn's role as Lincoln Place designer and the state commission's vote finding the complex historically significant. They also attacked the city's conclusion that the Lake Street demolitions weren't part of the approved redevelopment project and thus not subject to any of its conditions.

On July 13, five days before the deadline for all Lincoln Place tenants other than seniors or the disabled to move out, the court issued its decision. In a major disappointment to the LPTA, the justices ruled that the city had no obligation to revise the EIR before approving the redevelopment. But the ruling in the second lawsuit gave Lincoln Place advocates reason to cheer, because it said the city could not ignore the conditions originally placed on the project unless those conditions were changed or removed through a new environmental review. The project conditions were not "empty promises" or "mere expressions of hope," the justices said, but requirements that the city was obligated to enforce.

In a statement released under the names of the Los Angeles Conservancy and attorneys Chatten-Brown and Brandt-Hawley, the court ruling was called "a key decision that will block the demolition of Venice's Lincoln Place Apartments." And Bill Rosendahl, just two weeks into his first term as a city councilman, said, "I am pleased with this decision because it gives me the tools I need to keep Lincoln Place standing." On the Sunday following the ruling, tenants gathered outside in warm summer sunlight to celebrate what they believed was a major and long-overdue victory. A few who were musicians played guitars and conga drums and sang upbeat songs that dispelled the fear and anxiety that had been a kind of dirge pervading their lives ever since the eviction notices arrived in the mail.

But Aimco's reaction was starkly different. In an article in the *Santa Monica Daily Press*, Patti Shwayder said the ruling cleared the way for Aimco to carry on with its redevelopment plans.[67] Regarding the fact that the court found the Lake Street demolitions to be illegal, Shwayder contended that the ruling only involved one of the original conditions. "All we have to do is take pictures of the buildings and put them on the national market to see if anyone wants to buy the buildings," she said. "Clearly, the court ruling favors our position."

Who was right? The condition cited by Shwayder was a relatively minor element in the city planning commission's 1995 debate; at that time, center stage was taken by the issue of tenant displacement. The commission president, George Lefcoe, had insisted on an ironclad guarantee that the landlord wouldn't evict any tenants to make way for demolition of their buildings, and TransAction had agreed to that condition, which was approved by the commission and later by the city council. It read as follows: "Prior to the issuance of each building permit or demolition permit associated with the proposed project, the applicant will submit a Relocation Plan for review and approval."

That plan, among other things, included offering current tenants the legally mandated relocation payment and assistance in finding comparable apartments in the Venice area. But most importantly, it required the owner to offer any tenant who wanted to stay at Lincoln Place "a comparable or better vacant unit on site at no cost either for the move or in additional rent above the amount paid in the unit scheduled for demolition."

The appeals court justices didn't specifically mention this condition, but the fact that it had to be met before the city could issue demolition permits surely meant that it was covered by their ruling. Of course, legal rulings and concepts one party finds crystal clear may be regarded by another as ambiguous and even opaque. If that wasn't the case, what need would there be for nearly two hundred thousand lawyers in California and well over a million in the United States, and various court systems humming day after day with disputation? Aimco believed it was free to evict the tenants and tear down the buildings as long as it first snapped some photographs and put ads in real estate publications or otherwise reached out to what would obviously be a very small pool of potential buyers. And if nobody wanted the buildings, they could fall under the proverbial wrecking ball. But if that was true, then the agreement by TransAction attorneys sitting at the table with the city planning commissioners and reaffirmed seven years later before the city council was nothing more than a worthless scrap of paper.

Even if the ruling could be interpreted to mean the Lincoln Place buildings couldn't be torn down before Aimco jumped through some relatively minor hoops, it didn't touch on the most imminent threat to tenants, the Ellis Act. Two weeks before Aimco invoked that act to evict all tenants, the *Santa Monica Mirror* had published an op-ed piece by Laura Burns that painted a vivid picture of the fears the law had aroused.[68]

"When a landlord drops the 'E-word,' from one day to the next, your whole life changes. You realize that any Johnny-come-lately landlord can uproot you and throw you out of your home and community. It is a painful realization, fraught with anguish and desperation for many who see full well that, at today's rent levels, their income will not even suffice for rent, let alone food, clothing, utilities, or medicine. Many seniors have said, 'What am I going to do? I have no place to go. I barely get by now.'"

In her op-ed, Burns called on people to tell their elected representatives in Sacramento that the Ellis Act had to go. The powerful influence of the real estate industry in the state capital made that a very heavy lift, and Jan Book and Elena Popp had another idea. Despite the obstacles posed by past court rulings upholding the law, they believed a legal attack could be mounted that would stop the Lincoln Place evictions. Book recruited a pair of tenants to act as plaintiffs, and on July 15, just two days after the appeals court issued its decision, she and Popp filed a complaint for declaratory relief in superior court, asking for a ruling on the question of how tenants could be legally evicted from Lincoln Place under the Ellis Act when Aimco was still renting apartments in more than fifty other properties in California and clearly not getting out of the rental business. The plaintiffs were that loyal and steadfast LPTA supporter, Frieda Marlin, and her son Leslie, who everyone called Spike.

If any of this gave Aimco pause, it wasn't obvious, because a week later, and just four days after tenants gathered outside to celebrate what they regarded as their victory in the appeals court, Aimco filed legal actions called "unlawful detainers" against eighty tenants who hadn't been granted one-year extensions. The next stop? The county courthouse in nearby Santa Monica, where eviction hearings for residents on the west side of Los Angeles were held. The tenants would get their day in court, with Book and Popp arguing that they shouldn't be thrown out of their homes and Aimco asserting its legal right to do just that. The two women got busy putting together the nuts and bolts of their arguments, confident that they could prevail against the company and its high-priced lawyers. But were they just whistling in the dark?

21

WEARING GLASSES
IS A DISABILITY?

If capitalism's dark side is becoming the norm, if mercy is no longer part of people's vocabulary, let alone, practice, it is time for serious revisions here in Venice, Los Angeles, California, this country, and elsewhere.

— Ingrid Mueller, declaration to eviction court

ON JULY 2, 2005, Bill Rosendahl was inaugurated as one of fifteen members of the Los Angeles City Council. As a candidate, he had portrayed himself as man of the people not beholden to the real estate lobby and development interests so dominant in city politics, and his supporters at Lincoln Place and elsewhere in Venice and the district were eager to see if he would make good on his campaign promises or revert to the stereotype of the politician who, in the words of Emma Goldman, "promise you heaven before election and give you hell after." Many considered it a positive sign that instead of holding his inauguration in a hotel ballroom or other upscale venue, the ceremony took place outdoors at Venice Beach where anyone who happened by could stop and watch. A stage and rows of folding chairs were set up on the plaza at the end of Windward Avenue, the main street leading to the beach, and by the time the ceremony got under way, the chairs had filled and people stood in the back. A Los Angeles gay band called The Great American Yankee Freedom Band warmed up the audience, followed by a local Japanese synchronized drumming group and a longtime Venice poet named Philomene Long who read an inauguration poem she had written. The only sour note in this festive atmosphere came from a small group of antiabortion protesters brandishing signs with photos of mangled, bloody fetuses.

Wearing a short-sleeved shirt with paisley tie and a purple lei around his neck, the new councilman was sworn into office by superior court judge Katherine Mader. When applause died down he launched into a speech that opened with what had become his signature exhortation, a rapid-fire "Great, Great, Great!" Sheila Bernard, Ingrid Mueller and several other Lincoln Place tenants were in the crowd gathered beneath a warm, sunny sky with fluttering palm trees in the background, and they were pleased when Rosendahl spoke of his intention to pursue a "people first" policy and alluded to Lincoln Place and other apartment complexes by declaring, "When you look at the affordable housing we have, I don't want you bulldozing it down and putting up high-end condos." After the ceremony, he posed for photographs with a number of people, including Mueller, the two of them broadly smiling while holding up a large Preserve Lincoln Place poster.

Bernard had come to believe that the best, and possibly last hope for tenants lay with the city council, and making sure the sometimes-blustery Rosendahl's promise to do all he could to protect Lincoln Place would be followed by action. The new councilman clearly saw his role as that of a peacemaker, and during his first month in office he talked with both the LPTA and Aimco about trying to move the needle on the settlement offer made by the company in June but quickly rejected by the tenants. One of several sticking points in that offer was Aimco's insistence that the historic preservation effort led by Amanda Seward be dropped. The company had already succeeded in getting two hearings before the historical resources commission postponed, but a third, scheduled for August 5 in Sacramento, looked as if it would go forward despite efforts to have it delayed. It wasn't a surprise, then, that two days before the commission meeting, Aimco agreed to suspend eviction activity if the LPTA and preservationists were willing to talk—with Rosendahl acting as mediator—about a settlement. The only precondition was that Seward ask the commission to table action on the Lincoln Place nomination.

The offer was transmitted by Rosendahl's chief of staff, Mike Bonin, in an email to Bernard, Seward, Jan Book, and Laura Burns, who had come to comprise a kind of executive committee representing the LPTA and preservationists. Seward was loath to have come so far just to see the hearing postponed a third time with no guarantee that Lincoln Place would even be standing the next time it could be put on the commission's quarterly agenda. And given what many saw as a trail of broken promises, nobody really trusted Aimco's word. Book, in particular, was having none of it. Just half an hour after Bonin sent his email, she emailed Bernard and the other recipients to say that tenants "aren't afraid to go into eviction court and stand up against Aimco. If we compromise now, we will be betraying everything that [the tenants] are fighting for. They know that they are taking a risk and that the road will be bumpy and uncertain. But they believe in Lincoln Place and they believe that the goal is worth the gamble." All quickly agreed that the commission hearing should go ahead as scheduled. Whether this meant they had slammed the door on future negotiations with Aimco couldn't be immediately answered.

The hearing was again held in the auditorium of the state resources building in Sacramento. Seward and Burns made the trip from Los Angeles to speak in favor of the nomination, and they were joined by Gail Sansbury, then teaching at San Jose State University. Speaking in opposition were Aimco executive Patti Shwayder, attorney William Delvac, and Lincoln Place tenant Mary Roberts, who had been the major spokesperson in the 1990s for Lincoln Place Tomorrow, the tenant group that supported TransAction's redevelopment plan. Delvac, who worked for Latham & Watkins, one of the city's largest and most powerful law firms, had written a letter to the commission arguing that redevelopment of Lincoln Place would provide badly needed housing and prevent blight. If the commission were to deem it eligible for the historical register, he wrote, "the adverse effects would not be limited to Lincoln Place; rather the impact would be widespread, affecting countless similar structures throughout California." This latter argument had been echoed in a letter by State Senator Tom Torlakson, a northern California Democrat and chairman of the Senate Committee on Transportation and Housing. There were at least three garden apartment complexes similar to Lincoln Place in his district, he wrote, and he wondered if they and others in the state might also claim historic status. This, he warned, could seriously impact the need to redevelop such properties with more units and greater density. He urged postponement of the hearing and further study of the statewide implications of a Lincoln Place designation.

Aimco's recruiting of political help to thwart historic preservation brought back memories of 2003, when Robert Bisno solicited the aid of a congressman to stop Lincoln Place from being listed as eligible for the national register. Threats of adverse legislation had alarmed preservation groups and undoubtedly helped keep Lincoln Place in a kind of official limbo, with the nomination neither approved nor rejected. However, in her effort for state recognition, Seward had the support of an impressive list of elected officials, including US Senators Dianne Feinstein and Barbara Boxer; US Congresswoman Jane Harman; Los Angeles Mayor Antonio Villaraigosa, and Councilman Bill Rosendahl. Individuals and organizations involved in architecture, urban planning, and historic preservation had also weighed in in favor of the Lincoln Place nomination.

Seward and others had repeatedly stressed that such a listing would mean that Aimco couldn't demolish any buildings unless a new EIR found there were no viable alternatives. But when the commission hearing got underway, both Delvac and Shwayder refuted the idea that historic recognition would save those buildings. Repeating her contention that the July appeals court ruling in the 20th Century Architectural Alliance case had cleared the way for redevelopment, Shwayder said, "So if you designate [Lincoln Place on the California Register of Historical Resources], we believe we can still redevelop the property after complying with additional regulatory guidelines." This obviously referred to her earlier contention that all the company had to do before tearing the buildings down was to photographically document and offer them for sale.

That didn't sway the commission, which sided with the preservationists and voted unanimously to find Lincoln Place eligible for the state register. In a press release, Seward said, "Now that the historic importance of Lincoln

Place is settled, it's time for Aimco to accept the designation and do the right thing—withdraw the evictions and work amicably with the community to craft a preservation plan." But the landlord stuck to a hard line. In a *Los Angeles Times* article about the commission action, Patti Shwayder said of tenants, "I wouldn't be sipping champagne if I were them. They all have to be out of there by next March."[69] A day later, in an article in the *Santa Monica Daily Press*, she said that anyone who believed tenants could now stay at Lincoln Place were "grossly misreading" the commission's action. She described those who had failed to move out when their 120-day notices expired as "squatters."[70]

At the end of that notice period on July 18, 2005, there were 174 households still at Lincoln Place, which was both a testament to their determination as well as a grim reminder that the complex had once been home to nearly two thousand people. Aimco had granted one-year extensions to seventy-three tenants, and filed unlawful detainers against the rest. A few had since moved out, or weren't contesting their evictions, leaving Jan Book and Elena Popp with ninety-one to defend in court. For Book, that meant long hours getting declarations, assembling a myriad of court-required documents, and helping Popp craft arguments the attorneys hoped would convince a judge that Aimco was illegally trying to force people from their apartments. A major argument would be the one they put forward in the Marlin lawsuit—the misuse of the Ellis Act. While the law allowed landlords to evict tenants if they were going out of the rental business, Aimco would still be renting thousands of apartments even if they completely demolished Lincoln Place. Furthermore, the company's claim that the Ellis Act allowed it to leave the rental business at a single property conflicted with past statements and actions showing that it actually intended to pursue the redevelopment approved by the city in 2002, which called for 144 rental units in addition to 706 condominiums.

In the midst of preparing for the eviction hearings, Book and Popp got an unwelcome surprise. Aimco had filed a motion to dismiss the Marlin lawsuit on the grounds that it was a Strategic Lawsuit Against Public Participation, or SLAPP suit, filed to inhibit a constitutional right to free expression. This stirred memories of TransAction's lawsuit back in 2000 against Sheila

Bernard and other LPTA members for allegedly obstructing its Village at Venezia plans. Like that lawsuit, most SLAPP suits and ensuing anti-SLAPP actions attracted only minor media attention, but that wasn't the case in 2003, when Barbra Streisand made national headlines by suing a photographer for $10 million, claiming he had invaded her privacy and violated California's Anti-Paparazzi Act by taking an aerial photograph of her blufftop estate in Malibu and posting it on an internet website. But the photographer, Kenneth Adelman, wasn't a member of the paparazzi and the website didn't traffic in the private details of famous people's lives; he was an environmental activist who had set out to document the entire California coastline. The website that would eventually provide access to more than twelve thousand photographs, including the one showing Streisand's property, was intended for use by government agencies, universities, and environmental groups researching such issues as coastline development and beach erosion.

Adelman's attorneys succeeded in getting the lawsuit thrown out of court on the grounds that it was a SLAPP suit. Streisand's desire for privacy didn't nullify Adelman's right to take aerial photographs of the coast, just as TransAction's desire to maximize its profits didn't take precedence over the rights of Bernard and the LPTA to speak out and demonstrate against the landlord's redevelopment plans. But in cases like those, wealthy individuals and corporations were seen as trying to squelch the free speech rights of relatively powerless people and organizations, while Aimco, the largest owner of apartments in the country, was claiming that an elderly widow and her disabled son were the oppressors. In their anti-SLAPP motion, the company argued that the Marlin's lawsuit was intended only to "harass" the company and "chill valid exercise of its constitutional right to petition." That right to petition, the motion claimed, included giving the Marlins and other tenants notice that they would be evicted if they didn't vacate their apartments.

At that point, Book had never appeared as an attorney in a court proceeding. She had never heard of an anti-SLAPP motion, but when she learned what it was, her reaction bordered on disbelief.

"I thought it was silly and ridiculous," she says. "They were just trying to intimidate us." Her legal career had been confined to the intricate points of financial law, but she knew better than to assume that the court would dismiss the motion out of hand. In litigation the outcome was never certain. Still, she was determined not to be bullied. "We weren't giving up," she says, emphatically. "We were going to keep fighting with everything we had."

Book had no experience in land-use law, but a memo written shortly after the historical resources commission approved Lincoln Place's eligibility for the state register convinced her that a potentially more powerful argument could be used to defend tenants against eviction. That memo was written by Laura Burns, who wasn't a lawyer but had thoroughly educated herself about Lincoln Place legal issues by reading court documents and talking to Amanda Seward and the other attorneys handling litigation. The five-page memo set forth in detail the reasons why the July 13 appeals court ruling meant that Aimco had to comply with all the conditions attached to the project approved by the city, including the one giving every tenant the right to stay at Lincoln Place without any rent increase. The only way for the company to avoid this proviso would be to get the city to eliminate or change it, which in the view of the attorneys would require a new EIR. If this reading of the court ruling was correct, then Aimco's ongoing attempt to evict tenants was manifestly illegal.

A hearing on the first twenty-five unlawful detainer cases was held September 13 at the Santa Monica courthouse. Popp and Book had expected to defend those tenants in separate trials, but Aimco had thrown a wrench into that plan by filing for summary judgment, which meant that a judge would hear arguments from the attorneys on both sides and then decide to either hold trials or let Aimco proceed with the evictions. If the judge sided with Popp and Book, each of the tenants would get their day in court. If not, all twenty-five would be ordered to immediately vacate their apartments or face being locked out or even forcibly removed by the county sheriff.

The hearing was held before superior court judge Paul Flynn, whose name had been in the news ten years earlier when he presided over the murder trial of Calvin Broadus, better known as the rapper Snoop Dogg. The judge opened the hearing by complaining about the number of issues raised and the "hours and hours and hours" he and the court's research attorney had spent on the twenty-five cases. "You have put our staff and our court through a wringer," he said. Indeed, Popp and Book had taken a kind of "everything-but-the-kitchen-sink" approach, citing the appeals court ruling and what they believed was misuse of the Ellis Act but also raising questions of procedure. Had tenants been notified according to the letter of the law? Had security deposits and relocation payments been properly handled? Had tenant requests for one-year extensions been legitimately denied? As just one example, Aimco had deposited the legally mandated payments to evicted tenants in an escrow account at a bank in Glendale, thirty miles from Venice. The law required these payments to be "accessible" to tenants, but was it reasonable to expect elderly tenants who didn't drive or others without cars to spend two or more hours on multiple buses to get to the bank and collect their money?

Judge Flynn proceeded one-by-one through the issues, listening to arguments by Popp, Book and Linda Hollenbeck, the attorney representing Aimco. He had little comment on most of the arguments the tenant attorneys made on procedural grounds, but when the issue of entitlement to one-year extensions was raised, he became more vocal. "I'm sure that many of these claims for an extension due to disability are bogus, okay?" Alluding to one claim based on the need for corrective lenses, he said, "Corrective lenses? I mean, I've got corrective lenses. That is a disability?"

Popp replied that needing corrective lenses would qualify under the state's definition of disability if the person was legally blind without them. But like the judge, Hollenbeck pointed out the fact that she wore corrective lenses, as well as sometimes having backaches, but neither prevented her from going to work. She protested that "the legislature could not have intended for people who wear eye glasses to get a one-year extension the same as somebody who is currently undergoing chemotherapy or somebody who had their leg amputated."

Eventually, the two claims that overshadowed all others came up— Aimco's alleged abuse of the Ellis Act and the appeals court ruling requiring the property owner to comply with redevelopment project conditions. Popp argued that even if invoking the Ellis Act didn't require Aimco to stop renting apartments everywhere in California, any reasonable interpretation of law meant that the company had to take all units at a single property like Lincoln Place off the rental market. But instead of doing that, she argued, there was ample evidence that the company intended to pursue the redevelopment project approved by the city in 2002. That project, she said, "requires the plaintiffs [Aimco] to relocate folks within the development in order to move forward. They applied for it, they fought for it, they bought into it, and now they are trying to evict people in violation of that project."

Hollenbeck echoed Aimco's Patti Shwayder by accusing Popp of misreading the appeals court opinion. All the company had to do before demolishing buildings, she said, was to meet some requirements involving taking pictures of the buildings and offering them for sale. And those requirements had nothing to do with the landlord's right to proceed with evictions under the Ellis Act. When she sat down, the judge said that he hadn't heard anything from Popp to show that Aimco couldn't legally evict the tenants, and while a few other issues were argued, the air, so to speak, had gone out of the tenants' balloon. By the time he announced that he was ruling against the tenants, it was a foregone conclusion that it might be only a matter of days until the Lincoln Place chapter of their lives came to an end.

Because the hearing only involved arguments by attorneys, none of the twenty-five tenants were in the courtroom. In an email message the next day, Popp explained to them what had happened and what she expected to happen next. She would appeal Judge Flynn's ruling for all who wanted to continue to fight, and she would ask that those tenants be allowed to stay during such an appeal, but she warned that the answer would most likely be "No." She laid out a scenario for the immediate future: One, Aimco would ask the county sheriff to execute the judge's order. Two, the sheriff would post a five-day notice to vacate on each tenant's door. Three, any time after the end of that five-day period the sheriff could come and lock tenants out of their units. Typically, she said, this entire process took from fourteen to twenty-one days.

What should the twenty-five tenants do? Popp, who had been dealing with tenant evictions for years, didn't equivocate or try to cast an obviously dire situation in a positive light. "My suggestion," she wrote, "is that these families start looking for housing."

With this decisive loss in eviction court, some observers thought that the LPTA and preservationists may have miscalculated, and that a statement Book made in her email opposing settlement talks with the landlord—"We have

Aimco where we want them"—might come back to haunt her. But she and others believed that the evictions could be stopped if the city would just do its job and enforce the development project conditions. Bernard and others had talked to Mike Bonin about the urgency of this, and the day after the September 13 hearing, Bill Rosendahl sent a letter to City Attorney Rocky Delgadillo, asking for help in preventing "a grave injustice from being done" to Lincoln Pace tenants. He cited the condition that required tenant relocation within the property and urged Delgadillo to "immediately advise the appropriate city agencies to enforce the conditions of approval and halt any evictions."

A response came nine days later, in a letter from Assistant City Attorney Susan Pfann. She wrote that the appeals court ruling did nothing to stop evictions, but only prohibited the city from issuing any demolition permits at Lincoln Place until certain conditions were met. Since there weren't any pending applications for demolition permits, she wrote, the conditions hadn't been triggered. She also cited the 1997 appeals court ruling that gave TransAction the right under the Ellis Act to evict the sixteen tenants of the building on Elkland Place. As to the unlawful detainer actions, she called them "civil disputes between private parties" and said that since the city wasn't a party to those disputes there was nothing it could do to stop Aimco from forcing tenants out.

Rosendahl's office shared this response with tenant leaders, and attorney Jan Chatten-Brown produced a vigorous and impassioned rebuttal. Contrary to Pfann's claim that the conditions hadn't been "triggered," Chatten-Brown argued that they were triggered in 2003 when the city issued permits to demolish seven buildings, including the five on Lake Street, and again in 2004 when Aimco applied for permits to demolish the two buildings saved by the last-minute court injunction. She accused the owner of lying to the city with the promise that no tenants would be involuntarily displaced by the redevelopment, and urged the city council to direct the city attorney to seek an injunction to stop the evictions and to prosecute the landlord for a criminal misdemeanor.

"If the council allows itself to be defrauded," the attorney wrote, "every developer in Los Angeles will offer conditions knowing that they are meaningless, and every neighborhood will fight development tooth and nail, knowing that the City will not stand behind its own process."

During this back-and-forth, LPTA leaders decided to make a counter-offer to the settlement tendered by Aimco in June. For several reasons, the landlord's proposal had been considered unpalatable, but that was before the appeals court decision which appeared—in theory, at least—to strengthen the tenants' position. Chatten-Brown wrote up the offer and outlined it in a September 21 letter to William Delvac.

Seventy-five percent of the units designated as eligible for the California Register of Historical Resources, or a total of 522, would be preserved. Of those, 144 rental units and fifty-six condominiums would be set aside as permanently affordable for current tenants and anyone who moved out after March 18, 2005, but hadn't taken the enhanced relocation benefits and signed a voluntary termination agreement. Aimco could choose to rent the 322 remaining units at market rates or convert them to condominiums.

What about the rest of the property, including the vacant lots where buildings had already been demolished? Aimco could do what it wanted, either build new apartments or condominiums; the LPTA and other parties to the lawsuits would agree not to oppose those plans. For its part, Aimco would have to stop the current eviction proceedings and promise not to invoke the Ellis Act in the future. This settlement, Chatten-Brown wrote, would protect tenants and Lincoln Place's historic integrity while giving Aimco a satisfactory return on its investment.

Delvac responded a week later with Aimco's counteroffer, which was essentially a restatement of its earlier offer with some added details. Only 240 units would be preserved, with 144 set aside for current tenants and designated as affordable for twenty-five years. Units converted to condominiums would be available to tenants at a five percent discount. Aimco would demolish the remaining units—456 at that date—and build a minimum of 768 new units on the property, with a height limit of sixty feet in areas then limited to thirty feet. Tenants and their leaders would be obligated to support this redevelopment, but if the city failed to approve it the company would have the right to terminate the entire agreement. If that wasn't enough of a poison pill, preservationists would have to ask the state to rescind the eligibility for the state historic register and promise not to seek any future historic designation. In return, Aimco would stop evictions and agree not to evoke the Ellis Act for a period of twenty-five years.

The two sides appeared so far apart that it was hard to glimpse any middle ground. It was back to the courts—of law and public opinion. In early October, Aimco filed a lawsuit against Seward and the historical resources commission, seeking to nullify the August action. The LPTA , meanwhile, organized a demonstration at city hall to demand that Rocky Delgadillo enforce the condition prohibiting tenant eviction. Some thirty tenants and community members gathered across the street from city hall in the courtyard of the annex building that housed the city attorney's offices, holding signs with such messages as Stop Hurricane Aimco, Stand Up 2 Aimco, and Rocky, Will You Uphold the Law. Reflecting the fact that a number of Spanish-speaking tenants were facing eviction, a tenant carried a sign that said *Exigimos Vivienda Justa*. The demonstrators and a small number of curious onlookers listened to Sheila Bernard, Elena Popp, and several other speakers before forming a line and marching around the courtyard voicing their demand that the city enforce the law and stop the evictions. As common with such demonstrations, there was a festive air but also an atmosphere of dread, because so many wondered if it would be a matter of weeks or even days before they would have to hurriedly pack and leave their apartments. They hoped that Delgadillo or someone from his staff would appear and listen to their pleas, but that hope didn't turn into reality.

The hearing on Aimco's motion for summary judgment in the unlawful detainer cases against the second and last group of tenants was scheduled for October 20. Of the ninety-one tenants served unlawful detainers, sixteen had since moved out or decided not to contest the eviction proceedings and a few had been granted one-year extensions, including Sheila Bernard and her disabled daughter, and Ingrid Mueller, who was a cancer survivor and had turned sixty-two before the hearing. This left fifty cases. The hearing had been assigned to a different judge, Jacqueline Connor, and while Jan Book and Elena Popp hoped for a different result, they weren't going to be shocked if this second judge also sided with the landlord. As in the September hearing, the two central questions were whether the company intended to completely stop renting apartments at Lincoln Place as required by the Ellis Act, and whether the conditions attached to the redevelopment project prohibited tenant eviction.

The judge disposed of both questions by concluding that Aimco wasn't pursuing the project approved by the city council in 2002. Never mind that Aimco's Patti Shwayder and the company's attorneys had made statements in just the past several months that seemed to directly contradict that view. For example, William Delvac's aforementioned letter to the historical resources commission referred to the "approved" redevelopment of Lincoln Place, which could hardly mean anything other than the project with the conditions since it was the only one approved by the city. And Shwayder had told commissioners that Aimco believed it could proceed with redevelopment because the court of appeal had upheld the city's approval of "the new tract map," a reference to the document that set forth all the project conditions.

After dispensing with that issue and the others raised by Popp and Book, the judge ruled that Aimco was within its rights to evict the tenants. Afterward, Popp said that the Eviction Defense Network was willing to keep representing anyone who wanted to appeal the ruling, but as before, her advice to those tenants was to start looking for housing. The same afternoon, Sheila Bernard put out a message to tenants with practical advice about when they might expect to be forced to leave and what they should do with their possessions. But she ended on an aspirational note in keeping with her signature attitude of never-say-die: "Be strong and keep the faith. We knew the battle would be bumpy. To fight the bully in the playground, requires dedication, determination, and some bruises."

By the time of that hearing, the twenty-five tenants whose cases were the subject of the September 13 hearing had found the dreaded notices in the form of door hangers at their apartments. In large black letters below the heading of "County of Los Angeles Sheriff's Department," they read:

NOTICE TO VACATE
By virtue of a *Writ of Possession of Real Property,*
a copy of which is attached,
YOU ARE ORDERED TO VACATE THE PREMISES DESCRIBED IN THE
WRIT NOT LATER THAN: _____,20____

The handwritten date was 10/22/05. This meant that any time after that date, sheriff's deputies could come and force everyone in the apartment to leave and then stand by while the landlord changed the locks. Hence the term "lockout" commonly used to describe these actions. The fact that the deadline came and went without any lockouts could be attributed to Bill Rosendahl. The councilman had been working to bring all parties to the table to negotiate a settlement, and after the notices were posted on apartment doors he persuaded the company to ask the sheriff's office to hold off on actual enforcement of the orders while a last-ditch effort was made to reach an agreement.

Time was short, though. In a presumed effort to make a deal, Aimco had dropped its demand that Amanda Seward ask that the listing of Lincoln Place as eligible for the state register be rescinded. Instead, it would agree to the designation for 242 units. This, in Aimco's view, was a win-win for the company and preservationists—a significant number of buildings would have the protections of historic recognition, and Aimco would get to redevelop a large chunk of the property. And those like Rosendahl who were clearly more interested in the fate of tenants than in preserving Lincoln Place's architectural and cultural history would see those tenants living in the preserved buildings instead of being forced out.

In anticipation of all parties reaching agreement, Aimco had petitioned the historical resources commission for what was called a "redetermination" of the Lincoln Place listing. The commission had put the matter on the agenda of its quarterly meeting on November 4, and Rosendahl and the mayor's office had arranged for a room at city hall for representatives of Aimco and the other parties—the LPTA, the 20th Century Architectural Alliance, the preservation groups that had joined its lawsuit, and the city attorney's office—to meet and hammer out the final details. Nobody on the LPTA and preservationist side of the table was happy with what Aimco had proposed, though. Amanda Seward and Laura Burns would have to swallow the reality that two-thirds of what they considered Ralph Vaughn's remarkable creation would be torn to the ground, and Sheila Bernard would have to abandon her long-held dream of a Lincoln Place owned and run by tenants or a nonprofit committed to tenant welfare instead of the pursuit of profit. But glaring in their faces was the fact that seventy-five tenants had lost in court and were facing imminent eviction and another seventy-three—all elderly or disabled—faced the same fate in less than five months. The majority of those tenants were people of limited means who had believed in the leadership of Bernard, Jan Book, and others who had urged them to stay and fight. Could those leaders now, in good conscience, reject a deal that would allow them to live for the rest of their lives at Lincoln Place?

Aimco had conceded a major point of contention by agreeing to historical designation for the 242 units, but the two sides were still at odds on other issues, most notably the development of the rest of the property. The company was proposing to build 766 new apartments or condominiums up to a height limit of sixty feet, but wanted to revise the tract map for the original redevelopment instead of submitting a new application and conducting a new environmental impact report. As in the landlord's original offer, parties to the settlement would have to agree not to object to this and, in fact, would be required to actively support the project through public statements and the writing of letters to public officials. However, Aimco had dropped what might have been the single biggest deal breaker in its first offer, the right to terminate the entire settlement if the city failed to approve its plans.

That new development would increase Lincoln Place's density by more than twenty percent and double the height of existing buildings in some places without a new EIR to study the impact on such things as local traffic, parking, neighborhood schools, and water and sewer services. Many community residents and organizations had supported the LPTA over the years, but what if they had legitimate reasons to oppose what Aimco wanted to build? They would be pitted against tenant leaders like Sheila Bernard, who would be obligated by terms of the settlement to publicly support the property owner. That was an entirely plausible scenario, and a hard one to swallow for someone like Bernard who strongly believed that people should have a voice in whatever was built in their own community.

The negotiations came down to the wire, with Patti Shwayder and William Delvac at the table with Bernard, Amanda Seward, Laura Burns, Jan Book and Assistant City Attorney Susan Pfann. Others came and went—an aide to Bill Rosendahl, a deputy to Mayor Antonio Villaraigosa. By late in the afternoon of November 3, less than twenty-four hours before the historical resources commission meeting, there seemed to be general—if reluctant—agreement by the LPTA and preservationists that they had gotten the best they could from Aimco. Seward would go to the commission meeting and say she wanted the historic designation withdrawn for all but 242 units and Aimco would tell the county sheriff to stop the eviction process. Book and Bernard would tell distressed tenants that they would be able to stay at Lincoln Place after all. Rosendahl and Villaraigosa would proclaim victory for tenants and the cause of affordable housing and extol the virtues of negotiation and compromise.

But none of those things happened. Seward and Burns left city hall as darkness was falling and early the next morning made the four-hour drive to Fresno, the San Joaquin Valley city where the commission was meeting that quarter. Also making the trip were Delvac and Shwayder. When the meeting got underway, the Aimco attorney told commissioners about the negotiations and said there was a pending settlement that would be presented to tenants on the Sunday following the commission meeting. Seward, however, disputed this, saying the parties hadn't reached agreement. Aimco wanted to tear down three-fourths of Lincoln Place without public comment, she said, adding that the settlement included a gag order prescribing what she could or couldn't say about the new development. "Aimco is trying to ram its version down everyone's throat," she told the commissioners. Burns echoed Seward's statement and added a complaint about Aimco's "gun-to-the-head" style of negotiating.

When it came time for discussion, commissioner Claire Bogaard said she understood her role as limited to deciding whether a property was eligible for listing on the state register, and since the commission had done that at its August 3 meeting, she saw no basis for Aimco's redetermination request. Several other commissioners spoke up in agreement, and the ensuing vote to deny the request was unanimous.

That constituted a victory for preservationists, but nobody who had driven up from Los Angeles that morning or who had been part of the negotiations was in a celebratory mood. Some tenants had moved out since the last eviction court hearing, but more than sixty remained and faced imminent eviction. And Aimco's redevelopment plans still faced serious hurdles, even if the company succeeded in emptying all of Lincoln Place's buildings. Given the charged atmosphere, it was hardly surprising that recriminations followed. In the landlord's telling, Seward and Burns were the villains, having sabotaged any possibility of stopping evictions. In a statement posted on Aimco's Lincoln Place website, the two were accused of working against wishes of the tenants and city officials. "Their actions destroyed the opportunity to achieve a settlement," the statement said.

Others were unhappy as well. Just days after the commission hearing, the Venice Neighborhood Council took up a motion calling for Aimco to immediately halt Lincoln Place evictions and for the city attorney to enforce the redevelopment project conditions. One of the speakers was Larry Frank, a Venice resident and the deputy mayor who had represented Villaraigosa in the failed negotiations at city hall. An account of the meeting in a community newspaper called *Venice Paper* quoted Frank as saying that the deal to preserve units and protect tenants was agreed to by all parties except one.[71] "I care less about the buildings than I do about the tenants," he said, adding that the person who stood in the way of agreement "is in the room." That reference was obviously to Amanda Seward, who then rose to speak in her own defense, saying she resented the insinuation that she cared only about preservation of the buildings. "No one has spent more time with Lincoln Place tenants than I have," she said, a statement that, according to the article, drew cheers and applause from a large contingent of tenants in the audience. Seward was further quoted as saying that if Aimco had signed the deal on the table the night before the state commission meeting, she wouldn't have opposed the change to give historical status to only 242 buildings. But, she added, Aimco's disregard of the no-evictions condition of the redevelopment project meant there was little reason to believe that the company would adhere to any deal that wasn't actually signed by all parties and legally enforceable.

Looking back now, Seward says she doesn't believe Aimco actually wanted to make a deal. Even given her distaste for the "gag order" and other aspects of the company's settlement offer, she says she was serious about dropping the historic nomination for everything but the preserved buildings. "But I had to have a signed agreement," she says. "I would not accept anything less." By the time she left city hall to go home and prepare for the commission hearing the next morning, Aimco's attorneys still hadn't drafted anything that could be signed. "I know when people want to make a deal. If they wanted a deal, they could have had a deal."

While Aimco and some others continued to cast Seward and Burns as renegades who torpedoed any chance to save tenants from eviction, the person who had arguably fought the hardest for tenants over the years came to the pair's defense. In the November issue of the *Beachhead*, Sheila Bernard wrote that preservationists had been "erroneously accused of caring more about buildings than about people, when in fact without those organizations, Lincoln Place would be dust today and everyone would have already been evicted." She added her appreciation of the Lincoln Place design extolled by Seward, Burns, and others in the preservation fight, writing that "it is the ingenious design of these buildings that is partly responsible for the united and feisty community that has for years gone head-to-head with the biggest landlord in the United States."[72]

With the Thanksgiving holiday approaching and Rosendahl's office scrambling to keep the flickering flame of negotiations alive, tenants got more bad news in the form of a superior court ruling in the Marlin vs. Aimco case. To the surprise of many legal observers, Judge Andria Richey sided with Aimco and found that the lawsuit filed by Jan Book and Elena Popp was a SLAPP suit, and therefore had to be dismissed. Book and Popp had argued that Frieda Marlin and her son had every right to ask the court if the landlord could legally use the Ellis Act to evict them, and that simply asking that question in no way infringed upon the company's right to petition the government, as Aimco lawyers claimed. But Judge Richey disagreed. In her ruling, she said that the sending of required notices to the city as part of the eviction process was a protected "petitioning activity" and therefore the Marlin lawsuit was indeed an attempt to interfere with the company's constitutional rights.

Rebuffed in courts of law, tenants kept up efforts to pressure political leaders to stop the evictions. Two days after the ruling in the Marlin case,

Amanda Seward and several tenants went to city hall and buttonholed Mayor Villaraigosa and Councilman Rosendahl outside the city council chamber. Both politicians promised to push Aimco to re-open talks, and the mayor agreed to call the company's CEO, Terry Considine, and ask him to suspend evictions while the parties got back to the negotiating table. Later that day, Villaraigosa and Rosendahl had a conference call with Considine and Patti Shwayder. They reported that the company head agreed not to push forward with evictions until after the Thanksgiving holiday, although he wouldn't commit to restarting talks with tenant leaders and preservationists.

The LPTA continued to make its case in the court of public opinion. On the afternoon before Thanksgiving, about fifty tenants and others gathered at Elkgrove Circle in the middle of Lincoln Place and marched the two blocks to Lincoln Boulevard and California Avenue with signs warning of the imminent evictions and calling on Rocky Delgadillo to enforce the no-evictions condition. Sheila Bernard and others had been brainstorming ways to draw more public attention to the plight of tenants, and some who owned camping tents had suggested, with varying degrees of seriousness, that they would be forced to live in them if they couldn't find apartments they could afford. This had led to the idea of setting up a kind of tent city in a conspicuous place like the grounds of city hall. There had also been talk of demonstrating outside Delgadillo's home in the Wilshire Park neighborhood west of downtown, and the two ideas came together the Friday after Thanksgiving Day when many of the same people who had marched to Lincoln Boulevard two days earlier gathered in front of the city attorney's house and pitched tents in the grassy parkway between the sidewalk and the street.

A tenant and photographer named Elke Weiss had been taking black-and-white portraits of residents for a project she called "The Many Faces of Lincoln Place," and she brought a large poster printed with fifty of these portraits, along with individual enlargements in clear plastic sleeves. These enlargements, with the names of the people pictured, were hooked to the finials along the top of the wrought iron fence surrounding Delgadillo's large two-story house. Two dozen tenants and supporters paraded back and forth in front of the fence with signs that bore, among other messages,

Homeless for the Holidays; Where Is the City Attorney?; Renters Have Rights, Too; and Rocky, Stand Up To Aimco. One tenant carried a sign that said *Aimco Es Un Sin Virguensa Mentiroso,* an expression of what many Latino tenants felt about their landlord and a nod perhaps to Delgadillo's Mexican heritage and fluency in Spanish. Several older persons hoisted signs while seated on lawn chairs by the pitched tents, including the doughty Frieda Marlin and her son Spike.

Two police cars showed up but officers just kept watch and didn't attempt to break up the demonstration. After two hours or so a Delgadillo aide in a brown suit and tie emerged from the house and spoke briefly to Sheila Bernard and Laura Burns before inviting them inside. A few minutes later, Amanda Seward arrived, her appearance prompting cheers from the demonstrators, who clearly didn't embrace the view that she had wrecked the negotiations because she cared more about buildings than people. She was also ushered through the wrought iron gate and up a flight of steps to the front door of the house.

The city attorney's office had steadfastly maintained that the condition prohibiting displacement of tenants could only be enforced when the property owner applied for demolition permits related to the new construction. In the meantime, there was nothing the city could do to stop the landlord from evicting every tenant under the Ellis Act. But Seward and the others wanted to convince Delgadillo that the appeals court ruling that past July meant that redevelopment conditions had been triggered by the Lake Street demolitions and applications for permits to tear down the two buildings that were still standing.

All remember the meeting as congenial, with the city attorney sitting on one side of a large dining room table and Seward, Bernard and Burns on the other. Coffee was served, which Burns recalls as being hazelnut-cream flavored. Delgadillo appeared sympathetic, but seemed to want to know what legal options the city had. Seward agreed to send him a letter outlining the issue in detail and describing steps the city could take to stop the evictions.

Delgadillo followed the three back outside. The forty-five-year-old had been a star high school and college football player, and dressed in jeans and dark blue sweatshirt he still looked fit enough to run up and down a field.

By that time, a crew from Channel 4 News had shown up, and the reporter dressed in a dark suit and tie briefly interviewed Delgadillo and tenant leaders. The city attorney then chatted with some of the demonstrators, including Frieda Marlin, before going back inside his house. In an article the same day in the online version of *Venice Paper*, he was quoted as telling tenants that he would "earnestly pursue" the Lincoln Place issue, although he wouldn't commit to trying to enforce the tenant displacement condition.[73] Instead, he echoed the calls by Bill Rosendahl, Antonio Villaraigosa, and others for renewed negotiations with Aimco. Bernard was quoted in the article, and to the surprise of nobody who knew her, she sounded an optimistic note. "I'm very encouraged by the fact that Rocky invited us in and talked to us and came out and talked to the tenants and wants to get talks going again."

Three days later, Seward sent Delgadillo the promised letter, which laid out six pages of detail about legal steps the city could take to stop the evictions and enforce the conditions. At the same time, Rosendahl got the city council to schedule an executive session with the city attorney the following Friday, December 2, to discuss possible legal actions. In its July ruling, the appeals court had directed the superior court to issue a permanent injunction against tearing down any Lincoln Place buildings until predemolition conditions were met, and a hearing on that order was scheduled for December 6. The hope was that council members would instruct the city attorney to ask the judge to include a statement in his order that evicting tenants violated the appeals court ruling. There were mixed opinions on whether the judge would do this, even if the city attorney agreed to press the matter, but without Aimco agreeing to return to negotiations there seemed no other immediate recourse.

The hiatus in eviction activity promised by Terry Considine was about to expire, and tenants who had gotten notices to vacate were on edge, wondering when they would look out their windows and see sheriff's cars and hear ominous knocks on their doors. A few, including Laura Burns and Bernard Perroud, had rented curbside moving and storage containers, and Jan Book had stolen a few moments in the midst of putting together tenant appeals of evictions to pack up some of her artworks. There was fear and anxiety, but there was also hope. The leaders who had stood by tenants for so long still seemed to believe that they could win the fight, and their city councilman was adamant about bringing the city's resources to bear to protect them. And finally, a rich, powerful corporation like Aimco wouldn't be so heartless as to throw people—including families with children—out of their homes right at the beginning of the Christmas season, would it?

22

A TRAVESTY, AN INJUSTICE, AND A GREAT SHAME

AMID THE SUSPENSE AND turmoil that marked the fall of 2005, Sheila Bernard and Arrie Bachrach were moving ahead with marriage plans made earlier that year. They had set a date of December 10 for a wedding and reception at the Santa Monica home of a friend; a few days later they were to fly to Israel for a traditional Jewish wedding in the country where all three of Bernard's brothers now lived. She was aware of some recent grumbling about the LPTA's leadership and the failure to reach a settlement with Aimco that would banish the specter of eviction, and she knew that a few might look askance upon her absence from Lincoln Place at such a fraught time. What if tenants were forced from their apartments while she was nearly eight thousand miles away, happily celebrating her nuptials? But there was no way of knowing when, or even if, sheriff's deputies would show up and start knocking on doors. Bill Rosendahl was still pushing hard on two fronts—getting Aimco and the other parties back to the negotiating table, and persuading City Attorney Rocky Delgadillo to initiate some action to enforce the no-evictions condition. She also felt confident that the rest of the LPTA brain trust of Jan Book, Laura Burns and Amanda Seward could hold down the fort and deal with anything that might arise during the week she would be away.

But the first order of business after the post–Thanksgiving Day demonstration outside Delgadillo's house was to organize the same kind of "tent city" on the grounds of city hall on December 2, the day the council was scheduled to discuss the Lincoln Place situation and hopefully tell the city attorney to take some action. If Bernard had learned anything from her long tenure as LPTA president, it was that legalistic arguments carried the most weight with lawyers and judges; the public, and by extension, politicians, were moved by scenes and stories with an emotional appeal. The sight of gray-haired tenants like Frieda Marlin sitting outside camping tents with signs protesting eviction had gotten the attention of the press, and it probably helped persuade Delgadillo to invite the tenant leaders into his house and at least give the appearance of sympathy and a willingness to do something. Bernard hoped that the tents pitched on the south lawn outside the main entrance to city hall would have the same effect on a majority of city council members.

Time was of the essence, though, because of the hearing in superior court the following Tuesday. If the judge, David Yaffe, could be persuaded to rule that the current eviction attempts were illegal under the terms of the appeals court ruling, tenants would have a big weapon in their fight. Amanda Seward and others had been repeatedly making that argument, but they believed it would carry much more weight if it came from the city attorney. Although Delgadillo was an elected official and not directly under the city council's authority, the council was his client in the legal sense and he couldn't simply ignore a formal request that he ask the judge for an injunction to stop Aimco from putting anyone out of their Lincoln Place apartments.

The date of the council meeting fell on a Friday, which was traditionally set aside for members to deliver proclamations lauding organizations and individuals from their respective districts. These often took an hour or more before the council could get to the business on its agenda. Furthermore, the item calling for discussion of the Lincoln Place evictions was at the very end of the agenda, which meant a considerable wait for the two dozen tenants and their supporters who had gotten to city hall that morning before the council's ten a.m. starting time. Still, expectations were high that after the members listened to public comment and then went into executive session with a lawyer from Delgadillo's staff, they would heed the pleas for action and vote to direct the city attorney to initiate legal action to at least temporarily halt the evictions.

It's likely that almost everyone in the chamber that day knew that on Saturday the city's two major universities, UCLA and USC, would be playing their annual football game. The latter was undefeated and rated number one in the country; UCLA had lost twice and was rated number eleven. More than seventy-five thousand spectators were expected to pack USC's home field, the Memorial Coliseum, and in the past week, sports sections and radio and TV programs had been replete with articles and discussions about the upcoming contest. Although organized betting on football and other college sports wasn't legal in California, lots of wagers, ranging from the small and friendly between friends to the high-stakes by professional gamblers, were made on the game.

But nobody who had come to city hall on Friday morning imagined that all this passion and hoopla over that football game would spill into the council chamber and end up influencing the proceedings. Once the proclamations were dispensed with, the council got to its agenda, but it wasn't long before council president Alex Padilla interrupted discussion to announce that Councilman Bernard Parks would be making a presentation. A USC graduate, Parks was wearing a long scarf in the university's colors of cardinal and gold, and as he stepped to the speaker's podium the "Trojan Fight Song" played by the USC marching band blared over the public address system. Mayor Antonio Villaraigosa had appeared, and as he moved toward the podium he caught a football thrown from across the chamber by Councilman Eric Garcetti. The mayor was a UCLA graduate, and he was joined at the podium by fellow graduates and council members Ed Reyes and Wendy Greuel. Councilman Greig Smith, a USC alumnus, also joined the group.

Parks and then Villaraigosa read lengthy testimonials to the accomplishments of their respective universities, after which friendly wagers were made on the game, with winners getting such things as restaurant meals, dance lessons, and horseback rides. It was all good fun and comity, but not everybody in the chamber was amused or touched by the feel-good spirit. Their feelings were succinctly captured the following day in a headline in the Metro section of the *Los Angeles Times*: "Council Fiddles, Tenants Burn." The strapline read, "Residents facing eviction wait and wait while the panel makes USC-UCLA wagers and tosses a ball," and the article, written by city hall reporter Steve Hymon, opened with the question, "Which is more important to the Los Angeles City Council—dealing with tenants about to be evicted from their apartments or wagering on the USC-UCLA football game?" The question was rhetorical, but tenants and others who had sat seething at what they regarded as council antics had no trouble regarding it as emphatically answerable.

When the council finally reached the last item on the agenda, nearly three hours after Padilla called the session to order, Rosendahl asked that the public be given ten minutes to comment prior to the private session with a deputy city attorney. The first speaker was Sheila Bernard, who said the city attorney should go to Tuesday's court hearing with an injunction in hand and be prepared with an emergency appeal if the judge turned it down. She was followed by a Lincoln Place neighbor and homeowner named David Ewing, who chided the council members. "A lot of people have taken time off work and interrupted their lives to speak to you," he said, "I know there have been a lot of feel-good issues this morning but this is a serious one—this is going to affect people's lives and the future of our community." Next was seventy-four-year-old tenant Gloria Morales, who had been a faithful LPTA supporter and now faced eviction in March after living in her Lincoln Place apartment for thirty-one years. When she began to speak in Spanish of the predicament faced by herself and fellow tenants, she broke down in tears.

Also speaking on behalf of tenants were Elena Popp and Amanda Seward. Popp accused Aimco of holding tenants hostage in order to extract development concessions from the city, while Seward demanded that council members tell the city attorney to find a way to stop evictions. "If there is a moral wrong, there is a legal remedy," she said. The only speaker from the other side of the aisle was Aimco attorney William Delvac, who argued that the tenants' dilemma was of their leadership's own making, since the landlord had offered them the right to stay at Lincoln Place for as long as they wanted. When the ten minutes expired, a number of persons were still waiting to speak, but Rosendahl said members needed to immediately adjourn to executive session because some had other commitments and he didn't want the council to lose its quorum.

Even though it was well past lunch time, almost everyone was prepared to wait for council members to emerge from a private meeting room off the chamber. But when Rosendahl and a handful of others shortly reappeared, an announcement was made that only seven had attended the executive session, one short of the quorum needed to conduct business. They had listened to an informal legal briefing, but couldn't legally discuss the Lincoln Place issue or take any action. This didn't sit well, obviously, with the waiting tenants. One of them, Yael Korin, who had taken time off from her job to be at city hall, was quoted by *Times* reporter Hymon. "This is a humiliating joke. It's our taxpayer money that allows them to play football during a meeting." A graduate of the University of Pittsburgh, Rosendahl hadn't participated in the betting and football tossing, but he told the reporter that he wasn't going to "throw stones" at his colleagues. He would take the blame, he said, for not trying to move the Lincoln Place issue to an earlier spot on the agenda.

As for those colleagues who didn't escape stone-throwing from the public, Councilman Parks and the other USC partisans were undoubtedly happy on Saturday afternoon, because that university's team trounced UCLA by a score of 66–19.

On Sunday, the LPTA held its regular monthly meeting at Penmar Park. Tenants crowded into the room, both those who had gotten five-day notices to vacate and those who had been granted one-year extensions due to age or disability. Almost everybody had the same questions—what did the city council's nonaction two days earlier mean for them? What was the status of legal steps being taken on their behalf? And foremost in many minds, how long did they have before being locked out of their apartments?

Elena Popp couldn't be at the meeting, but she sent an email "status report" for Sheila Bernard to read aloud. In her message, Popp said that Aimco had requested lockouts but the company's eviction attorney, Linda Hollenbeck, refused to tell her when sheriff's deputies might actually show up. "Aimco wants you all on pins and needles," Popp wrote, "so that you will go into a panic and put pressure on Amanda [Seward] to agree to sign the agreement that is on the table." This referred to the stalled negotiations with Aimco over its offer to preserve 242 units and allow 180 tenants to stay at their current rents. But Seward hadn't been shown an enforceable agreement she could sign, and Aimco had walked away from negotiations after the historical resources commission confirmed the eligibility of all Lincoln Place buildings for the state historical register. "My sense," Popp wrote, "is that Amanda believes that we can get a much better deal out of Aimco than is on the table, if we hang tough." Striking a possibly rueful note, she wrote, "I am unwilling to speculate as to whether this is true because I fear that minimally [tenants not given one-year extensions] will be locked out if we continue on the present course. I would be thrilled to be wrong and glad that decision is not in my hands."

On the legal front, she brought up the superior court hearing that coming Tuesday. She had learned that the city attorney intended to ask the judge if the appeals court ruling allowed the city to do anything to stop the current evictions. But just asking this question, she said, would be "grossly inadequate." If the city attorney's office stuck to its contention that project conditions could only be enforced when the company applied for demolition permits, the no-evictions condition wasn't worth the paper it was written on. Aimco could just wait until all the tenants were out before applying for those permits, which created an absurdity—the city enacting legal protections for tenants but unable to enforce them until there were no longer any tenants to protect. She concluded by writing that attorneys and tenant leaders were talking about mounting a completely new lawsuit to compel the city to enforce the condition. Unfortunately, even if such a lawsuit were filed and resulted in a favorable ruling, it would come too late to save tenants facing immediate lockouts.

The next day, December 5, Sheila Bernard got a call from a producer for KCRW's *Which Way, L.A.?* The host, Warren Olney, had read the *Times* account of the betting and football tossing at Friday's city council meeting, and he wanted to discuss it with her and Councilman Rosendahl on that evening's half-hour program.

"It was hard being there for so long and watching that happen and knowing we had urgent business before the council," Bernard told Olney at the beginning of the ten-minute segment given over to Lincoln Place. "I have a football player son, so I'm not against football. But I want them [the council] to deal more seriously with the serious issues confronting Los Angeles."

When Olney turned to Rosendahl, the councilman sounded—for him, at least—subdued, and repeated what he told the *Times* reporter, that it was his fault for not insisting that the Lincoln Place issue be moved up on the agenda. But he didn't seem confident that his colleagues would have ridden to the rescue of tenants even if they had kept a quorum. In the closed session, he said, the deputy city attorney had been unable to offer a legal rationale for challenging the evictions. The best immediate hope for Lincoln Place tenants, he said, lay in renewing negotiations with Aimco.

Bernard had the last word, and sounded a skeptical note about these talks. In her view, Aimco's overriding goal in settlement negotiations was to get everyone involved to support a redevelopment project with more units and greater height than the one originally submitted in 1993 and ultimately approved by the city council in 2002. "I don't think the council really understands the gravity of what's going on [at Lincoln Place]. The tenants are being held for ransom, the city council is being expected to pay that ransom in development concessions over and above what they received in a public process." This, she declared, was not only morally wrong but dangerous. But another fact was clear, certainly to the tenants Aimco was trying to evict. They had fought for and been granted the right to stay at Lincoln Place, and the city needed to do everything in its power to stop the landlord from brushing aside that right as if it didn't exist.

Bernard had been staying in Camarillo with her husband-to-be and driving to Los Angeles for her adult school teaching job. Her youngest son, then twenty-one, was staying at the Lincoln Place apartment with her thirty-year-old daughter. On Tuesday, she expected to do some work on wedding preparations, go to her teaching job, then come back and find out by telephone or email what had happened at the court hearing. The optimism that had followed the meeting with Rocky Delgadillo at his house had mostly dissipated, and without a strong statement by the city attorney on behalf of tenants, it seemed unlikely that Judge Yaffe would go beyond the appeals court ruling and explicitly say that Aimco's eviction activity was illegal. Some were also calling Delgadillo's loyalties into question. According to official filings, he had gotten $3,000 in campaign contributions from Aimco attorney William Delvac between 2000 and 2005, and $20,800 from Delvac's law firm, Latham & Watkins. Those inclined to draw a direct line between campaign contributions and an elected official's actions also pointed to $3,000 in contributions from the Apartment Association of Greater Los Angeles. But the biggest red flag had gone up in late October, when the *Los Angeles Times* published an article titled, "Alleged Slumlords Donated to Delgadillo." The article detailed more than $16,000 in campaign contributions from two landlords who had been sued by the city for health and safety violations. According to the article, the lawsuit filed by Delgadillo's predecessor had been settled by Delgadillo on highly favorable terms to the alleged slumlords. Delgadillo had also surprised people just months after winning a second four-year term in 2005 by announcing his candidacy for the Democratic nomination for California Attorney General. He would face former governor Jerry Brown in the June 2006 primary, and those who regarded campaign contributions as an obvious source of corruption believed that he needed the support of the real estate industry and related interests and wouldn't want to do anything to alienate them.

The most realistic hope, at that point, was for Aimco to temporarily suspend eviction activity and join the other parties in settlement talks, even if the company's motive in those talks, as Bernard declared, was less than honorable. But as people at Lincoln Place were eating breakfast and sending their kids off to school and getting ready to go to work, and while various attorneys were preparing to go downtown for the superior court hearing, sheriff's deputies were gathering directly west of Lincoln Place on the rooftop parking area of the Staples office supply store on Lincoln Boulevard. They were joined there by Aimco's eviction attorney, Linda Hollenbeck, and Maria Lopez, the Lincoln Place manager, who laid out copies of more than fifty eviction notices on the hood of a car. With the Santa Monica mountains visible in the distance and the tops of nearby palm trees motionless in the morning air, the deputies in their tan shirts and green trousers organized their plans for the next few hours and then got in their cars and made the brief drive down the parking area ramp and across Lincoln Boulevard past the shopping center into the heart of Lincoln Place.[74]

When Laura Burns first looked out her kitchen window and saw those black-and-white cars, she called and emailed as many people as she could before a deputy loudly rapped on her door. One of her calls was to Jan Book, who quickly got in her car and drove to Lincoln Place from the condominium she shared with her husband in Marina Del Rey. The tenants who had been given five-day notices were scattered throughout the complex, and she tried to keep a step ahead of the deputies and warn those tenants that they should immediately pack whatever belongings they needed for the next few nights at a motel or the home of friends or relatives or wherever else they might have to stay. In her rounds, she came upon Frieda Marlin, waiting at the curb for a taxi to take her to a doctor's appointment. The eight-one-year-old wasn't in danger of eviction until spring, but she was still visibly upset as Book tried to assure her that the fight against the landlord was far from over. As Book helped Marlin into the taxi, the older woman planted a kiss on the younger woman's cheek and repeated, over and over, "I love you guys. I love you guys."

The news of what was going on spread into the surrounding neighborhoods, reaching two persons who would soon play a significant role in the long-running battle over Lincoln Place's future. David Ewing, who had spoken at the past Friday's city council meeting, and Laura Silagi, a homeowner on the first street south of Lincoln Place, were among the leaders of the Venice Community Coalition, the group that had organized opposition to the plan to turn the shopping center adjacent to Lincoln Place into a complex of upscale stores and high-rise apartments.[75] A number of Lincoln Place tenants had supported the successful effort to stop that project, and Silagi and Ewing had become friends with some of them, notably Sheila Bernard, Ingrid Mueller, and Carol Beck, the tenant who had blocked the asbestos removal crew with her car. Bernard and other LPTA leaders had long considered support from the broader community to be a vital part of their fight, and they welcomed the presence of neighbors at the LPTA's monthly meetings at Penmar Park. Ewing and Silagi, along with several others, had been coming to those meetings for the past year and volunteering to help in media relations, letter-writing campaigns to public officials, and outreach to other neighborhoods and organizations. They had also joined the demonstrations outside Delgadillo's office and home, as well as attending the December 2 city council meeting.

Silagi, an artist and founding member of a feminist art collective called Mother Art, grabbed her Panasonic camcorder and made the short walk to Lincoln Place after Ewing called her with news that the lockouts were starting. She saw Mueller, who like Frieda Marlin wasn't in danger of eviction until spring, and the two of them followed a phalanx of deputies up a stairwell to an apartment door. One of the deputies was filming the activity, presumably as a record to protect against liability, and Silagi remarked to him that his camcorder was the same model as hers. He didn't comment. She also asked how many deputies were on the property, but he refused to answer. One rapped sharply on the door and delivered the loud announcement that would be repeated throughout the complex, "Sheriff's department, we're here for eviction, open the door!" When the door finally opened and three deputies went inside, Silagi kept filming through the door, but when one of them saw her, he slammed it shut.

At another building, she filmed a maintenance worker changing the locks on an apartment door while a deputy stood by. When the worker finished and the door was closed and locked, the deputy took a door hanger from a sheaf in his hand and hooked it over the knob. In bold red letters, it read:

Notice of Eviction

To the Judgment Debtor(s) and All Claiming under Same:

You are hereby notified that pursuant to the Order of the Court and Notice to Vacate heretofore delivered to you or your agent, or posted upon these premises, your occupancy of these premises has been terminated. Any property which you may have left

upon the premises is now under the legal control of the judgment creditor referred to below.

Information regarding legal procedures to follow to regain possession of your personal property is set forth in the above-mentioned Notice to Vacate. For further information, you should consult an attorney.

As Silagi filmed other deputies moving through the complex, an off-camera voice called out, "Merry Christmas, officers, I hope you enjoy kicking people out of their homes." She filmed a man carrying plastic bags of possessions from a building while his wife and a locked-out neighbor wept with their arms around each other. She saw Gloria Morales, the woman who had broken down in tears at the December 2 city council meeting. The longtime LPTA supporter wasn't in danger of being locked out that day, but the sight of younger neighbors being forced from their apartments clearly upset her. "I don't have no place to go," she said. "No money to pay higher rent." A woman in pajamas and bathrobe hurriedly pushed a shopping cart toward an unruly stack of possessions on the lawn outside her building. Five deputies trooped into an apartment, then filed back out while a Lincoln Place security guard on a bicycle waited on the sidewalk, leisurely leaning on the handlebars as if he were witnessing something of only mild interest. A young child in a bright red jacket jumped out of a stroller and joined a group of other small children playing on the sidewalk in front of a building, oblivious to the drama around them. Silagi wondered if their parents had told them they couldn't go back inside their apartments, and if so, what they understood, if anything, of such strange news.

She stopped to film a rack with clothing like a stray department store display in front of a door with an eviction hanger on the knob. Moving along, she approached Elkgrove Avenue, the street that runs through the heart of Lincoln Place. It was after eleven o'clock, and the sheriff's deputies had finished the lockouts at fifty-two apartments and were getting into their cars and pulling away. A gray Honda Civic sat at the curb; the front seat passenger was Bill Rosendahl, who rolled down the window and told her to follow the car up the block to where he would be holding an impromptu news conference with some media people, including a crew that had shown up from Channel 7 News.

The councilman's presence attracted a small crowd, many holding signs from previous demonstrations with such messages as Aimco Lies! and Aimco=Bad Faith and the old favorite, Preserve Lincoln Place. Among those gathered to hear Rosendahl were some of the sixty-five adults and twenty-one children who had lived until moments before in apartments that now displayed red-lettered eviction notices and were locked with keys that only the landlord possessed. Laura Burns, wearing the jeans and sweatshirt she had thrown on after first seeing the sheriff's deputies out her window, stood alongside Amanda Seward, who was dressed in the brown business suit she had worn to the superior court hearing downtown. Seward had still been at the courthouse when she got the news that the lockouts had started, and she couldn't help remembering back to 2003 when machines were reducing the five Lake Street buildings to rubble at the very moment she and other attorneys were in court to get an injunction to stop them. It was, to quote Yogi Berra once more, like "déjà vu all over again."

She had gotten back to Lincoln Place in time to see the deputies still going from apartment to apartment while a helicopter hovered in the sky above, and she was even more appalled than she had been two years earlier. "It looked like a sting operation for a drug cartel," she says. "It was the worst thing I'd ever seen in my life." As more people were drawn to the crowd around Rosendahl, Seward gave the councilman an account of that morning's court proceeding. As directed by the appeals court, Judge Yaffe had approved an order barring the city from issuing any demolition permits until the property owner complied with the redevelopment project conditions. But that was all. Despite Delgadillo's promise to help the tenants, a lawyer from the city attorney's office had declined to ask the judge for an injunction or other sort of order to enforce the no-evictions condition. That, in essence, left Aimco free to keep doing what it had started while attorneys were waiting to address the judge—emptying the complex of tenants who had every reason to believe that they had been promised the exact opposite—an unequivocal right to stay.

Seward's account prompted a few shouts of displeasure aimed at the judge. Burns had been standing by listening, and Rosendahl beckoned her over, put his arm around her, and identified her as a locked-out tenant. With the top of her head at the middle of the six-foot-four councilman's chest, she looked small and vulnerable, although most people at the scene that morning knew her as feisty and always ready to fight for what she believed was right. Addressing the crowd, Burns said outrage should be directed at Rocky Delgadillo. That prompted yells of "Delgadillo's a criminal!" and "Recall Delgadillo!" When the clamor died down, Rosendahl, wearing a dark suit and paisley tie identical to the one he had worn at his inauguration ceremony on Venice Beach, said, "I'm disappointed and sorry to hear what the city attorney did today. I hoped the city attorney would side with the tenants, not the landlord." That brought more angry shouts of displeasure from the audience, and he added that what Aimco was doing was "totally unacceptable behavior. I'm offended by this. It hurts all of us who care about people."

With most of the crowd following, he walked the short distance to the Lincoln Place management office in one of the single-story bungalows appended to each of the complex's buildings. Someone shouted that the manager was inside, but when Rosendahl knocked, nobody came to the door. A typed notice taped to the door said, "If you were locked out, please contact the office tomorrow to make arrangements to get the rest of your belongings." Rosendahl took out his cell phone and called the number at the bottom of the notice but got no answer. As soon as he walked away, four security guards who had been standing by took up positions on the steps to the door, presumably to stop anyone who might get the idea of expressing their displeasure by committing vandalism or other mischief. By that time, the sheriff's cars were gone and the pulsing beat of the helicopter no longer disturbed the late morning air. Rosendahl got back into the car driven by his chief of staff, Mike Bonin, and headed to his city hall office. By mid-afternoon, the councilman had put out a formal statement that read, in part:

"These evictions are a travesty, an injustice, and a great shame. They represent an assault on affordable housing, a slap in the face to renters everywhere, and insult to the community of Venice and its elected representatives. For months, I have called on AIMCO to halt these evictions. I reiterate and underscore that statement today, and I urge AIMCO to allow tenants to return to their homes. AIMCO, do the right thing. Unlock those doors. Return to the bargaining table and negotiate in good faith with these tenants."

By the time Sheila Bernard got word that the sheriff's deputies had descended upon Lincoln Place, she was preparing for her teaching shift at University High School in West Los Angeles. She had spoken to Laura Burns and told her that she and her husband could stay at the Bernard apartment, but there seemed nothing more she could do. Despite her innate optimism, the future for tenants looked as dark as it ever had in her seventeen years as leader of the LPTA. After her classroom stint was over at seven she made the twenty-minute drive to Lincoln Place, now more of a ghost town than ever, with over six hundred apartments completely empty. Almost all the remaining tenants were seniors and people with disabilities, and she couldn't help remembering the time she walked into her first LPTA meeting and saw a sea of gray and white heads. Her initial motivation in going to that meeting had been to pursue a dream of tenant ownership, but she also found it abhorrent that people who wanted to live out their remaining years in the homes they had made for themselves were in danger of being cast out because a wealthy landlord wanted to make more money. Back in her apartment, she got a call from an *Argonaut* reporter wanting her reaction to the day's events, and she told him that the tenants had sincerely believed that Aimco would return to the negotiating table before proceeding with evictions.[76] "The overall feeling," she said, "is that a great injustice has been done to them and they will fight."

As the sun sank toward the horizon and unseen ocean, Laura Burns and Bernard Perroud lingered on the street in front of their building. A photograph taken by Amanda Seward's husband, Hans Adamson, paints a melancholy picture—Burns sitting on the open tailgate of her maroon Volvo station wagon while Perroud sits on the curb beside it, staring into the distance with his elbows on his knees. As soon as they could get the rest of the things inside their apartment, hopefully in the next day or two, they would head off on the fourteen-hundred-mile drive to Austin, Texas. Would the Lincoln Place they had known for the past nine years just become one item in a catalog of memories? Would the buildings that had gotten historical recognition in large part because of her tireless research simply disappear?

Those who didn't live at Lincoln Place but had hurried there that morning had either gone home or were on their way. As Jan Book drove south on Lincoln Boulevard, she felt what others involved in the fight against the evictions felt, an indelible mixture of sadness and anger. She had handled the paperwork for the unlawful detainer cases heard by judges in September and October, and in the course of this work, she had met and talked to every one of the tenants now locked out of their apartments. She had sat beside them at the table in her art studio apartment, explaining the procedures and helping them fill out forms and paying the fees for those who had no money. She felt that she genuinely knew them, and seeing them forced from their homes deeply hurt her. Back in her own home, she composed an email she hoped would get to most of them—instructions about how to retrieve their belongings and get the relocation payments still due them even though they hadn't voluntarily left. When she was finished the sadness overwhelmed the other emotions, and she sat and sobbed in her husband's arms.

That evening, KCRW's Warren Olney again devoted a segment of *Which Way, L.A.?* to Lincoln Place. His first guest was Claire Sassoon, who had lived at Lincoln Place with her husband and fifteen-year-old daughter until that morning, when the sheriff's deputies rapped on their door. Olney asked why they had stayed so long when the writing had been on the wall, so to speak, for months. Undoubtedly reflecting the opinions of almost everyone who had been forced out, she referred to the no-evictions condition and said, "We believed that we had a right to be there. We were not going to let them take away our rights."

Asked by Olney to respond to Sassoon's contention that the property owner had agreed not to evict anyone, Aimco's Patti Shwayder said that the company had bought the property after the city council approved the redevelopment in 2002, and thus had never agreed to any conditions. At best, that statement was misleading, since conditions the city places on a development project still apply even if the property changes hands. Furthermore,

Aimco had owned a half interest in Lincoln Place since 2001, and had joined in defending the city against the LPTA lawsuit to overturn the council's approval. But neither Olney nor the other guests, including Bill Rosendahl, challenged her on the point. She said that it was "very unfortunate that today's events had to happen," but added that the locked-out tenants were in violation of the law and had been living at Lincoln Place rent-free since July. She didn't say that Aimco had refused to accept any rent after that date, a fact pointed out by Rosendahl, although he didn't elaborate on the reason, which was that if Aimco had accepted rent from tenants after their deadline to move out, the landlord would have had to initiate the eviction process all over again, including filing paperwork with the city and giving four-month notices.

A third guest, Deputy City Attorney Rich Llewellyn, sidestepped a question from Olney about enforcing the no-evictions condition, saying that Rocky Delgadillo believed the matter would be resolved through nego-tiations between tenants and Aimco. The city attorney was on the tenants' side, he said, and was doing everything possible to bring the parties back to the negotiating table. When Olney again turned to Shwayder, the Aimco executive rebutted any notion that Aimco was the villain in this saga.

"We were willing to allow every resident, just to say it again, to live there for the rest of their lives at below-market rent and people couldn't agree," she said. On the subject of invoking the Ellis Act to evict tenants, Shwayder said the law gave a landlord "an unfettered right to do whatever you want with your own property." Renters' groups and tenant advocates would certainly argue with such a broad interpretation of that law, but her statement went unchallenged by Olney and his guests.

Immediately after that radio program, Rosendahl headed for a com-munity meeting sponsored by a homeowner's association in the Del Rey area immediately south of Venice. The featured speaker was Mayor Antonio Villaraigosa, and Rosendahl was to make the introduction. Some locked-out Lincoln Place tenants had heard about the meeting and saw an opportunity to air their plight to the mayor in a face-to-face setting. It might also be a way to enlist the sympathies of people beyond Lincoln Place and Venice in the ongoing effort to get Aimco to stop the evictions and resume negotiations.

Sheila Bernard didn't join them. She thought that confronting the mayor in such a setting could be counter-productive, since the meeting was billed as a way for Del Rey residents to meet their newly elected mayor and share their concerns. But some twenty tenants and Lincoln Place neighbors showed up with the familiar protest signs, eager to be seen and have their voices heard by the mayor who had enjoyed the strong support of the LPTA in his election campaign.

When Villaraigosa took the microphone, he acknowledged the presence of the Lincoln Place contingent standing with their signs at the back of the middle school auditorium, saying that members of both his and Rosendahl's staffs had "spent a lot of hours trying to resolve this situation at Lincoln Place." This prompted a few shouts of disapproval from those who felt that the mayor was exaggerating his role and could have done more. As the mayor went on to speak of what he hoped to accomplish during his four-year term, he was interrupted by questions from tenants wanting to know what he intended to do to help them now that a total of eighty-six residents were locked out of their apartments.

"I understand that you're upset," the mayor responded. "There's a lot of people who you can be upset at but I'm not one of them." He added that "unfortunately [Aimco] has certain rights under the law to evict." When he alluded to the fact that tenants had refused the settlement Aimco had proposed, with the preservation of 242 units, a number of the tenants shouted, "That's not true!"

As Bernard had feared, a sizable portion of the audience of Del Rey residents appeared to think that the Lincoln Place group had hijacked their meeting. One told the *Argonaut* reporter that he had felt "shortchanged" because he hadn't been able to air his concerns to Villaraigosa. And he expressed a sentiment that was likely shared by at least a few others in the audience when he said, "The only reason they're fighting is because they're paying cheap rent by the beach."[77]

That night, as if to further punish locked-out tenants, one of whom was forced to sleep in his car, the temperature fell to thirty-nine degrees. A crescent moon hung over Lincoln Place, which was almost totally dark—only a few scattered windows showing rectangles of light, hardly any cars parked along the curbs, long stretches of time without any signs of life like traffic on the streets or pedestrians on the sidewalks other than security guards making their rounds. Although evening had settled over the surrounding neighborhoods, there were lights in the houses and cars on the streets and a drone of traffic from Lincoln Boulevard that never entirely died, no matter the hour. From the eastbound airliners that took off west from Los Angeles International Airport and turned back over Venice on their way to Denver or Chicago or Miami or New York, Lincoln Place must have looked like a park or golf course, a dark vacancy in the midst of a sparkling urban grid.

But on closer look, there was a scene that belied the atmosphere of emptiness. At the corner of Frederick Street and California Avenue, a dozen people were gathered around a large brazier with burning logs that pushed back the darkness with a blaze of light and heat. Behind them, three of the tents that had been used for demonstrations were pitched in the wide, grassy area between the street and the parking lot of the Ross Dress for Less store on Lincoln Boulevard. A large, hand-lettered sign propped against a light standard said, Homeless for the Holidays. Thanks, Aimco! Laid out along the curb were two large boxes of pizza, a case of bottled water, and two six-packs of soda. Most people stood, but a couple of elderly tenants had brought lawn chairs. There was a woman with a child and a young woman strumming a guitar. A van from Channel 4 News was parked at the curb, and a cameraman was shooting footage of the people bundled in winter coats and warming their hands over the fire.

Whether this latest "tent city" was just symbolic or locked-out tenants would actually spend the night in the impromptu campground was uncertain. The next day, Bill Rosendahl submitted two city council motions, one urging Aimco, the LPTA and historic preservationists to return to negotiations, and one directing city departments to review the Ellis Act and make recommendations for legislative reforms. "Everyone must come together and find a resolution," Rosendahl said. "These evictions are intolerable." As to the Ellis Act, he contended that it had been "abused and misinterpreted," resulting in a reduction of affordable housing throughout the city. "It is time we stood up for renters and for the middle class," he said.

The motions were scheduled for the following Tuesday, December 13, and tenant leaders worked to get a large contingent of tenants, community members and other supporters to city hall. Undoubtedly mindful of the poor public relations that had followed the account in the city's major newspaper of the football tossing and wagering, the items were placed in an early spot on the agenda. Rosendahl asked that everyone who wanted to speak be given time to do so, and more than twenty came to the microphone, including Gloria Morales, Claire Sassoon, and a locked-out tenant named Doug Ertman who told council members that he had now joined the ranks of the city's homeless. At the conclusion of this public comment, the council unanimously approved both motions, but the action elicited only brief, polite applause from tenants and community members who were steadily growing more skeptical that the city would take the legal action needed to restore tenants to their homes and stop Aimco from evicting those who remained.

For reasons that weren't entirely clear, seven tenants who had gotten five-day notices to leave in November hadn't been locked out on December 6, but on December 14, the day after the city council adopted Rosendahl's motions, a smaller number of sheriff's deputies appeared on the property to order those tenants to immediately leave their apartments. Many saw this as Aimco thumbing its nose at Rosendahl and the rest of the city council, although the timing may have been a coincidence. Whatever the case, the inescapable fact was that just two weeks before Christmas, everyone who had gotten a notice to move out on or before July 18 but hadn't left voluntarily or been granted an extension for age or disability was now locked out of his or her apartment.

Those tenants had all authorized Jan Book and Elena Popp to appeal the eviction court rulings that preceded the lockouts, but it would be months or longer before any decision came down from the court's appellate division. Of immediate concern was the fate of the elderly and those with disabilities who faced a March 18, 2006, deadline. With Sheila Bernard in Israel getting ready for her wedding and Laura Burns back in her childhood home in Texas, it fell to Book and Popp, along with Amanda Seward, to put together a plan of action. All three believed that a new lawsuit needed to be filed to compel the city to enforce the no-evictions condition, but that would take time and money. In the meantime, negotiations with Aimco seemed to offer the best chance of keeping the eighty-three remaining tenants in their homes and allowing the others to return. This was the approach favored by city politicians, who clearly didn't want to be embroiled in yet another Lincoln Place lawsuit. The tenant population also seemed to have grown more fractious, and the three lawyers believed it would be good strategy to go into any negotiations with Aimco knowing in advance what kind of outcome a majority of tenants favored.

They put together a ballot with four settlement options and called a tenant meeting for Sunday, December 18, at Penmar Park. Option one was similar to the settlement on the table when negotiations ended in November, the day before the historical resources commission meeting. Aimco would preserve 242 units and allow current tenants to stay and locked out tenants to return with no rent increases. Under this option, tenants would be obligated to support Aimco's plans for redeveloping the rest of the property and the company would have the option of canceling the settlement if the city failed to issue demolition permits by March 2006.

Option two was essentially the same as the first, but with a critical difference; the deal would remain in force even if Aimco failed to get the city permits to proceed with the redevelopment. Option three was also the same in most respects as the first two, but it didn't specify a number of units to be preserved. Instead it would leave that up to negotiation between Aimco and Amanda Seward. The fourth option, recently put forward by a pair of tenants, was much different than the others. The only units preserved would be for tenants granted one-year age or disability extensions. And the units would all be located in buildings on Penmar Avenue, which was considered the least desirable of Lincoln Place locations because of the volume of traffic on that street.

That last option was considered most likely to be readily approved by Aimco, but it had virtually no support in the LPTA leadership or among preservationists. As for the first option, it might also be agreeable to Aimco, but the provision allowing the landlord to cancel the deal would leave tenants high and dry if there was a hitch in getting permits. On the other hand, without that escape clause Aimco might refuse to sign any settlement agreement. Allowing Amanda Seward to negotiate details of a settlement appealed to a number of tenants, preservationists, and community members. Her refusal to agree to a deal in November without having something ironclad in writing had gained her a reputation for toughness and resistance to intimidation. If anyone could get the best deal for everyone involved, she was seen as the one who could.

Jan Book ran the meeting, but as it turned out, there wasn't any vote on the options. In an email to Sheila Bernard the following day, she reported that a motion was made and unanimously passed to *not* vote on specific proposals. "We just voted to keep the status quo," Book wrote, "which returns to the tenants' statement to Aimco—come back to the negotiation table and let's talk." She also observed that some tenants were angry and wanted a more forceful reaction by the LPTA to the evictions and lockouts, whatever that might be. "I don't want our leadership to fall apart and be taken over by the radicals," she wrote. "I would like to see us all work together. We are all pulling the same train."

On the Sunday afternoon following that meeting, the Los Angeles Conservancy led walking tours of Lincoln Place. With so many apartments empty and buildings boarded up and bearing No Trespassing warnings, the place Ralph Vaughn designed to give residents the feeling of being in a garden-like setting where they could readily interact with their neighbors was bleak and uninviting. And indeed, the tours seemed as if they might be a final effort to show off the creative work of Vaughn and his associates before it turned into a 38-acre pile of rubble and existed only in photographs, some movie footage, and the memories of the thousands of people who had called it their home.

People gathered at the tent city, which now had a table for food and drink, many more chairs, a festoon of protest signs, and a "Tree of Keys," a nearby juniper decorated with 180 keys cut from packing material, a representation of the 180 families either evicted or facing that fate. People were led in groups of ten to fifteen through the complex by conservancy members, who warned everyone to stay on public sidewalks and only enter apartments if invited by tenants. That warning was punctuated by the highly visible presence of Aimco security guards in their black pants and white shirts. Also joining the tours were Bill Rosendahl and Aimco attorney William Delvac. A reporter at the tour wrote that the attorney "ignored suspicious stares from organizers and politely declined a cookie from a man wearing a sign on his back that read Corporate Greed Is Spelled AIMCO.[78] Another wrote that Delvac decided to go on one of the tours "to see what was historic about the buildings," but declined to comment on the long-running dispute between tenants and landlord. But the loquacious Rosendahl repeated his earlier critical comments to that reporter, including his characterization of the evictions and lockouts as "intolerable."

One of the tour stops was at the apartment of Michael Palumbo, who had drawn Amanda Seward into the Lincoln Place preservation effort. He showed people his apartment and described the way the building designs encouraged neighborliness and community; illustrating that with the story of a nurse who lived next door, knew that he was diabetic, and "saved" him when he had a severe insulin reaction. Another stop was at Ingrid Mueller's apartment, which was the only one still occupied in her building on Elkgrove Avenue. In contrast to the forbidding No Trespassing signs, she had nestled a sign reading, There's No Place Like Home, against some potted plants on the landing in front of her door. Like everyone else still living at Lincoln Place, she was facing eviction in March, almost exactly three months away. But she had been at the front lines of the LPTA's efforts for seventeen years, and she had never shrunk from wading into whatever battles commenced. She told the reporter that if she were forced to leave, the sheriff would have to carry her out in a pine coffin that she would have custom-made for the occasion.[79]

23

LIMBO AND HEARTACHE

FROM THE BALCONY OF her second-floor apartment on Elkgrove Avenue, Ingrid Mueller could stand among her carefully tended bromeliads and other potted plants and look out over a wasteland of brown grass, brittle shrubbery, weeds poking up between sidewalk cracks, and plots of bare earth where people had dug up and carried away bushes and flowers. The sixty-two-year-old was physically active and sociable, but there was no one else in her building to greet with a cheerful "Good morning" and "How are you?" on a landing or stairwell or sidewalk outside. Nobody to chat with for a few moments about goings-on at Lincoln Place or downtown in city hall or elsewhere in the world. Likewise, the building across the courtyard had only a single occupant, a Vietnam war veteran who suffered from PTSD and was almost always unfriendly, more than once calling Mueller a "Nazi bitch" even though the native German was outspokenly progressive in her social and political views.

When she left her apartment to walk to her car on the street or to another building to visit old LPTA comrades like Frieda Marlin and Carol Beck, she would see trash and debris that never seemed to get cleaned up. If she walked into the alley behind her building she would see all manner of junk in the open carports, as well as mattresses, blankets, and other evidence that some of Venice's homeless population were camping out there. She might see used condoms, crack pipes and hypodermic needles, evidence that empty carports had become convenient retreats for prostitutes and drug users. Now and then a resident would see one of those prostitutes conducting business with a client, or persons lighting crack pipes or shooting up, but complaints to management or directly to the police never seemed to bring any change. One morning Mueller opened her door to find a strange man sleeping on the landing outside; other tenants had similar stories to tell. Graffiti was everywhere, including the tags of Venice gangs that a few years earlier had engaged in a bloody war over the turf each claimed for the selling of drugs.

"I was always on high alert, day and night," Mueller says. She had respites from the dreary, unsettling atmosphere by house sitting in another part of the city for her youngest daughter, a TV and movie actress who periodically had to go out of town on location. But others weren't as fortunate. Frieda Marlin, who had always enjoyed spending time outdoors and watching children play on the lawns, only left her apartment to go to doctor's appointments; her son Spike shopped for food and ran any needed errands. Others who had been attracted to Lincoln Place because of its garden-like setting and design that encouraged neighbors to interact with one another became near-recluses in their buildings.

By mid-summer of 2006, Mueller was one of only forty-five tenants in the thirty-eight-acre complex. After the lockouts the prior December, they had faced a deadline of March 20, 2006 to vacate their apartments, but at the beginning of that month, Bill Rosendahl announced that Aimco had agreed to halt eviction proceedings until the end of May and resume negotiations over Lincoln Place's future. Those negotiations would be overseen by a professional mediator, and the councilman urged everyone involved to move with dispatch, saying that the tenants, all seniors or people with disabilities, "cannot continue to live in this state of limbo and heartache."

Aimco's willingness to return to the bargaining table was seen as having a twofold purpose. One, throwing elderly and disabled tenants out of their homes would be a public relations disaster, and two, Lincoln Place was a major money loser and the company wanted to proceed with redevelopment as soon as possible. But there were complications. After the state historical resources commission approved Lincoln Place's eligibility for the state register, Aimco sued, and in February 2006, the commission settled that lawsuit by agreeing to rescind the designation and take up Amanda Seward's application as if it were brand new, or in legal terms, conduct a *de novo* hearing. That hearing was put on the agenda of the commission's next quarterly meeting on May 5. The original approval had been unanimous, but Governor Arnold Schwarzenegger had since appointed six new members and nobody knew if they would hold Lincoln Place's historical qualities in the same esteem as their predecessors.

In addition, Sheila Bernard and Jan Book had begun talking to an attorney who believed that the 2005 Appeals Court decision in the 20th Century Architectural Alliance case clearly meant that the city was obligated to enforce the redevelopment project condition forbidding evictions, even if the ruling hadn't explicitly said so. The attorney, John Murdock, wasn't the slick, fast-talking lawyer of stereotype, but an idealistic man who had left a high-paying job in a prominent Beverly Hills law firm to set up his own practice, taking on clients with causes he strongly believed in, from street vendors to neighborhood groups fighting deep-pocketed developers. He worked from an office in his modest house in a middle-class Santa Monica neighborhood, doing without all the lawyerly trappings, including a secretary. His mild demeanor contrasted with that of many of the lawyers Bernard and other LPTA members had seen in action in courtrooms and in city hall, but he had built a solid reputation for his arguments involving constitutional disputes and land-use and environmental laws. In his view, a lawsuit to compel the city to enforce the condition had a good chance of success. This prospect enthused Bernard and others in the LPTA's inner circle, but to hire him they'd have to raise more money than they'd ever raised before, and they'd have to do it quickly, before Aimco succeeded in completely emptying out the property.

The negotiations began in April at a satellite campus of Malibu's Pepperdine University, which consisted of a pair of modern, high-rise buildings alongside the I-405 freeway five miles south of Venice. The mediator was Peter Robinson, a Pepperdine law professor and expert in dispute resolution who had the daunting task of getting people who hadn't been able to agree on fundamental issues and profoundly mistrusted one another to reach a settlement of the long-running dispute. There would be twenty-four seats at the negotiating table, with representatives of Aimco, tenants, preservationists, the city, and the Venice community. Given such a large group with disparate and often passionate interests, the mediator's task might have seemed in the nature of herding cats. But there was optimism that the urgency of the situation and the gathering of all interested parties face-to-face for the first time would result in a settlement that everyone could accept.

Bringing the community into the talks was seen as major key to success. Aimco had made clear that it wanted to go beyond the project originally proposed by TransAction, which called for demolition of all existing buildings and the construction of 706 new condominiums and 144 apartments. While Aimco had since offered to preserve some existing buildings, it also wanted more than 850 total units, and it wanted to build above the legal height limit. In earlier negotiations, the company had insisted that all parties to a settlement, including the city, support this revised project even though exact details—the total number of units, the mixture of apartments and condominiums, the locations of taller buildings—hadn't been specified. This was a major sticking point. As Sheila Bernard and others made clear after negotiations broke down in November 2005, the company's desire to bypass public review and essentially have the city rubber stamp its final plan would deny residents of neighborhoods around Lincoln Place and the larger Venice community their rightful voice in the process. And that was a bridge too far, even for Bernard and others in the increasingly desperate fight to protect the remaining tenants from eviction.

Everyone knew that if Bill Rosendahl supported Aimco's plans when—or if—they came before the city council, the other council members would in all probability go along. They also knew that Rosendahl repeatedly promised during his campaign to put community concerns ahead of the desires of real estate developers, so he was unlikely to lend his endorsement to Aimco's plans without first being sure of support in Venice and the neighborhoods around Lincoln Place. Hence, the community contingent at the negotiations, with representatives of the Venice Community Coalition, the nonprofit Venice Community Housing Corporation, and the Venice Neighborhood Council. As usual in such cases, the devil would be in the details, but Amanda Seward and others representing preservationists had already agreed in principle that Aimco could demolish a portion of Lincoln Place and the company had already agreed to allow current tenants to remain and to let at least some evicted tenants return. Many details would still have to be discussed, but resolving the questions important to the community—the height, the density, the number of affordable units in the new development—would be a crucial element in the talks.

How did things work out? In mid-April, people gathered in a classroom in one of the Pepperdine buildings to hear Robinson lay out the goals and terms for the negotiations, and over the next two weeks the five groups met both jointly and in smaller pairings. There were varying degrees of optimism, but at the final session on April 28, the elusive goal of a settlement actually seemed to be within reach. Aimco and the community had agreed upon a total of 1,284 units and a height limit of forty-five feet in certain areas. The company would preserve 453 existing units, which was fewer than the 502 preservationists wanted although the numbers appeared close enough for compromise. Current tenants could remain and those evicted in 2005 could come back. Details of when they would be allowed to return and where on the property they would live had to be worked out, as did a question that arose at the last minute over the number of affordable units Aimco had to provide to qualify for a density bonus provided for by state law. Finally, Aimco agreed to historical designation as long as Amanda Seward didn't oppose the demolition of buildings beyond those slated to be preserved. However—and this proved to be a big however—it wanted to delay that designation until after the city issued permits for the new development. Seward, conversely, wanted historic listing immediately. When, and if, Aimco signed an agreement on the number and location of units to be preserved, she would go to the historical resources commission and ask that the listing be revised to reflect the change.

At that point, the commission meeting was less than a week away. Aimco wanted Seward to ask for a postponement, but the previous fall she had been unwilling to do that without first having a legally enforceable agreement, and she was again unwilling to put her trust in the company's verbal assurances. For the second time in nine months, she made the trip to Sacramento to tell commissioners why all of Lincoln Place deserved recognition, while Aimco's Patti Shwayder and William Delvac once again challenged the idea that Lincoln Place had historical significance.

In response to a question from a commissioner, Delvac said that if Lincoln Place was given historical status Aimco would just conduct a new EIR and then demolish some or all of the complex. If, however, the commission rejected the nomination, all parties would continue to negotiate a mutually agreeable plan for Lincoln Place's future. This threat didn't sway the commission's majority. The three holdover commissioners voted again for the designation, along with two of Governor Schwarzenegger's appointees. Another pair of new members abstained, and one voted no. For the third time in less than a year, the historical significance of all forty-five buildings with 696 units was confirmed.

As for prospects of a negotiated settlement, the company indicated to Bill Rosendahl after the commission's action that it had no interest in further talks. The councilman, who had worked for months to get the parties to sit down with one another, issued a written statement that said, "After exhaustively exploring the variety of needs and interests necessary to reach a consensus development plan, the parties were unable to articulate a package of terms that adequately met the variety of needs." This dry, bureaucratic language obscured what must have been serious disappointment on his part. A statement issued jointly by all the negotiating groups repeated the same language but added some detail. "The participants invested more than fifty hours in joint session meetings and fifty hours of confidential consultations with the facilitator," it said in part, concluding with, "The participants agree that all entities now need to pursue their independent options."

Who was at fault? Sheila Bernard blamed Aimco. In an email to John Murdock, she said she believed that the company hadn't negotiated in good faith because it wasn't going to accept any settlement that included historic designation. "We are exhausted with this," she wrote. "We don't want to break ranks with the community, or with Amanda. We want Aimco to take back the people they wrongfully evicted, and then seek a new entitlement under an open process prescribed by law." In closing, she said, "Our experience with Aimco so far does not bode well for a settlement. I'm sure they feel the same way about us."

Tenants now faced a May 31 deadline to either leave their apartments or defend themselves against eviction proceedings in court. Many suffered health problems and lived on fixed incomes that would make finding new places anywhere in the area extremely difficult. But it was obvious that Aimco still wanted to avoid the spectacle of forcing these people from their homes, so once again Shober-Livas Relocation was brought onto the scene to offer "enhanced" relocation packages. The offers were the same as before—$12,000 plus moving expenses and help relocating to an available apartment in another Aimco-owned complex—although word quickly got around that if tenants bargained they could get more. That compared with the $8,000 landlords were then required to pay in Ellis Act evictions. But the long-standing disincentive for taking these so-called Shober deals remained—tenants would have to sign away any right to return to Lincoln Place if their units were put back on the market.

Aimco appeared to believe, or hope, that if the tenants had enough time to consider, they would all take the Shober deals. Thus, on May 31, Bill Rosendahl announced that the company was extending the deadline for leaving to August 31. "I am thrilled by this news," Rosendahl said. "It gives everyone involved a little time to take a deep breath and assess their options." Sheila Bernard was less sanguine, though. She told an *Argonaut* writer that she believed most of the tenants then remaining would reject the relocation offers and keep fighting to stop the evictions. As for herself, she said, "They will have to pry me out of here with a crow bar."[80]

When Bernard made that statement, the LPTA brain trust had already decided to hire John Murdock to file a new lawsuit against the city. They drafted a letter to tenants and LPTA supporters asking for help in raising $20,000 to retain the attorney to prepare the lawsuit and seek an injunction against further evictions. Bernard had never relished the task of raising money, but she knew a local woman named Suzanne Thompson who worked professionally as a fundraiser for progressive causes, and with Thompson's help in finding donors, she was able to hand Murdock a $20,000 check and set the latest phase of the Lincoln Place battle into motion. On June 8, the lawsuit seeking to compel the city to enforce the condition requiring tenants to be relocated on the property instead of being evicted was filed in Los Angeles County Superior Court. The plaintiff was the LPTA, but Murdock had also wanted at least one tenant to also be named, and Ingrid Mueller, the longtime LPTA warrior who had vowed to leave Lincoln Place only by being carried out in a coffin, readily volunteered. Because the project conditions were technically mitigations to the environmental impacts of the redevelopment, which included displacement of residents, Murdock alleged that Aimco's eviction activity violated the California Environmental Quality Act and hence the lawsuit came to be commonly called the "CEQA suit" to distinguish it from the numerous others involving Lincoln Place, both past and present.

Regardless of how the lawsuit fared in superior court, one side or the other would appeal, and there would be hours spent on filings and court hearings over a period that could stretch to several years. Murdock estimated that all this could cost as much as $100,000, and the LPTA set out to raise that daunting amount. One idea was to hold house parties where people could be educated about the Lincoln Place situation, meet some of the tenants, and hopefully, take out their checkbooks and wallets and donate to the legal effort. Suzanne Thompson arranged for the first of these at the home of Stanley Sheinbaum, a well-known peace and human rights activist married to the daughter of Harry Warner, the Warner Brothers Studios mogul whose former horse ranch, in an ironic twist, had figured in the infamous Warner Ridge case that had once been raised as a threat to Lincoln Place. Among those signing on as sponsors were actors Jane Fonda and Elliot Gould, so hopes were high that other luminaries would come and open both their hearts and pocketbooks to the cause.

Two dozen people showed up at Sheinbaum's estate in the upscale Brentwood community. Laura Silagi and David Ewing, who had represented the Venice Community Coalition in the failed negotiations with Aimco, aired a nine-minute video they put together from footage that Silagi and others had shot during the mass December lockouts. John Murdock, a lanky sixty-one-year-old with long, graying sideburns, gave a summation of the LPTA lawsuit, and afterward attendees ate hors d'oeuvres and drank wine while mingling outside on the spacious grounds of the Sheinbaum home. A group photograph shows Fonda in jeans, orange shirt, orange baseball cap, and oversize sunglasses, flanked by Sheila Bernard in a black dress and Amanda Seward in a stylish black ensemble and gold necklace. Others in the photograph are Lincoln Place tenants Gloria Morales, Ruth Holzgreen, and Ingrid Mueller, along with locked-out tenants Sara Sakuma and Laura Burns, who had come from Austin and was staying in Bernard's apartment. All looked cheerful, perhaps responding to an exhortation from the photographer, or perhaps genuinely optimistic about a potential turn in their fortunes after so many years of fear and uncertainty.

But the affair, while obviously raising people's spirits at that moment, was a major disappointment in terms of fundraising. After paying for valet parking, catering, and renting audiovisual equipment, the LPTA netted just over $5,000. And that didn't account for the many volunteer hours that went into organizing the event. It was glaringly obvious that raising twenty times that amount was going to be a very steep hill to climb, especially since most charitable organizations that might have considered the Lincoln Place effort worthy had policies against funding lawsuits.

Eleven days after that fundraiser, John Murdock and attorneys representing the city and Aimco gathered in a courtroom in downtown Los Angeles. It was another in a string of unseasonably mild days free of the smog that often shrouded downtown's skyscrapers at that time of year, and the white, granite facade of the county courthouse just uphill from city hall gleamed with morning sunlight. If any in the steady stream of people entering the building had watched the old Perry Mason TV series, they might have recognized that facade dominated by a large bas-relief sculpture of a robed female figure with a sword in her hand and the scales of justice above her head. For Sheila Bernard, Ingrid Mueller and several other tenants who made the trip downtown that morning, the promise of justice embodied in the sculpture was at best uncertain, but with Murdock's confidence in their case they allowed themselves to hope that when they left the building they would be the bearers of good news for a change.

The judge was David Yaffe, the same judge who ruled in 2004 that demolition of the five Lake Street buildings was lawful, only to have his decision overturned on appeal in 2005. Judge Yaffe had subsequently issued an order prohibiting the city from issuing any demolition permits unless the property owner complied with the development project conditions or got them changed, and now the LPTA was coming before him to argue that

Aimco's eviction of tenants was as much a violation of those conditions as tearing down the buildings and therefore an injunction should be issued to stop the landlord from forcing any more tenants to leave.

When the attorneys got to the courtroom they were handed the judge's tentative ruling, which denied the injunction request on the grounds that arguments over eviction issues belonged in eviction court. As attorney for the plaintiffs, John Murdock was the first to respond. He pointed out that Elena Popp and Jan Book had argued in eviction court the previous fall that the project conditions were being violated, but the judge had rejected those arguments as irrelevant. Furthermore, the city wasn't a party to eviction proceedings between landlords and tenants, so that judge couldn't have ordered it to do anything. Murdock spelled out the issue as plainly as possible for Judge Yaffe. The city had a duty to enforce the conditions imposed on development projects, but in the case of Lincoln Place, it was failing to do so. Therefore, he was asking the judge to order the city to fulfill its duty.

Susan Pfann, from the city attorney's office, countered with the claim first aired in 2003, that the city only had to enforce the conditions when Aimco applied for demolition permits. Greg Ozhekim, the attorney representing Aimco, characterized Murdock's claims as "wild," telling the judge that "I had to bite my tongue at times." Aimco was evicting tenants under the Ellis Act, he said, which gave the landlord the "unfettered right to go out of the rental business." What Murdock was asking the court to do was to interfere with that right.

The judge gave Murdock the final word, and he delivered an appeal that belied the image of a cool, unflappable lawyer. Referring to the tenants sitting in the courtroom, he said, "They have nowhere to go. They have no income. They are on fixed incomes. They are disabled." He said those tenants would be "scattered to the four winds," after which Aimco would say, "Okay, now we have to demolish those buildings because they are attracting vagrants, they have rodents in them..." At that point, the city would invoke the court order requiring compliance with the conditions. "And they [Aimco] are going to say, well, the tenants are gone. It's moot." He concluded with, "I apologize, Your Honor. I'm just worked up."

Prior to the hearing, Murdock had filed declarations from many of the forty persons still living at Lincoln Place. Gloria Morales, then seventy-five and disabled by a back injury and glaucoma, said that she lived on Social Security and had looked but hadn't found any apartments in the Venice area that rented for less than her total income. Celia Harriman, an eighty-four-year-old living on a fixed income had suffered a stroke and said she didn't believe she could survive the rigors of moving. Lucy Siam, who was seventy-seven and had trouble walking any distance, said she could not afford rents in the area on her income of $869 a month from Social Security. Michael Palumbo, the tenant who first brought Lincoln Place to the attention to Amanda Seward, said he had Type I diabetes and was currently living on unemployment insurance and couldn't afford to move.

There were more, but the judge didn't indicate whether he had read any of them. In any event, he wasn't swayed by Murdock's legal arguments or emotional plea and stuck with his tentative ruling. It was bitterly disappointing to the handful of tenants in the courtroom, and if Sheila Bernard and Ingrid Mueller and the others who afterward trudged out the courthouse doors and down the steps had stopped and looked back at the sculpture of Lady Justice, they might have imagined the scales badly tilted, themselves teetering high on one side and Aimco and the industry it was part of heavily weighing down the other. But Bernard also knew that the LPTA would somehow raise the money to take the case to the appeals court, where the tenants would hopefully get a more equitable hearing. And the lawsuit filed in 2005 by Frieda and Spike Marlin questioning the use of the Ellis Act to evict them was still pending in that court. But would be anyone left at Lincoln Place if and when favorable rulings were handed down?

The immediate concern for the forty households was deciding to either continue to fight while lawsuits dragged out, or to take the Shober deals and move elsewhere. Pressure was intense, given the looming August 31 deadline and the fact that some tenants said they had gotten offers for more than $20,000. A few, like Ingrid Mueller, declined to even speak with a Shober representative, vowing to stay after the move-out date even if she was the only person left in the complex. Others, like Dicie Meyers, who was one of sixteen tenants threatened with eviction from her Elkland Place building in 1995, was eighty-three-years-old and had seen younger neighbors who fought their evictions being locked out of their apartments by sheriff's deputies. She had lived at Lincoln Place for twenty-four years, but she couldn't face that prospect; she took a Shober deal and moved to an apartment her son found for her in the Palms district east of Venice.

Still others were torn. Sheldon Turchin, who was seventy-one and had lived at Lincoln Place for thirty-four years, was afraid that if he was locked out of his apartment he would become homeless. When he finally spoke to a Shober representative, he was given a list of available apartments in three Aimco complexes in other areas of Southern California, but the rent for all of those exceeded his monthly income of $863 from Social Security. If he took a Shober deal anyway, the money would hold off immediate homelessness but it would eventually be consumed by the higher rent, and what then? Sixty-four-year-old Bob Bass decided to take a Shober deal but when he looked for apartments he could afford he discovered that landlords wanted prospective tenants to have income at least two-and-a-half times the monthly rent, a requirement he couldn't come close to meeting with his earnings as a musician. Seventy-two-year-old Kenneth Christiansen was haunted by the specter of the December 2005, lockouts and actually signed a Shober deal, but his search for housing was fruitless and he decided to back out of the agreement, saying in a later court declaration that he had "come to the conclusion that I would be better off placing my trust in the courts than in placing my trust in Aimco or in Shober's relocation company."

On August 31, the deadline for all tenants to vacate their apartments, Aimco issued a press release that was also posted on its Lincoln Place website. It said, "Aimco offered, in October of 2005 and in April of 2006, to allow all existing residents to remain at Lincoln Place at their current rents for life. These offers were rejected by the Lincoln Place Tenants Association, which went against the wishes of many residents, and shut other residents completely out of the process." It included a quote from Aimco's Patti Shwayder: "It's time to put this matter to rest. A few extremists have continually distorted the facts surrounding Lincoln Place and misled innocent residents, the community and the general public. We look forward to a positive new chapter in the history of Lincoln Place, so that it provides the kind of housing that the community needs, desires and deserves."

The next day, Sheila Bernard found an unlawful detainer notice taped to the door of the Doreen Place apartment she shared with her daughter. Even though she was now married to a man who lived in another city, she had hoped the apartment she had occupied for eighteen years would be her home as long as her daughter needed care and the Lincoln Place situation was unresolved. Would she finally be forced to move? The other thirty-nine residents scattered around the property—including LPTA stalwarts Ingrid Mueller, Frieda Marlin and Carol Beck—were asking the same question. At that point, Aimco was no longer accepting rent, but the company was clearly eager to avoid the public spectacle of sheriff's deputies rapping on the doors of elderly and disabled residents, so the enhanced relocation packages were still being offered. Among those taking the "Shober deals" that ranged as high as $23,000 were Gloria Morales, Celia Harriman, and Michael Palumbo. In a rare alignment of interest with Aimco, the LPTA also wanted to avoid the dismal scene that unfolded that past December and Bernard put out a call for volunteers to help elderly and frail tenants pack their belongings and move to a relative's home or whatever accommodations they had managed to find. And she added a plea for donations to help defray the costs of an appeal of Judge Yaffe's unfavorable ruling, which John Murdock had filed with the California Court of Appeal six days after the hearing.

Almost forgotten in the rapid swirl of events over the past several months was the lawsuit filed against Aimco by the Marlins, who were represented by Jan Book and Elena Popp. An appeal to the superior court judge's dismissal of that suit under the anti-SLAPP law had been pending for the past eight months. Book and Popp had also filed appeals on behalf of the seventy-five tenants who lost their cases in eviction court in the fall of 2005, and those were awaiting a hearing in the appellate division of the superior court. But Popp had decided to run for a seat in the California State Assembly and had left the Eviction Defense Network to campaign for the June 6, 2006 primary. It appeared unlikely that she would be further involved in the legal battles over the eviction of Lincoln Place tenants.[81]

Whatever needed to be done was essentially left up to Book. She had gotten a crash course in landlord/tenant law and felt confident of her knowledge, but in her own words she "hated litigation" and thus was thrilled when Amanda Seward volunteered to help with cases that had to be argued in upcoming eviction court hearings. John Murdock had also agreed to take charge of the appeal in the Marlin vs. Aimco case, which greatly lessened Book's anxiety about being overwhelmed, although Murdock would be charging a fee and the LPTA would have to redouble its fundraising efforts. At that point, almost $50,000 had been raised, mostly in the form of small donations between $100 and $500 although a few, including Book, had given substantially more. Whenever Sheila Bernard and other tenant leaders got the opportunity to speak to community organizations and other groups, they made a plea for money to defray the rapidly mounting legal costs. Volunteers made phone calls to solicit donations and checks came in from people who had heard of the tenants' fight through newspaper articles and other media outlets.

By the time another eviction court hearing was held on October 30, 2006, all but thirteen tenants had taken Shober deals and either moved out or were in the process of doing so. Aimco had filed for summary judgment against those thirteen, and Seward and Book represented twelve of them—a tenant named Barbara Eisenberg, who had moved to Lincoln Place in 1971, had thrown her lot with an attorney named Noel Weiss, who was representing, in addition to Eisenberg, a small number of tenants locked out in 2005. In the courtroom, Seward reprised two earlier arguments—Aimco was acting in bad faith under the Ellis Act because it didn't really intend to go out of the rental business, and the redevelopment project conditions forbade tenant evictions. She spelled out in blunt terms to Judge Patricia Collins what she believed to be the underlying issue. "They [Aimco] have got all of these long-term tenants who are paying way below-market rates. How do they get rid of them and stay in the rental business?" The answer, she argued, lay in the fact that the landlord had "pushed and pushed and pushed" to get tenants to take the Shober deals, which required them to sign away their right of return if their units were put back on the rental market. To bolster the bad faith argument, Seward also brought up remarks allegedly made by Aimco

CEO Terry Considine at the company's annual shareholders meeting that past May. David Ewing, one of the Venice Community Coalition leaders and a participant in the failed April mediation, had bought the minimum amount of stock needed to gain admission to the shareholders meeting—just over $2,000 worth—and flown to the company headquarters in Denver, hoping to question Considine about Lincoln Place. Back home in Venice, he said that when he brought up the subject, Considine answered by calling the Lincoln Place tenants "scammers," characterizing their efforts to fight eviction as "trying to scam the system." This, Seward argued, was further evidence that Aimco wanted to get current residents out so that they could rent their units to new tenants at market rates.

Aimco attorneys also brought up previous arguments. The 2005 appeals court decision requiring compliance with conditions had nothing to do with the evictions, they claimed, but only meant that the company had to take pictures of buildings and offer them for sale before proceeding with demolition. Aimco Venezia, the legal entity that owned Lincoln Place, was going out of the rental-housing business, as required by the Ellis Act, and the entire property would be demolished and redeveloped.

Unlike the two judges in the previous eviction hearings, Judge Collins didn't issue a ruling on the spot, but took the matter under submission. This gave Book and Seward hope that she wasn't giving their arguments short shrift. That hope proved to be more than just whistling in the dark—on December 15, the judge ruled that the twelve tenants were entitled to a jury trial on the issue of whether Aimco was acting in good faith in evicting them. This wasn't a guarantee against eventual eviction, but they would get their day in court. While Lincoln Place in that holiday season was a desolate place, appearing to the casual eye to be abandoned, and while most of the thirteen tenants lived like recluses, trying to distract themselves from dark, obsessive thoughts about their futures, there was hope, a light at the end of a long tunnel, no matter how faint and in danger of being snuffed out it might be.

The jury trial was scheduled to get underway on January 19. In the meantime, the battle of words between Amanda Seward and Patti Shwayder continued in the press.[82] Seward, whose manner was typically polite and even gracious but who didn't mince words when making a point, said, "You're talking about the largest apartment company in the country can come in and say, 'We don't like rent control. We want the rent up to market rate, and we want you out." In turn, Shwayder called this allegation "absolute hogwash." The tenants still fighting eviction, she said, could have accepted Aimco's generous relocation offers but had instead chosen to make "a political statement." Those dueling claims didn't reach the courtroom that January, though, because Aimco's attorneys filed a series of motions to exclude almost all the evidence Seward had planned to present to a jury to prove that Aimco was acting in bad faith. This raised the possibility that the landlord was actually afraid that a jury might return a verdict on behalf of the tenants. Whether or not this was the case, each of the motions would have to be argued before a judge and rulings would have to be made, which meant that the tenants' day in court was going to have to wait.

On March 8, 2007, John Murdock and attorneys for Aimco gathered at the Ronald Reagan State Building in downtown Los Angeles to argue the appeal in the case of Marlin vs. Aimco. The plaintiffs had gotten a boost late in 2006 when California Attorney General Bill Lockyer had filed an amicus brief on their behalf. The Marlins had every right to ask the court to rule on whether Aimco could use the Ellis Act to evict them, he argued, and by granting Aimco's anti-SLAPP motion, the lower court was actually inhibiting the tenants' right to petition the courts and seek redress of grievances. Murdock argued the same point, and went further in asking the panel of three justices to rule that what was requested in the Marlins' lawsuit—an injunction against pending evictions—should be granted.

The case had garnered statewide attention because rapid inflation in real estate values the past several years had resulted in property owners increasingly using the Ellis Act to evict tenants and convert rental units to condominiums. The issue was especially critical in Los Angeles and San Francisco, both with low vacancy rates and some of the highest rents in the country. There were moves both on the local and state level to try to slow down these Ellis Act evictions, but as usual it was an uphill battle in the face of opposition by the politically powerful real estate industry. City council president Alex Padilla and Councilman Bill Rosendahl had called for a moratorium on condominium conversions, citing the thousands of apartments lost during the first half of the decade.[83] There were ongoing discussions among the city's elected and appointed officials about ways to increase the chronically short supply of affordable housing, which struck some as ironic given City Attorney Rocky Delgadillo's intransigence in taking legal steps to stop Aimco from emptying out Lincoln Place.

Those tenants and others in Los Angeles did win a small victory in late spring of 2007. The current law exempted rental units built after 1979 from rent control, but the city council adopted a new ordinance on May 23 that removed that exemption from any new units built on the site of a demolished rent-controlled building. That meant that if Aimco demolished Lincoln Place and built new rental units, they would be subject to rent control, although the initial rents could be set at market rates.

Exactly two months later, news of much greater significance came in the form of a ruling from the state appeals court in the Marlin case. The justices rejected the argument that the lawsuit was a SLAPP suit and sent it back to the superior court. Although the three-judge panel didn't deal with the question at the heart of the lawsuit—did Aimco have a legal right to evict Lincoln Place tenants?—the ruling was cheered by renters groups and advocates statewide who were alarmed about landlords increasingly invoking the anti-SLAPP statute against tenants fighting Ellis Act evictions. And Frieda Marlin and her son would have the actual merits of their lawsuit argued before a judge.

The thirteen persons still living at Lincoln Place would have to wait awhile for their day in court, though, because the judge presiding over their unlawful detainer cases had granted Aimco's request to postpone a jury trial until after the appeals court ruled in the "CEQA suit" that John Murdock had filed against the city. That case had the earmarks of finality, the potential to put an end to the long Lincoln Place eviction drama. If Aimco lost, it would have no legal basis for any of the evictions. If it won, the sheriff could force the thirteen holdouts to leave their apartments. Then the company could tear down Lincoln Place and proceed with the original redevelopment or seek city permission for some other project. In which case the tenants would be, as Murdock told the superior court judge that prior summer, "scattered to the four winds."

In August, the thirteen tenants, joined by some of the previously evicted and a number of community supporters, gathered at the Penmar Park recreation center to celebrate the twentieth anniversary of the LPTA. Jan Book and Amanda Seward were there, along with David Ewing and Laura Silagi; holdout tenants Spike Marlin and Bob Bass brought their guitars to provide live music. There was cake, a giant birthday candle, and drinks—nonalcoholic since the site was city property. Bill Rosendahl dropped in for a few minutes to give the group a pep talk and chat with some of the attendees. Only a handful like Frieda Marlin and Barbara Eisenberg had been living at Lincoln Place in 1987 when Ethel Shapiro-Bertolini had urged her neighbors to organize and fight the attempts by their new landlord to evict them so their apartments could be rented to people willing and able to pay much higher rents. The few who had then walked the two blocks to Penmar Park and written a fifteen-dollar check or paid cash for membership in the new Lincoln Place Tenants Association could scarcely have imagined that twenty years later they would still be fighting a landlord who wanted to get them out.

The Labor Day weekend that year was marked by scorching heat that brought crowds of people to Venice and other Los Angeles beach communities. The torpor-inducing heat might have served as a metaphor for the gloom that had been part of the mental state of Lincoln Place tenants for years, but on the Friday after the holiday the appeals court was scheduled to hear oral arguments in the CEQA suit. The three justices who would listen to Murdock and attorneys representing the city and Aimco were the same three who had handed down the ruling in the Marlin case, and the same three who had ruled in July 2005, that the Lincoln Place property owner had violated conditions of the approved development project by tearing down the five Lake Street buildings. Murdock hadn't wavered in his belief that the tenants had a strong case, and now it wouldn't be long until they found out whether he was right.

Sheila Bernard and Jan Book were in the dark wood-paneled courtroom on the third floor of the downtown state building, along with tenant Spike

Marlin and Lincoln Place neighbor David Ewing. All remembered leaving the county courthouse just over a year earlier after the judge refused to order a stop to evictions and feeling that the scales of justice had tilted badly against the tenants. It was only a ten-minute walk from the courthouse with the sculpture of Lady Justice to the nineteen-story state building, but it felt like a different world. As counsel for the plaintiffs, Murdock spoke first, summarizing the arguments he had made in detail in written briefs. When he finished, the justices didn't ask any questions. But when Deputy City Attorney Gerald Sato countered Murdock's argument that the city had a duty to enforce the no-evictions condition, saying it was only obligated not to issue building permits and demolition permits, Justice Laurie Zelon broke in.

"So someone can submit a tract map [the official document detailing conditions] and say 'I'm going to do all these things, and they can violate that right up to the point of demolishing the property, then you can say, 'Oh, gee, we can't enforce this anymore because everybody's gone.' I mean, doesn't that take all of the meaning out of the conditions that the city imposes?"

It was the very question that had been asked over and over again, all the way back to the losing battle in 2003 to save the Lake Street buildings from the wrecker's claw. And Sato's answer was the same answer that came out of the city attorney's office then and numerous times since—the conditions hadn't been "triggered." It might be generous to call this answer to the Justice's question a nonanswer, but she didn't press him further.

Greg Ozhekim, the attorney representing Aimco, used his time to also make familiar arguments, that the tract map with the conditions was just a proposal that the property owner wasn't obligated to follow, that the landlord was exercising rights under the Ellis Act in evicting the tenants, that the place for the tenants to challenge those evictions was in the court that dealt with unlawful detainer actions. Both Zelon and presiding Justice Earl Johnson seemed skeptical about these claims, which Murdock disputed in his rebuttal. "The City has the power and the duty to protect my clients. Those are the persons being displaced by the so-called withdrawal of rental units, and we don't even know if it is a withdrawal. They're not telling anyone; they're just saying 'We can do this.'"

The tone of the hearing raised people's spirits, although it was always dangerous to speculate too closely about what judges are going to do in a given case. But a ruling was expected within the month, so they wouldn't have long to wait. As it turned out, the wait was mercifully brief, because the court issued a ruling on September 19, just twelve days after the hearing. The headline in the next day's *Los Angeles Times* told the story in succinct terms: "Court Victory for Tenants in Long Battle." The *Santa Monica Mirror* headline added some more detail: "Lincoln Place Evictions Halted," and the *Argonaut* headline added even more: "Remaining Lincoln Place Apartment Tenants Hail Appeals Court Decision That They Can Stay."

The unanimous decision written by Justice Zelon flatly rejected the arguments advanced by Aimco and the city attorney. The Ellis Act didn't preempt the conditions the city placed on the redevelopment project. The conditions were environmental mitigations and therefore the evictions violated CEQA. The unlawful detainer proceedings were not a place for the tenants to seek a remedy. The ruling directed the lower court judge to issue an injunction halting further evictions and to order the city to enforce the project conditions. It was an unambiguous victory long in coming, although Aimco and the city still had one more bite of the apple, albeit uncertain, in the form of a petition for review by the California Supreme Court.

In the meantime, tenants and others savored the unfamiliar taste of success. Laura Burns was quoted in the *Los Angeles Times* article, saying, "I'm ecstatic. We have said since the very beginning that those evictions were not legal and that the city had the duty to enforce these conditions, and nobody would listen to us." A bit of hyperbole, perhaps, because a few officials, like Bill Rosendahl, had listened and tried to do something. In the *Times* article, he said the court ruling called into question the quality of advice the city attorney had given the city council. "I look forward to the city attorney's office's explanation," he said. "And frankly, I wouldn't mind an apology." In a *Santa Monica Mirror* article, David Ewing and Laura Silagi jointly called the case "an important lawsuit which will have far-reaching effects on how our city and other cities enforce their agreements with developers." And in an LPTA press release, Sheila Bernard wrote, "We are jubilant. This points the way for council members to assist longtime renters being pushed out of gentrifying neighborhoods by condo conversions where the developer wants to evict them rather than include them in redevelopment plans."

John Murdock was obviously happy, but as he studied the twenty-nine-page ruling he had a kind of "Aha!" moment. "As I read the opinion," he says, "it became immediately clear that if tenant rights were being trampled on we had a case for damages." While the ruling had ordered a halt to evictions, it hadn't addressed the question of what should happen to those already gone, and he began thinking about how to compel Aimco to allow those tenants to come back. But he had to wait to see if Aimco and the city would try to take the case to the supreme court. If those justices decided to review the case, it would be at least a year and probably longer before a ruling, and if they reversed the appeals court, a case for damages would be out the window.

Aimco indicated that it would indeed take the case to the state's highest court, and Rocky Delgadillo advised the city council to do the same. But Bill Rosendahl immediately began lobbying his colleagues to ignore the city attorney's advice and show that they stood with the Lincoln Place tenants. On October 2, the council discussed the issue in closed session, then voted 11–1 against joining Aimco in the appeal. Quoted in the *Daily Journal*, John Murdock said he was "dumbfounded" by the city attorney's position. "What does the court have to do? Hit them over the head with a hammer? I think finally the message has gotten through, though, as indicated by the vote of the council." He brought up the subject of damages, saying that a case could be made against the city as well as Aimco. But he added that the council's decision not to pursue further appeal made it likely that tenants wouldn't sue the city. "If they had dragged it out with an appeal for another year," he said, "then my clients would feel otherwise." It was also a measure of atonement for the notorious council meeting two years earlier when tenants had waited to be heard while council members tossed around a football and made bets on the USC-UCLA game.

Three weeks later, as expected, Aimco filed the petition with the supreme court. That court only took a small percentage of cases in any event, but many legal observers thought the fact of the city's refusal to join the action made the odds against success even longer. The Thanksgiving holiday passed in a kind of limbo for the thirteen tenants who were free of the fear of the sheriff appearing at their doors, but they still didn't know what the long-term future might be. Then on December 12, a day when the overnight temperature had plunged to a frigid 38 degrees in downtown Los Angeles, the supreme court denied Aimco's petition for review. People involved in the past battles over such a long period of time could scarcely allow themselves to believe it, but, as the old saying goes, it was all over but the shouting.

Still, there were questions. Would any tenants be able to come back? Would buildings be preserved? What would happen with the vacant lots? Many questions, yes, but instead of the uncertainty that had darkened the holidays at Lincoln Place for years there was the uncertainty created by questions founded in hope, in a sense of justice having been done. In the handful of apartments with people living in them and in other apartments and homes in Venice and elsewhere, spirits were lifted, both literally and figuratively, to a brighter future for Lincoln Place.

24

COMING HOME

BY THE BEGINNING OF 2008, the subprime mortgage crisis had pre-cipitated what would be called the Great Recession. In the coming year, the country's financial system would teeter on the edge of collapse, home foreclosures would become rampant, and corporations as large as General Motors would face bankruptcy. Hillary Clinton would win California's votes in the Democratic presidential primary, but Barack Obama would later win the party's nomination and go on to become the country's first Black president. As if to show that for every step forward there's a step back, California voters would approve Proposition 8, which amended the state constitution to ban same-sex marriage.

But the most far-reaching moment of 2008 for Lincoln Place tenants, preservationists, and community supporters came when John Murdock, with the help of an attorney named David Lefkowitz, filed the threatened lawsuit for damages against Aimco. The "mass action" suit named 191 plaintiffs, a group that included the thirteen tenants who had never left, most of the fifty-nine who had been locked out in 2005, and many of those who had voluntarily left after getting eviction notices, either taking the enhanced "Shober deals" or the relocation payments mandated for Ellis Act evictions. The suit asked for an unspecified amount of monetary damages, plus an order giving the plaintiffs the right to return to their Lincoln Place apartments.

In a press release jointly issued by Sheila Bernard and Murdock, the LPTA president said, "Aimco took a bad business gamble. They broke the law and hurt a lot of people. They threw families out of their homes, little children, frail elderly ladies, and people with life-threatening illnesses. You bet it's going to cost them." The release quoted Laura Burns, who along with her husband, Bernard Perroud, was among the plaintiffs. She accused Aimco of having used the tenants as hostages to "extort more height and density" for their Lincoln Place redevelopment. "But," she said, "this Goliath has met its match." Amanda Seward added her voice, saying, "Aimco abused its power. The company underestimated the tenants at Lincoln Place and they are not going away." And Jan Book, the fourth member of the LPTA leadership team, said, "We are now playing offense instead of defense. Aimco has done serious damage to our community and to people's lives, and Aimco must be held accountable."

Despite the tide seemingly having turned against the landlord, Aimco's legal team went on the offensive just days after Murdock and Lefkowitz filed the lawsuit for damages. After the city council voted that past October against petitioning the state supreme court for review, the company had sent a letter to the city giving notice that it was abandoning the tract map, the official document with all the details of the Lincoln Place redevelopment project. Then in March 2008, Aimco filed a lawsuit against the city in US District Court, asserting that this abandonment of the redevelopment meant that none of the tract map conditions could be enforced. In other words, the company was claiming that despite the appeals court decision, the Ellis Act still gave it the right to evict every last tenant. It was the fourteenth lawsuit involving Lincoln Place since TransAction first sued the city in 1995.

Many legal observers saw the action as a Hail Mary on Aimco's part, and indeed, a judge dismissed it three months later on the grounds that the federal court lacked jurisdiction in the matter.

Every domino seemed to be falling in the tenants' favor, but there was a question about how many of the elderly would live to see the conclusion of the long, arduous struggle. Eighty-six-year-old Celia Harriman, who had come to LPTA meetings even after suffering a stroke and who had willingly lent her voice to legal proceedings, died in May. Frieda Marlin, the spirited widow who had been seen so often in demonstrations with her cane in one hand and protest sign in the other, had broken her hip and moved to the Jewish Home for the Aging in the San Fernando Valley, twenty miles from her beloved Lincoln Place. The eighty-four-year-old adamantly insisted she would return some day, but her friends and others who had come to know her wondered if this was wishful thinking.

That left eleven households on the desolate, thirty-eight-acre property. But their conditions began to improve when demands from Bill Rosendahl led to city inspectors citing the landlord for health and safety violations and ordering improvements in maintenance and security. Workers showed up to fix long-standing plumbing and electrical problems. Broken glass and missing window screens were replaced. Junk abandoned by former tenants was hauled out of carports. Gardeners cut weeds and trimmed overgrown shrubbery. The place was just a little less bleak than it had been the past few years.

As the lawsuit for damages and restitution moved forward in superior court, attorneys for Aimco began discussing a settlement with Murdock and Lefkowitz. Nobody was surprised by the company's willingness to negotiate. A jury trial pitting the biggest landlord in the country against a group of mostly working-class and elderly tenants who had been evicted from their longtime homes wasn't likely to generate sympathy for Aimco. Jurors could end up awarding many millions in actual and punitive damages to the tenants, and even if the company dragged the matter out for a number of years with appeals, Lincoln Place would remain in limbo and generate red ink for its balance sheets.

On November 10, 2008, Bill Rosendahl called Sheila Bernard and left her a voicemail message. He said he had just gotten a call from one of the attorneys representing Aimco, who had outlined the major elements of a settlement the company was willing to make. It was remarkably different than anything it had demanded in the past. One, nothing would be torn down—all the existing buildings would be preserved and renovated. Two, tenants who had left under duress or been evicted could come back at their old rents, and those who didn't want to come back would get compensation. Three, Aimco would put up new structures on the lots where the seven buildings had been demolished. In his message, Rosendahl said he told the attorney that it was really up to Sheila and Murdock. "You're our leader on this issue," he said, "and we work for you."

After the *sturm und drang* of the past number of years, the voice mail seemed an especially attenuated way of announcing that the Lincoln Place battle was, for all practical purposes, over. The tenants had won. David had slain Goliath. Sheila Bernard's dream of a community of people who each owned a piece of Lincoln Place and were masters of their own destinies where housing was concerned would not be realized, but she had already resigned herself to that fact. If the tenants living at Lincoln Place could stay as long as they wanted, if others who had left under various forms of pressure could come back, if the buildings that fostered a sense of community that gripped her imagination from the moment she moved in would be saved, then she would say yes to the settlement even though she was only one of the 191 plaintiffs in the lawsuit.

Within the general outline reported by Rosendahl, there were many details to be worked out before anything could be put in writing, signed by all the parties, and approved by the court. Another complication was that attorney Noel Weiss had filed a separate lawsuit against Aimco and the city on behalf of a dozen tenants who hadn't supported the LPTA's hiring of John Murdock. A court-appointed judge would mediate between the attorneys and interested parties, and it was hoped there wouldn't be a clash between the two groups of tenants that could potentially throw an overall settlement into jeopardy. Bernard, Jan Book and Laura Burns represented the LPTA in these negotiations, and Amanda Seward participated on behalf of preservationists. To the casual observer, it might have looked like yet another quixotic attempt to get the warring parties to actually vanquish the devil in the details, but there was a big difference this time. If an agreement couldn't be reached, the tenants fully intended to proceed to trial on their claims for millions in damages.

In April 2009, Murdock and Lefkowitz sent a letter to the 191 plaintiffs telling them that agreement had been reached on the total amount of monetary compensation and the number of tenants who would be allowed to return. The agreement confirmed the preservation of all existing buildings and the construction of new buildings that would bring the total number of units back to the original 795, all to be maintained as rentals. The new buildings would be the same height and mass as existing buildings, all of which would be renovated with new plumbing and electrical systems but not altered in their outward appearance. A total of eighty-three units would be set aside for the eleven current tenants and those evicted in 2005 and 2006 who wanted to return. There would also be a financial settlement, including attorneys' fees for Murdock and other lawyers involved in the various Lincoln Place litigations, but specific amounts were subject to confidentiality agreements and would not be disclosed to anyone other than the parties involved.

It took another year to get everyone, including the small group represented by Noel Weiss, to sign off on the details of the complex settlement. But on May 26, 2010, a *Los Angeles Times* headline displayed the words all had been hoping to see—"Deal Reached on Lincoln Place." Bill Rosendahl called it a "historic day for the city," and Aimco's Patti Shwayder was quoted as viewing the settlement as "a big group hug," a comment that both amused and annoyed tenants who remembered her calling them "squatters" when they were fighting eviction. In a *Santa Monica Daily Press* article the next day, Rosendahl was quoted at greater length, saying, "This is a great day for tenants, for preservationists, for Venice, and for anyone concerned with fairness and justice." Sheila Bernard told the newspaper that she was "delighted" by the settlement and looked forward to the day when many of her old neighbors would return to their homes.[84] The entire front page of the *Argonaut* was taken up with a photograph of Jan Book, Laura Burns, Amanda Seward and Ingrid Mueller standing outside a Lincoln Place building. Overlaying the photo were the words "Back Home," and the four women who had played such important roles in the long battle were broadly smiling.

Before any tenants could return, however, more questions had to be answered. One of the most fraught concerned the issue of where they would live. The settlement called for eighty-three units to be set aside, but Sheila Bernard wanted the units to be scattered throughout the complex, to avoid creating a kind of ghetto, while Aimco wanted to restrict them to a specific area. Aimco prevailed on that point, and a cluster of six buildings was designated at the southwest corner of the property. But only sixty-five tenants exercised their right to return, and Aimco reduced the number of designated buildings to four. That complicated matters further, because the settlement specified that eligible tenants could return to units comparable to their prior apartments, something that proved difficult with only four buildings. Sheila Bernard, who headed a "unit selection committee," believed that the settlement language clearly meant that a tenant who originally had a two-bedroom apartment should return to a two-bedroom apartment. If the tenant's old apartment had a balcony or patio, then the new one should as well. And so forth. That issue was eventually resolved, albeit with some acrimony between Bernard and Aimco, but there were other conflicts as well. For example, Aimco wanted to make the entire property smoke-free, and several returning tenants were smokers. Under the terms of the settlement, they were not to be deprived of any rights they previously had. So how were they to be accommodated?[85]

While back-and-forth continued on those and other issues, renovation of the buildings for returning tenants got underway. Units were to be kept in their original condition, with repairs rather than replacement of the original ceramic tile, hardwood floors, and cabinetry. Aimco even applied to the city for historic-cultural monument status, an irony given how strenuously the company had fought efforts at the city, state, and national level to recognize Lincoln Place as historically significant. And it would later apply for listing on the National Register of Historic Places, extolling all the virtues, including Ralph Vaughn's role as designer, that had been denigrated so vigorously by Robert Bisno and others.

In May 2012, seven years after Aimco had first informed all tenants that they would have to move out, people began moving into the four buildings with their freshly renovated apartments. Ingrid Mueller parked her Scion in the alley behind the Elkgrove Avenue building where she had been the lone occupant for almost six years and carried possessions to the car and drove the two blocks to her new apartment in a building at the corner of Doreen and Elkland Place. She was happy to have gotten an apartment like her old one, on a second-floor corner with a balcony where she could tend her plants and sit and enjoy the sight of a Brazilian pepper tree and a jacaranda in the building's courtyard. Barbara Eisenberg moved into an apartment in a different wing of the same building. Carol Beck moved into a ground-floor unit in the building across the courtyard. Returning tenants

Sara Sakuma and Gloria Morales moved into buildings on Elkland Place closer to the Lincoln Center shopping mall.

Frieda Marlin, who always spoke with passion about how she loved living at Lincoln Place, didn't come back. On April 10, 2011, she died at the Jewish Home for the Aging, leaving empty spaces in the hearts of those who had been on the front lines with her in twenty-plus years of fighting to keep their Lincoln Place homes. Among eligible tenants who chose to take monetary compensation instead of returning were Dicie Meyers, who was eighty-eight-years-old and would eventually move to a nursing home, and Michael Palumbo, who moved back east where he had grown up. One locked-out tenant who had long dreamed of living again at Lincoln Place was Laura Burns, but she had been diagnosed with chronic obstructive pulmonary disease (COPD) and she and her husband made the difficult decision to take the compensation and stay in Austin, where the air quality was significantly better than in Los Angeles. Sheila Bernard would not be taking up residence in one of the four buildings, either. She had hoped her daughter could stay at Lincoln Place, but to do that would involve another fight with Aimco, and she decided to take the money instead. She would use it for a down payment on a duplex in a desert city east of Los Angeles where real estate was much cheaper and where her daughter could live with some sense of security.

On the first Sunday in July of 2012, Bernard walked into the Penmar Park community room for the regular monthly meeting of the LPTA. She had done this hundreds of times since taking over leadership of the organization in 1989, but it was a poignant moment because this day would be her last as LPTA president and it might be the last time she'd walk through those doors and see her friends and neighbors on rows of folding chairs, waiting for her to tell them the latest Lincoln Place news and introduce speakers and ask for volunteers for the formidable, never-ending task of fighting their landlord's attempts to get rid of them.

Bill Rosendahl was there, and he presented her with an official city certificate of appreciation. He also gave her a half-dozen eggs from the flock of hens he kept in the backyard of his Mar Vista home. The councilman's effusive personality was on abundant display, and there was vigorous applause from tenants who had depended for so long on Bernard's leadership, and who had come to see Rosendahl's advocacy not as political posturing but as a genuine concern for their welfare. What they and others in the room didn't know was that he had been suffering severe back pain and just a month later would publicly announce that he had been diagnosed with cancer in his pelvic area. To the dismay of those who saw him as a human being who cared about the homeless, the poor, the elderly and working families displaced by gentrification, he wouldn't run for a third term on the city council and less than four years after the Penmar Park meeting, he would be dead.

When Bernard left that meeting, she left Lincoln Place behind. She had retired from her teaching job, and there was no reason to keep making the drive from Camarillo to Los Angeles to preside at LPTA meetings or attend to the organization's business. The Doreen Place apartment where she had raised three children and hosted innumerable meetings with everyone from distraught tenants to lawyers and landlords, was empty. Like others that had stood vacant, some for as long as a dozen years, the apartment would be stripped to bare walls and remodeled, with a new, modern kitchen, bathrooms with the latest fixtures, laundry with stacked washer and dryer, and central heating and air conditioning. It would be rented at market rate, likely upward of $3,000 a month. All of the 696 preserved units would fall under city rent control once they were leased, but the new occupants wouldn't be seniors living on Social Security or workers in the many restaurants and other small businesses in Venice. They wouldn't be the people that the Bialacs and Ralph Vaughn had in mind when they set out to build an apartment complex that gave working people on strict budgets a home with the amenities associated with places only the well-to-do could afford.

That fact is made glaringly obvious by the rents currently being advertised on the website of the re-branded Lincoln Place Apartment Homes. The cheapest apartment listed is a one-bedroom, one-bath for just over $2,600 a month. The most expensive is a two-bedroom, two-bath for $4,600. Like many corporate landlords, Aimco requires prospective tenants to have income at least three times the monthly rent, which translates to $75,000 for the cheapest unit and $165,000 for the most expensive. In 2019, the median household income in Los Angeles was approximately $68,000, meaning that considerably more than half the households in the city couldn't rent a Lincoln Place apartment. Ingrid Mueller, Barbara Eisenberg, Gloria Morales and all the other tenants who returned now pay the same rent they paid in 2005, plus annual increases allowed by the city's rent control law. A few are paying as little as $600 a month, but when they leave—most likely when they die or are too old to live independently—the law's vacancy decontrol provision will mean that the landlord can then charge the new tenants whatever the market will bear.

Ralph Vaughn and others involved in the design and construction of Lincoln Place would surely be pleased that the original buildings—with a few exceptions—are still standing, but what would they make of the sleek, glass-walled management office at the intersection of Frederick and California Avenues, the spot that Sheila Bernard considered the face of the complex? What would they think of the modern recreation building with swimming pool and roof deck and fitness center furnished with exercycles and treadmills? How would they regard the sight of dogs frolicking with their masters on the lawns where so many children used to play?

Aimco got mostly high marks for its renovation work, financed with a $190 million FHA-insured loan, an interesting bookend to the fact that Samuel Bialac and Philip Yousem got an FHA-insured loan to build the complex. Although Aimco got some criticism for failing to maintain the original diversity of the landscaping, it did preserve most of the existing trees, plant new trees and shrubbery, and re-sod the dead and dying lawns. Several picnic areas were constructed, with gas barbecue grills, benches and tables. Bag dispensers and receptacles for dog waste were set at intervals along the sidewalks. A charging station for electric vehicles was installed in a corner of the management office parking lot.

But those who returned to the sixty-three apartments in the four buildings at the corner of the property sometimes felt that the landlord considered them second-class citizens. The most overt expression came in 2014, when they were informed by management that they couldn't use the just-completed recreation center with the swimming pool and fitness equipment. The reason? The settlement agreement signed by all parties allowed the tenants to return to Lincoln Place with the same amenities they enjoyed prior to the evictions. And since there hadn't been a pool or fitness facility before, these would be off-limits. This action looked both petty and spiteful, and Aimco relented—wisely, no doubt—after getting complaints and a threatening letter from Jan Book, who was still giving free counsel to people having legal issues with their leases or other aspects of their tenancies. But the message most of those tenants got was clear—Aimco only tolerated their presence on the property because it was legally forced to do so.

Sara Sakuma, who was locked out in 2005 but never wavered in her desire to return, had kept asking herself, "What are we going back to? What's going to be there?" When she finally moved into a second-floor apartment on Elkland Place, she was happy until the electricity suddenly went off. That marked the beginning of months of problems that maintenance crews seemed either unable or unwilling to fix. Ingrid Mueller had the same experience. The breaker for the electrical circuit to her refrigerator tripped so often that she finally taped it down. That probably wasn't prudent, but it did succeed in getting the attention of maintenance personnel who gradually got everything into working order. Others had similar experiences, but an initial flood of complaints gradually slowed to a trickle. People couldn't help thinking, though, that this sort of thing wouldn't happen to the tenants in the rest of the complex who were considered more desirable and thus worth keeping satisfied.

A few of the returned tenants also felt that they were viewed in a condescending manner by people paying much higher rent for their apartments, although a more common feeling was that they were simply invisible to the newcomers, virtually all of whom were considerably younger and more affluent. Mueller, for one, didn't care what the others thought, or if Aimco hoped that tenants like her who had caused so much trouble over the years would get fed up and move. When one of the original LPTA members, Adolphe Griffith, died in 2005, she bought a ninety-nine cent ficus tree in a little pot and planted it in an open space behind his building, having every intention of watching it grow into the densely crowned fifteen-foot-high tree it is today. When she was just fourteen months old, the Russian Army mounted a siege on her birthplace of Königsberg, Germany, which forced her parents and many others to flee to the west in the middle of one of the coldest winters of the century. While she doesn't remember the details of that harrowing journey, she believes it instilled in her an adult compulsion to flee from her past. But once she moved to Lincoln Place and got involved with the LPTA, her instinct for flight was overwhelmed by an urge to fight. "I said, 'Don't mess with me. I'm not leaving.' And I dug in." She's sure she could have developed her career in film translation and made more money in the time she devoted to the LPTA, but she's not sorry. The Lincoln Place saga instilled in her a desire to work on behalf of worthy causes, and she's involved in various community actions, most notably an effort to save a historic Black church in Venice's Oakwood neighborhood from the relentless forces of gentrification. She's not sorry she stayed for years when Lincoln Place was a ghost town, when it evoked memories of growing up in a country deeply scarred by the aftermath of war. "No," she says, standing in her living room and looking into the verdant limbs of the pepper tree outside the window, one of those planted when Lincoln Place was originally built. "I'm not sorry I did what I did."

Jan Book, who grew up in the suburban San Fernando Valley playing the piano and dreaming of becoming an artist, now lives with her husband in a tract of 1960s ranch-style houses not far from Los Angeles International airport. Speaking in her characteristically rapid and energetic style, she says she long resisted getting too deeply involved with the Lincoln Place struggle, but when she saw that the community was in real danger of being destroyed, she felt she had no choice. "You don't abandon people in need," she says. But the unrelenting stress from being involved with the tenants both personally and professionally for all those years took an emotional toll that she feels even now, when she has time to in indulge in her passion for painting and relax by playing her piano. "But I loved living at Lincoln Place," she says. "My heart is still there."

Amanda Seward never lived at Lincoln Place, but her involvement with the tenant struggle and preservation had a profound effect on her life. During those years, she still did legal work in the field of entertainment law, but her feelings about social justice issues and the effect of defending tenants in eviction court led her to change the path of her legal career and make a practice of representing renters facing eviction and other disputes with their landlords. She was happy, of course, that her efforts to save Lincoln Place from demolition finally bore fruit, even to the extent of Aimco seeking and getting the complex listed on the National Register of Historic Places. All of it, she told the *Argonaut*, in a 2012 interview, was "very, very rewarding. It's seldom in life that we get a chance to fight for what we believe in and see it work and I think this could have happened only in Venice."[86]

The four women—Seward, Jan Book, Sheila Bernard, and Laura Burns— all played key roles in saving Lincoln Place, but they all recognize that it couldn't have happened without the indefatigable research by Burns. Speaking from her childhood home in Austin, she says that she and her husband would still be living at Lincoln Place if it had been possible. But from the time they decided not to return because of her COPD, her health deteriorated to the point where she underwent a double lung transplant. She believes that the stress of the Lincoln Place fight contributed to her health problems, and the aftermath of the transplant with its myriad tests and medications and visits to doctors turned into what she describes as "a full-time job." As for Lincoln Place, she says she's very happy that the buildings she fought so hard for have been preserved. But she also remembers the place nearly filled when she and her husband moved in, and says, "I think it's a pity that so few people were there to move back in."

That fact bothers others who had some role in the Lincoln story as well. One of the most outspoken is Elena Popp, who went back to heading the Eviction Defense Network, and still represents tenants in fighting landlords who want to get them out to raise rents or convert their apartments to condominiums. She calls herself and staff of seven lawyers "the ragtag defenders of the downtrodden," and in the fifteen years since the grimness of watching people she had represented being locked out of their Lincoln Place apartments, she says she has seen no significant moves to protect renters and preserve affordable housing in Los Angeles and the rest of California. "The Ellis Act continues to be the boogeyman," she says. "We see the same thing over and over, landlords trying to get rid of tenants. If we eradicated the Ellis Act and vacancy decontrol, we could stop gentrification in its tracks. But it won't happen while elected officials are in the pockets of landlords."

Laura Silagi, who has lived within sight of Lincoln Place for thirty-four years, set forth points during the 2006 negotiations with Aimco that she believed important to the neighborhood people she represented, including the return of all evicted tenants and priority in any redevelopment given to the housing needs of the lower and middle classes. Now, reflecting upon that time, she says it was important to her that Lincoln Place be kept intact as a community and an integral part of that Venice neighborhood. Like others, she is happy that the buildings have been preserved, and she made some lasting friendships with tenants and others involved in the struggle. But, she says, "Most of the people who lived there have been scattered all over, and the people who came back are a very small part of the population. That sense of Lincoln Place as a community where a lot of people knew each other and had common goals doesn't really exist anymore."

David Ewing, who along with Silagi was one of the most active community members in the Lincoln Place struggle, later played a key role in setting up and running a neighborhood association that represents all of Venice east of Lincoln Boulevard, including Lincoln Place. He became close friends with some of the tenants, including Frieda Marlin, who he visited when she was in the nursing home, and her son Spike, who died three years after his mother. He can see a corner of Lincoln Place from the window of his upstairs home office, and is happy that almost all of what the architect and builders envisioned still exists. He also believes that the Lincoln Place struggle has an important lesson.

"I disliked the idea that this company could come in and dictate terms and screw the tenants," he says. "But it showed that if people organized they could win fights. Lincoln Place was a long, drawn-out, uphill fight, but in the end they made a huge corporation do something it didn't want to do."

Anne Murphy, the longtime Venice resident and affordable-housing advocate, reacted to TransAction's redevelopment plan in 1994 by standing up at a community meeting and saying it was "unthinkable to me that we could just destroy eight hundred units of affordable housing." Like almost everyone who supported the Lincoln Place tenants, she is glad the place wasn't razed to the ground, but the fact that ninety percent of the complex doesn't presently meet the definition of affordable housing looks to her like a failure. The city, she says, had an opportunity to help the LPTA's "Let's Own It" campaign with financial support, and it could have done more to convince TransAction to sell the property to a nonprofit entity run by the tenants. "If the city had done its job, Lincoln Place could have been preserved as affordable housing, absolutely. They were complicit, they knew we had an affordable-housing crisis but didn't do anything about it. Gentrification was exploding, it was a prime time in which leaders of L.A. could have gotten together and made sure there was housing for everyone who needed it."

But what of laws like the Ellis Act, which landlords are still using to empty out affordable rental units, and the Costa-Hawkins Act, which forbids California cities from limiting the amount of rent a landlord can charge for vacated rent-controlled apartments? Murphy believes that if the city had seriously pushed for changes in those laws and other tenant protections, its sheer size would have meant that legislators had to listen. "The city could have led," she says, "Instead of just being dragged along. It's like we know about climate change but don't do anything about it. It's a big lack of leadership." She acknowledges that council members Ruth Galanter and Bill Rosendahl genuinely cared about Lincoln Place tenants and tried to protect them. But, she says, "Ruth was a lonely voice in the wilderness," and Rosendahl couldn't get the city council to go along with the kind of bold actions that were needed to keep Lincoln Place from turning into the mostly upscale housing complex it is today.

Did the tenants and their supporters indeed win the battle but lose the war? The person who most closely fits the imperfect analogy of a general leading troops in battle is Sheila Bernard, and her feelings are clearly mixed. She's glad the buildings weren't all torn down, although she was less interested in historic preservation than the other LPTA leaders, seeing it as a way to save the tenants rather than an end in itself. When she was first seized by the idea of tenant ownership, she thought it might take two or three years to realize her dream, but she had no doubt that it was possible. Now she is blunt about that dream that burned so brightly for so long but waned and finally flared out. "The fact we were defeated in that endeavor is one of the enduring disappointments of my life."

Was the entire "Let's Own It" venture a quixotic exercise, a lost cause? Marcia Scully, the attorney who put untold hours of unpaid time into that effort, believes that the owner, then TransAction, clearly didn't want to sell to the tenants. "It wasn't impossible," she says, "But hard. It was going to take a lot of work." Scully says she was also worried about the LPTA's ability to manage such a large apartment complex even if they succeeded in buying it. "It would have been a big obligation. A big job, not like somebody buying twenty units. And it would have been really awful if they owned the place and ran into serious problems. I think that would have been worse than never having owned it at all. I expressed this, I didn't harp on it, but I hoped they knew it was a really big deal."

But despite Sheila Bernard's disappointment, despite the toll her twenty-three years as head of the LPTA took on her and her family life, despite the financial losses and the emotional pain of seeing friends and fellow tenants forced from their homes, despite the fact that in the settlement phase rifts opened between her and other LPTA leaders, she doesn't look back with regret on the July day in 1989 when she agreed to take the job of leading the tenant organization. For one thing, she can point to victories that sprang from her tireless organizing and leadership. Stopping the major rehabilitation evictions in the 1980s and successfully pushing for reforms that made such evictions much more difficult. Resisting TransAction's plan to evict everyone and turn the place into the upscale Village at Venezia. Raising the money to hire a skilled attorney whose arguments eventually led to court decisions stopping the Ellis Act evictions and the landlord's use of the anti-SLAPP law to silence tenant protests. And in general, organizing a disparate group of tenants and community people to pursue a common goal of social justice.

In an email message to Amanda Seward shortly after the final approval of the settlement, she wrote, "I used to draw a lot, and it was always amazing to me that a drawing never turned out exactly as it started out in my mind's eye. But it always turned out to be interesting. LP [Lincoln Place] is like that. I had a different vision, and I failed to realize it. But what actually happened does contain a lot of success, and no matter how it turns out, we can walk away with our heads held high."

Now seventy-one, she and her husband own a small house in a senior living community in Camarillo, a city of seventy thousand at the edge of a broad coastal plain green with citrus groves and fields of artichokes, strawberries, and other fruits and vegetables. The dark brown hair of her youth is almost completely gray, and she walks with a slight limp as a result of a recent bout with multiple myeloma, which is now in remission but at its most severe kept her flat on her back in bed. She shows a visitor to a sunny, enclosed porch off one of the two bedrooms of the compact home. "There it is," she says. The space is crowded with stacks of boxes filled with files, folders, notebooks, photographs and other materials pertaining to Lincoln Place. "Twenty years. I worked and I took care of my kids, and I spent almost all the rest of my time on Lincoln Place." With a smile that looks a bit wistful, she waves an arm at the neatly labeled boxes. "Twenty years," she says again. "That was my life."

Since the returning tenants moved back in, she has come to Los Angeles only sporadically, but when she does, she tries to take a drive through Lincoln Place's curving streets. She has visited her old friend and compatriot, Ingrid Mueller, a few times, and she attended a memorial service at the complex for Carol Beck, who died in 2016 from complications that followed from being bitten by a dog. She hasn't lost her drive to lead people in an effort for positive change, though—at home with her husband in Camarillo she chairs a committee of her homeowners' association that works to plant trees and improve the landscaping in her retirement community. Not as exalted, perhaps, as leading tenants in a fight to save their homes, but with some of the same challenges—getting people to agree on a common goal and attracting volunteers and community support.

As always, a forward-looking and positive person, she says the entire Lincoln Place experience had a positive effect, on a spiritual and political level. "I viewed the whole effort as a mission," she says. "And I learned so much about the way things work, about organizing people around a cause."

She pauses a moment, then says, "I came into my own at Lincoln Place. I became the person I am."

END

AFTERWORD

IN THE EARLY 2000s, I was working for Venice Community Housing, supervising the renovation of apartment buildings for low-income families in Venice and other areas on the west side of Los Angeles. I didn't deal directly with prospective tenants, but I knew that the demand for affordable housing in the area far exceeded the supply, so much so that the waiting list for Venice Community Housing units had been closed to new applicants. People called or walked into the office almost every day to inquire about apartments, but they had to be turned away.

One day, I happened to be in the office reception area when a man and woman with two small children came in and asked about places to rent. When told there wasn't anything available, the woman turned and spoke to the man in Spanish, telling him something that eluded my uncertain grasp of that language, although I recognized the word *nada*. But instead of leaving, she looked at me and whoever else was there that day, and told us the family's story, perhaps in the faint hope that it might change the negative response, or more likely, just capture, for a moment, some sympathetic ears.

Her husband, she said, worked in a Venice restaurant, and she did housekeeping for some homeowners in the community. They lived in an apartment with relatives in another part of the city, but the crowded conditions were unbearable and the long commute was a strain on their old car. They had been looking for apartments in Venice and nearby communities, but the rents for the few places they had found actually exceeded their combined incomes. In a voice like a suppressed cry of anguish, she said they were desperate; was there something—anything—we could do? She stared at us, not with hostility but what seemed incomprehension at the gulf that obviously divided us from her and her family. Then a dam burst and tears flooded her face; in a choked voice she again spoke in Spanish to her husband, and they turned and ushered their children through the door and disappeared.

At the time, I was only vaguely aware of the details of the LPTA's "Let's Own It" campaign that had tried and failed ten years earlier to turn Lincoln Place into a tenant-owned and managed complex that would permanently maintain Lincoln Place as originally envisioned by its builder and architect, as comfortable homes in a garden-like setting for working families and others of modest means. A place where that desperate woman and her husband could have lived and raised their children without fear of sudden rent increases and eviction and the other assaults suffered by people of their social and economic class every single day.

In my research and writing of "The Battle of Lincoln Place," it became painfully clear that government, and in particular, the city of Los Angeles, not only failed to promote such a vision but treated it with a neglect that seems a kind of contempt. At the time of the "Let's Own It" campaign, city leaders knew there was an affordable housing crisis in the Venice community, but the tenant leaders' cries for assistance fell on deaf ears. It was up to them to raise many millions of dollars, negotiate with the landlord, and figure out how to manage one of the largest apartment complexes in the city. Notwithstanding resistance from city council members to the landlord's plan to demolish Lincoln Place, the result of the city's indifference to the tenants' desire for ownership was the ongoing specter of the complex turning into an enclave for the well-to-do, an indifference that ultimately upended lives and caused untold distress and psychic damage that lingers to this day. And while the fact that Lincoln Place still stands through the heroic efforts of some individuals counts as a kind of miracle, a family like the one in desperate search of an apartment couldn't afford to live there now. In fact, they couldn't afford to live anywhere in Venice or near it, despite working in its restaurants, keeping house and tending children for its increasingly affluent residents.

When I worked at Venice Community Housing, there was a sign on the wall near the entrance that read, "Housing is a Right, Not a Privilege." I'm not sure if any elected officials in Los Angeles ever voiced that sentiment, but action, or should I say, inaction, speaks louder than words. In 1986, when Lincoln Place was sold to a corporate developer who almost immediately tried to get rid of tenants paying below-market rents, there was an affordable housing crisis in the city. In 2002, when the city threw up its hands after a long court battle and approved a plan to demolish Lincoln Place, there was an affordable housing crisis. Three years later, when the largest owner of apartments in the country sent an eviction letter to every single Lincoln Place tenant, there was an affordable housing crisis. Likewise in 2012, when the tenants who weren't "scattered to the four winds," as attorney John Murdock put it, were finally able to return to Lincoln Place, there was an affordable housing crisis. And today, with Ellis Act evictions having eliminated 27,000 units of rent-controlled housing over the past two decades, and thousands upon thousands of people living on the streets, the city faces its largest affordable housing crisis since the end of World War II.

What has the city done in the face of this crisis? Along with the state legislature, it has embraced the idea of increased density and decreased regulation as the way to create a significant stock of affordable housing. Upzoning single-family neighborhoods, raising height limits, allowing homeowners to build accessory rental units on their property, making it faster and cheaper for developers to build new housing, in particular by de-fanging CEQA, the very law that saved Lincoln Place from being leveled and turned into luxury condominiums or apartments. In other words, the city's preferred solution is to keep the housing supply in the hands of private corporations that regard apartment complexes like Lincoln Place as commodities to be bought and sold and operated for maximum profit, not as necessities of life for hundreds of thousands of people.

Every apartment at Lincoln Place is still covered by the city's rent control law, which means that rent increases will be strictly limited and the complex will likely become more affordable over time. It has been officially listed on the National Register of Historic Places. But what will happen when the owner, or a subsequent owner, looks at the rent rolls and sees that new apartments exempt from rent control in Venice and elsewhere are fetching much higher rents? What will happen when another developer comes along with visions of the many millions that could be made by converting the units to condominiums? What will happen when the argument for increased density as the answer to the affordable housing crisis carries the day, and eyes turn to Lincoln Place, with its low-rise buildings spread over acres of lawns and trees and shrubs and flowers?

The past has shown that real estate speculators and other powerful interests who regard the value of property as the maximum amount of money that can be extracted from it will use their deep pockets to bend the system to their will, regardless of restraints like rent control and historic recognition. There are other Lincoln Places in the city, communities of working people and the elderly living on fixed incomes, people who reside at the whims of property owners who might decide at any moment to pull the levers of the eviction machinery and line up the bulldozers to get rid of impediments to greater profits. Who can these people turn to? Elected officials who have shown themselves unwilling or unable to resist the blandishments of the real estate and development lobby? People from their own ranks, like the tenant leaders at Lincoln Place, who made such great personal sacrifices in a long, exhausting struggle? In my writing of "The Battle of Lincoln Place," these questions kept hovering, like storm clouds gathered on the horizon, ready to douse people's hopes and dreams with the cold reality of our system.

"Housing is a Right, Not a Privilege." That simple statement contains depths of aspiration, but for that man and his wife and their children in search of a home that existed only in their imaginations, will it ever be true?

Dennis Hathaway
Venice, California
March, 2022

ENDNOTES

1. "Wyatt Gets Firsthand Facts on Housing Crisis," *Los Angeles Times*, September 29, 1946.

2. "Veterans: Haunted Houses," *Newsweek*, August 26, 1943.

3. "Statement by the President Outlining the Housing Program for 1947"; December 14, 1946. Gerhard Peters and John T. Woolley, The American Presidency Project.

4. "National Housing Act, Public Law 73-479 (6/27/34) Major Legislation on Housing and Urban Development Enacted Since 1932; US Department of Housing and Urban Development.

5. Jerry Bialac, in-person interviews by Laura Burns, August 20, September 11, and September 25, 2001.

6. Ibid.

7. "Housing Project's First Units Ready," *Los Angeles Times*, October 29, 1950.

8. United States Census Bureau.

9. U.S., Congress, Senate, Committee on Banking and Currency, "The Report on the FHA Investigation, pursuant to S. Res. 229, 84th Congress, January 6, 1955.

10. "Fantastic Profits Told in FHA Investigation," *Los Angeles Times*, September 2, 1954.

11. Digital Collections of Los Angeles Public Library, "Crowd at Nightclub."

12. "Four Pickets Arrested as Trespassers," *Los Angeles Times*, March 3, 1965; "CORE complaint Settled;" April 12, 1965.

13. "A Bit of History," Gail Sansbury, LPTA Newsletter, July 10, 1003.

14 Rental Rehabilitation Activity Under the Major Rehabilitation Program: 1985-1992. Los Angeles Housing Department. The numbers increased to 816 units in 172 buildings in 1986 and 1,431 in 167 buildings in 1987.

15 James Coxeter and Robert Bisno didn't respond to requests to be interviewed.

16 "Apartment Residents to Fight Evictions," *Los Angeles Times*, August 2, 1987.

17 "Finally an Amerian: 'Born Rebel' Becomes a Citizen at 75 after Battling McCarthy-era Deportation Proceedings Since 1950;" *Los Angeles Times*, August 9, 1985.

18 "Council Acts to Close Rent Control Law 'Loophole,'" *Los Angeles Times*, August 5, 1987.

19 "Agents Seize 20 Tons of Cocaine in Raid on Los Angeles Warehouse," *New York Times*, Sept. 30, 1989.

20 *The Struggle for Community*, Allan David Heskin, Westview Press, 1991.

21 "Who Lives at Lincoln Place," LPTA Survey, 1991.

22 "Looking to Buy," *Los Angeles Times*, September 15, 1991.

23 "Mr. Coxeter concluded that even extensive rehabilitation of the existing apartments could not bring the current plumbing and electrical systems in line with current demands," Lincoln Place: helping shape the future; brochure by TransAction Companies, Ltd.

24 Letter from Ruth Galanter to constituents, March 27, 1991.

25 Letter from Ruth Galanter to Jennifer Reif; April 21, 1992.

26 "Lincoln Place Fate Still up in the Air;" *Argonaut*, April 30, 1992.

27 "Kemp's Legacy as Housing Secretary: One of Ideas, Not Accomplishments"; *New York Times*, August 20, 1996.

28 "Surviving without Driving," *Los Angeles Times*, September 23, 1992.

29 Draft Environmental Impact Report no. 91-0458-SUB(DB)(VAC); Los Angeles Department of City Planning.

30 "When a House Is a Home" *Los Angeles Times*, July 26, 1994.

31 "Galanter Urges City to Block Redevelopment Project," *Los Angeles Times*, August 4, 1994.

32 "Man Who Attacked Galanter 7 Years Ago Paroled;" *Argonaut*, September 24, 1994.

33 "Vote on Venice Complex Put Off," *Outlook*, January 20, 1995.

34 "After a Long Battle, Three Office Buildings Are Scheduled for Construction at a Los Angeles."

35 "Chick Accuses Some of Her Male Colleagues of Sexism;" *Los Angeles Times*, June 24, 1995.

36 "L.A. Delays Vote on Venice Housing Redevelopment," *Outlook*, August 9, 1995.

37 "Lincoln Place Project Rejected," *Outlook*, September 13, 1995.

38 Jerome J. Nash, Plaintiff and Respondent, v. City of Santa Monica et al., Defendants and Appellants, L.A. No. 31798. Supreme Court of California, October 25, 1984.

39 "Lincoln Place Owners Sue City of L.A." *Outlook*, October 7, 1995.

40 "Let's Own It—Tenant's Struggle to Save Venice Homes" YouTube.

41 "1940s Apartment Complex Wins Landmark Status;" *Los Angeles Times*, July 12, 2000.

42 "Developer Wins Court OK to Tear Down Apartments," *Los Angeles Times*, September 29, 2000.

43 "Developer Wins Court Battle over Lincoln Place Project," *Argonaut*, October 5, 2000.

44 "ACLU Moves to Protect Venice Tenant Activists' Freedom to Organize and Speak Out," Press Release, ACLU of Southern California, November 2, 2000.

45 "ACLU to Help Defend Venice Tenants in Suit," *Los Angeles Times*, November 3, 2000.

46 "ACLU Motion Support Lincoln Place Residents in Suit Filed By Owners," *Argonaut*, November 9, 2000.

47 "Declaration of Frieda Marlin;" Pfeiffer Venice Properties, LLC v. Sheila Bernard, Laura Ponce, et al.; Los Angeles County Superior Court Case No. BC237108.

48 "Heritage Panel Takes No Action on Chase Knolls," *Los Angeles Times*, June 8, 2000.

49 "ACLU Wins Dismissal of Landlord's Retaliatory Lawsuit Against Los Angeles Tenant Activists," Press Release, ACLU, February 26, 2001.

50 "Being Forced Out by Low Incomes, Rising Rents," *Los Angeles Times*, September 29, 2001.

51 "REIT Invests in Venice Units," *Los Angeles Times*, June 26, 2001.

52 "Apartment Investment and Management Company Announces 795 Unit Acquisition in Venice, California," Aimco, June 22, 2001.

53 "Candidate Perfect until He Started Discussing Issues," *Washington Post*, June 6, 1986.

54 "Ralph Vaughn Succumbs," *Los Angeles Sentinel*, April 19, 2001.

55 "Brilliant Design Makes a Little House Big," *Los Angeles Times*, November 2, 1947

56 "Complaints of Police Harassment Peril Calm in Venice," *Los Angeles Times*, February 11, 1971

57 "Company Grows into Colossus," *Sacramento Bee*, January 28, 2002.

58 "Lincoln Place Tenants Demonstrate Against Aimco," October 9-15, 2002.

59 "City Council Okays Lincoln Place Project; Developer May Sue City," *Argonaut*, December 5, 2002.

60 The meeting transcript and minutes do not reflect who cast the negative vote or why.

61 "Developer Poised to Raze Lincoln Place," *Santa Monica Mirror*, February 26-March 4, 2003.

62 "Lincoln Place: What's at Stake," *Santa Monica Mirror*, April 7-13, 2004.

63 Long-time city councilman Joel Wachs didn't come out as gay until near the end of his final term.

64 "Race for Council Seat Goes Negative," *Los Angeles Times*, March 4, 2005.

65 "A Voice for the Westside," *Los Angeles Times*, February 15, 2005.

66 The 41 List: Ridge Gonzalez and Elena Popp (2015), YouTube, January 6, 2016.

67 "Renters Continue to Challenge Landlord," *Santa Monica Daily Press*, July 25, 2005.

68 "Rights and Wrongs," *Santa Monica Mirror*, March 2, 2005.

69 "Residents Say Apartments Will Be Saved, but Owner Disagrees," *Los Angeles Times*, August 9, 2005.

70 "State Group: Lincoln Place Should Be Saved," *Santa Monica Daily Press*, August 10, 2005.

71 "Neighborhood Council Won't Support Future Variances Unless Evictions Cease," *Venice Paper*, November 18, 2005.

[72] "Tenants Hang Tough at Lincoln Place Apts." *Beachhead*, November 2005.

[73] "Tenants Talk Turkey with City Attorney," *Venice Paper*, November 25, 2005.

[74] "Lincoln Place—A Month of Heartache, Anger and Determination," Jim Smith, *Beachhead*, January 2006.

[75] Laura Silagi is married to the author.

[76] "Evicted Lincoln Place Tenants Express Frustration to LA Mayor at Del Rey event," *Argonaut*, December 15, 2005.

[77] Ibid.

[78] "Endangered Lincoln Place Shows Off," *Santa Monica Mirror*, December 21, 2005.

[79] Ibid.

[80] "Lincoln Place Evictions Put on Hold for Three More Months," *Argonaut*, June 8, 2006.

[81] Popp lost that primary race to Kevin DeLeon, currently a Los Angeles City Council member.

[82] "Trial Will Start on Plans for Venice Complex," *Daily Journal*, January 17, 2007.

[83] On December 22, 2020, Padilla was appointed to the US Senate seat vacated by vice president-elect Kamala Harris.

[84] Settlement Reached in Lincoln Place Dispute," *Santa Monica Daily Press*, May 27, 2010.

[85] A small outdoors area with a bench and ash receptacles was eventually designated as a smoker's area.

[86] "Attorney Had Led Some Key Preservation Efforts in Venice," *Argonaut*, June 28, 2012.

INDEX

M

ABOUT THE AUTHOR

Dennis Hathaway has worked as a building con-tractor, director of construction and rehabilitation for a non-profit housing corporation, staff member of a YouthBuild program, and head of a non-profit organization fighting billboards and visual blight in Los Angeles. A former journalist, he has writ-ten nonfiction dealing with issues of housing and public policy for online magazines. His short stories have appeared in a number of print journals, and his story collec-tion, "The Consequences of Desire," won the Flannery O'Connor Award for Short Fiction. He was the publisher and editor of Crania, an early online literary and arts magazine, and his poetry collection, "The Taste of Flesh," was published by Crania Press. He was born and raised on a farm in Iowa, and now lives with his wife, artist Laura Silagi, in Venice, California.

www.ddhathaway.com

CPSIA information can be obtained
at www.ICGtesting.com
Printed in the USA
BVHW030924080722
641616BV00007B/146